THE
BRONX
KILL

VERTIGO
CRIME

WRITER
PETER MILLIGAN

ART
JAMES ROMBERGER

LETTERS
CLEM ROBINS

THE BRONX KILL

Karen Berger SVP – Executive Editor
Pornsak Pichetshote Assoc. Editor
Robbin Brosterman Design Director – Books
Louis Prandi Art Director

DC COMICS
Paul Levitz President & Publisher
Richard Bruning SVP – Creative Director
Patrick Caldon EVP – Finance & Operations
Amy Genkins SVP – Business & Legal Affairs
Jim Lee Editorial Director – WildStorm
Gregory Noveck SVP – Creative Affairs
Steve Rotterdam SVP – Sales & Marketing
Cheryl Rubin SVP – Brand Management

THE BRONX KILL
VERTIGO CRIME

THE BRONX KILL Published by DC Comics, 1700 Broadway, New York, NY 10019.

Copyright © 2009 by Peter Milligan and James Romberger. All rights reserved.

All characters, the distinctive likenesses thereof and all related elements are trademarks
of DC COMICS. VERTIGO and VERTIGO CRIME are trademarks of DC COMICS. The
stories, characters and incidents mentioned in this book are entirely fictional. DC Comics
does not read or accept unsolicited submissions of ideas, stories or artwork.

Printed in the USA. First Printing. DC Comics, a Warner Bros. Entertainment Company.

ISBN: 978-1-4012-2631-2

Certified Chain of Custody
SUSTAINABLE   80% Certified Fiber Sourcing and
FORESTRY   40% Post-Consumer Recycled
INITIATIVE   www.sfiprogram.org

SGS-SFI/COC-US10/81072

This label applies to the text stock.

100% Recycled

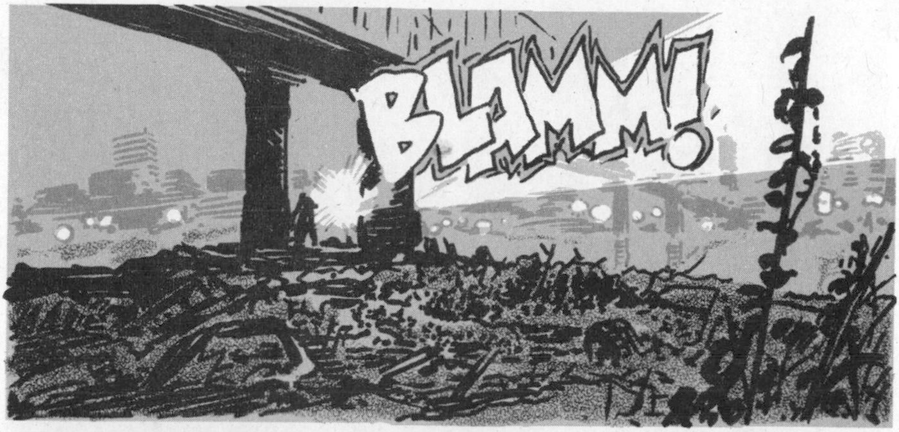
BLAMM!

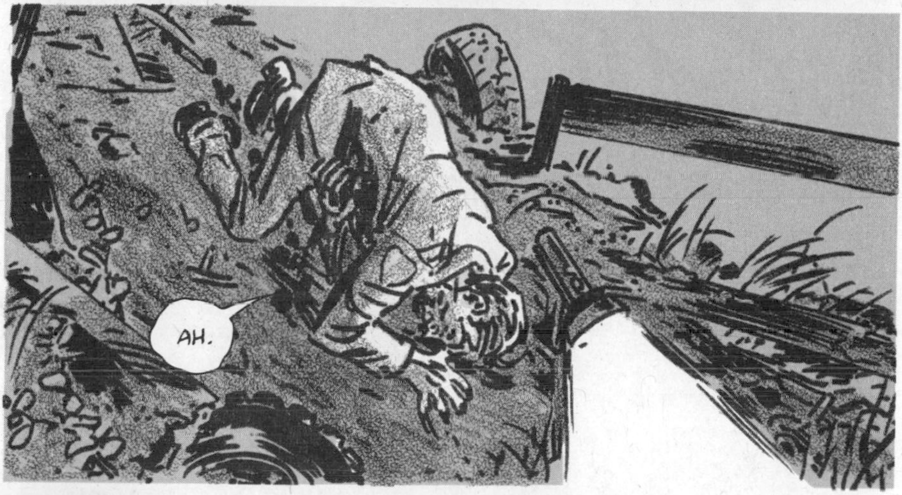
AH.

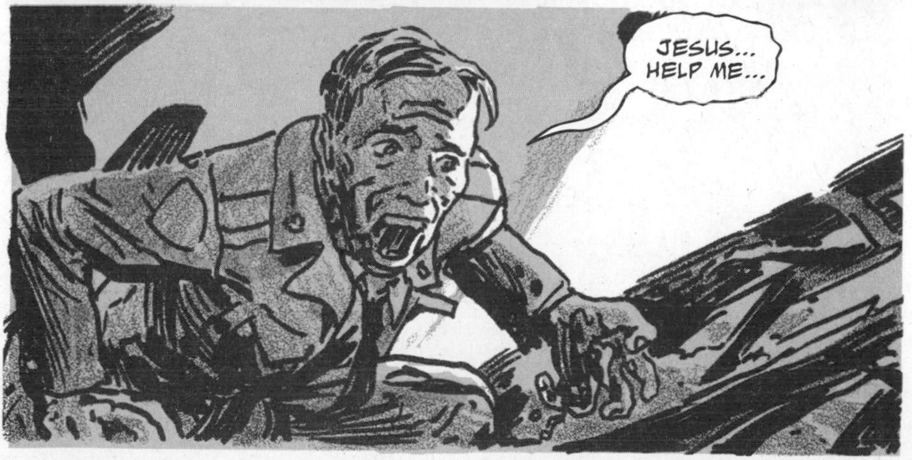
JESUS... HELP ME...

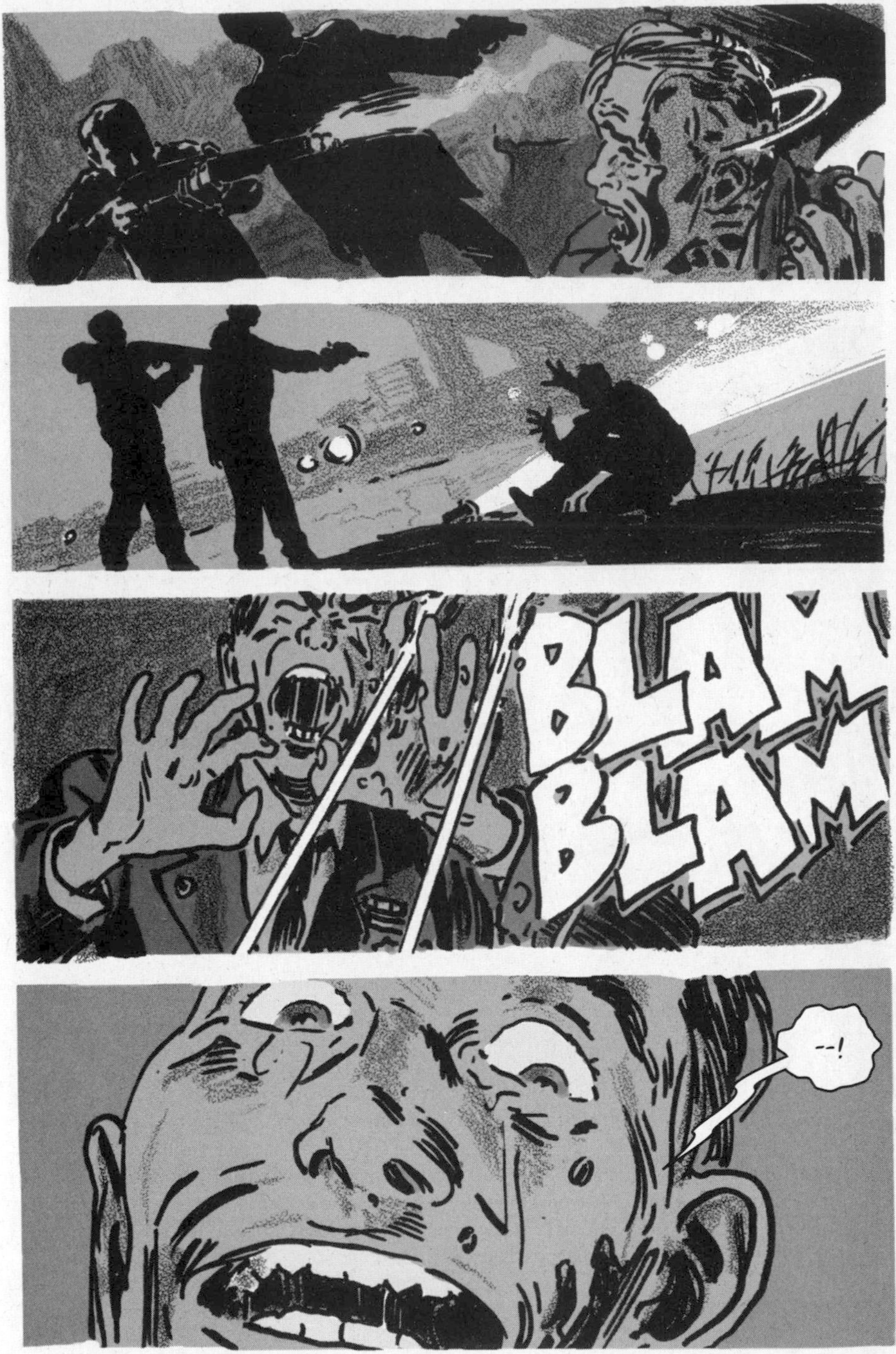

BLA
BLAM
--!

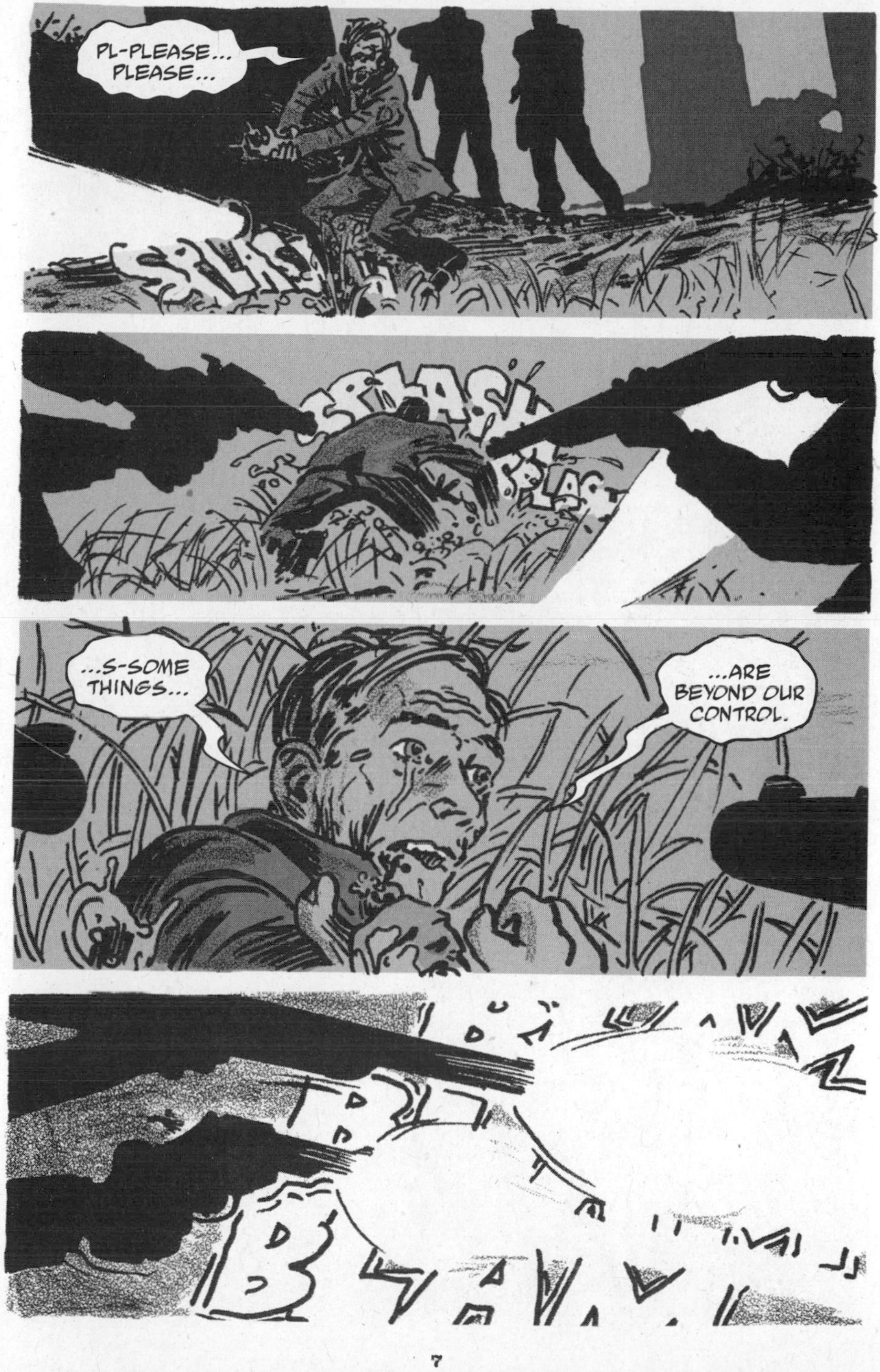
PL-PLEASE... PLEASE...
...S-SOME THINGS...
...ARE BEYOND OUR CONTROL.

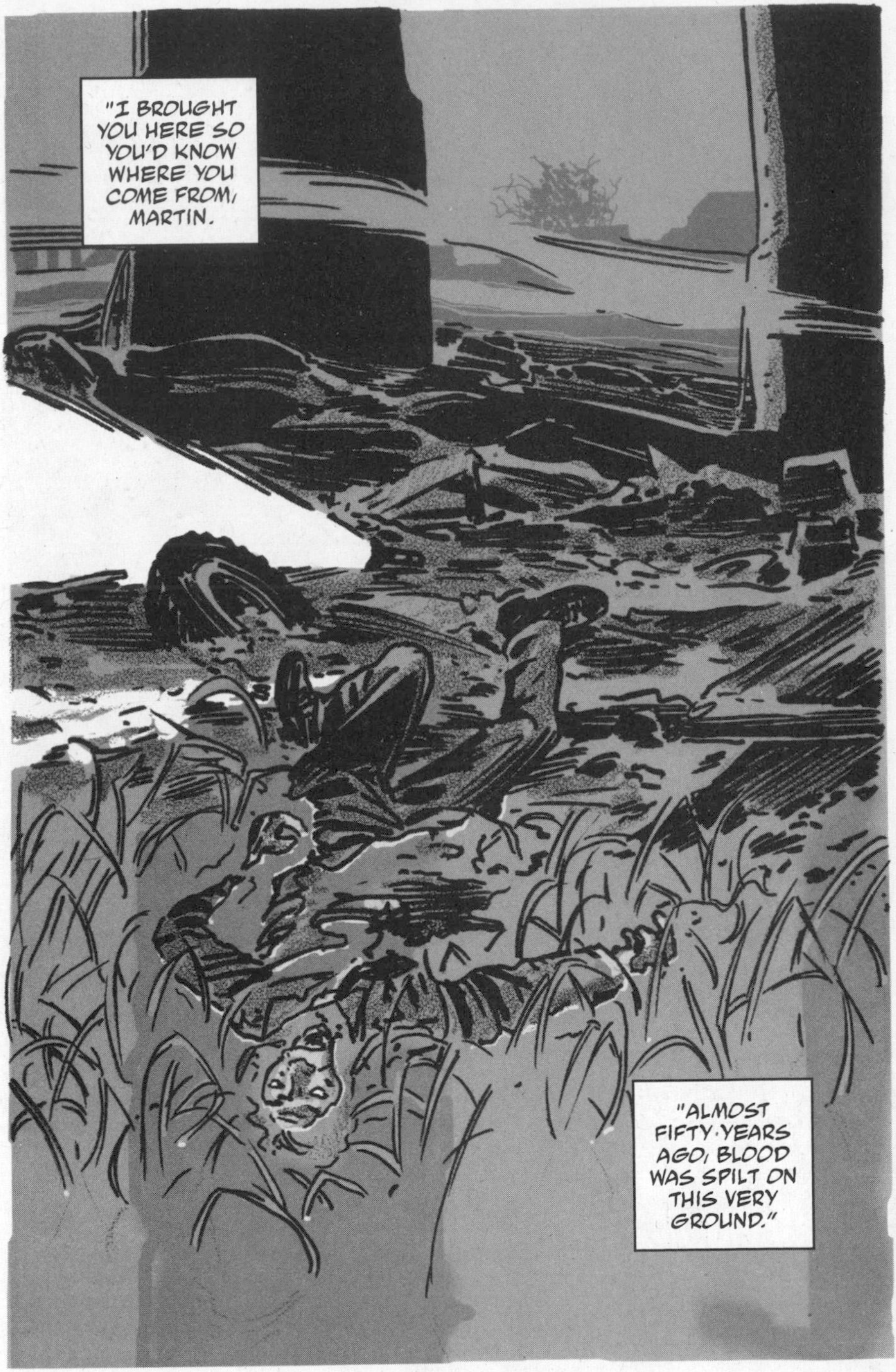
"I BROUGHT YOU HERE SO YOU'D KNOW WHERE YOU COME FROM, MARTIN.
"ALMOST FIFTY YEARS AGO, BLOOD WAS SPILT ON THIS VERY GROUND."

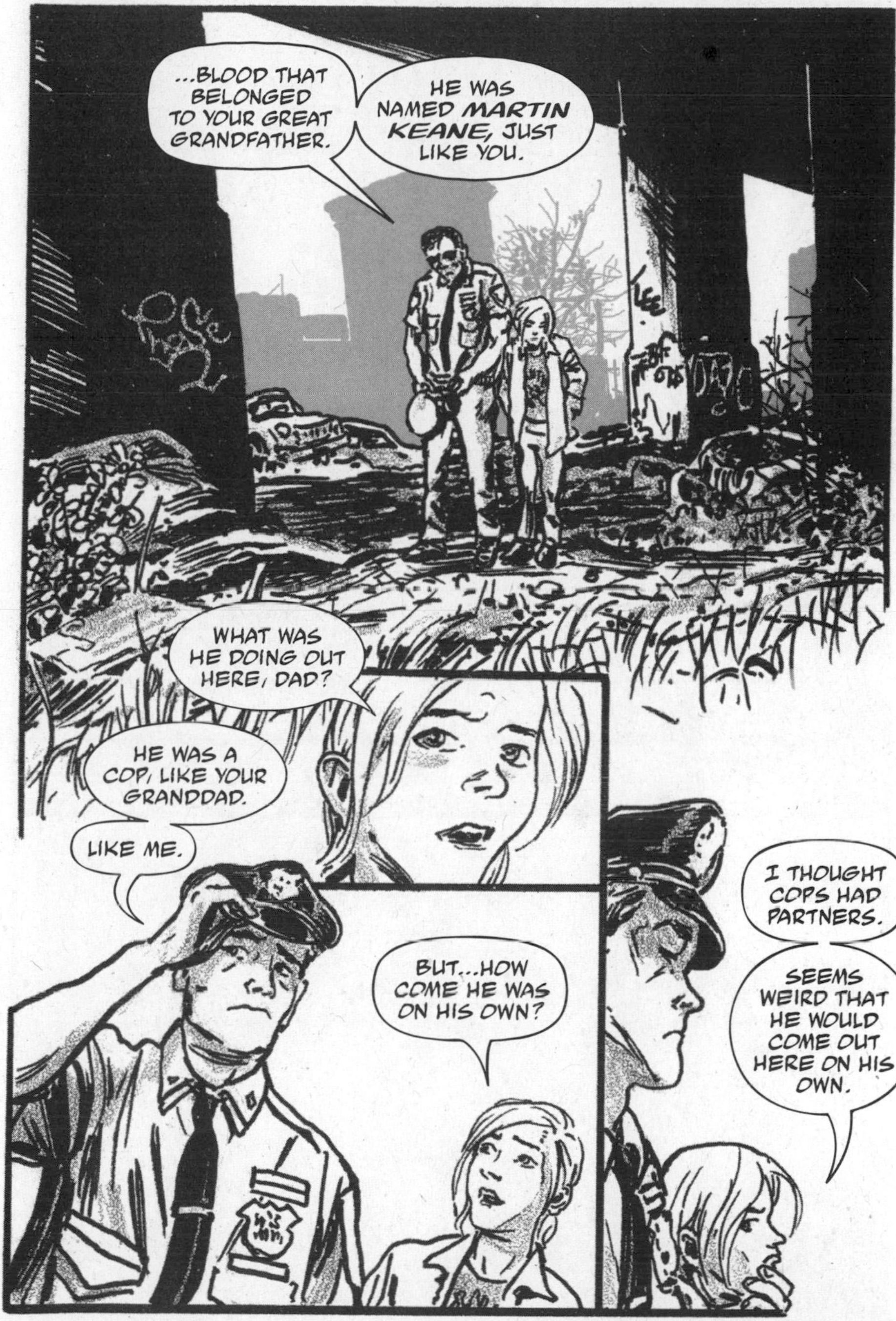
...BLOOD THAT BELONGED TO YOUR GREAT GRANDFATHER.
HE WAS NAMED *MARTIN KEANE*, JUST LIKE YOU.
WHAT WAS HE DOING OUT HERE, DAD?
HE WAS A COP, LIKE YOUR GRANDDAD.
LIKE ME.
BUT...HOW COME HE WAS ON HIS OWN?
I THOUGHT COPS HAD PARTNERS.
SEEMS WEIRD THAT HE WOULD COME OUT HERE ON HIS OWN.

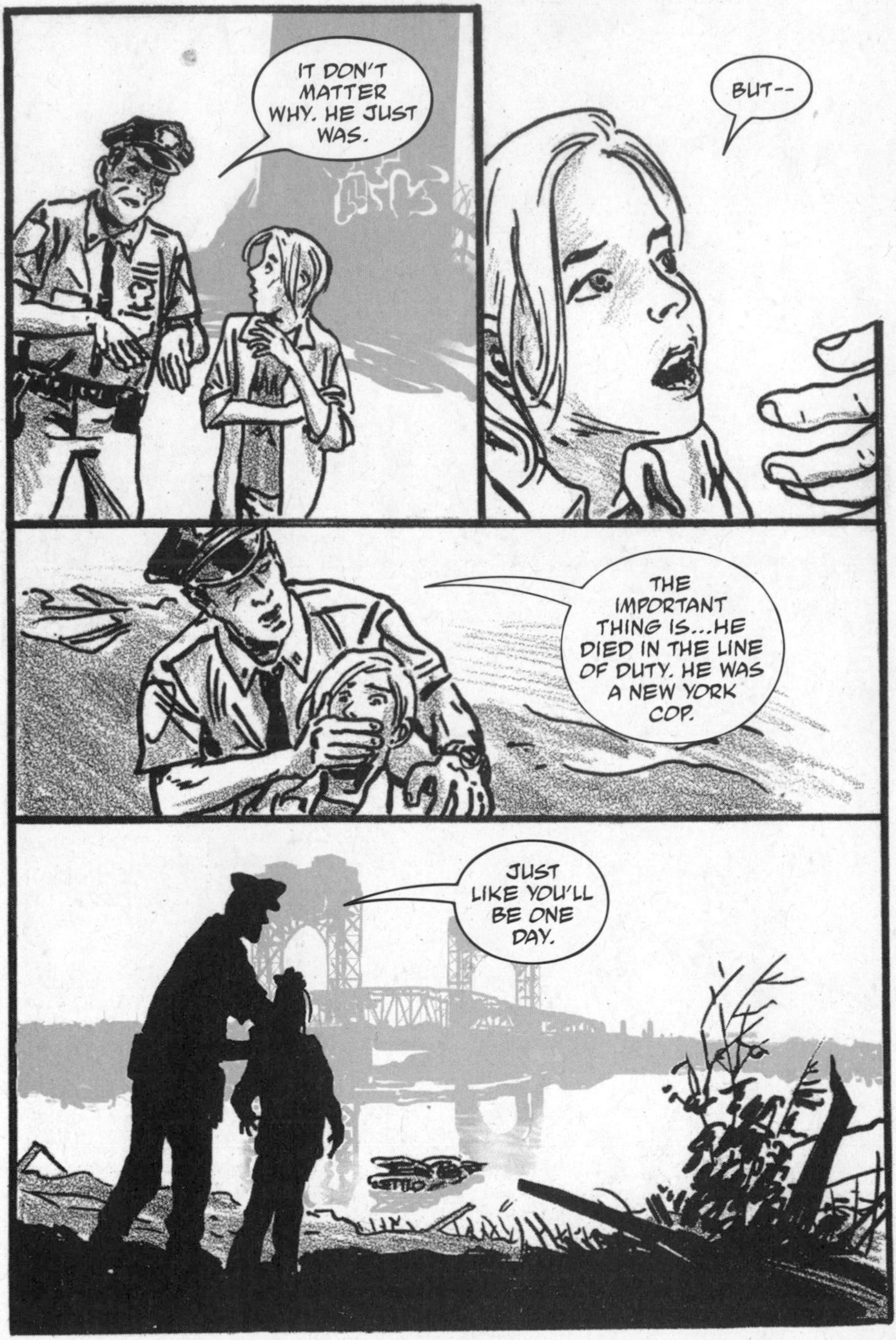
IT DON'T MATTER WHY. HE JUST WAS.
BUT--
THE IMPORTANT THING IS...HE DIED IN THE LINE OF DUTY. HE WAS A NEW YORK COP.
JUST LIKE YOU'LL BE ONE DAY.

I KNEW THAT DAY AT THE *BRONX KILL*...I WASN'T GOING TO BE A COP. I WOULDN'T DO WHAT WAS EXPECTED OF ME.

EVEN THEN, I KNEW I HAD TO ESCAPE.

ESCAPE FROM WHAT?

TURN AROUND, ERIN.

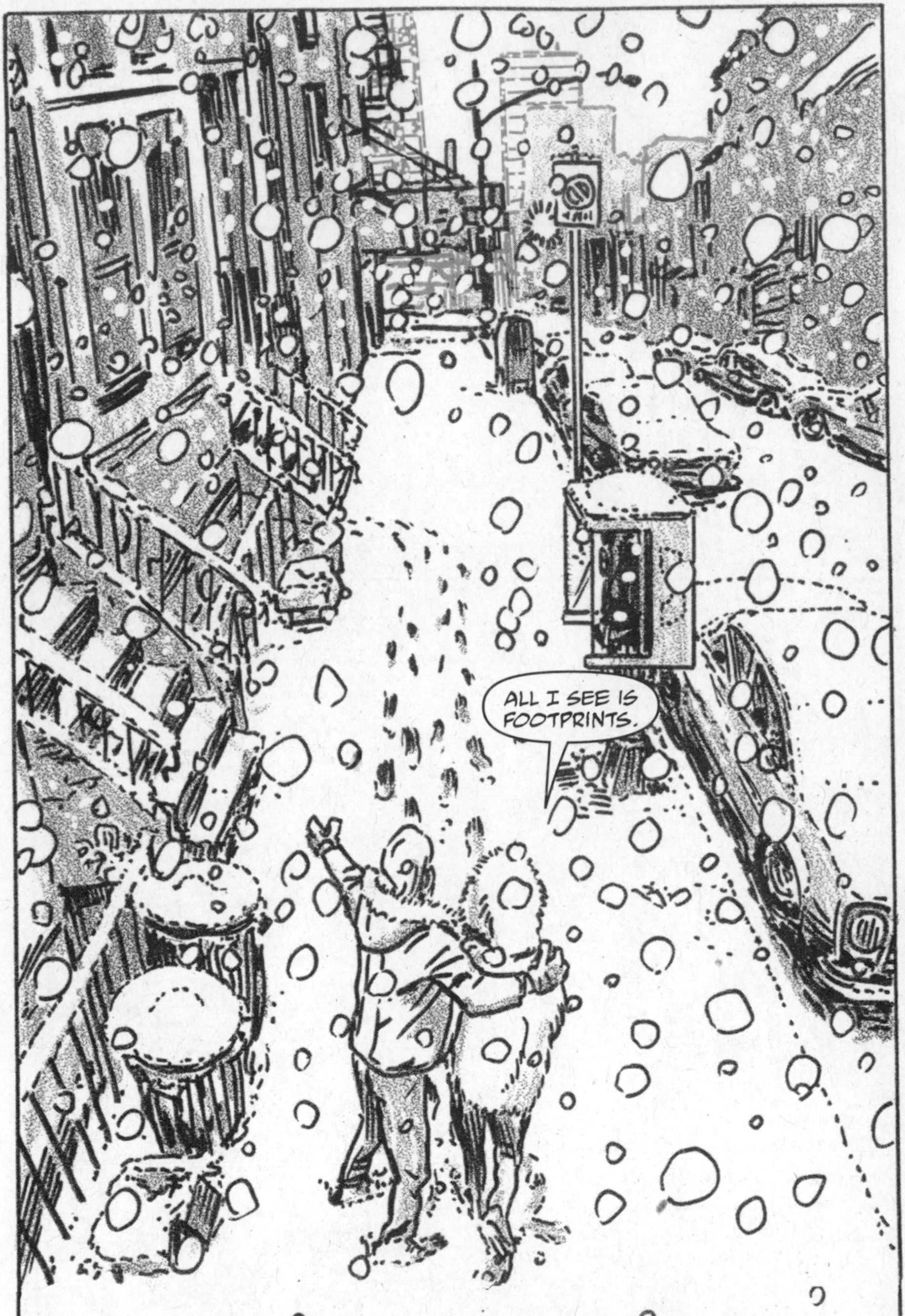
ALL I SEE IS FOOTPRINTS.

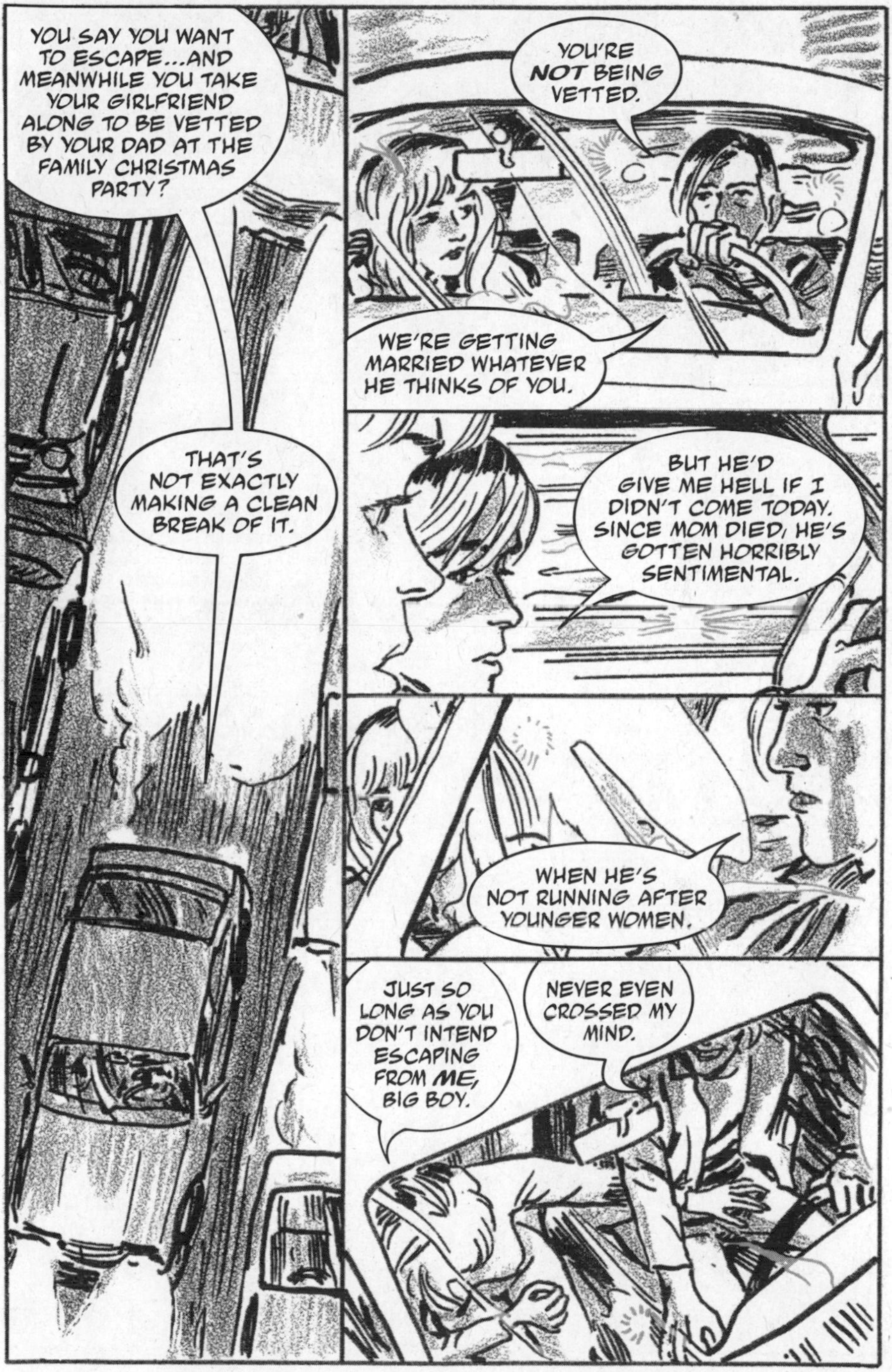
YOU SAY YOU WANT TO ESCAPE...AND MEANWHILE YOU TAKE YOUR GIRLFRIEND ALONG TO BE VETTED BY YOUR DAD AT THE FAMILY CHRISTMAS PARTY?
THAT'S NOT EXACTLY MAKING A CLEAN BREAK OF IT.
YOU'RE **NOT** BEING VETTED.
WE'RE GETTING MARRIED WHATEVER HE THINKS OF YOU.
BUT HE'D GIVE ME HELL IF I DIDN'T COME TODAY. SINCE MOM DIED, HE'S GOTTEN HORRIBLY SENTIMENTAL.
WHEN HE'S NOT RUNNING AFTER YOUNGER WOMEN.
JUST SO LONG AS YOU DON'T INTEND ESCAPING FROM **ME**, BIG BOY.
NEVER EVEN CROSSED MY MIND.

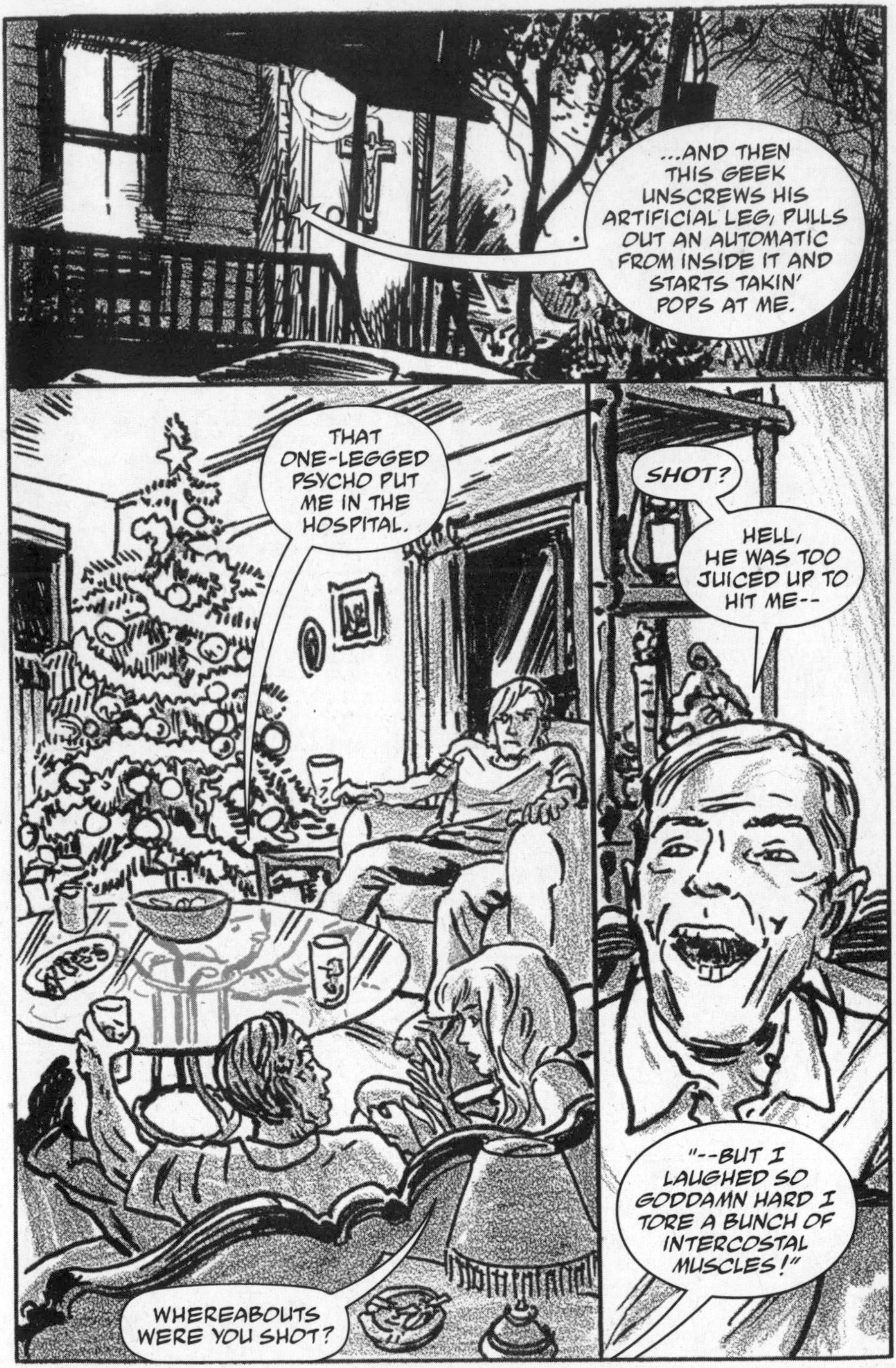
...AND THEN THIS GEEK UNSCREWS HIS ARTIFICIAL LEG, PULLS OUT AN AUTOMATIC FROM INSIDE IT AND STARTS TAKIN' POPS AT ME.
THAT ONE-LEGGED PSYCHO PUT ME IN THE HOSPITAL.
WHEREABOUTS WERE YOU SHOT?
SHOT?
HELL, HE WAS TOO JUICED UP TO HIT ME--
"--BUT I LAUGHED SO GODDAMN HARD I TORE A BUNCH OF INTERCOSTAL MUSCLES!"

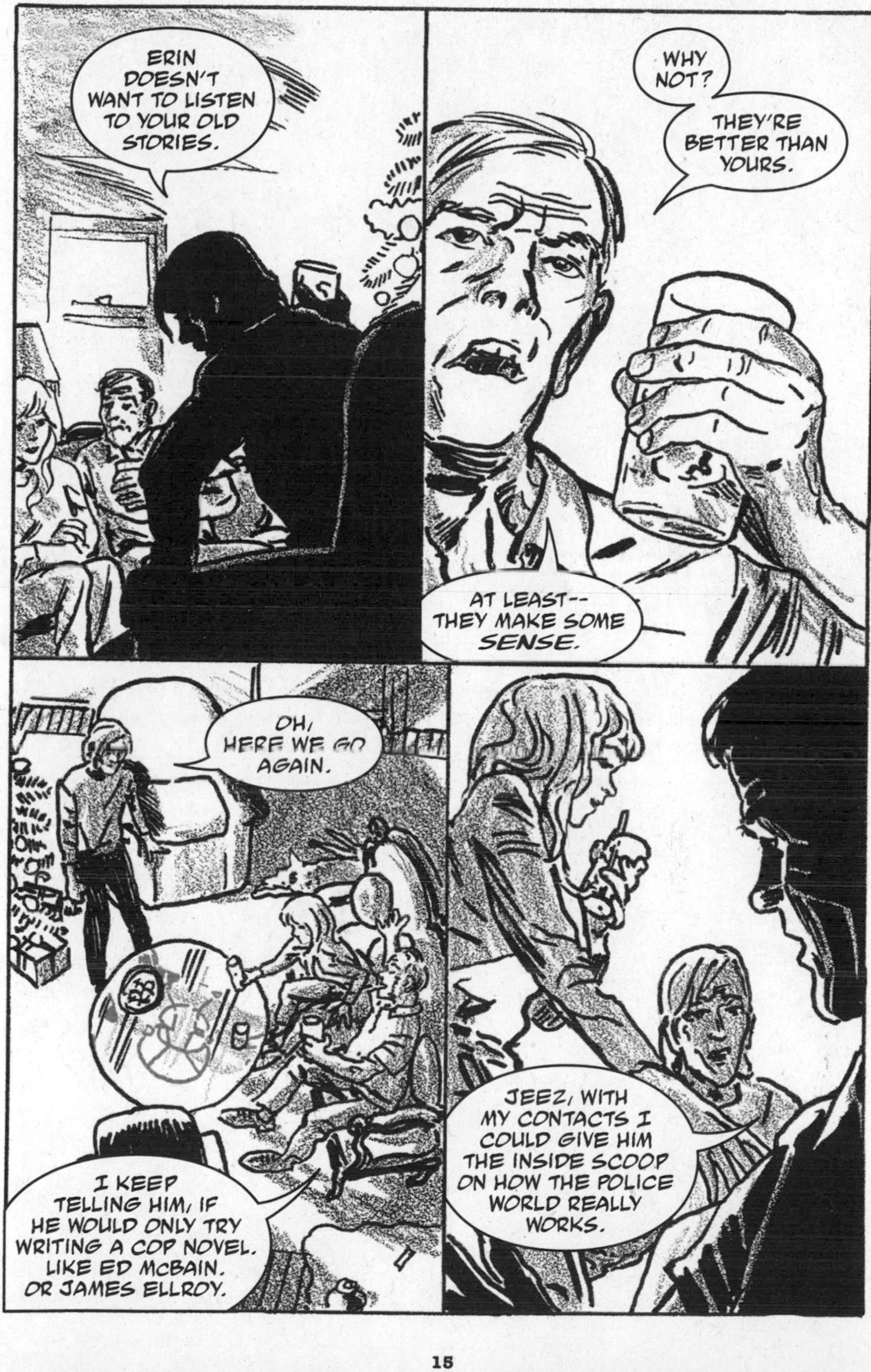
ERIN DOESN'T WANT TO LISTEN TO YOUR OLD STORIES.
WHY NOT?
THEY'RE BETTER THAN YOURS.
AT LEAST-- THEY MAKE SOME SENSE.
OH, HERE WE GO AGAIN.
I KEEP TELLING HIM, IF HE WOULD ONLY TRY WRITING A COP NOVEL. LIKE ED McBAIN. OR JAMES ELLROY.
JEEZ, WITH MY CONTACTS I COULD GIVE HIM THE INSIDE SCOOP ON HOW THE POLICE WORLD REALLY WORKS.

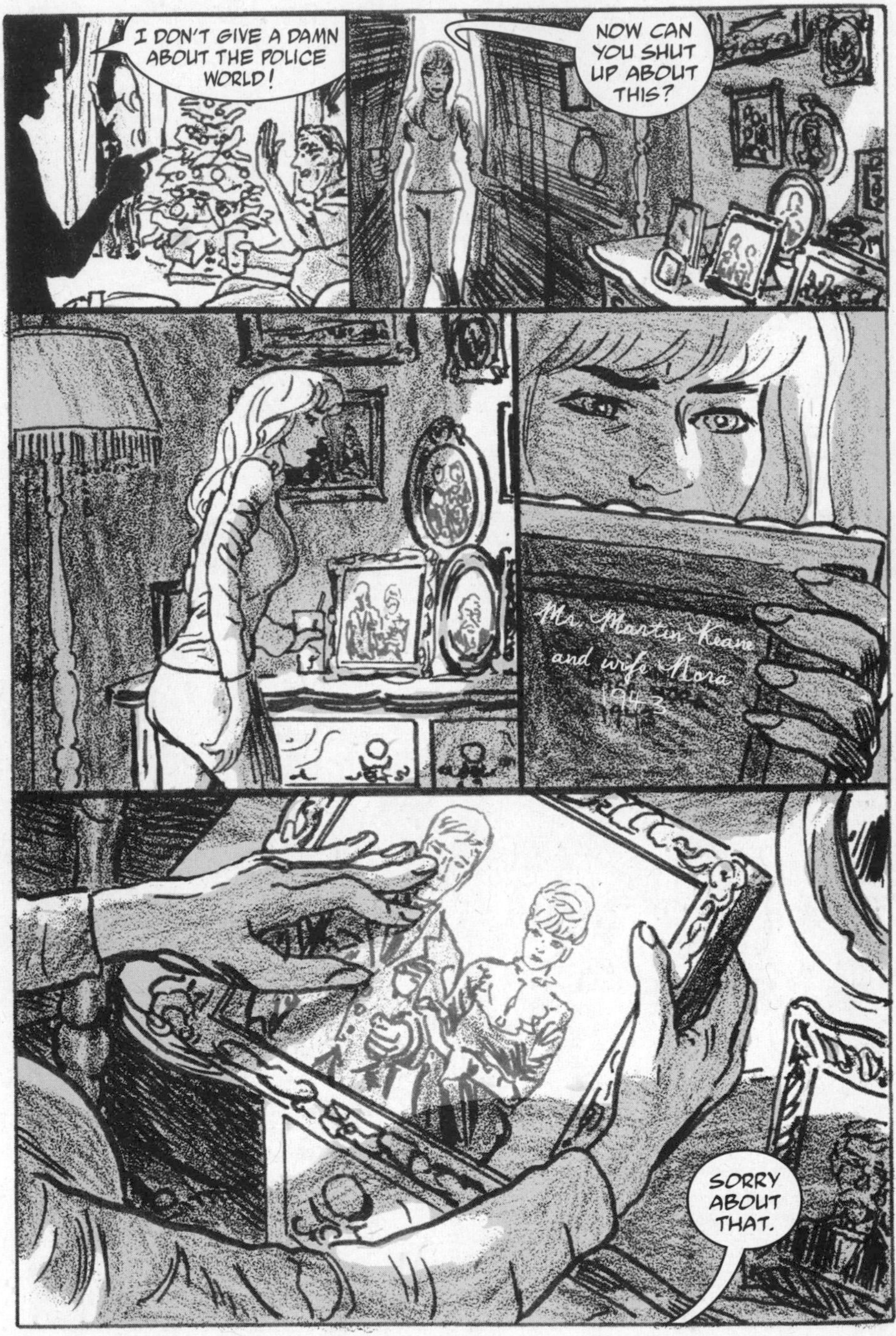
I DON'T GIVE A DAMN ABOUT THE POLICE WORLD!
NOW CAN YOU SHUT UP ABOUT THIS?
Mr. Martin Keane and wife Nora 1943
SORRY ABOUT THAT.

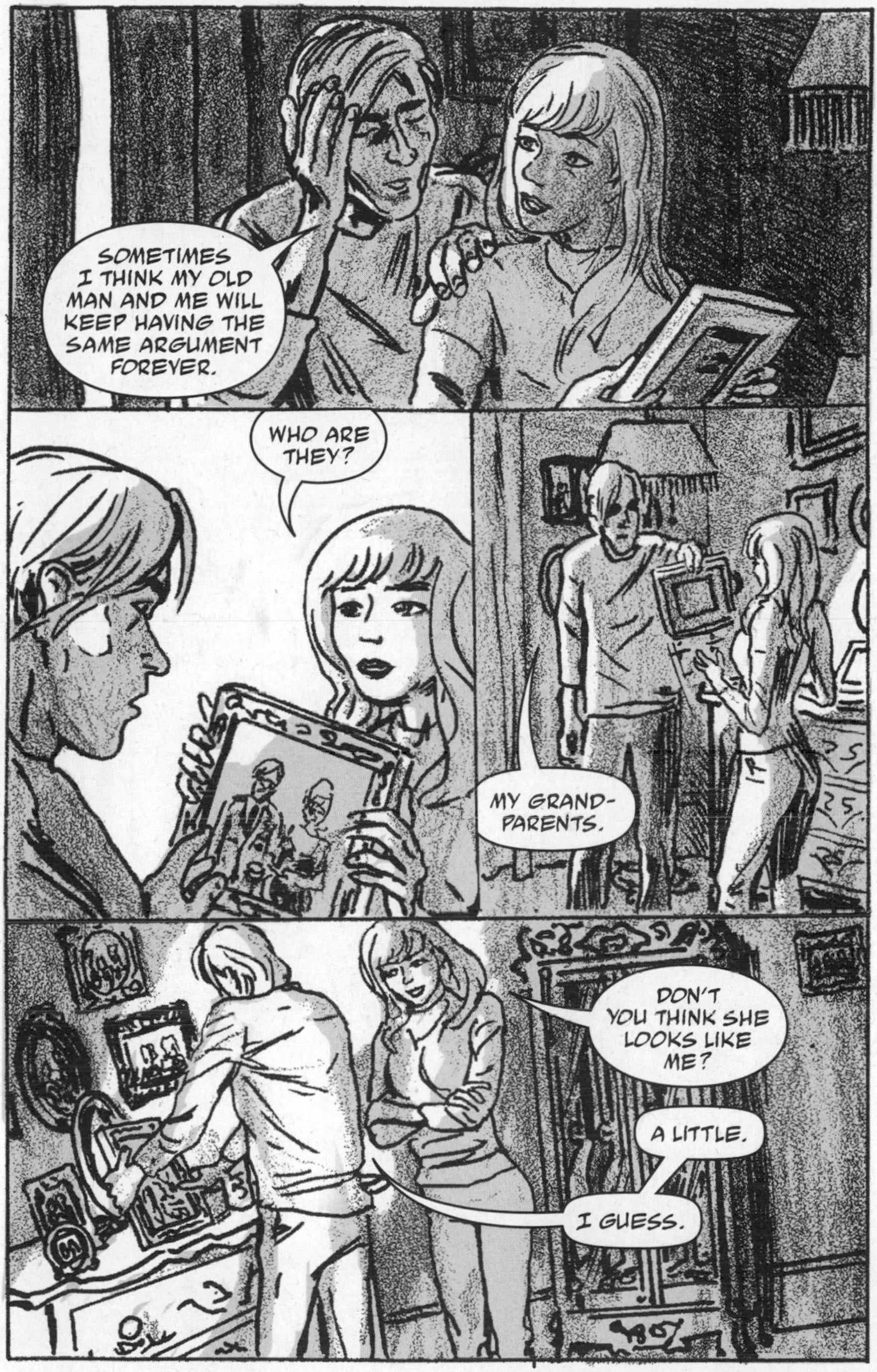
SOMETIMES I THINK MY OLD MAN AND ME WILL KEEP HAVING THE SAME ARGUMENT FOREVER.
WHO ARE THEY?
MY GRAND-PARENTS.
DON'T YOU THINK SHE LOOKS LIKE ME?
A LITTLE.
I GUESS.

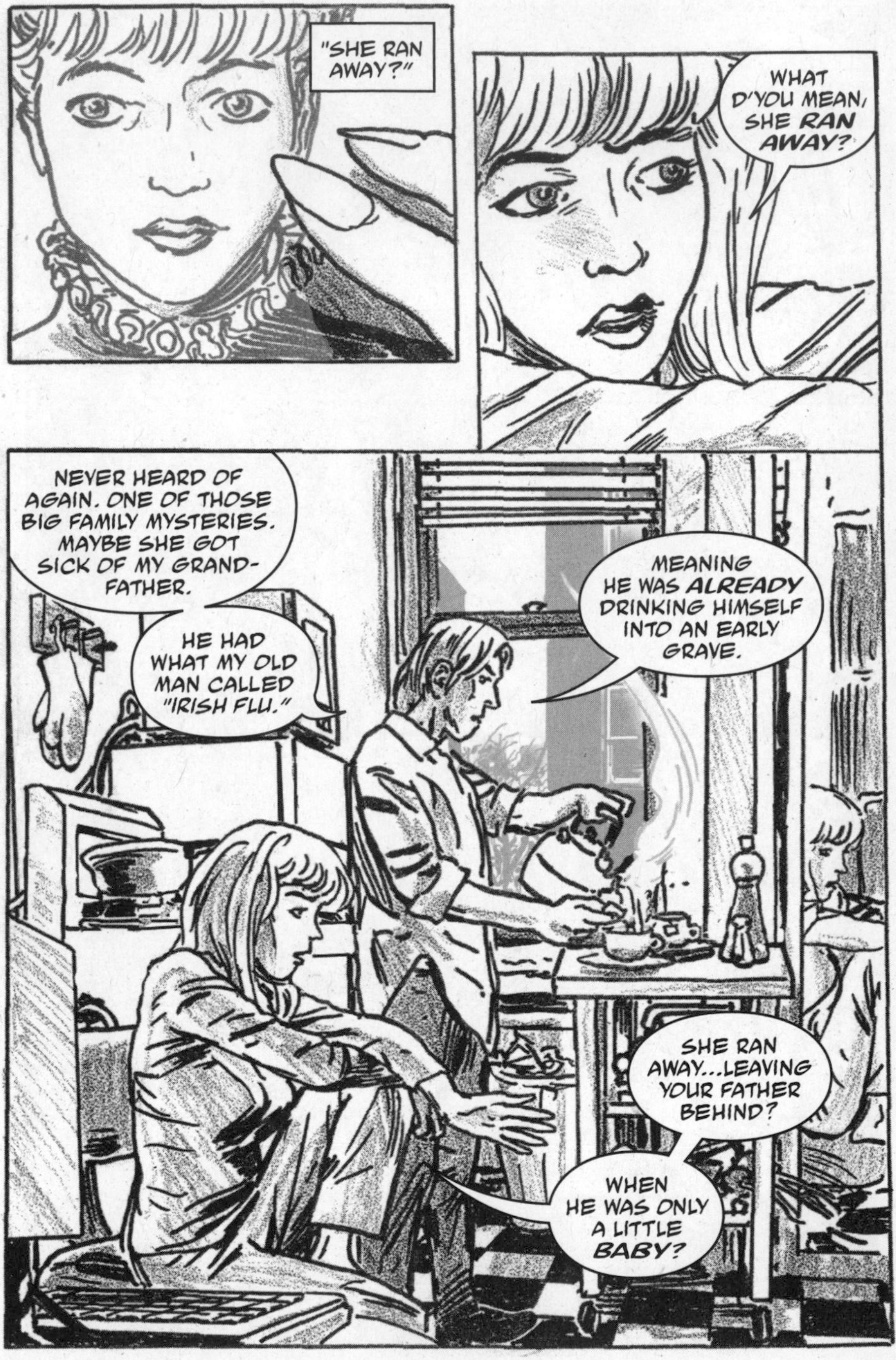
"SHE RAN AWAY?"
WHAT D'YOU MEAN, SHE RAN AWAY?
NEVER HEARD OF AGAIN. ONE OF THOSE BIG FAMILY MYSTERIES. MAYBE SHE GOT SICK OF MY GRAND-FATHER.
HE HAD WHAT MY OLD MAN CALLED "IRISH FLU."
MEANING HE WAS ALREADY DRINKING HIMSELF INTO AN EARLY GRAVE.
SHE RAN AWAY...LEAVING YOUR FATHER BEHIND?
WHEN HE WAS ONLY A LITTLE BABY?

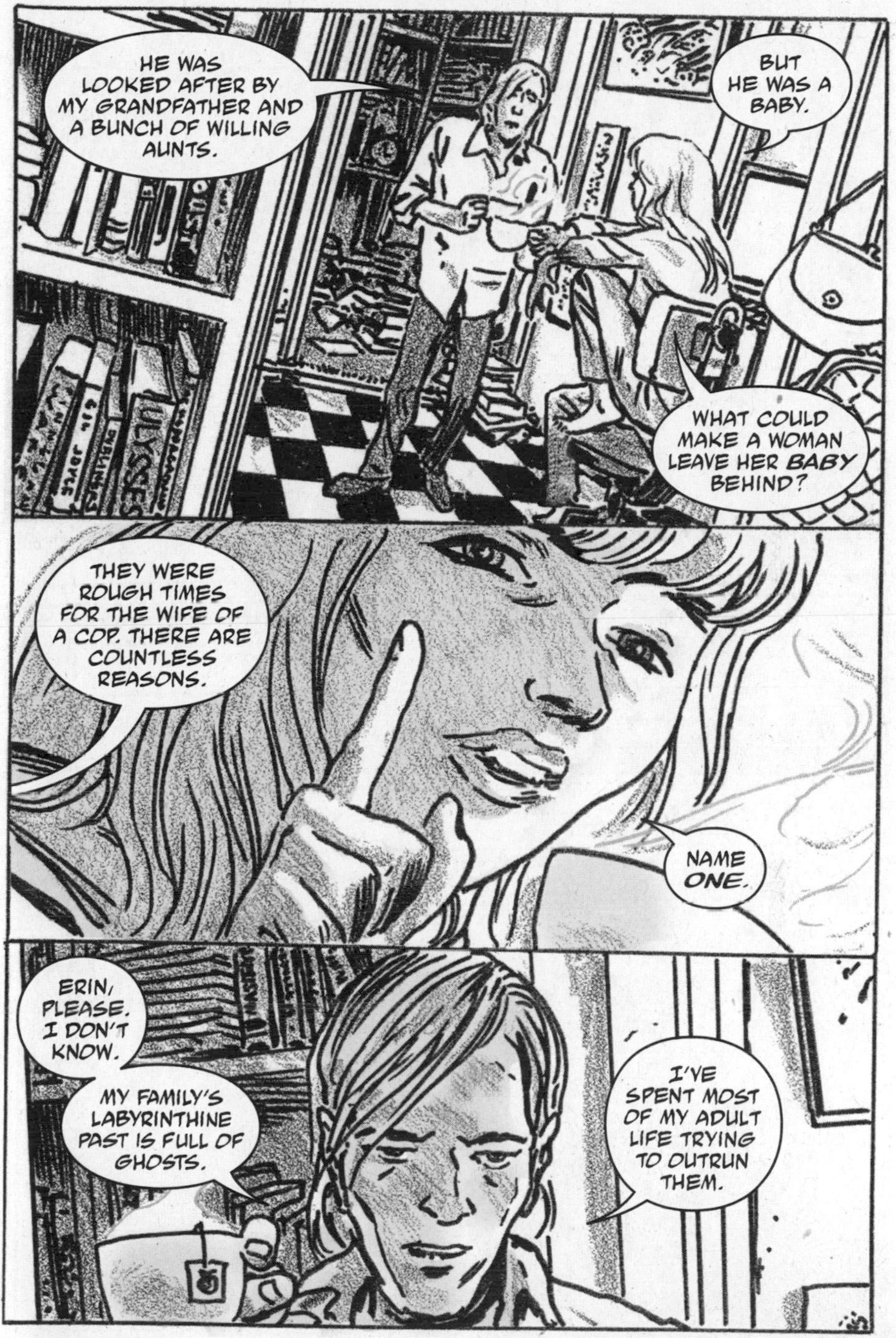
HE WAS LOOKED AFTER BY MY GRANDFATHER AND A BUNCH OF WILLING AUNTS.
BUT HE WAS A BABY.
WHAT COULD MAKE A WOMAN LEAVE HER *BABY* BEHIND?
THEY WERE ROUGH TIMES FOR THE WIFE OF A COP. THERE ARE COUNTLESS REASONS.
NAME *ONE*.
ERIN, PLEASE. I DON'T KNOW.
MY FAMILY'S LABYRINTHINE PAST IS FULL OF GHOSTS.
I'VE SPENT MOST OF MY ADULT LIFE TRYING TO OUTRUN THEM.

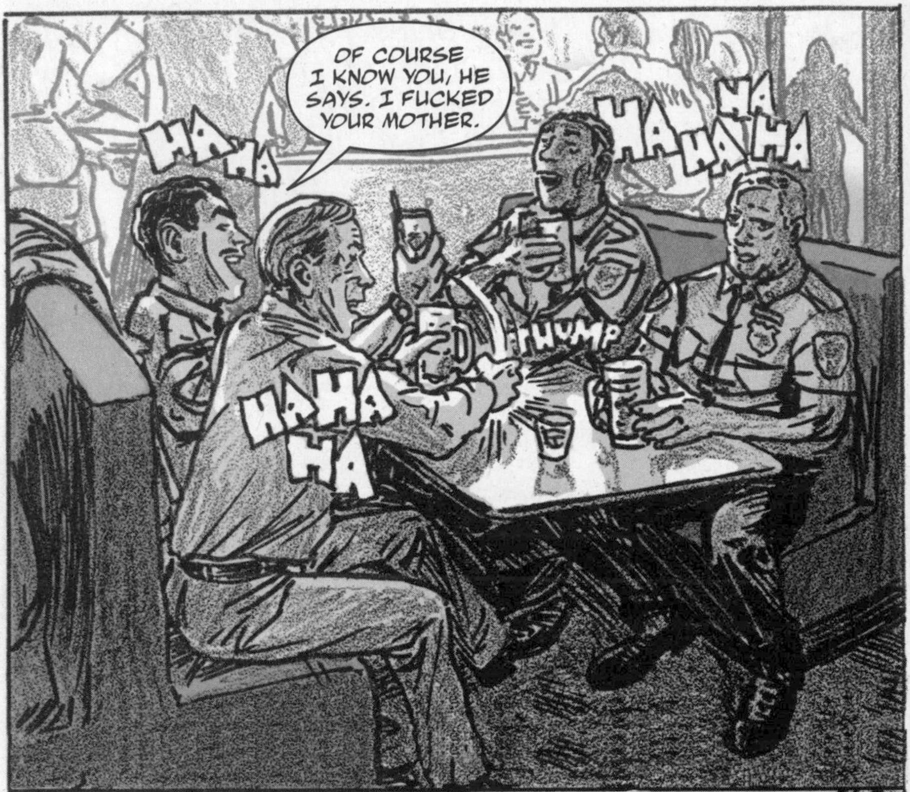
OF COURSE I KNOW YOU, HE SAYS. I FUCKED YOUR MOTHER.
HAHA
HAHAHAHA HA
THUMP
HAHAHA HA

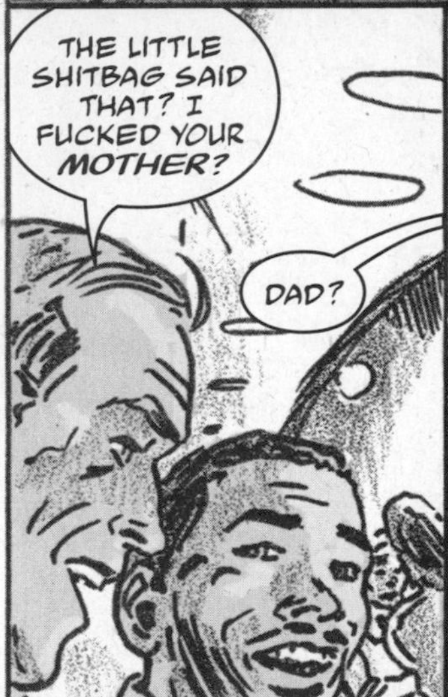
THE LITTLE SHITBAG SAID THAT? I FUCKED YOUR *MOTHER?*
DAD?

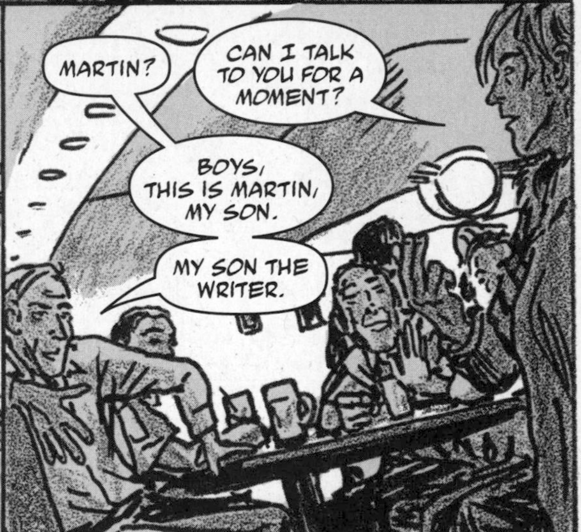
MARTIN?
CAN I TALK TO YOU FOR A MOMENT?
BOYS, THIS IS MARTIN, MY SON.
MY SON THE WRITER.

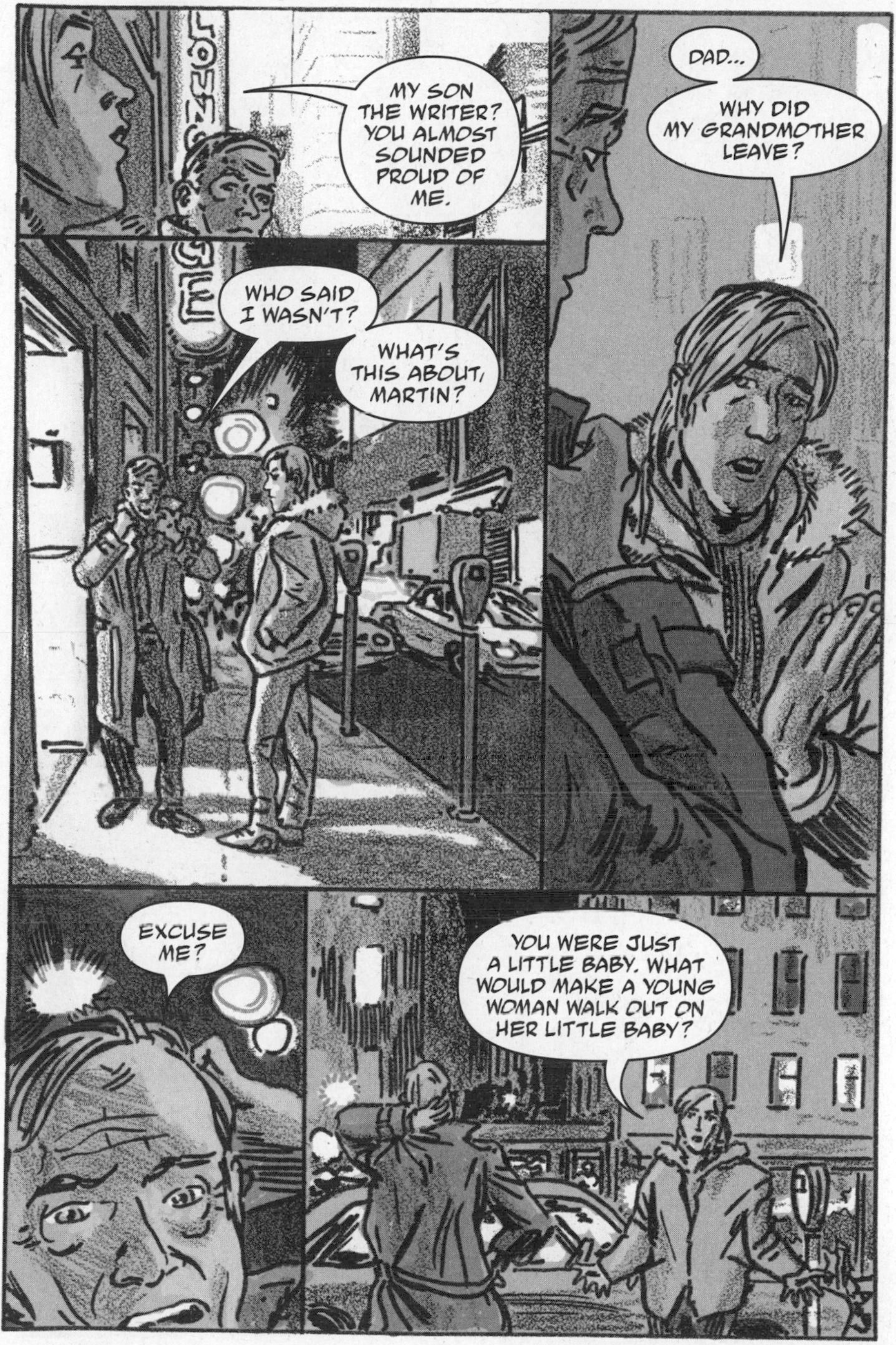
MY SON THE WRITER? YOU ALMOST SOUNDED PROUD OF ME.
WHO SAID I WASN'T?
WHAT'S THIS ABOUT, MARTIN?
DAD...
WHY DID MY GRANDMOTHER LEAVE?
EXCUSE ME?
YOU WERE JUST A LITTLE BABY. WHAT WOULD MAKE A YOUNG WOMAN WALK OUT ON HER LITTLE BABY?

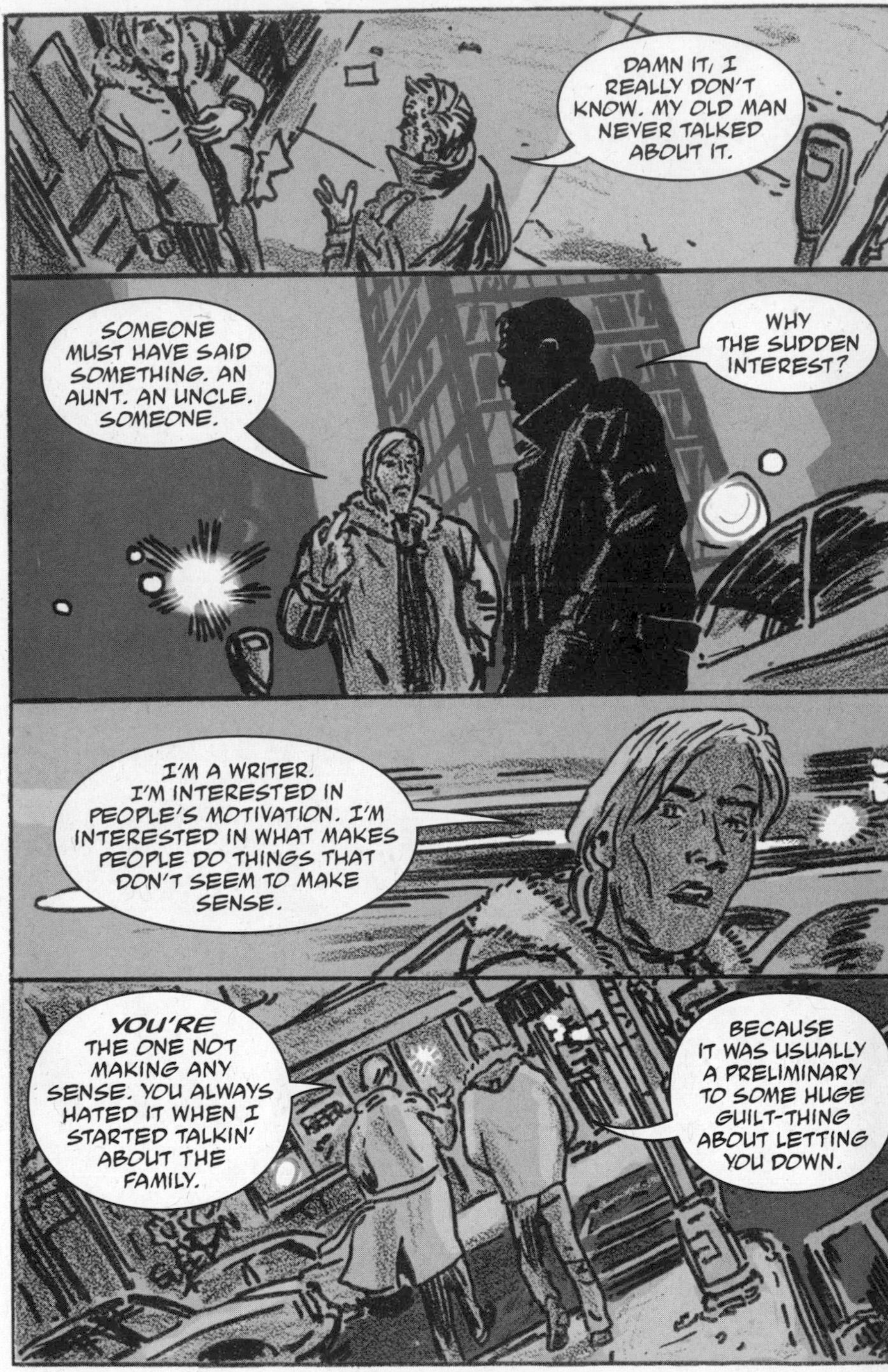
DAMN IT, I REALLY DON'T KNOW. MY OLD MAN NEVER TALKED ABOUT IT.
SOMEONE MUST HAVE SAID SOMETHING. AN AUNT. AN UNCLE. SOMEONE.
WHY THE SUDDEN INTEREST?
I'M A WRITER. I'M INTERESTED IN PEOPLE'S MOTIVATION. I'M INTERESTED IN WHAT MAKES PEOPLE DO THINGS THAT DON'T SEEM TO MAKE SENSE.
YOU'RE THE ONE NOT MAKING ANY SENSE. YOU ALWAYS HATED IT WHEN I STARTED TALKIN' ABOUT THE FAMILY.
BECAUSE IT WAS USUALLY A PRELIMINARY TO SOME HUGE GUILT-THING ABOUT LETTING YOU DOWN.

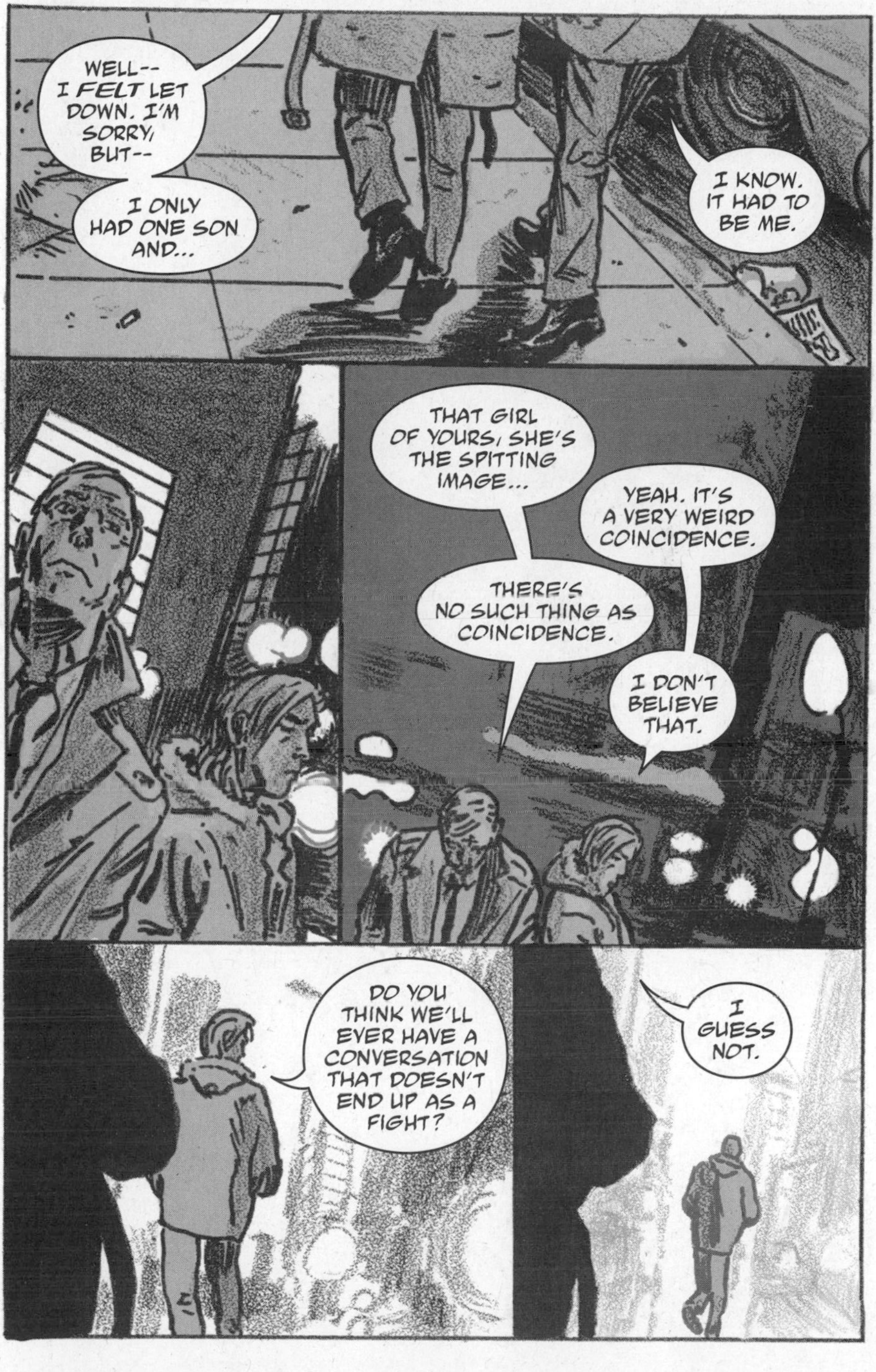
WELL-- I FELT LET DOWN. I'M SORRY, BUT--
I ONLY HAD ONE SON AND...
I KNOW. IT HAD TO BE ME.
THAT GIRL OF YOURS, SHE'S THE SPITTING IMAGE...
YEAH. IT'S A VERY WEIRD COINCIDENCE.
THERE'S NO SUCH THING AS COINCIDENCE.
I DON'T BELIEVE THAT.
DO YOU THINK WE'LL EVER HAVE A CONVERSATION THAT DOESN'T END UP AS A FIGHT?
I GUESS NOT.

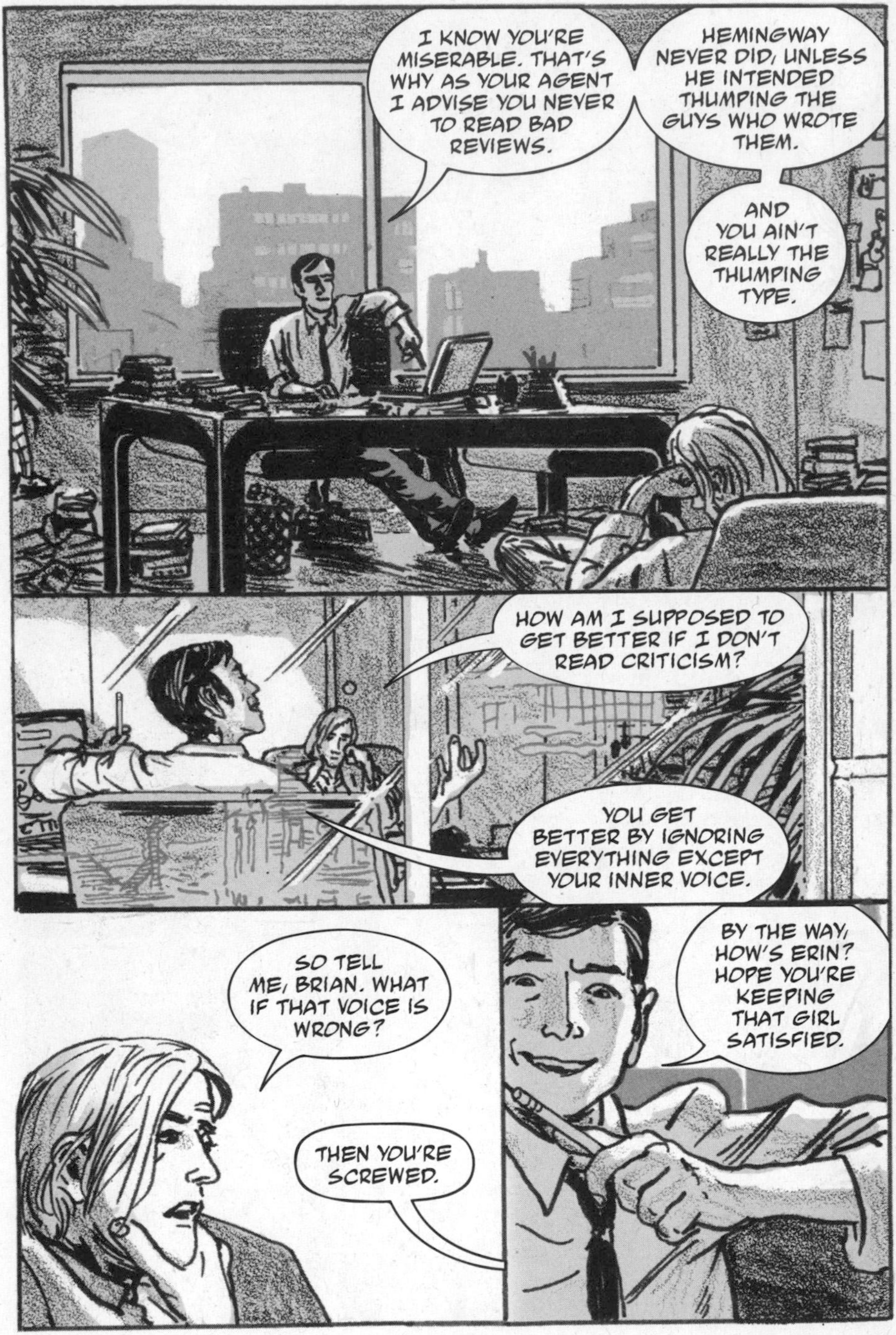
I KNOW YOU'RE MISERABLE. THAT'S WHY AS YOUR AGENT I ADVISE YOU NEVER TO READ BAD REVIEWS.
HEMINGWAY NEVER DID, UNLESS HE INTENDED THUMPING THE GUYS WHO WROTE THEM.
AND YOU AIN'T REALLY THE THUMPING TYPE.
HOW AM I SUPPOSED TO GET BETTER IF I DON'T READ CRITICISM?
YOU GET BETTER BY IGNORING EVERYTHING EXCEPT YOUR INNER VOICE.
SO TELL ME, BRIAN. WHAT IF THAT VOICE IS WRONG?
THEN YOU'RE SCREWED.
BY THE WAY, HOW'S ERIN? HOPE YOU'RE KEEPING THAT GIRL SATISFIED.

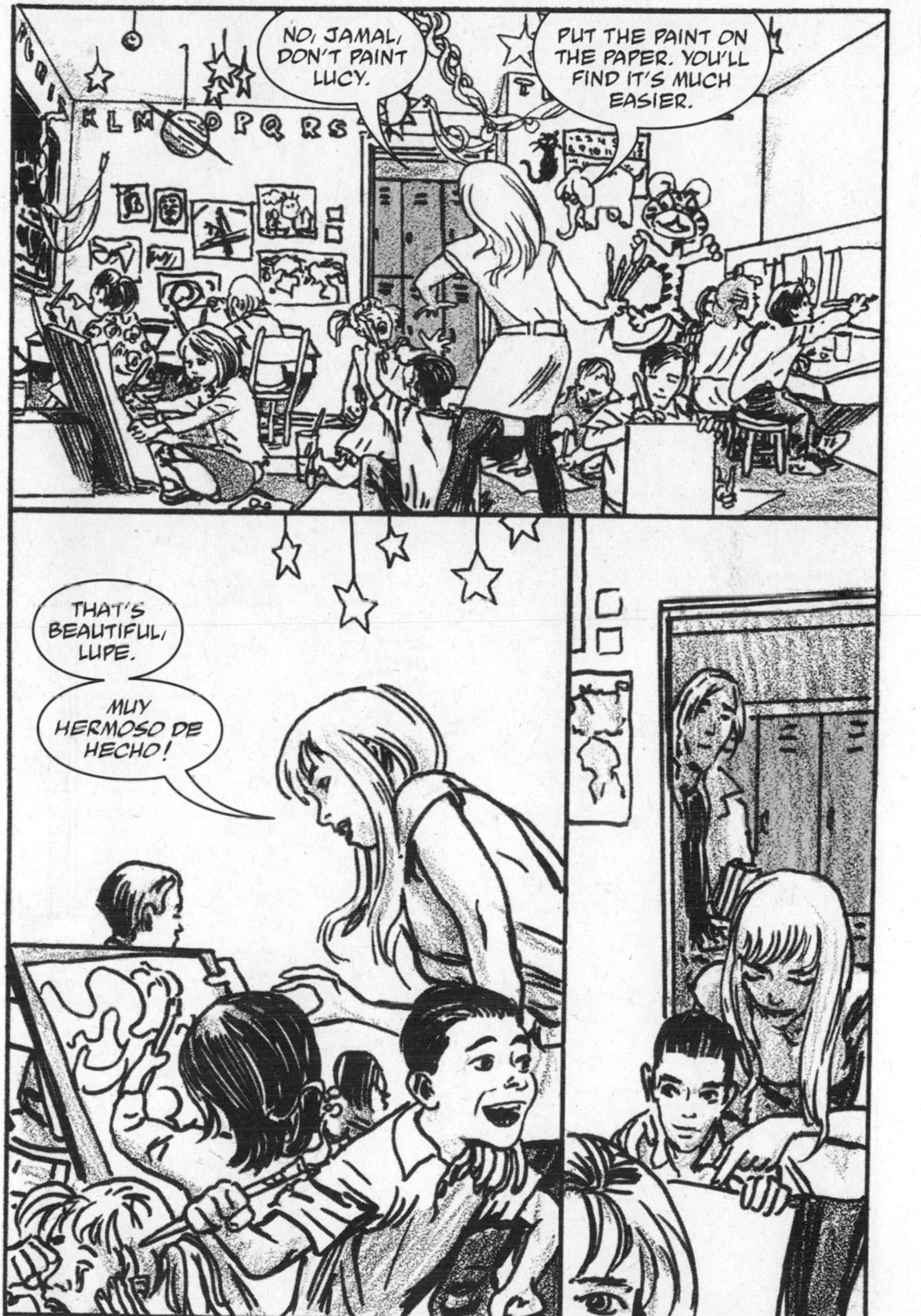
NO, JAMAL, DON'T PAINT LUCY.
PUT THE PAINT ON THE PAPER. YOU'LL FIND IT'S MUCH EASIER.
THAT'S BEAUTIFUL, LUPE.
MUY HERMOSO DE HECHO!

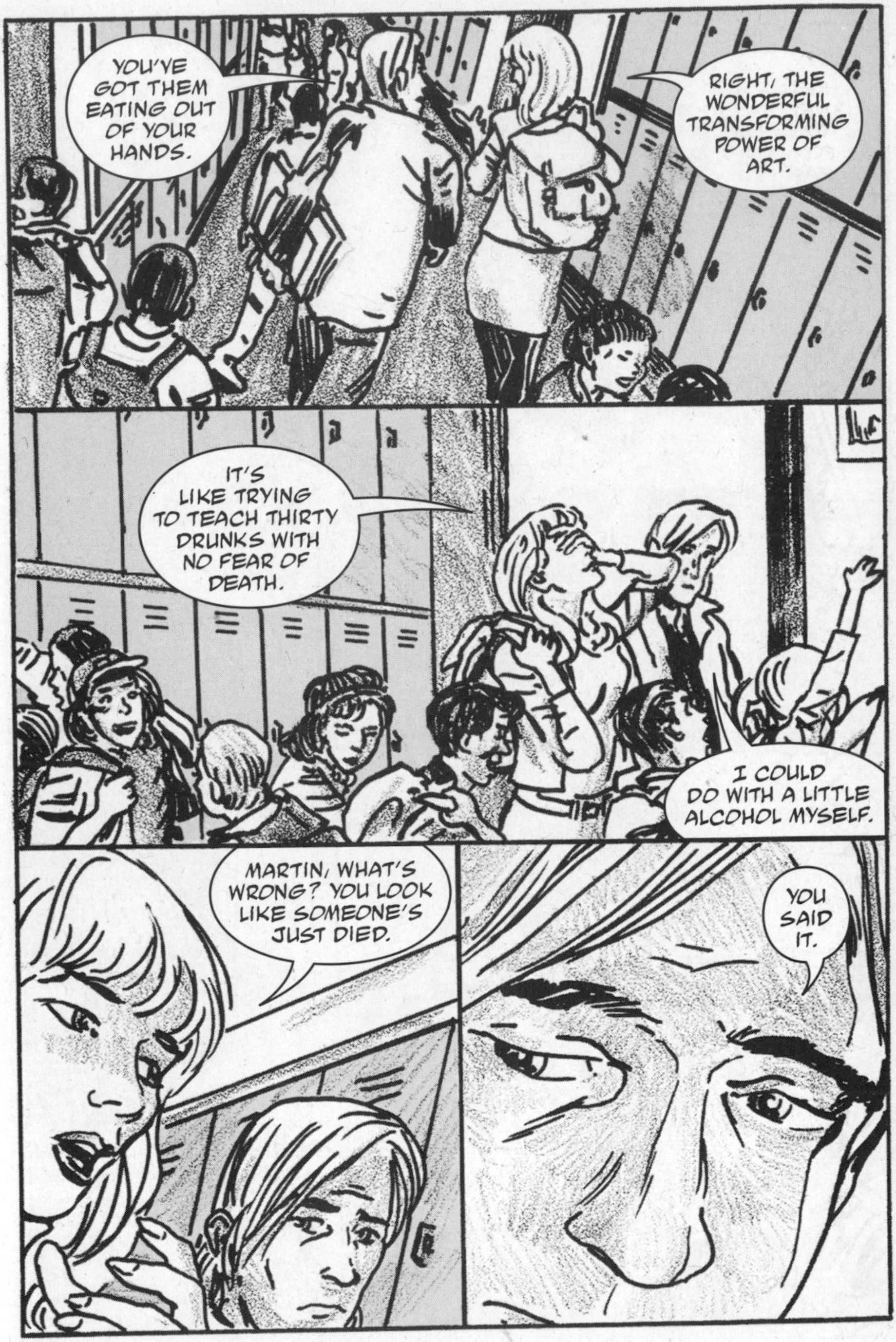

YOU'VE GOT THEM EATING OUT OF YOUR HANDS.
RIGHT, THE WONDERFUL TRANSFORMING POWER OF ART.
IT'S LIKE TRYING TO TEACH THIRTY DRUNKS WITH NO FEAR OF DEATH.
I COULD DO WITH A LITTLE ALCOHOL MYSELF.
MARTIN, WHAT'S WRONG? YOU LOOK LIKE SOMEONE'S JUST DIED.
YOU SAID IT.

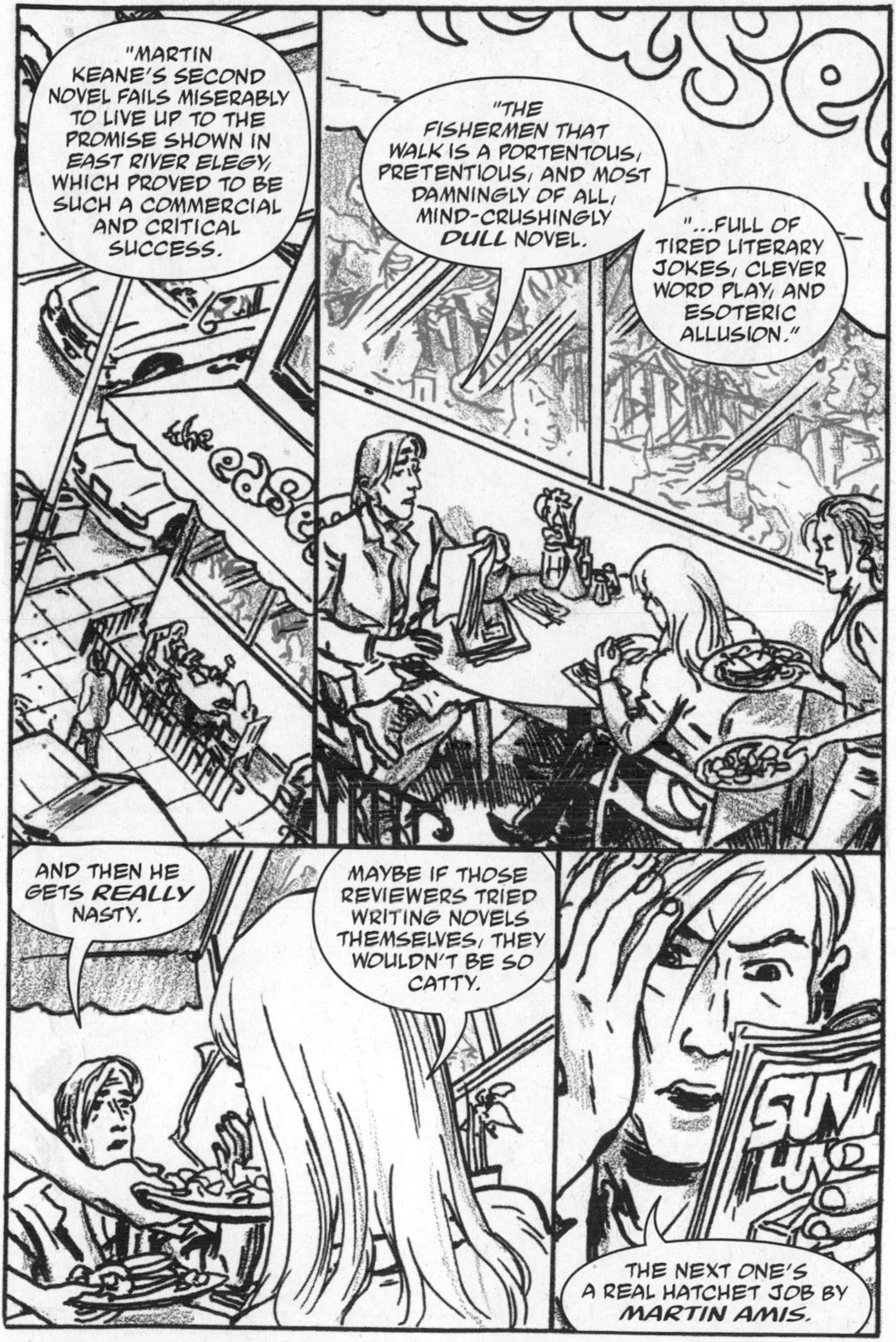
"MARTIN KEANE'S SECOND NOVEL FAILS MISERABLY TO LIVE UP TO THE PROMISE SHOWN IN EAST RIVER ELEGY, WHICH PROVED TO BE SUCH A COMMERCIAL AND CRITICAL SUCCESS.
"THE FISHERMEN THAT WALK IS A PORTENTOUS, PRETENTIOUS, AND MOST DAMNINGLY OF ALL, MIND-CRUSHINGLY DULL NOVEL.
"...FULL OF TIRED LITERARY JOKES, CLEVER WORD PLAY, AND ESOTERIC ALLUSION."
AND THEN HE GETS REALLY NASTY.
MAYBE IF THOSE REVIEWERS TRIED WRITING NOVELS THEMSELVES, THEY WOULDN'T BE SO CATTY.
THE NEXT ONE'S A REAL HATCHET JOB BY MARTIN AMIS.

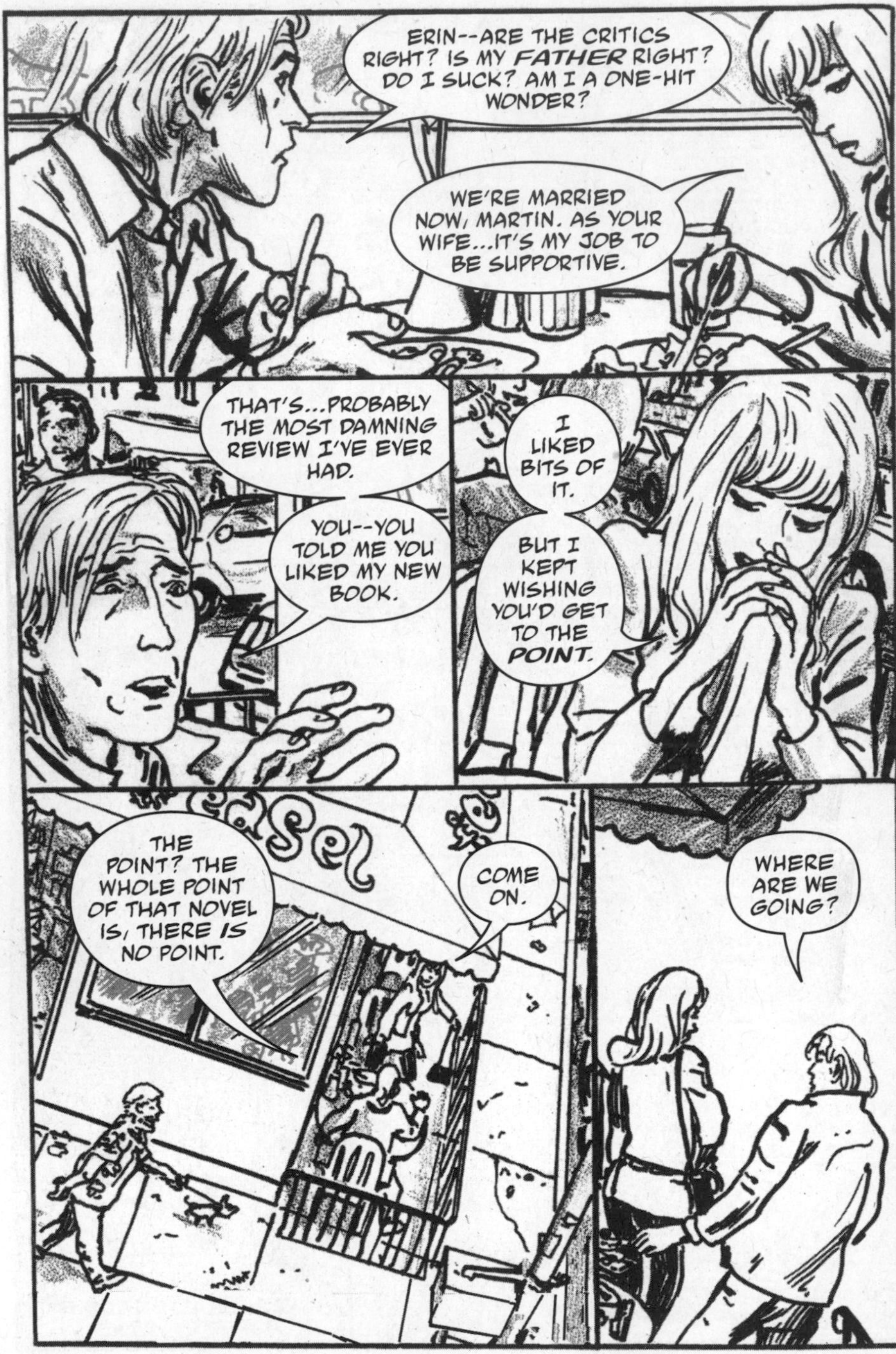
ERIN--ARE THE CRITICS RIGHT? IS MY FATHER RIGHT? DO I SUCK? AM I A ONE-HIT WONDER?
WE'RE MARRIED NOW, MARTIN. AS YOUR WIFE...IT'S MY JOB TO BE SUPPORTIVE.
THAT'S...PROBABLY THE MOST DAMNING REVIEW I'VE EVER HAD.
YOU--YOU TOLD ME YOU LIKED MY NEW BOOK.
I LIKED BITS OF IT.
BUT I KEPT WISHING YOU'D GET TO THE POINT.
THE POINT? THE WHOLE POINT OF THAT NOVEL IS, THERE IS NO POINT.
COME ON.
WHERE ARE WE GOING?

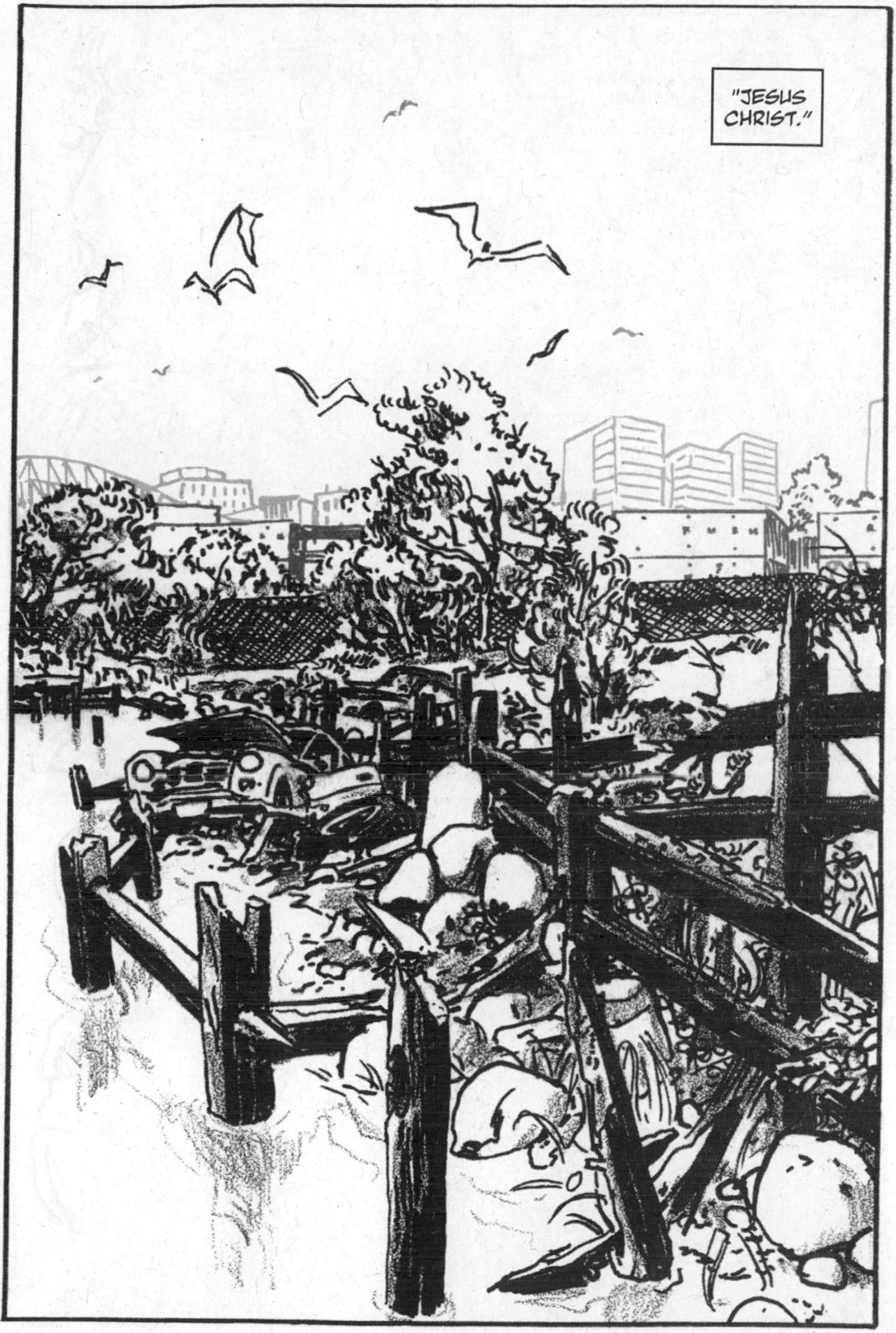
"JESUS CHRIST."

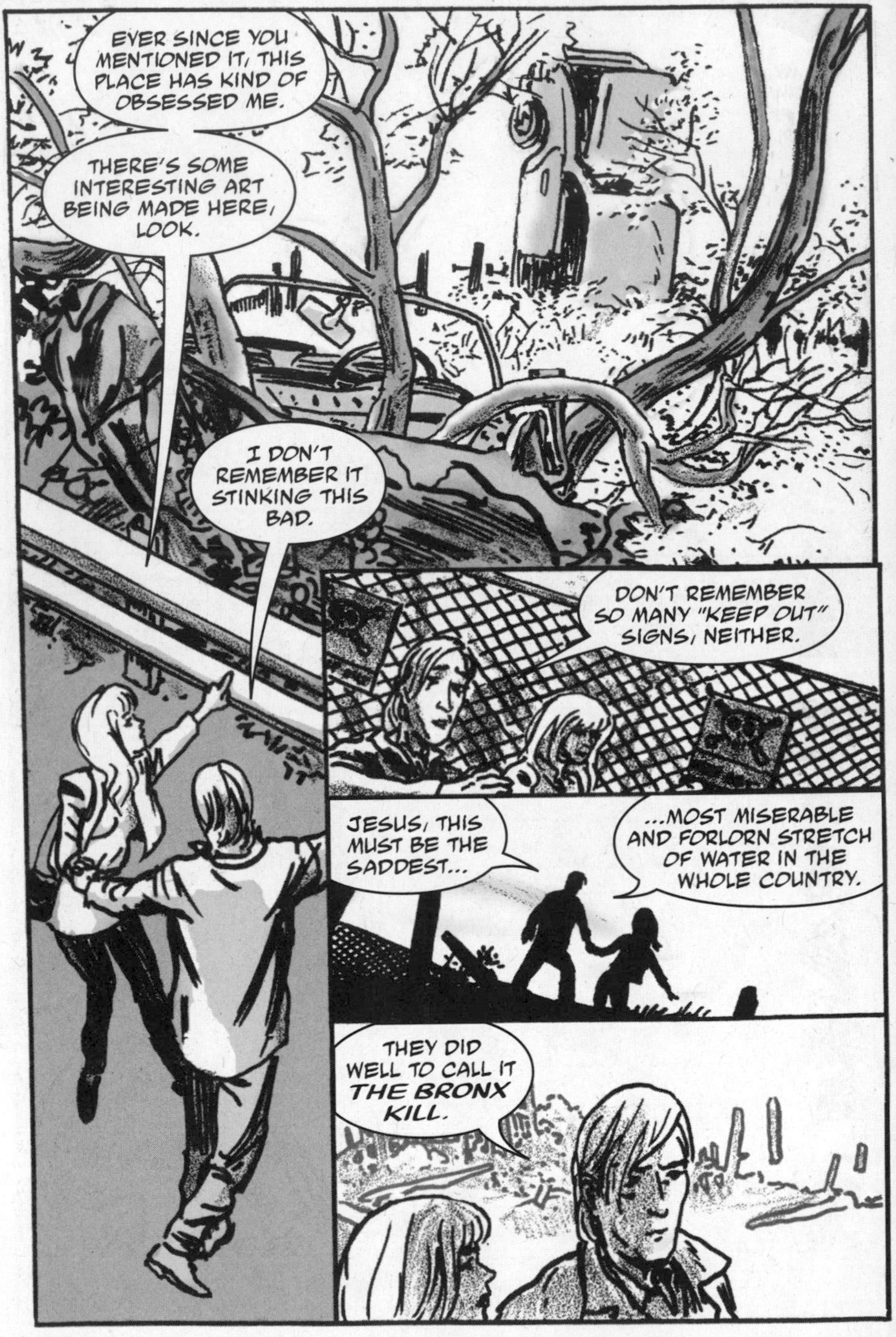
EVER SINCE YOU MENTIONED IT, THIS PLACE HAS KIND OF OBSESSED ME.
THERE'S SOME INTERESTING ART BEING MADE HERE, LOOK.
I DON'T REMEMBER IT STINKING THIS BAD.
DON'T REMEMBER SO MANY "KEEP OUT" SIGNS, NEITHER.
JESUS, THIS MUST BE THE SADDEST...
...MOST MISERABLE AND FORLORN STRETCH OF WATER IN THE WHOLE COUNTRY.
THEY DID WELL TO CALL IT THE BRONX KILL.

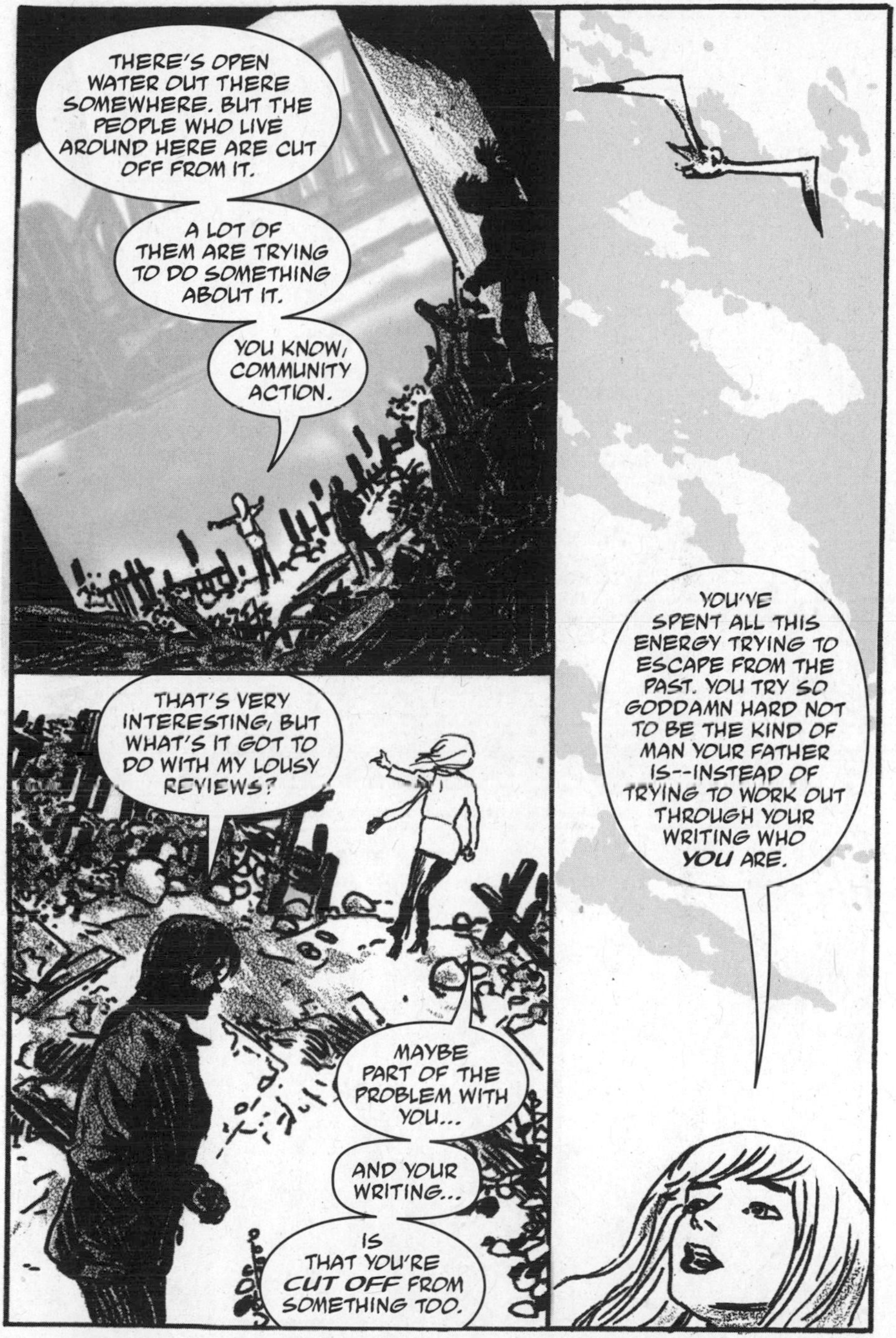
THERE'S OPEN WATER OUT THERE SOMEWHERE. BUT THE PEOPLE WHO LIVE AROUND HERE ARE CUT OFF FROM IT.
A LOT OF THEM ARE TRYING TO DO SOMETHING ABOUT IT.
YOU KNOW, COMMUNITY ACTION.
THAT'S VERY INTERESTING, BUT WHAT'S IT GOT TO DO WITH MY LOUSY REVIEWS?
MAYBE PART OF THE PROBLEM WITH YOU...
AND YOUR WRITING...
IS THAT YOU'RE CUT OFF FROM SOMETHING TOO.
YOU'VE SPENT ALL THIS ENERGY TRYING TO ESCAPE FROM THE PAST. YOU TRY SO GODDAMN HARD NOT TO BE THE KIND OF MAN YOUR FATHER IS--INSTEAD OF TRYING TO WORK OUT THROUGH YOUR WRITING WHO YOU ARE.

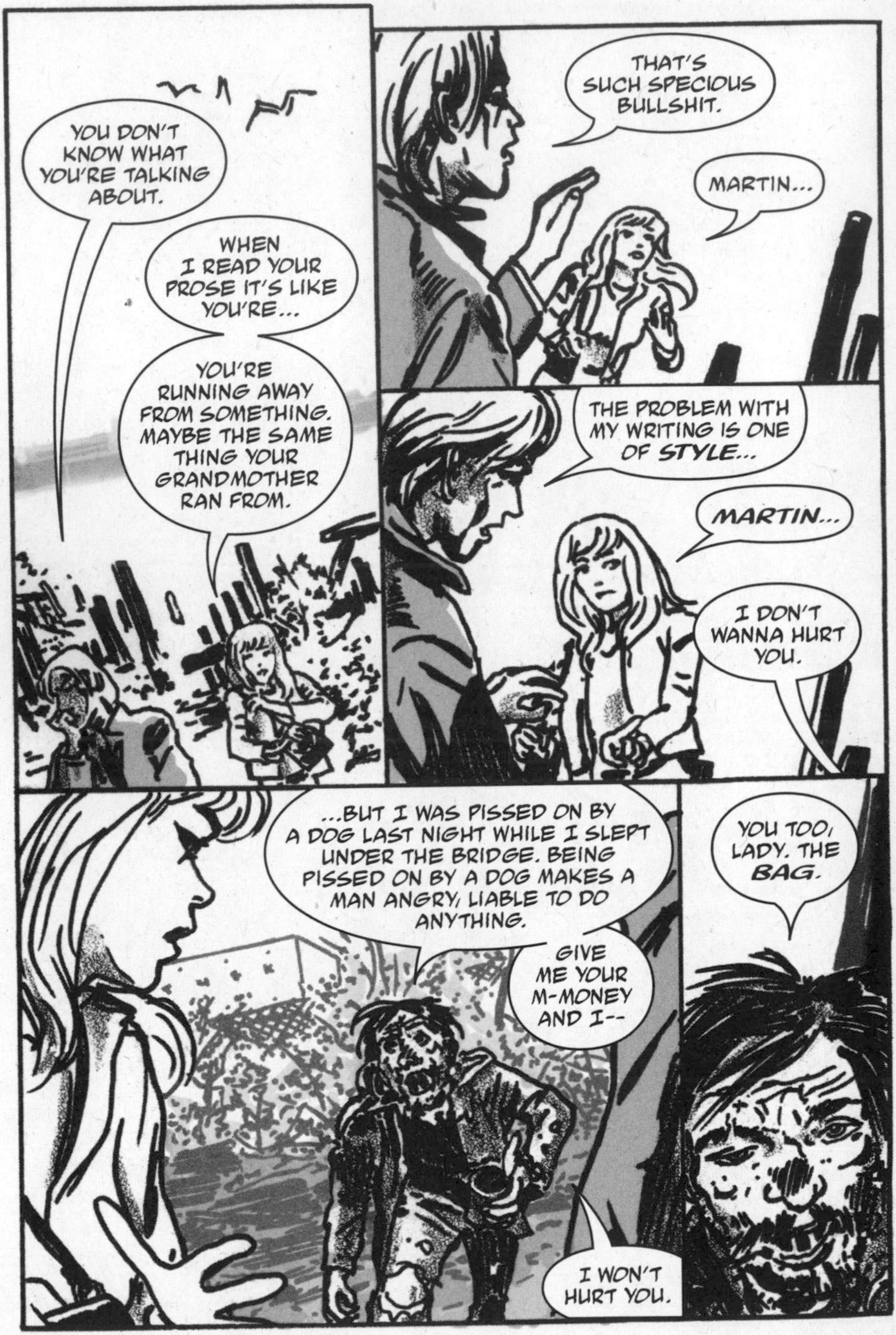

YOU DON'T KNOW WHAT YOU'RE TALKING ABOUT.
WHEN I READ YOUR PROSE IT'S LIKE YOU'RE...
YOU'RE RUNNING AWAY FROM SOMETHING. MAYBE THE SAME THING YOUR GRANDMOTHER RAN FROM.
THAT'S SUCH SPECIOUS BULLSHIT.
MARTIN...
THE PROBLEM WITH MY WRITING IS ONE OF STYLE...
MARTIN...
I DON'T WANNA HURT YOU.
...BUT I WAS PISSED ON BY A DOG LAST NIGHT WHILE I SLEPT UNDER THE BRIDGE. BEING PISSED ON BY A DOG MAKES A MAN ANGRY, LIABLE TO DO ANYTHING.
GIVE ME YOUR M-MONEY AND I--
I WON'T HURT YOU.
YOU TOO, LADY. THE BAG.

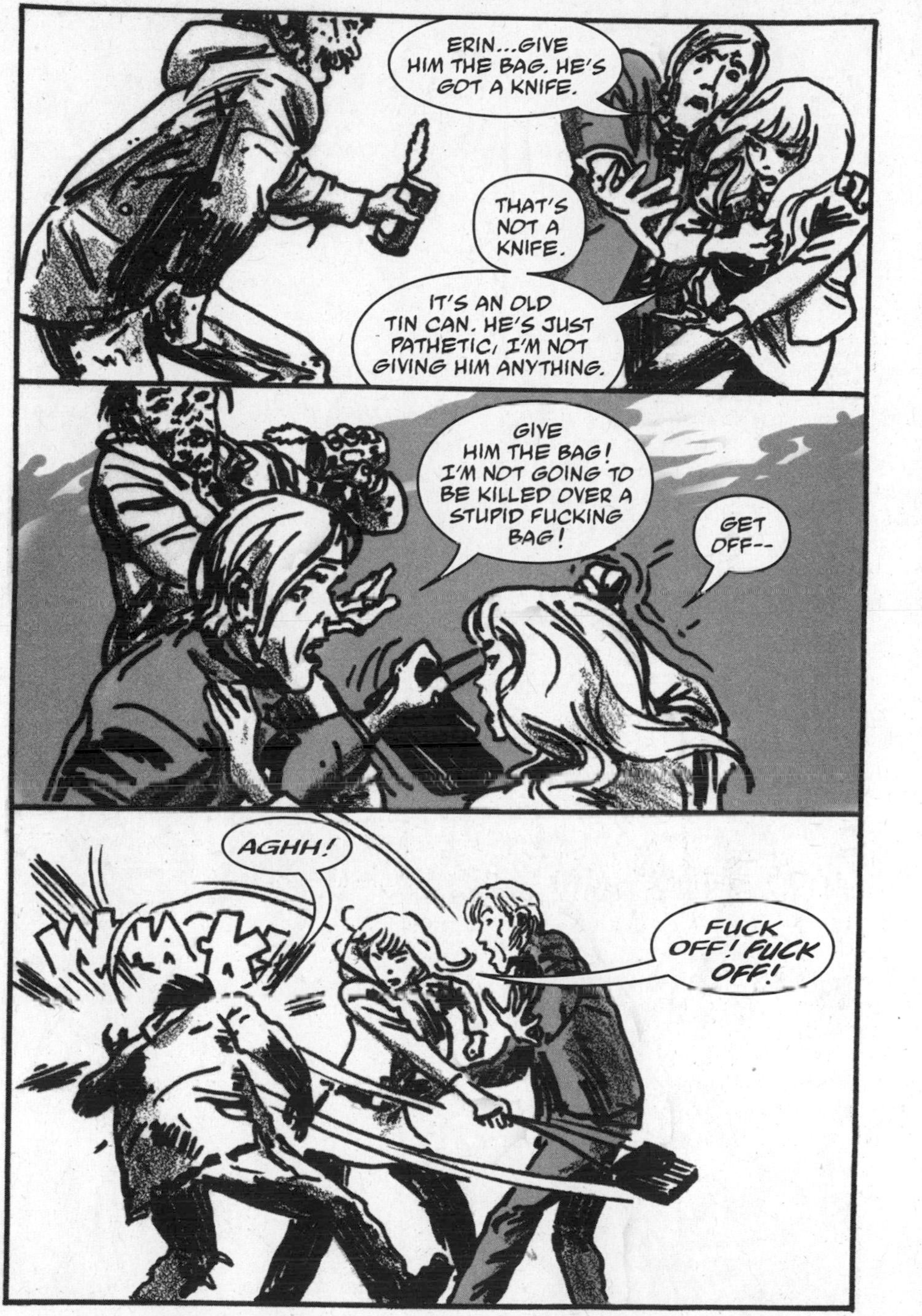

ERIN...GIVE HIM THE BAG. HE'S GOT A KNIFE.
THAT'S NOT A KNIFE.
IT'S AN OLD TIN CAN. HE'S JUST PATHETIC, I'M NOT GIVING HIM ANYTHING.
GIVE HIM THE BAG! I'M NOT GOING TO BE KILLED OVER A STUPID FUCKING BAG!
GET OFF--
AGHH!
FUCK OFF! FUCK OFF!

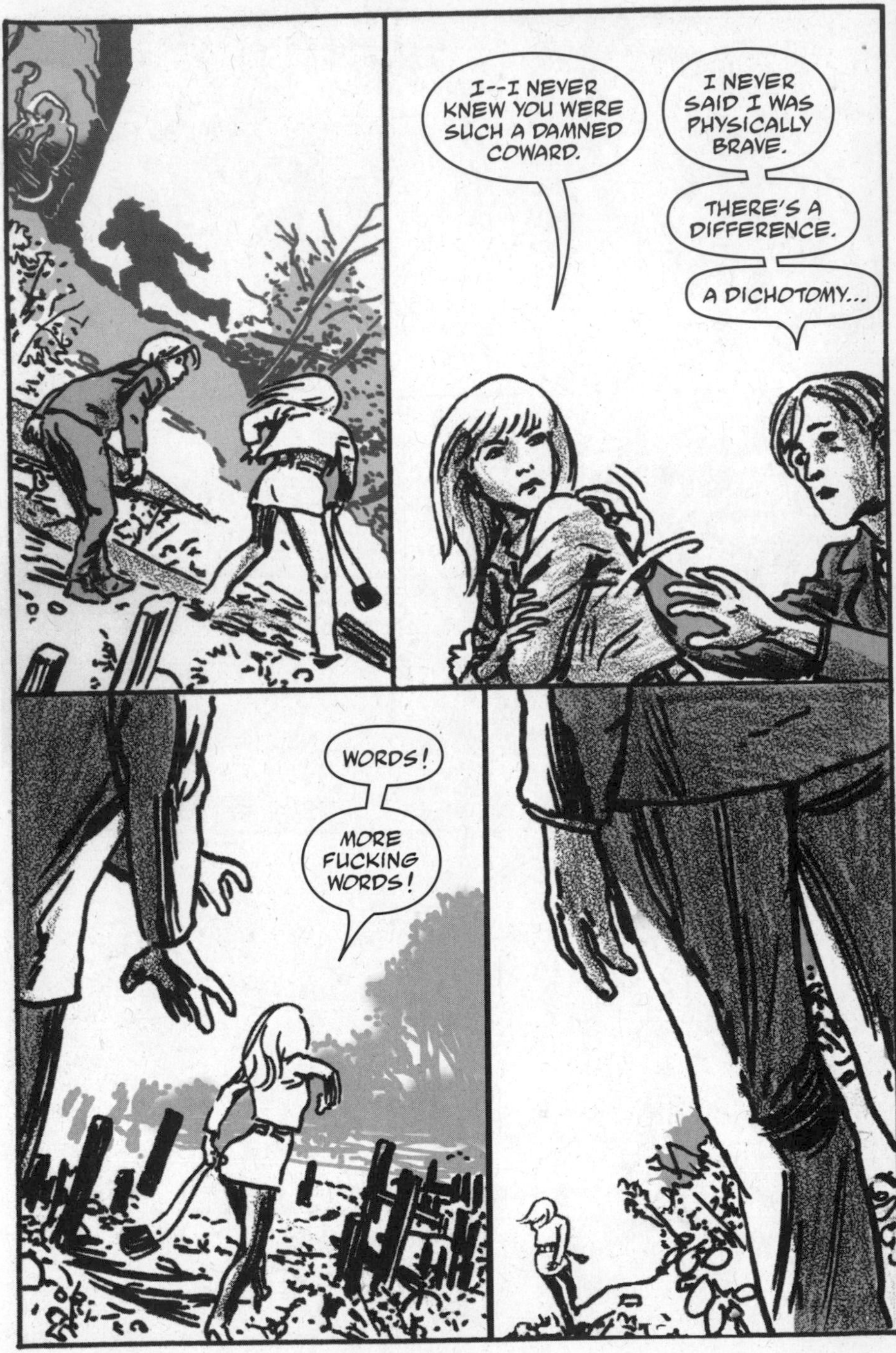
I--I NEVER KNEW YOU WERE SUCH A DAMNED COWARD.
I NEVER SAID I WAS PHYSICALLY BRAVE.
THERE'S A DIFFERENCE.
A DICHOTOMY...
WORDS!
MORE FUCKING WORDS!

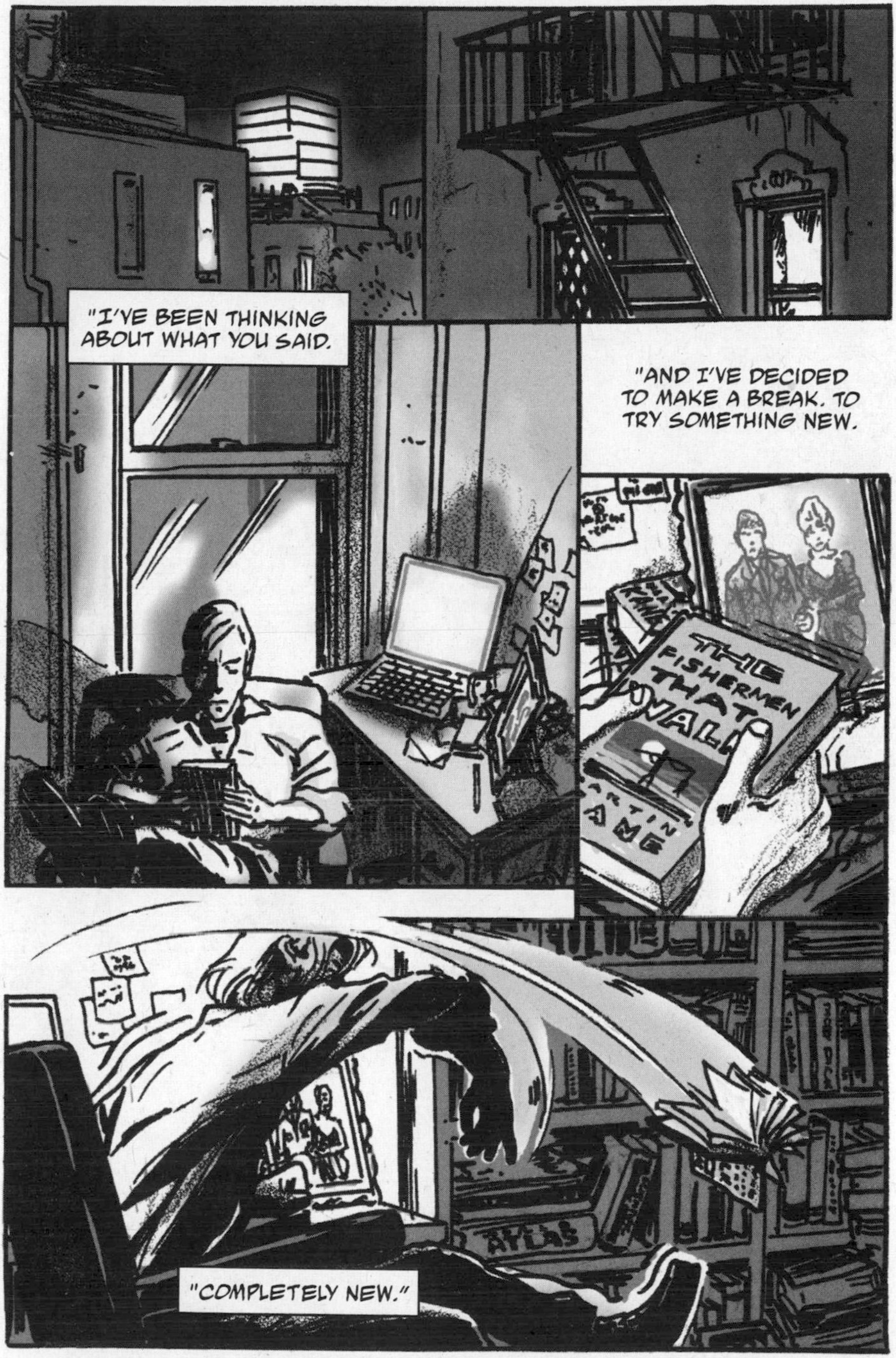
"I'VE BEEN THINKING ABOUT WHAT YOU SAID.
"AND I'VE DECIDED TO MAKE A BREAK. TO TRY SOMETHING NEW.
THE FISHERMEN THAT WAL
MARTIN AME
ATLAS
"COMPLETELY NEW."

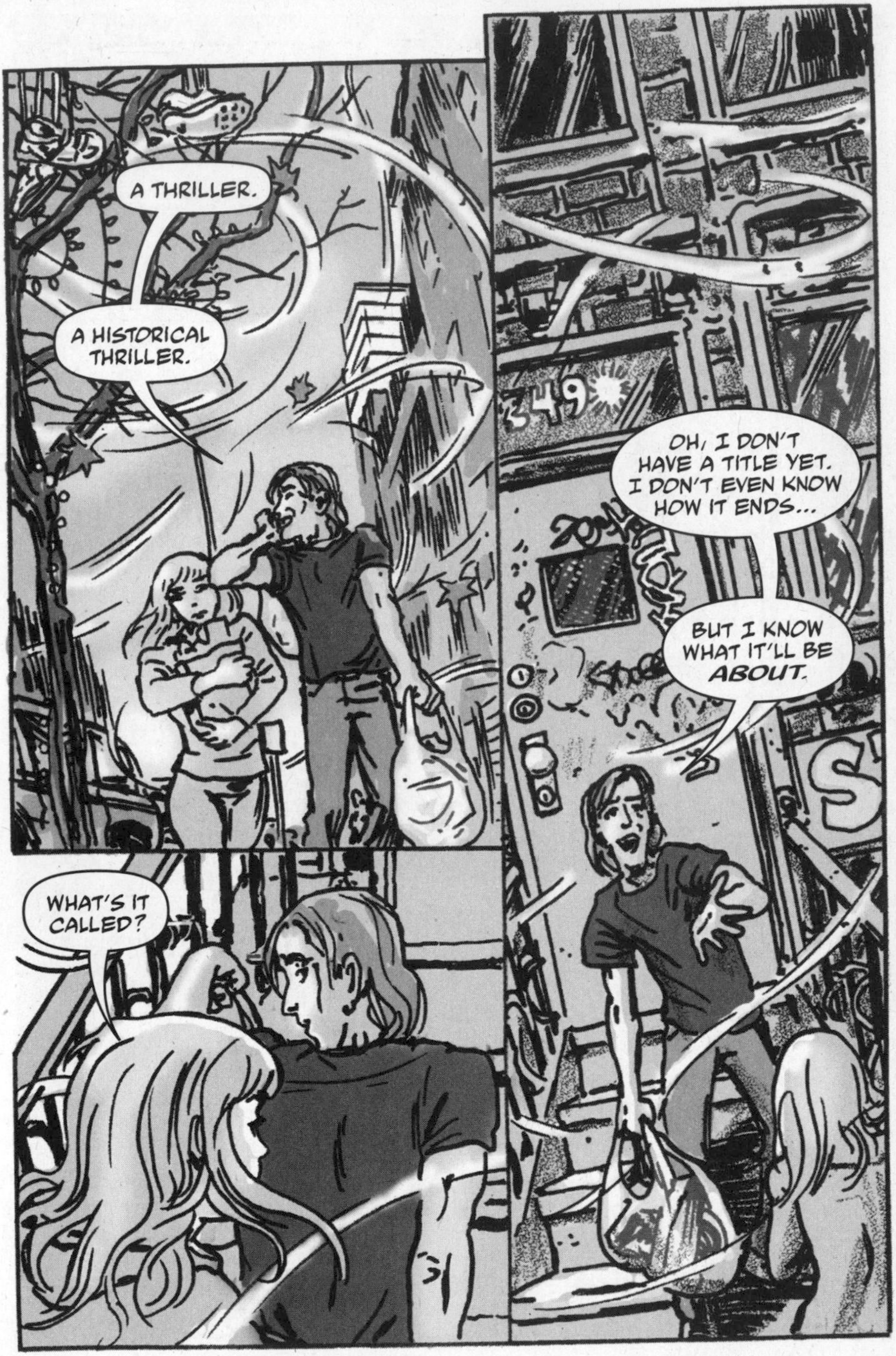
A THRILLER.
A HISTORICAL THRILLER.
WHAT'S IT CALLED?
349
OH, I DON'T HAVE A TITLE YET. I DON'T EVEN KNOW HOW IT ENDS...
BUT I KNOW WHAT IT'LL BE *ABOUT*.

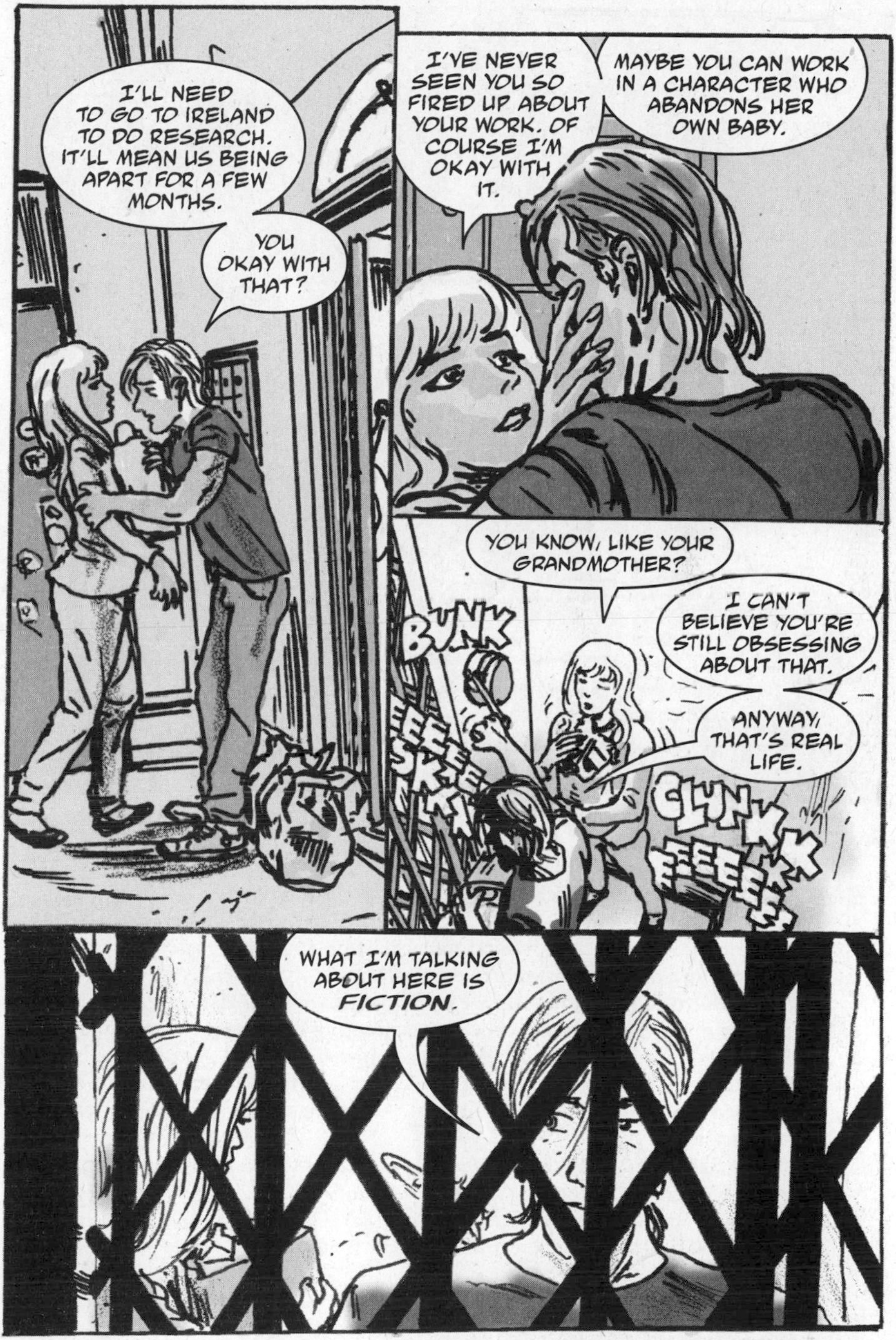
I'LL NEED TO GO TO IRELAND TO DO RESEARCH. IT'LL MEAN US BEING APART FOR A FEW MONTHS.
YOU OKAY WITH THAT?
I'VE NEVER SEEN YOU SO FIRED UP ABOUT YOUR WORK. OF COURSE I'M OKAY WITH IT.
MAYBE YOU CAN WORK IN A CHARACTER WHO ABANDONS HER OWN BABY.
YOU KNOW, LIKE YOUR GRANDMOTHER?
BUNK
I CAN'T BELIEVE YOU'RE STILL OBSESSING ABOUT THAT.
ANYWAY, THAT'S REAL LIFE.
CLUNKK
WHAT I'M TALKING ABOUT HERE IS *FICTION*.

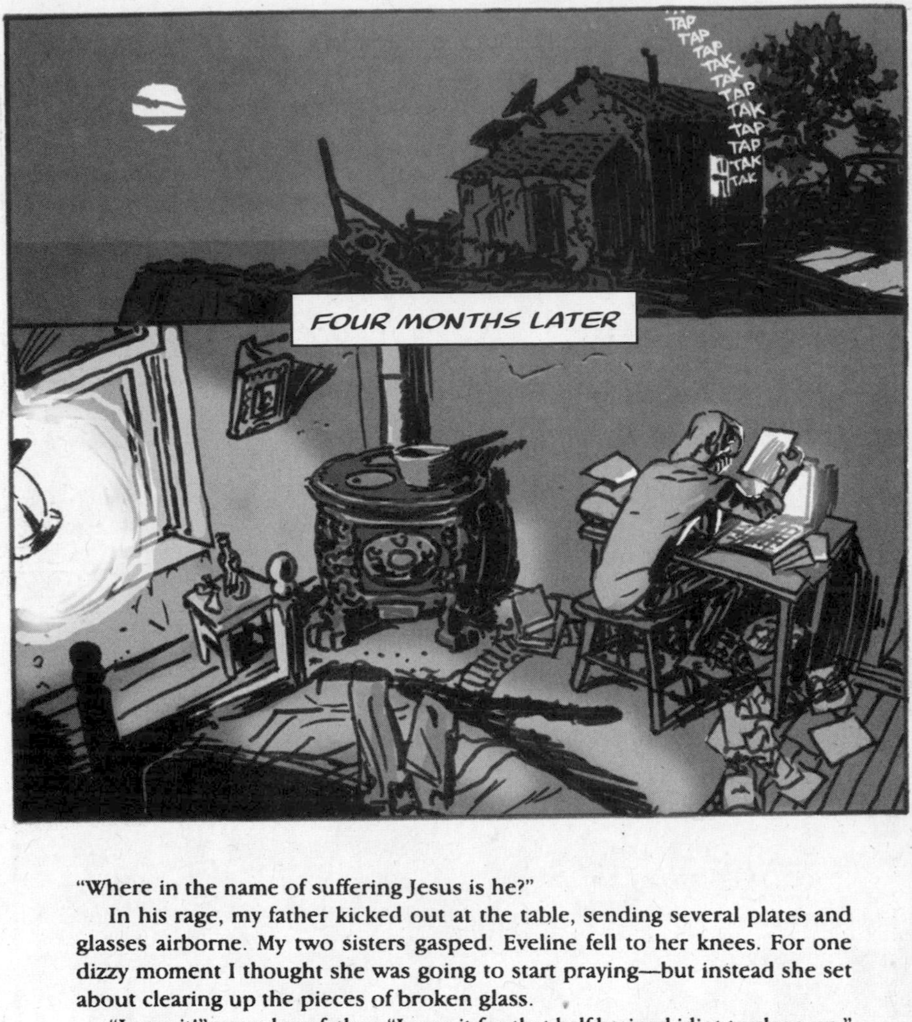
...
TAP
TAP
TAP
TAK
TAK
TAP
TAK
TAP
TAP
TAK
TAK
FOUR MONTHS LATER

"Where in the name of suffering Jesus is he?"

In his rage, my father kicked out at the table, sending several plates and glasses airborne. My two sisters gasped. Eveline fell to her knees. For one dizzy moment I thought she was going to start praying—but instead she set about clearing up the pieces of broken glass.

"Leave it!" roared my father. "Leave it for that half-brained idiot to clean up."

Eveline meekly withdrew to her chair, shooting me a helpless wounded look, crushed by the ferocity of Papa's face, which was pulled out of shape by anger and nameless inner turmoil. My father—so he claimed—had once been called the "handsomest man in Cork." But that was long ago. That was another man.

Check w/ Dad about Cork

The "half-brained idiot" Papa referred to was my brother Hugh, who had been sent out some time earlier to Cunniams to buy three pounds of *crubeens*—or pig trotters—which Papa was particularly fond of. I stood in the corner, at the edge of the candle's reach, there but not there, with one thought *scorching* through my soul.

Please God, ~~help me get away~~ from this.

let me be free

Four years earlier, the first black potatoes had been dug up in the West. The potatoes were soft and gave off the stench of Satan's eggy supper. Nothing would be the same again, for any of us. I am told that here in the city of Cork we were spared the worst apocalypses of the great hungers. But for me those filthy potatoes, and the lines of ragged stick people that soon followed them, were another reason to want to escape.

It seemed that I had wanted to escape since I could remember. Maybe it was something to do with never having had a mother around. My mother died when I was six. Seventeen hours she spent giving birth to Eveline and didn't live to see her. I still remember the screams. The silence. The sobbing. And then the silence again.

Then again, maybe my itch to escape was simply a symptom of our diseased times, which made potential emigrants of us all. Of course, from the outside we remained a respectable middle-class family. My father owned a brickfield, we lived in a house built in the time of Wolfe Tone. But in truth the house was falling apart, and so was the Furey family that lived inside it. The famine was over now, but we were still suffering. Sometimes it felt as though our history was squeezing the life out of the whole bloody lot of us.

I was sent out to look for Hugh. Was he lost? Had he gone drinking with the money Papa had given him? Had he — God Forbid! — forgotten all about his *crubeen*-hunt and headed for the Holy Ground, as our city's brothel district was called?

Most likely, he had simply wandered off. They always said that Hugh was a little soft in the head: There were those who ventured that a strain of something mentally rotten ran in us Fureys, as though certain of our brains, if dug out of their skulls, might be as black and foul-smelling as the tubers they'd been uncovering in the fields.

Whatever the truth of this, what had made Hugh worse, what had further rotted his mind, had surely been his obsession with the half-dead creatures on the quays in Queenstown. He used to watch them as they waited for the ships to take them away from this hungry land. Hours, he'd stand there. And then he'd tell me about them, in strange wide-eyed detail. I suppose I should have been warned, should have been concerned about my brother.

Ah, but I had my own worries. Papa was convinced I'd take over the running of the cursed brickyard; that I would become another version of him and my grandfather, who had started the family business. I was equally convinced that this wouldn't happen. If it hadn't been for poor Eveline I would have taken to the road before now. But Eveline, with her harelip and sweet nature that meant she was forever bullied, needed me.

[handwritten marginal notes:]
Better link to mother. Look at Woolf. The character who doesn't appear.

too much?

More? Ask Dad about Ireland

some

it

could not

Is he telling the truth?

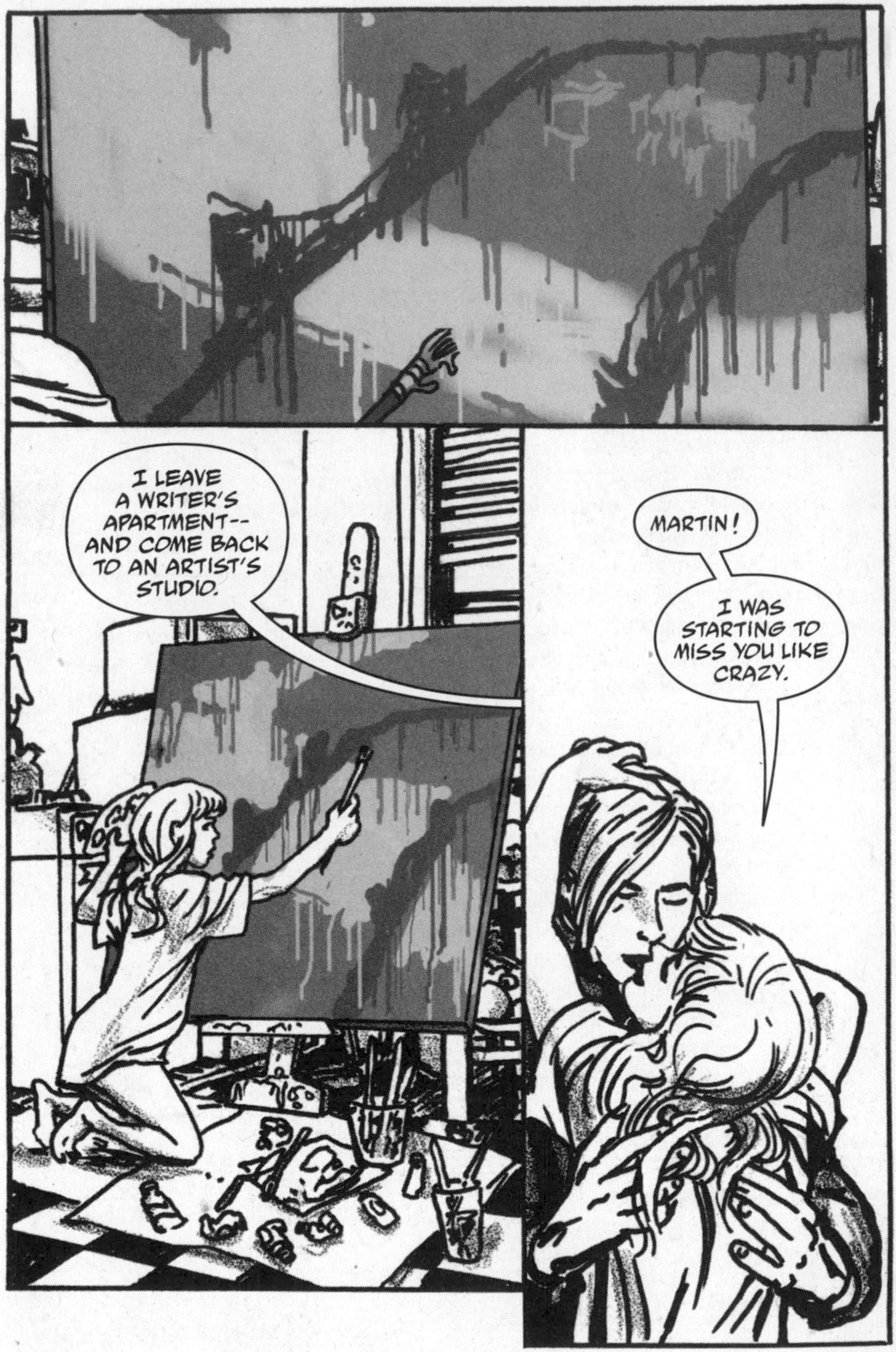
I LEAVE A WRITER'S APARTMENT-- AND COME BACK TO AN ARTIST'S STUDIO.
MARTIN!
I WAS STARTING TO MISS YOU LIKE CRAZY.

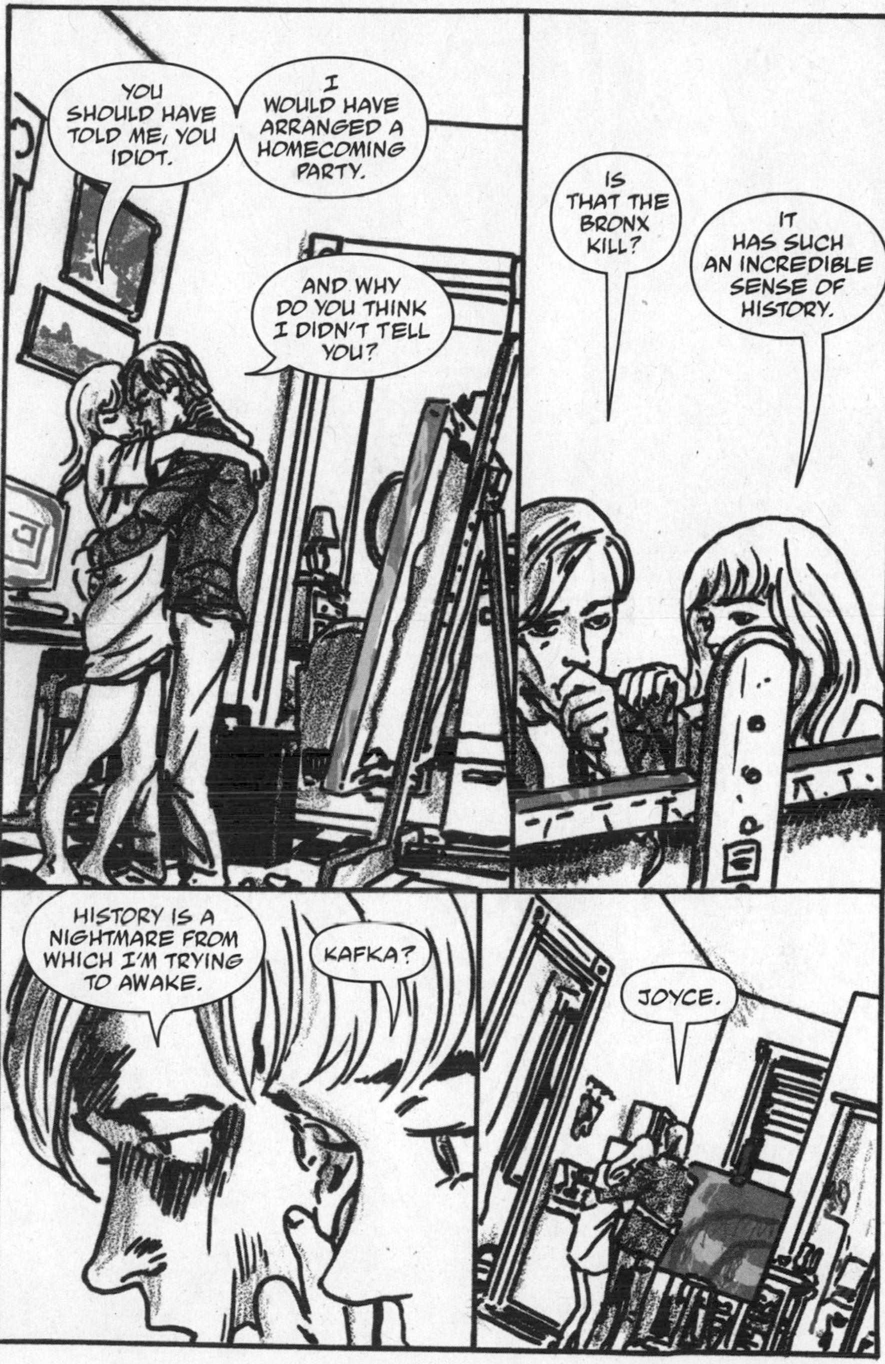
YOU SHOULD HAVE TOLD ME, YOU IDIOT.
I WOULD HAVE ARRANGED A HOMECOMING PARTY.
AND WHY DO YOU THINK I DIDN'T TELL YOU?
IS THAT THE BRONX KILL?
IT HAS SUCH AN INCREDIBLE SENSE OF HISTORY.
HISTORY IS A NIGHTMARE FROM WHICH I'M TRYING TO AWAKE.
KAFKA?
JOYCE.

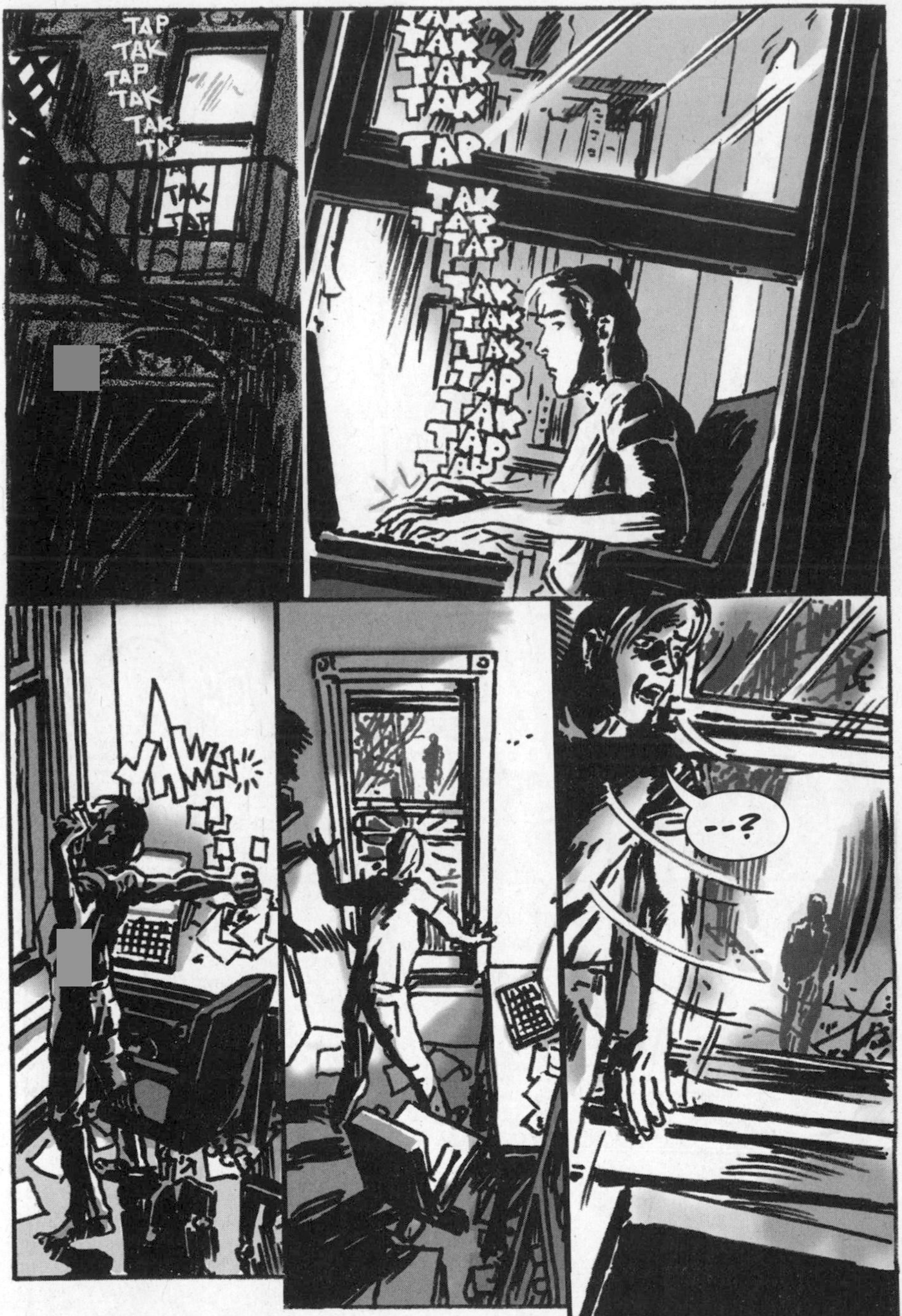
TAP
TAK
TAP
TAK
TAK
TAK
TAP
TAK
TAK
TAK
TAK
TAP
TAK
TAP
TAP
TAK
TAK
TAP
TAK
TAP
YAWN
--?

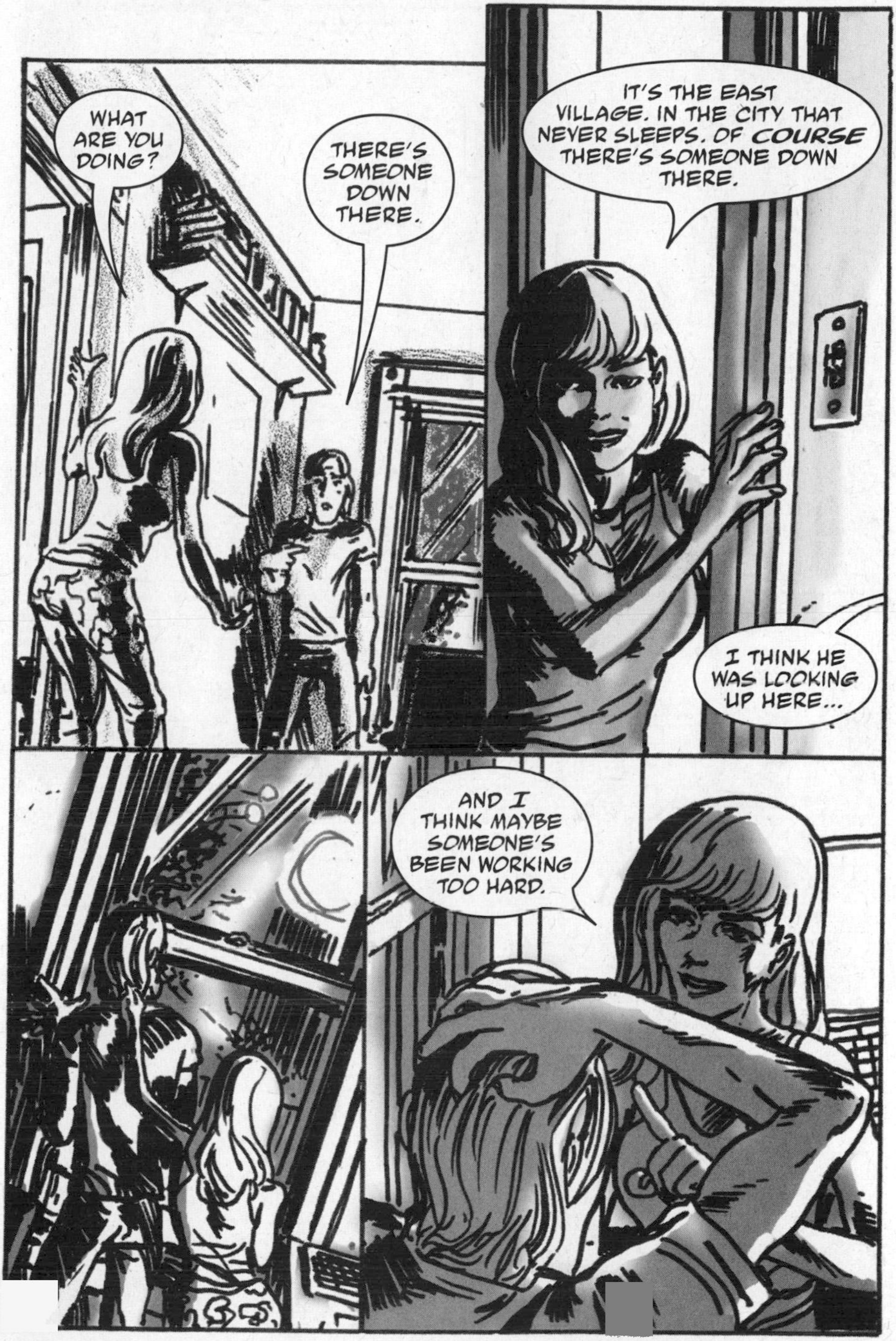
WHAT ARE YOU DOING?
THERE'S SOMEONE DOWN THERE.
IT'S THE EAST VILLAGE. IN THE CITY THAT NEVER SLEEPS. OF COURSE THERE'S SOMEONE DOWN THERE.
I THINK HE WAS LOOKING UP HERE...
AND I THINK MAYBE SOMEONE'S BEEN WORKING TOO HARD.

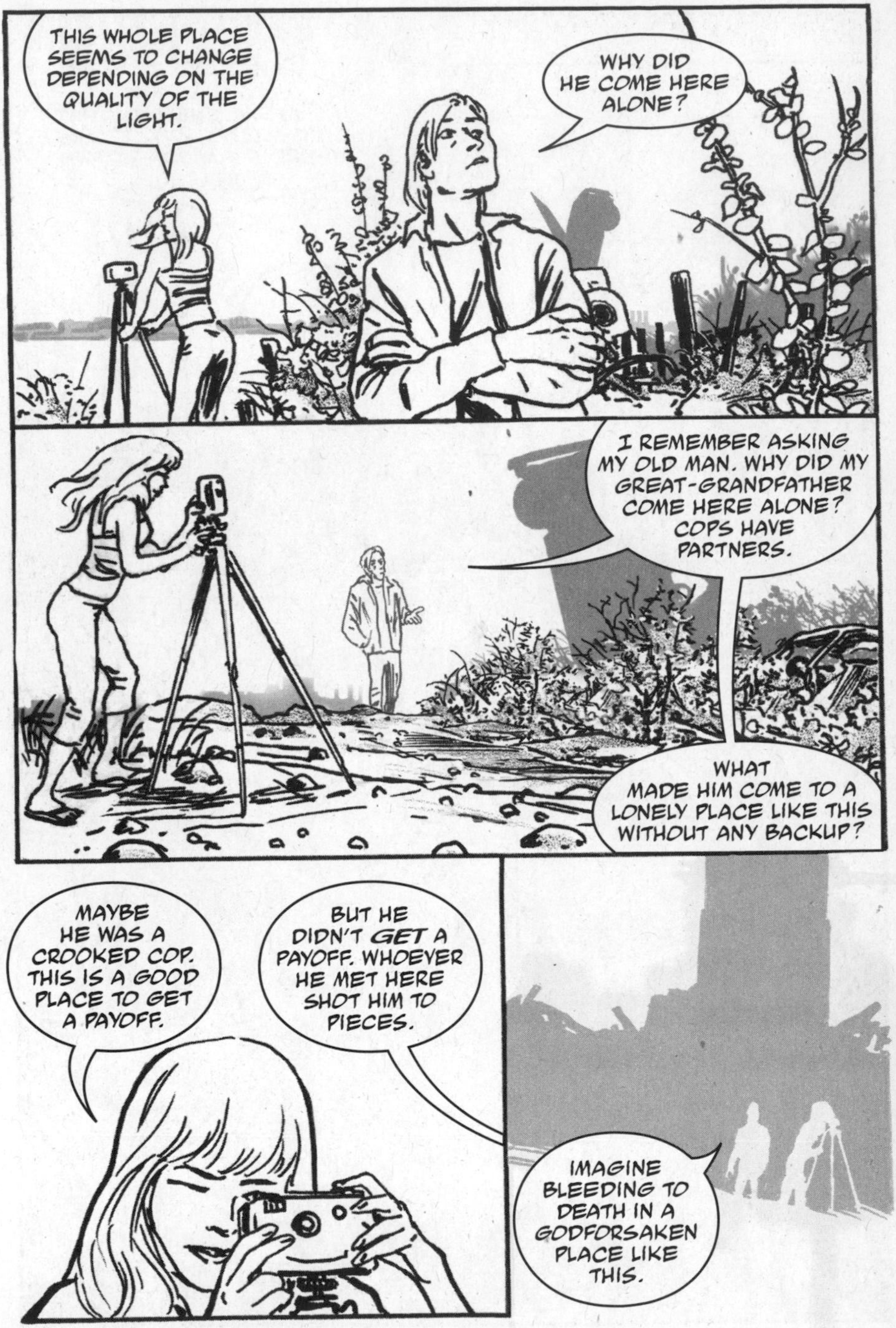
THIS WHOLE PLACE SEEMS TO CHANGE DEPENDING ON THE QUALITY OF THE LIGHT.
WHY DID HE COME HERE ALONE?
I REMEMBER ASKING MY OLD MAN. WHY DID MY GREAT-GRANDFATHER COME HERE ALONE? COPS HAVE PARTNERS.
WHAT MADE HIM COME TO A LONELY PLACE LIKE THIS WITHOUT ANY BACKUP?
MAYBE HE WAS A CROOKED COP. THIS IS A GOOD PLACE TO GET A PAYOFF.
BUT HE DIDN'T *GET* A PAYOFF. WHOEVER HE MET HERE SHOT HIM TO PIECES.
IMAGINE BLEEDING TO DEATH IN A GODFORSAKEN PLACE LIKE THIS.

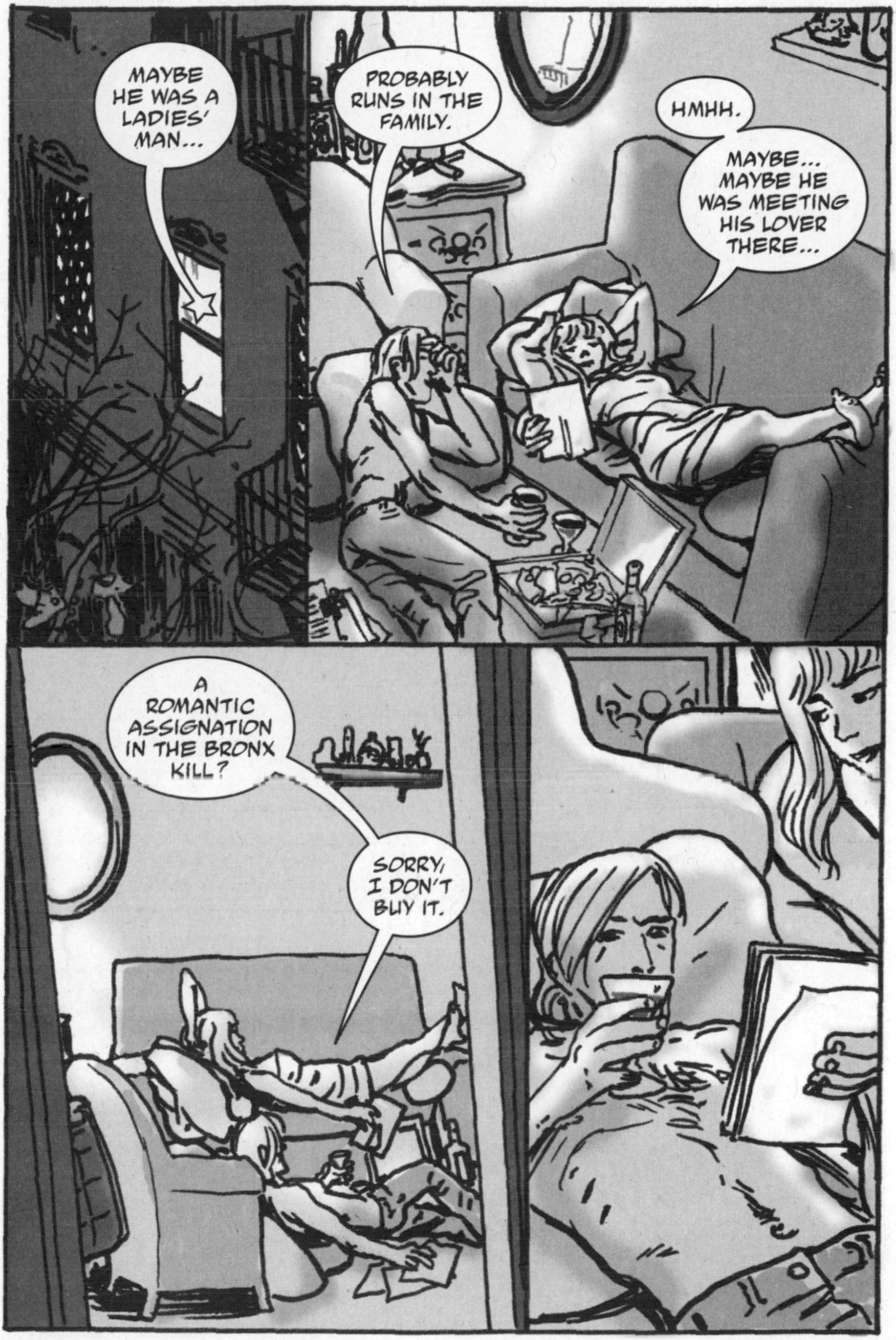
MAYBE HE WAS A LADIES' MAN...
PROBABLY RUNS IN THE FAMILY.
HMHH.
MAYBE... MAYBE HE WAS MEETING HIS LOVER THERE...
A ROMANTIC ASSIGNATION IN THE BRONX KILL?
SORRY, I DON'T BUY IT.

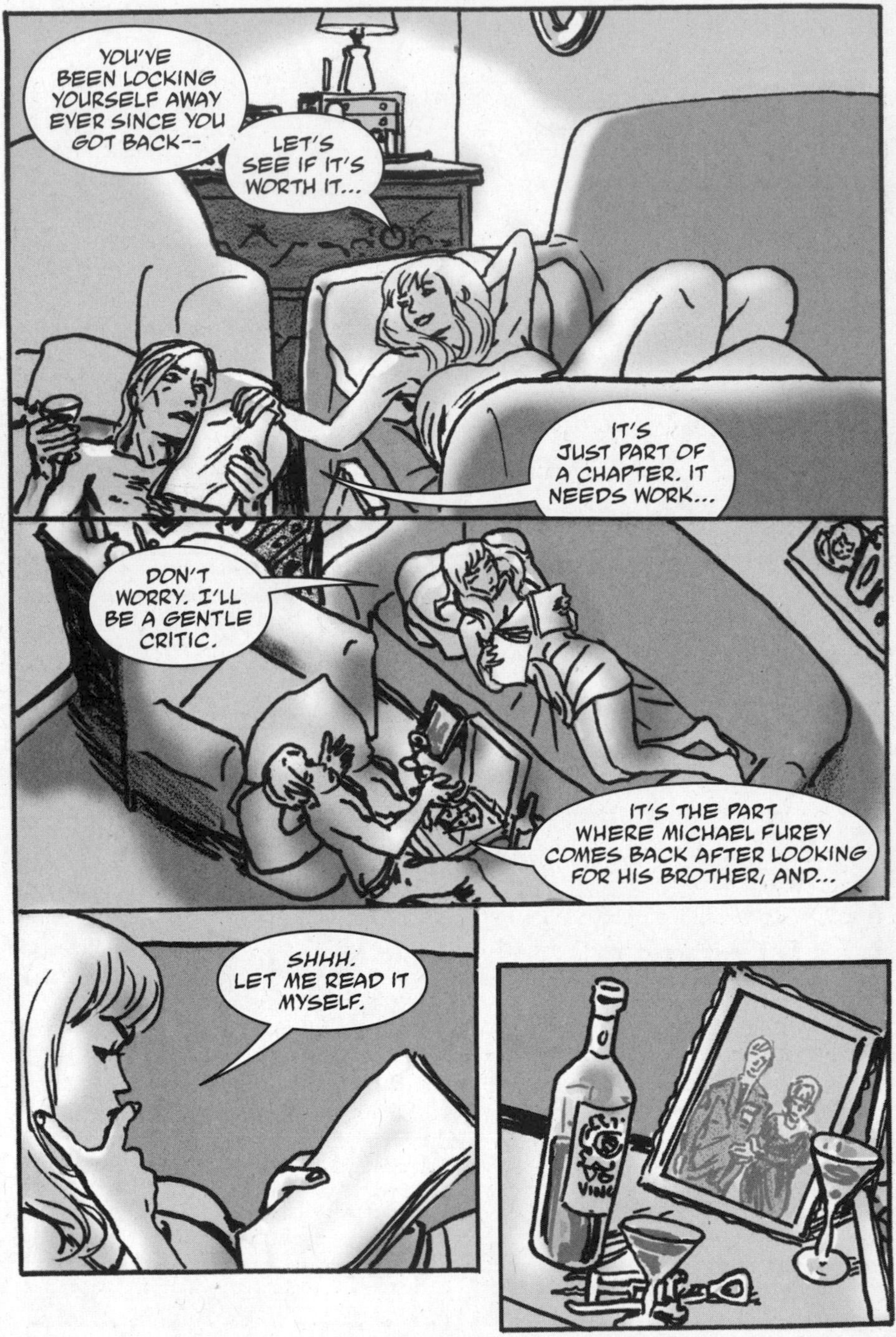
YOU'VE BEEN LOCKING YOURSELF AWAY EVER SINCE YOU GOT BACK--
LET'S SEE IF IT'S WORTH IT...
IT'S JUST PART OF A CHAPTER. IT NEEDS WORK...
DON'T WORRY. I'LL BE A GENTLE CRITIC.
IT'S THE PART WHERE MICHAEL FUREY COMES BACK AFTER LOOKING FOR HIS BROTHER, AND...
SHHH. LET ME READ IT MYSELF.

As I reached our street, I heard a piano playing softly behind one of those smug Imperial facades. That would be the army major's daughter. Stopping for a moment to listen, I took out my watch and saw that I had been gone almost two hours. Two hours! My heart sank as I anticipated my father's pitiless interrogation. Where had I been? Why had I taken so long? Where was my brother?

[handwritten: more?]

Indignation for what was to come spread like heartburn into my chest. I imagined myself turning around right now: I sent a ghost version of myself walking away with the few coins I had in my pockets, walking all the way to the pilots and liners of Queenstown, and then on to a vessel bound for Sydney or New York.

Only when I pushed open the door did the silence strike me. Later, looking back at this moment, I would imagine I sensed some awful foreboding, crouching like a fat beetle in the shadows of the quiet house.

[handwritten: re-writing history?]

"Papa!"

There was no reply. Thank God, I thought. Maybe he's fallen asleep.

"Eveline?" I started to say as I pushed into the kitchen.

The word turned to dry clay in my throat. My bowels opened and warm soup ran down my legs, the sour stink quickly brushing my nose. My brain could not take in what I was seeing. I was looking at a scene that seemed to break the very laws of nature. That refuted any possibility of the existence of God. There may have been no possibility of God, but there was still a Hell. There was most definitely a Hell.

[handwritten: indent]

[handwritten: Too much? Take back. Not a fucking melodrama!]

I was looking right at it.

The candle threw agitated shadows across the room, which I now moved into slowly. My father was still seated on the chair covered in green leather that had been reclaimed from the house of some gentleman that my grandfather had done work for many years earlier. The white shirt was so dark with what I took to be blood that in this fitful light it looked burnt and I thought of the crubeens that Hugh had been sent out for and how they would have been fired until the fat turned black.

Hugh! For the first time since I'd entered the house I thought of my brother.

I steadied myself and looked squarely at my father's face. The handsomest man in Cork at one time, if you believed him. The head was lolling back, the mouth just a little open. Two black coins had been placed over the eyes.

Coins over the eyes? *Black* coins?

I moved closer, and as I did, felt the already cooling shit sticking to the hairs of my legs. The candle spluttered, throwing a different yellowy light over his face.

I could see now that it wasn't coins that covered my father's eyes.

The eyes had been removed from their sockets. What I'd mistaken for coins were in fact holes.

I swallowed something like air that might have been bile and turned away. Spread on the floor, as though flung out from my father by some demonic force, were my two sisters. Mary-Ann was lying face down, her arms bent impossibly beneath her. Eveline was on her side, face turned towards me, and I saw—before I quickly looked away—that she too wore those terrible black coins over her eyes.

I'm free, I thought.

Even as I thought it, I knew it was the most shameful, the most evil of thoughts, but I thought it none the less. There is nothing keeping me here now. All the strings are cut. I am released. My prison bars have vanished, as in some biblical miracle. And the very moment I realized that I was free, I thought:

Do I want to be free?

The abrupt idea that I could go anywhere in the world and no one would try to stop me made me giddy. The room started to move around. I realized I had been holding my breath.

And then everything went black.

I gasped and turned and was immediately lost. Which way was the door? I stepped forwards and tripped over something, letting out a cry as I fell to the ground. By now, my eyes were adjusting a little to the darkness, and I could make out the stump of the dead candle; I could discern the shape of my dead father in the chair. Beyond him was the body of Mary-Ann. I had tripped over Eveline. Her dead face was just inches from me. In this light, you could not tell that she had a harelip. She looked pretty. I smiled.

Eveline. Still trying to stop me from leaving, even now. The thought made me laugh. And then someone started screaming. I looked around. Who had come into the room?

There was no one. There was no one screaming.

No one but myself.

I ran, spilling out of the house and down the steps to the street.

"Murder!" I cried. It sounded ridiculous but what else was I to cry? "Murder!"

My puny voice died in the thickening night. Dogs barked a few streets away. The army major's daughter was still playing the piano. Suddenly, she stopped. And the world was silent.

anyway

Is there a fucking clue in here?
Something I'm not seeing?

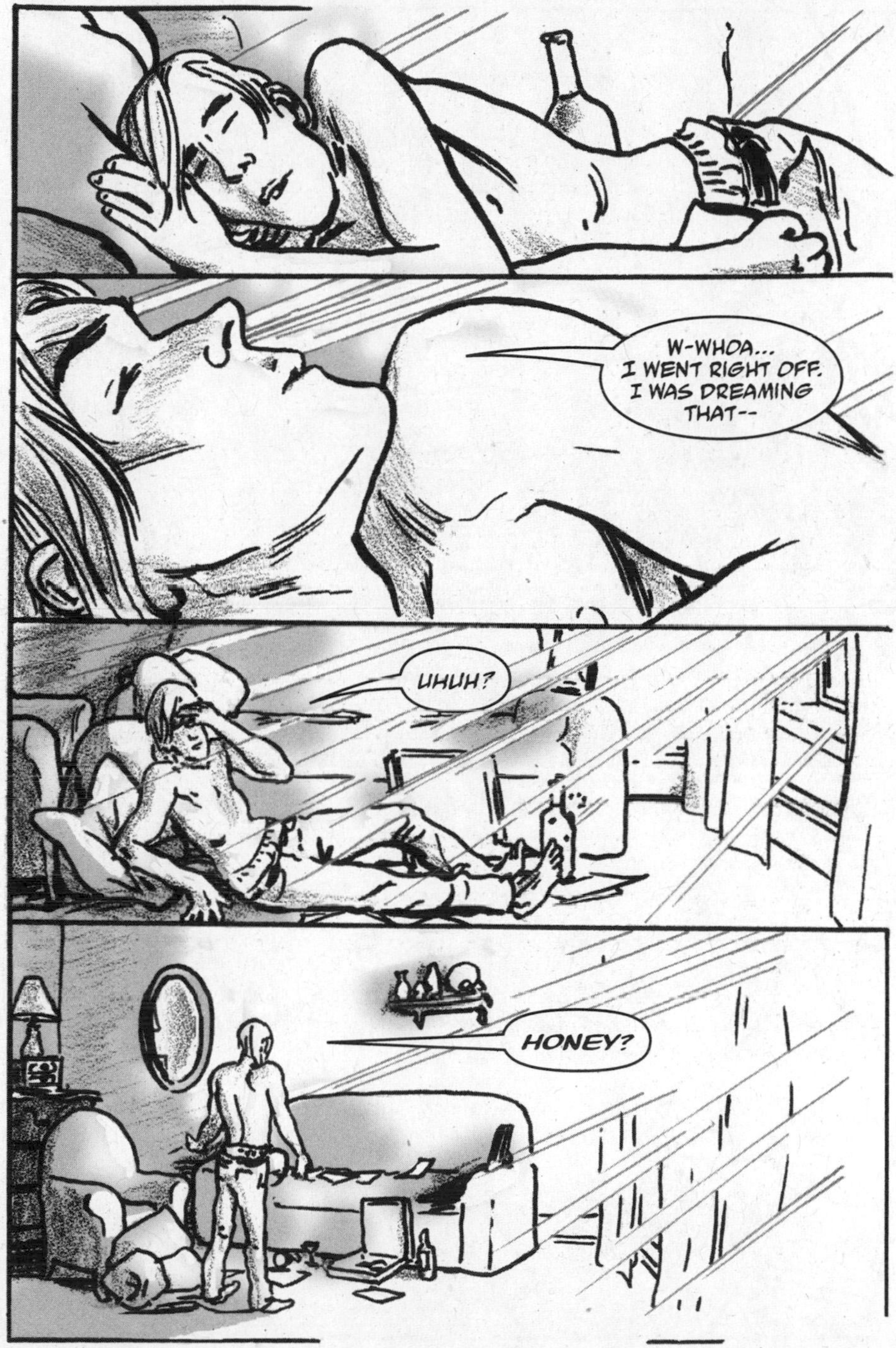
W-WHOA... I WENT RIGHT OFF. I WAS DREAMING THAT--
UHUH?
HONEY?

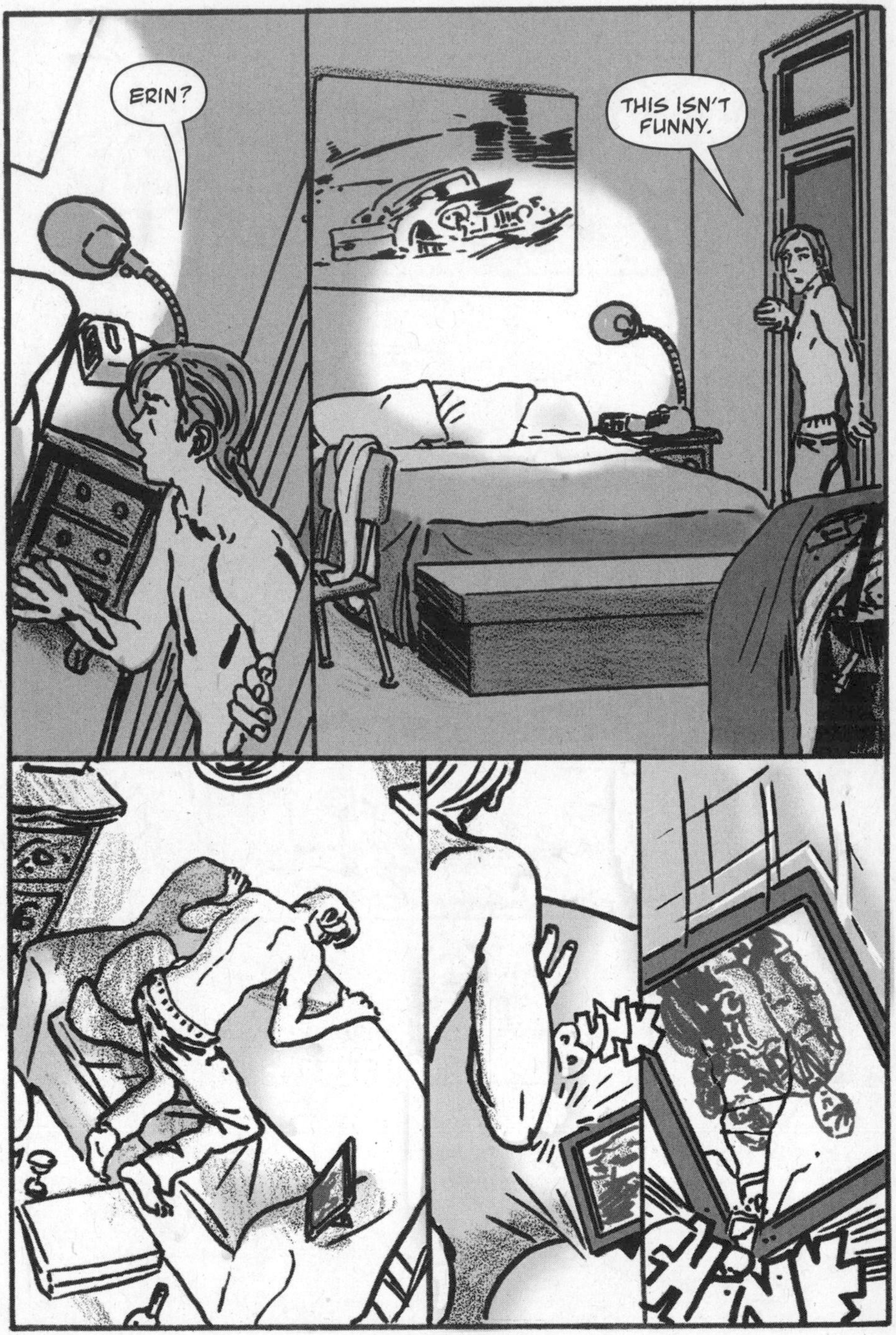
ERIN?
THIS ISN'T FUNNY.
BUNK

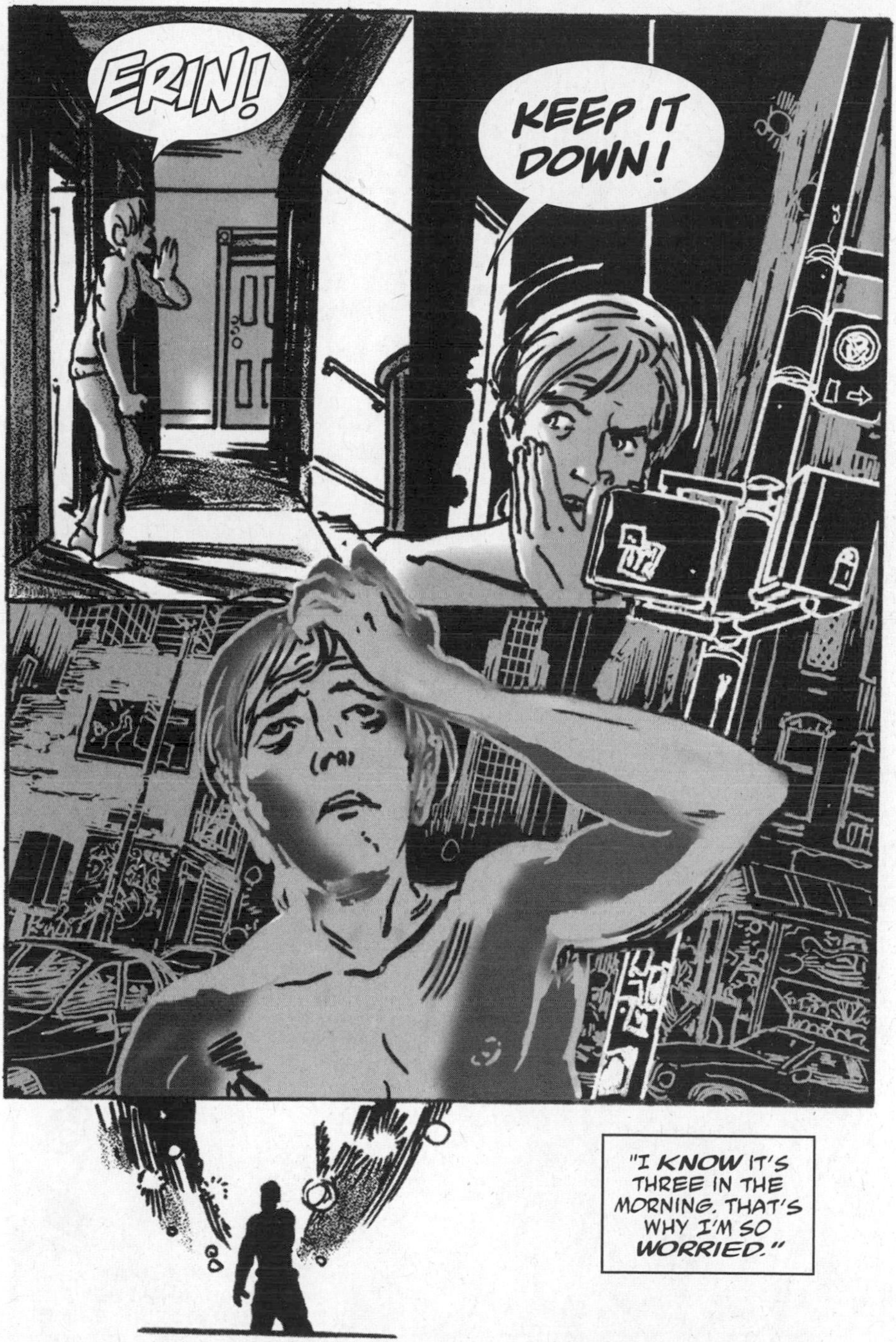
ERIN!
KEEP IT DOWN!
"I KNOW IT'S THREE IN THE MORNING. THAT'S WHY I'M SO WORRIED."

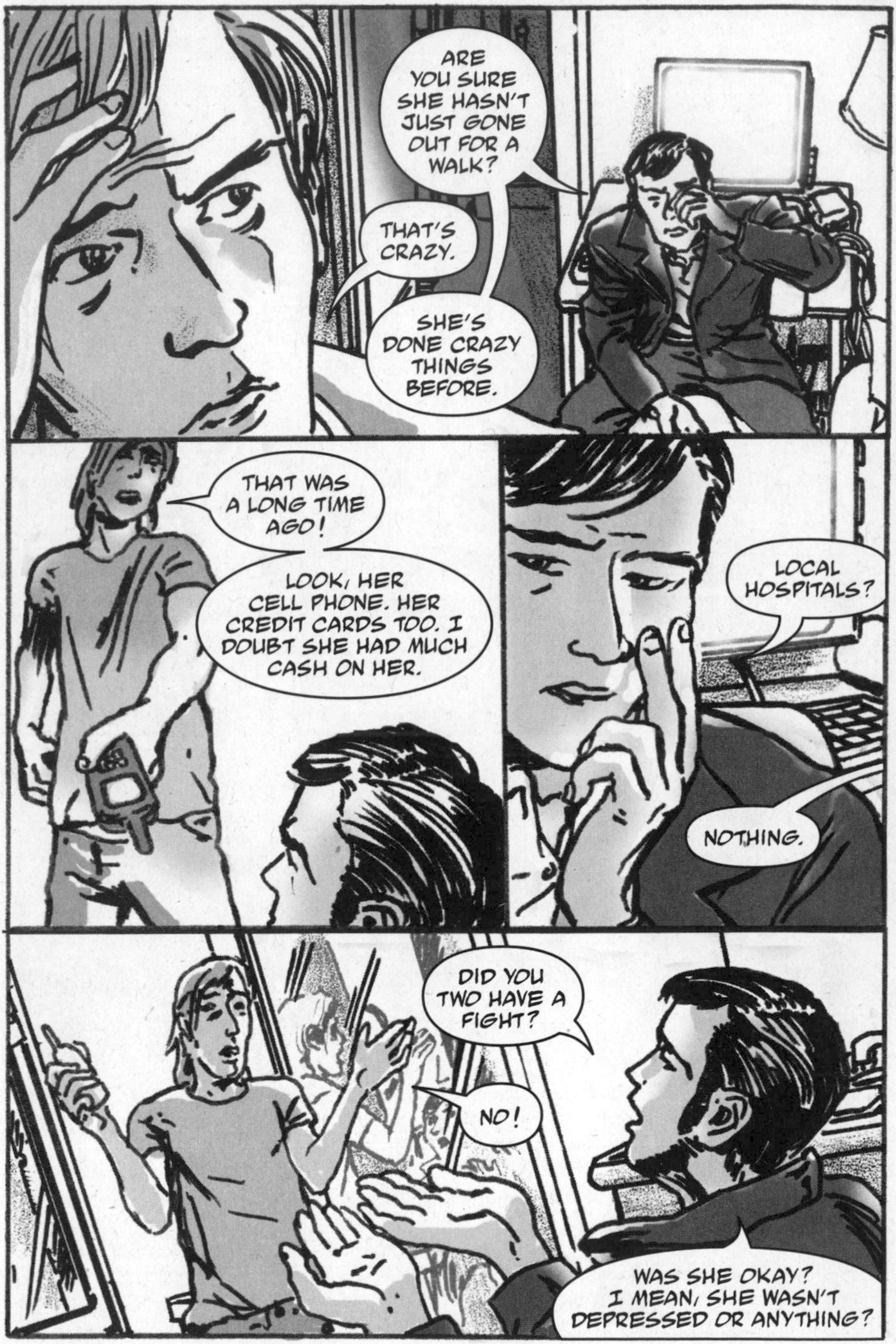
ARE YOU SURE SHE HASN'T JUST GONE OUT FOR A WALK?
THAT'S CRAZY.
SHE'S DONE CRAZY THINGS BEFORE.
THAT WAS A LONG TIME AGO!
LOOK, HER CELL PHONE. HER CREDIT CARDS TOO. I DOUBT SHE HAD MUCH CASH ON HER.
LOCAL HOSPITALS?
NOTHING.
DID YOU TWO HAVE A FIGHT?
NO!
WAS SHE OKAY? I MEAN, SHE WASN'T DEPRESSED OR ANYTHING?

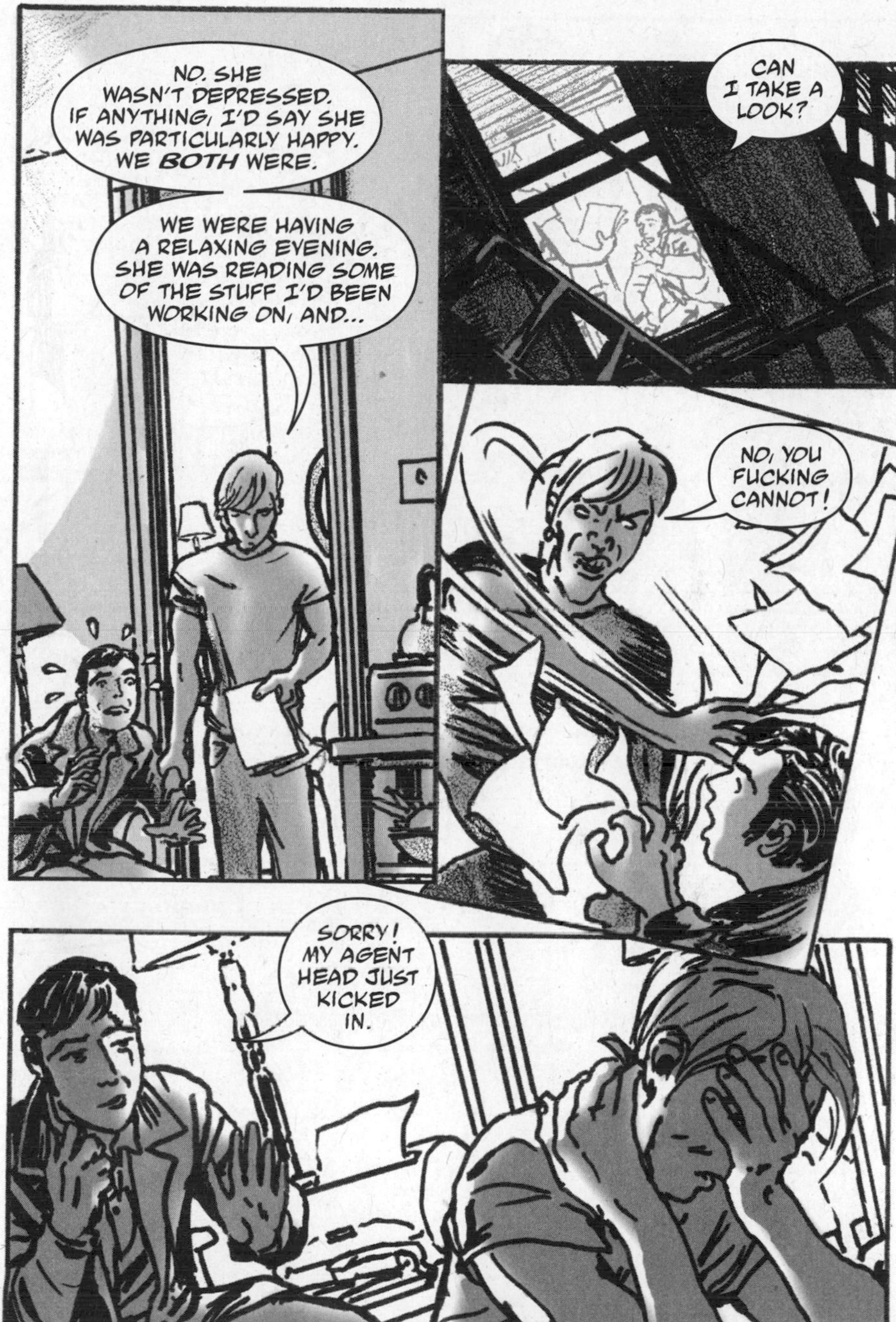
NO. SHE WASN'T DEPRESSED. IF ANYTHING, I'D SAY SHE WAS PARTICULARLY HAPPY. WE *BOTH* WERE.
WE WERE HAVING A RELAXING EVENING. SHE WAS READING SOME OF THE STUFF I'D BEEN WORKING ON, AND...
CAN I TAKE A LOOK?
NO, YOU FUCKING CANNOT!
SORRY! MY AGENT HEAD JUST KICKED IN.

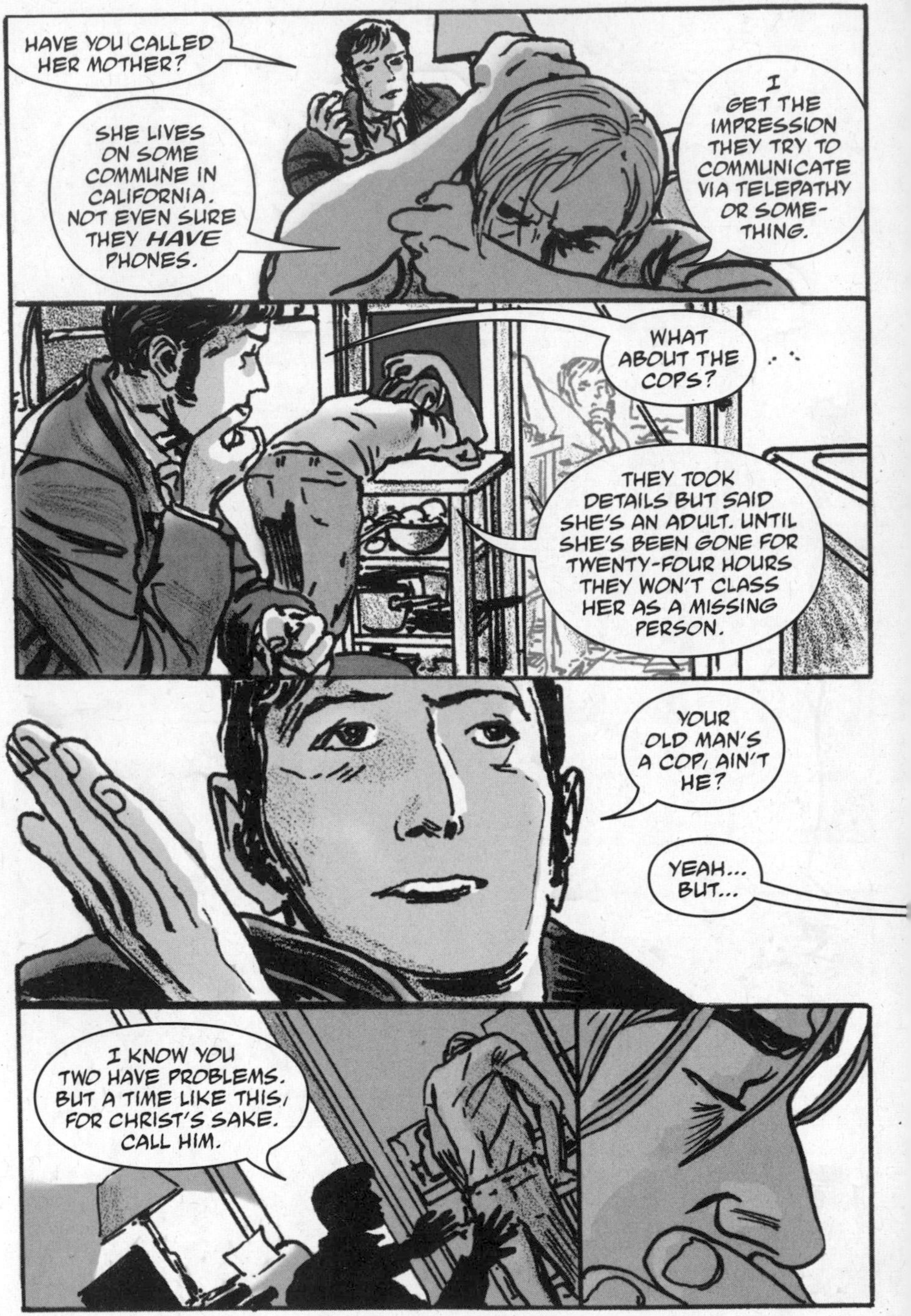
HAVE YOU CALLED HER MOTHER?
SHE LIVES ON SOME COMMUNE IN CALIFORNIA. NOT EVEN SURE THEY *HAVE* PHONES.
I GET THE IMPRESSION THEY TRY TO COMMUNICATE VIA TELEPATHY OR SOMETHING.
WHAT ABOUT THE COPS?
THEY TOOK DETAILS BUT SAID SHE'S AN ADULT. UNTIL SHE'S BEEN GONE FOR TWENTY-FOUR HOURS THEY WON'T CLASS HER AS A MISSING PERSON.
YOUR OLD MAN'S A COP, AIN'T HE?
YEAH... BUT...
I KNOW YOU TWO HAVE PROBLEMS. BUT A TIME LIKE THIS, FOR CHRIST'S SAKE. CALL HIM.

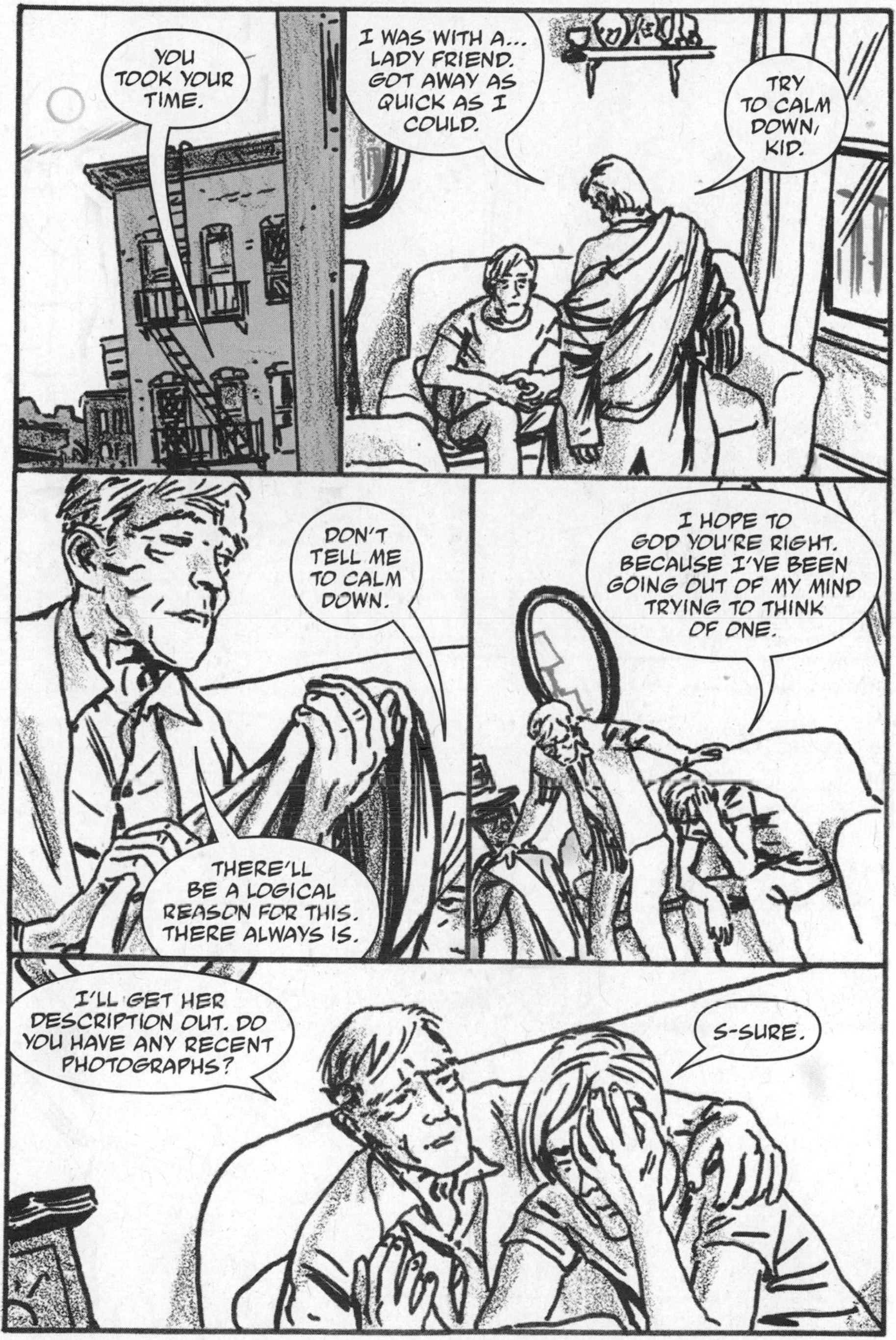
YOU TOOK YOUR TIME.
I WAS WITH A... LADY FRIEND. GOT AWAY AS QUICK AS I COULD.
TRY TO CALM DOWN, KID.
DON'T TELL ME TO CALM DOWN.
THERE'LL BE A LOGICAL REASON FOR THIS. THERE ALWAYS IS.
I HOPE TO GOD YOU'RE RIGHT. BECAUSE I'VE BEEN GOING OUT OF MY MIND TRYING TO THINK OF ONE.
I'LL GET HER DESCRIPTION OUT. DO YOU HAVE ANY RECENT PHOTOGRAPHS?
S-SURE.

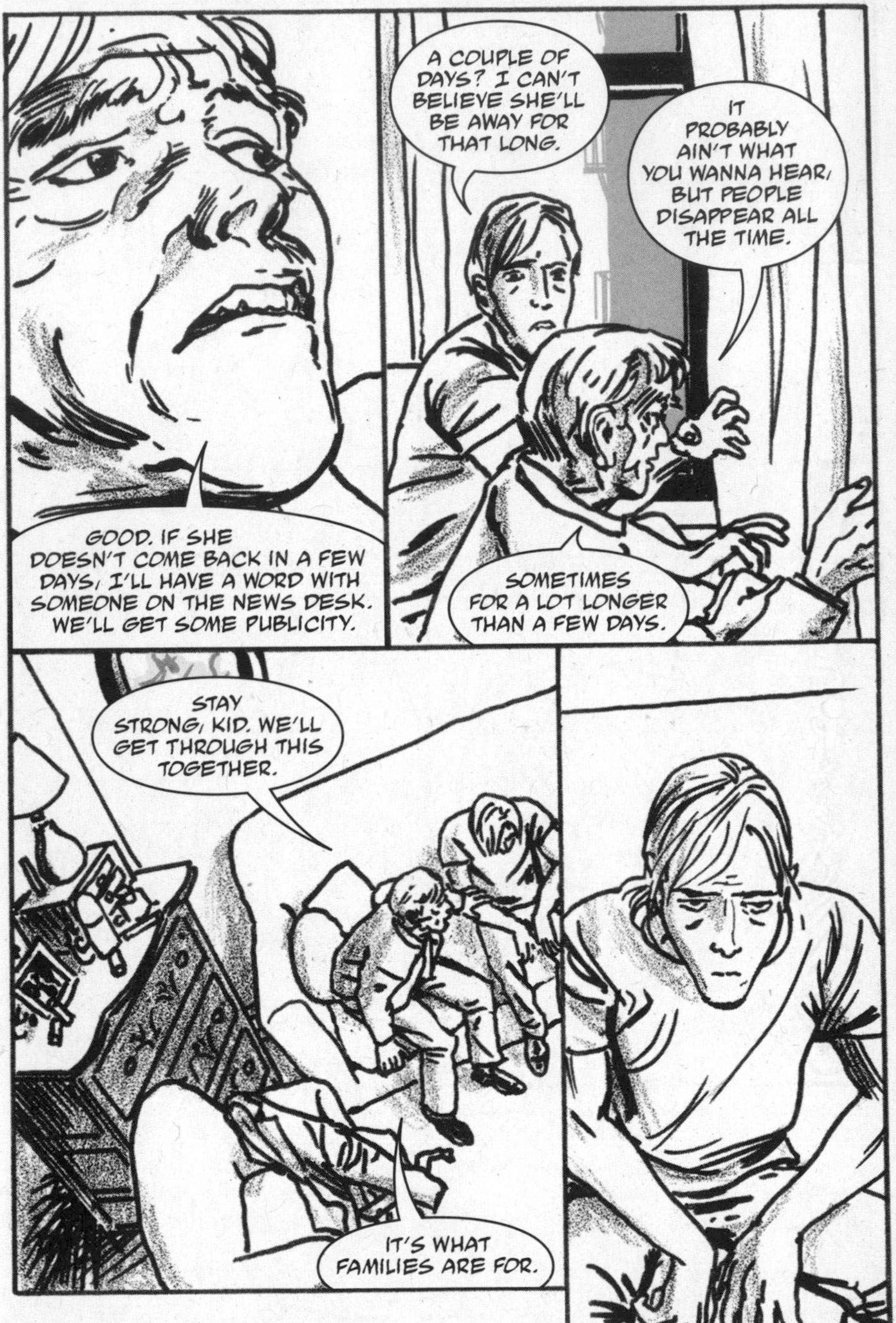
GOOD. IF SHE DOESN'T COME BACK IN A FEW DAYS, I'LL HAVE A WORD WITH SOMEONE ON THE NEWS DESK. WE'LL GET SOME PUBLICITY.
A COUPLE OF DAYS? I CAN'T BELIEVE SHE'LL BE AWAY FOR THAT LONG.
IT PROBABLY AIN'T WHAT YOU WANNA HEAR, BUT PEOPLE DISAPPEAR ALL THE TIME.
SOMETIMES FOR A LOT LONGER THAN A FEW DAYS.
STAY STRONG, KID. WE'LL GET THROUGH THIS TOGETHER.
IT'S WHAT FAMILIES ARE FOR.

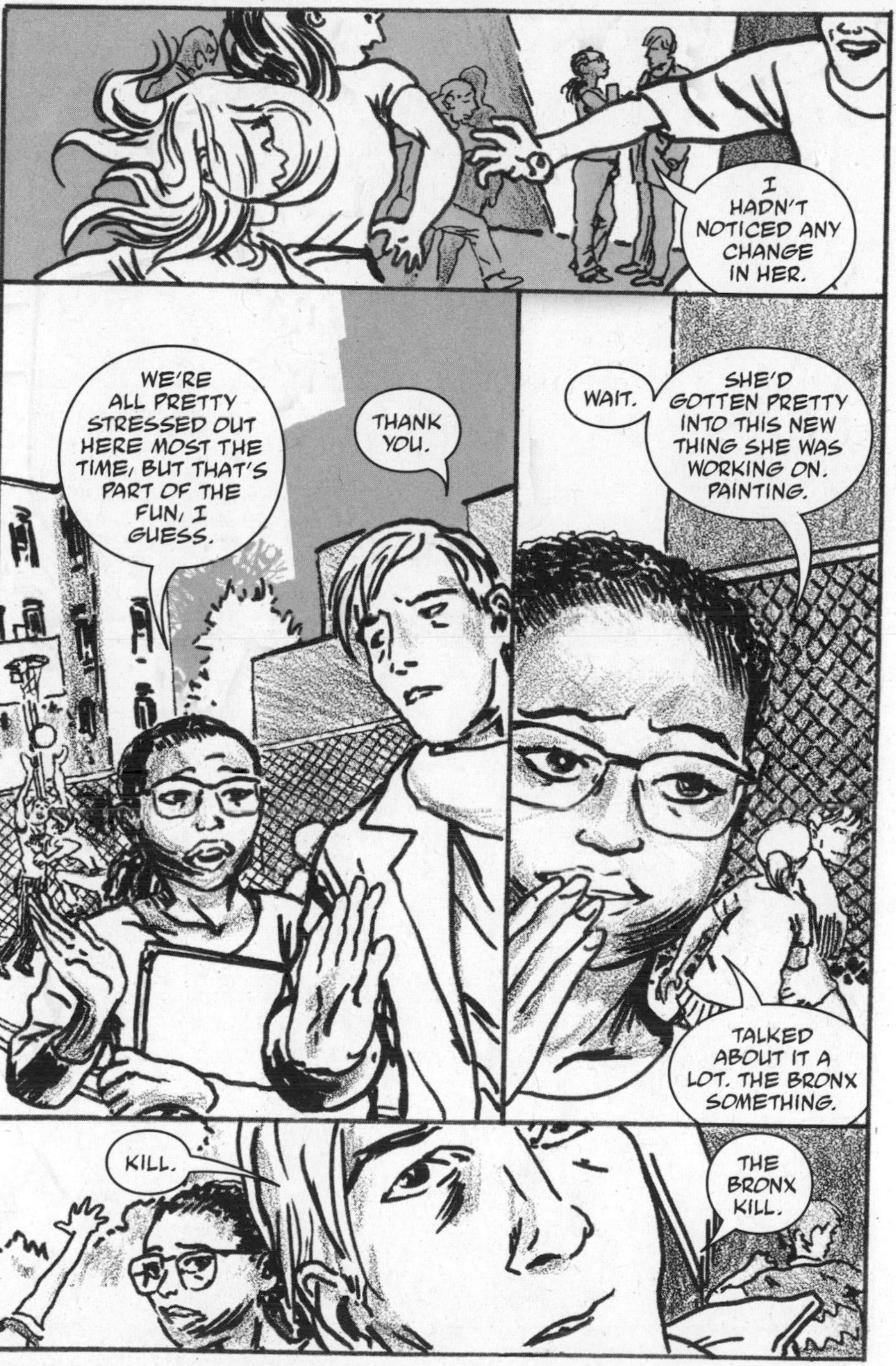
I HADN'T NOTICED ANY CHANGE IN HER.
WE'RE ALL PRETTY STRESSED OUT HERE MOST THE TIME, BUT THAT'S PART OF THE FUN, I GUESS.
THANK YOU.
WAIT.
SHE'D GOTTEN PRETTY INTO THIS NEW THING SHE WAS WORKING ON. PAINTING.
TALKED ABOUT IT A LOT. THE BRONX SOMETHING.
KILL.
THE BRONX KILL.

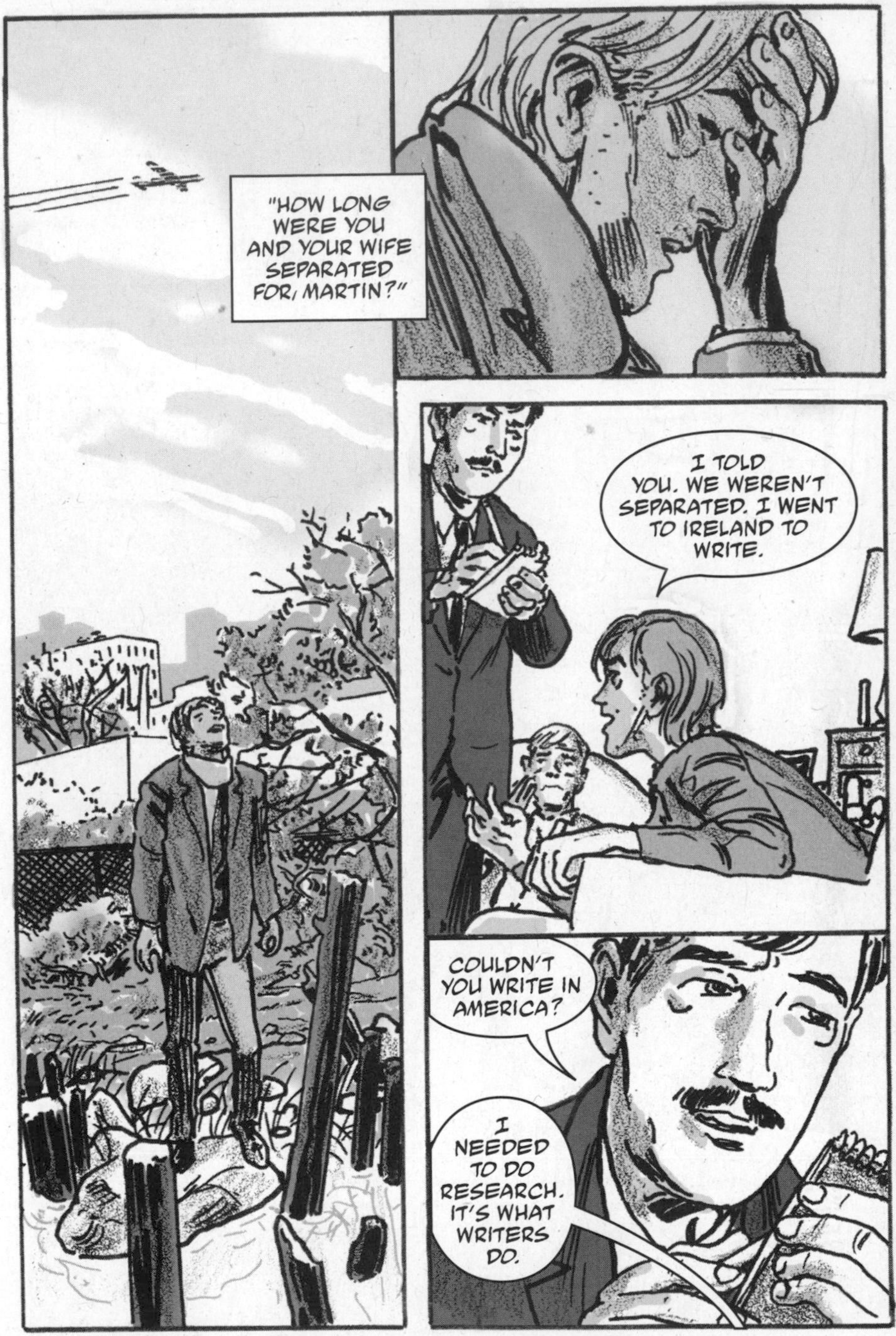
"HOW LONG WERE YOU AND YOUR WIFE SEPARATED FOR, MARTIN?"
I TOLD YOU. WE WEREN'T SEPARATED. I WENT TO IRELAND TO WRITE.
COULDN'T YOU WRITE IN AMERICA?
I NEEDED TO DO RESEARCH. IT'S WHAT WRITERS DO.

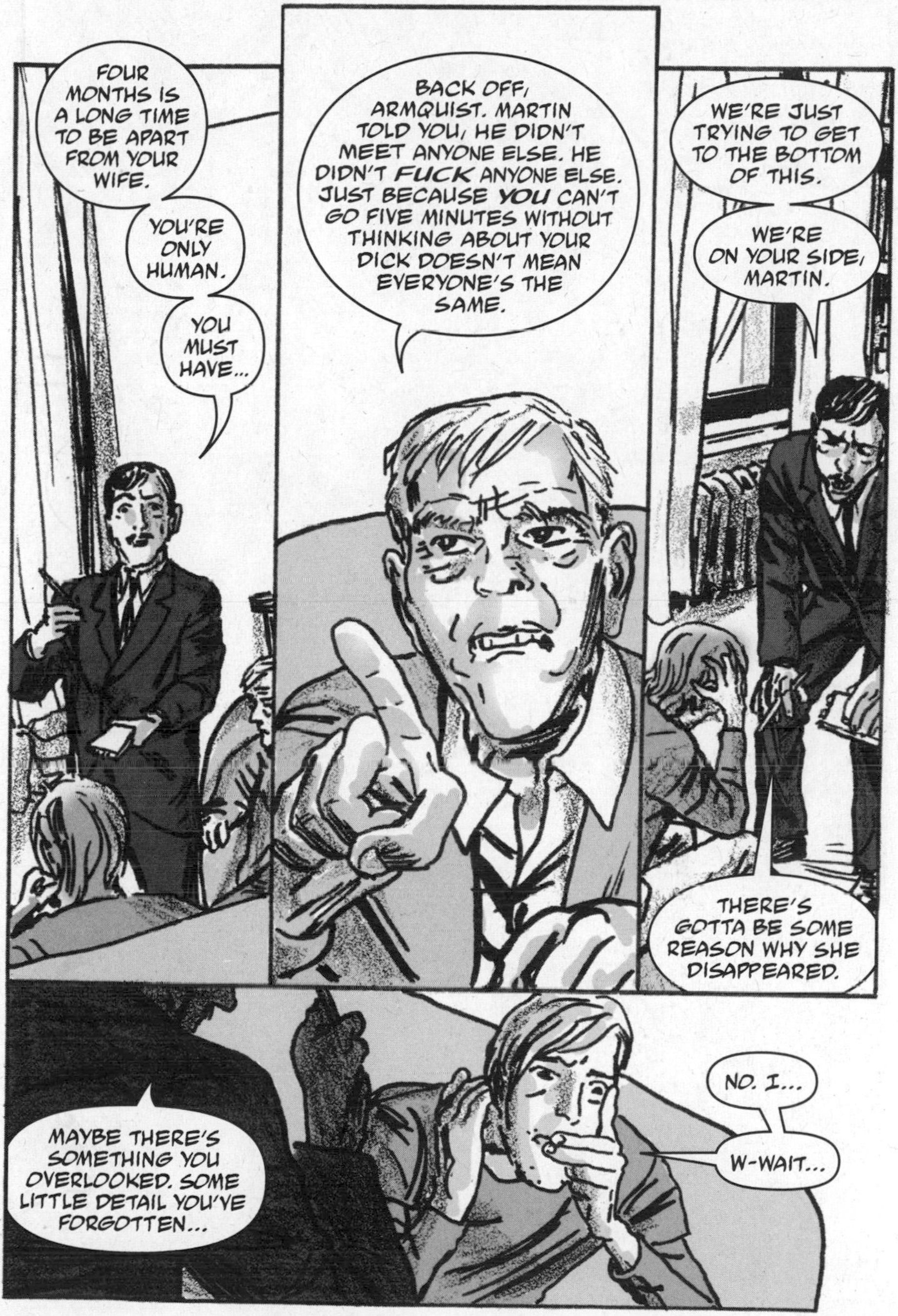
FOUR MONTHS IS A LONG TIME TO BE APART FROM YOUR WIFE.
YOU'RE ONLY HUMAN.
YOU MUST HAVE...
BACK OFF, ARMQUIST. MARTIN TOLD YOU, HE DIDN'T MEET ANYONE ELSE. HE DIDN'T FUCK ANYONE ELSE. JUST BECAUSE YOU CAN'T GO FIVE MINUTES WITHOUT THINKING ABOUT YOUR DICK DOESN'T MEAN EVERYONE'S THE SAME.
WE'RE JUST TRYING TO GET TO THE BOTTOM OF THIS.
WE'RE ON YOUR SIDE, MARTIN.
THERE'S GOTTA BE SOME REASON WHY SHE DISAPPEARED.
MAYBE THERE'S SOMETHING YOU OVERLOOKED. SOME LITTLE DETAIL YOU'VE FORGOTTEN...
NO. I...
W-WAIT...

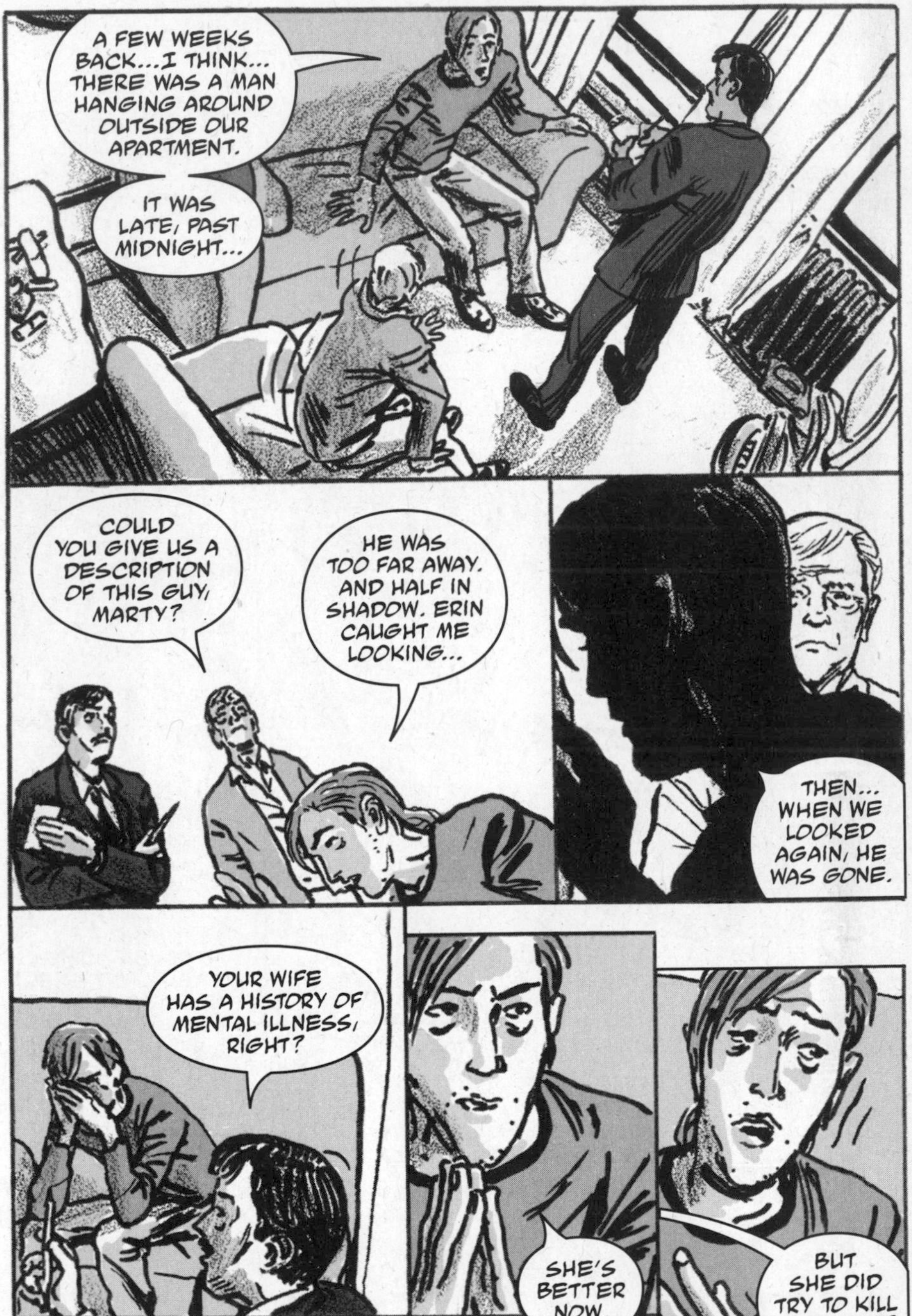
A FEW WEEKS BACK...I THINK... THERE WAS A MAN HANGING AROUND OUTSIDE OUR APARTMENT.
IT WAS LATE, PAST MIDNIGHT...
COULD YOU GIVE US A DESCRIPTION OF THIS GUY, MARTY?
HE WAS TOO FAR AWAY. AND HALF IN SHADOW. ERIN CAUGHT ME LOOKING...
THEN... WHEN WE LOOKED AGAIN, HE WAS GONE.
YOUR WIFE HAS A HISTORY OF MENTAL ILLNESS, RIGHT?
SHE'S BETTER NOW.
BUT SHE DID TRY TO KILL HERSELF?

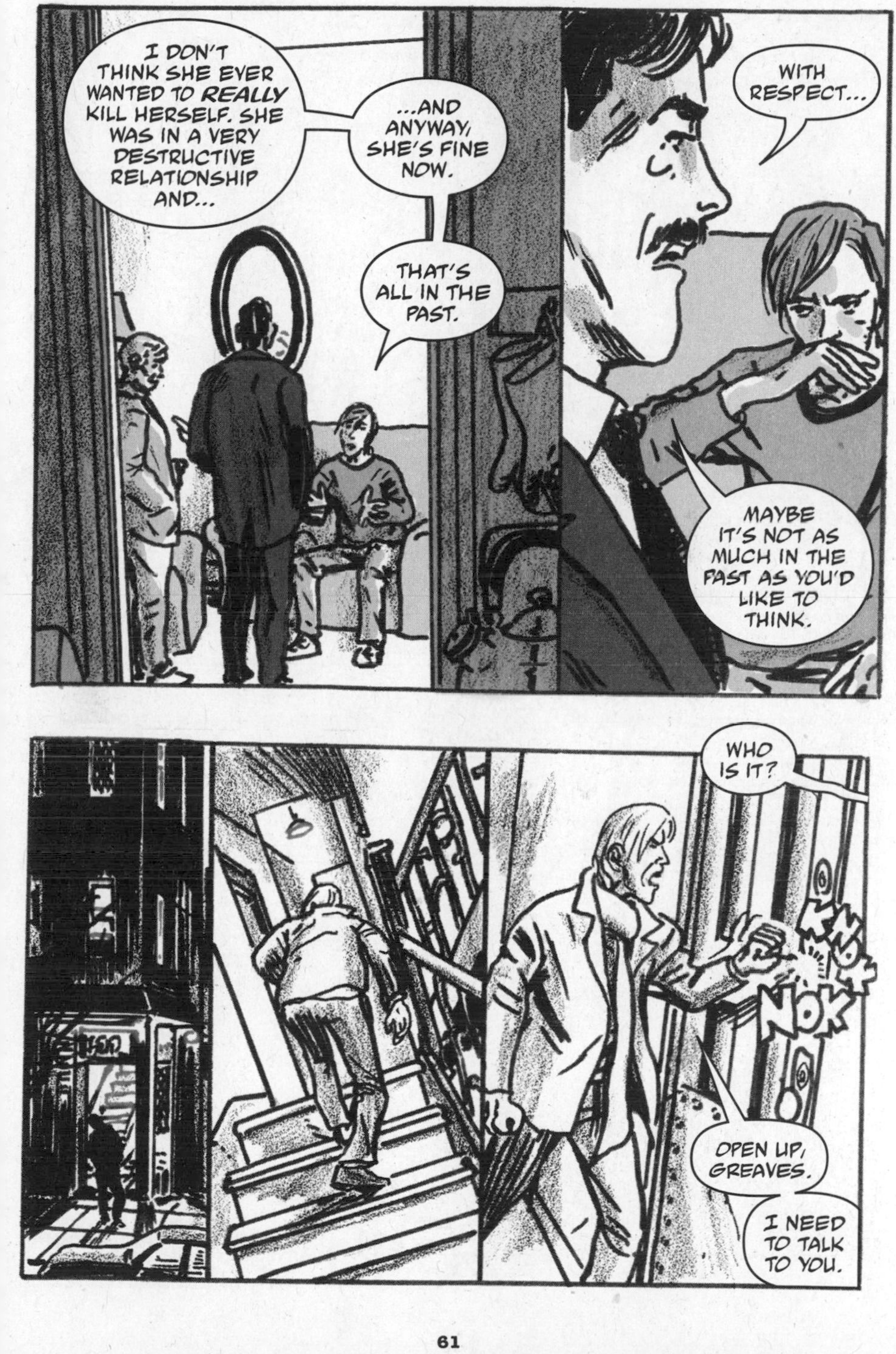

I DON'T THINK SHE EVER WANTED TO *REALLY* KILL HERSELF. SHE WAS IN A VERY DESTRUCTIVE RELATIONSHIP AND...
...AND ANYWAY, SHE'S FINE NOW.
THAT'S ALL IN THE PAST.
WITH RESPECT...
MAYBE IT'S NOT AS MUCH IN THE PAST AS YOU'D LIKE TO THINK.
WHO IS IT?
KNOK
NOK
OPEN UP, GREAVES.
I NEED TO TALK TO YOU.

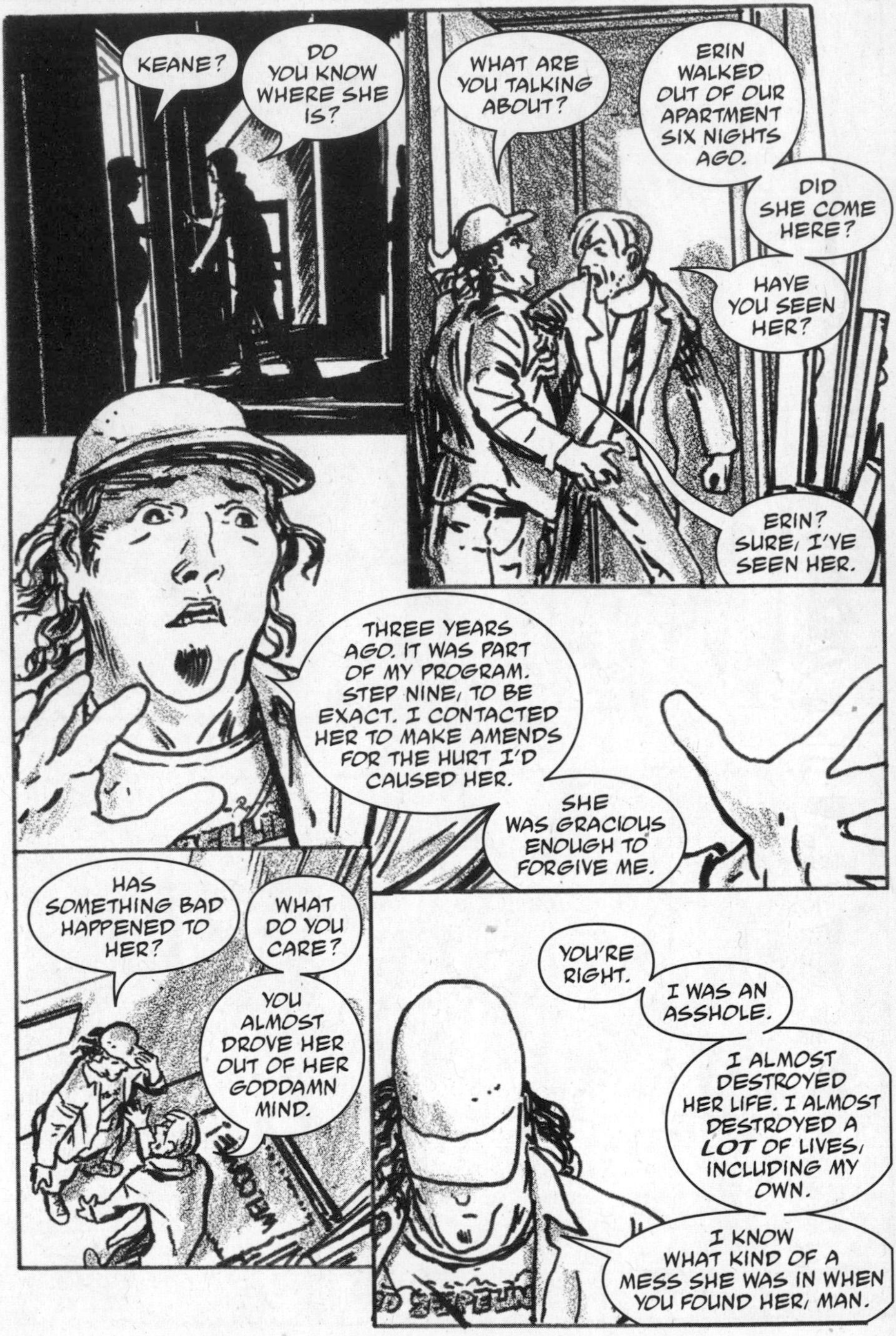
KEANE?
DO YOU KNOW WHERE SHE IS?
WHAT ARE YOU TALKING ABOUT?
ERIN WALKED OUT OF OUR APARTMENT SIX NIGHTS AGO.
DID SHE COME HERE?
HAVE YOU SEEN HER?
ERIN? SURE, I'VE SEEN HER.
THREE YEARS AGO. IT WAS PART OF MY PROGRAM. STEP NINE, TO BE EXACT. I CONTACTED HER TO MAKE AMENDS FOR THE HURT I'D CAUSED HER.
SHE WAS GRACIOUS ENOUGH TO FORGIVE ME.
HAS SOMETHING BAD HAPPENED TO HER?
WHAT DO YOU CARE?
YOU ALMOST DROVE HER OUT OF HER GODDAMN MIND.
YOU'RE RIGHT.
I WAS AN ASSHOLE.
I ALMOST DESTROYED HER LIFE. I ALMOST DESTROYED A *LOT* OF LIVES, INCLUDING MY OWN.
I KNOW WHAT KIND OF A MESS SHE WAS IN WHEN YOU FOUND HER, MAN.

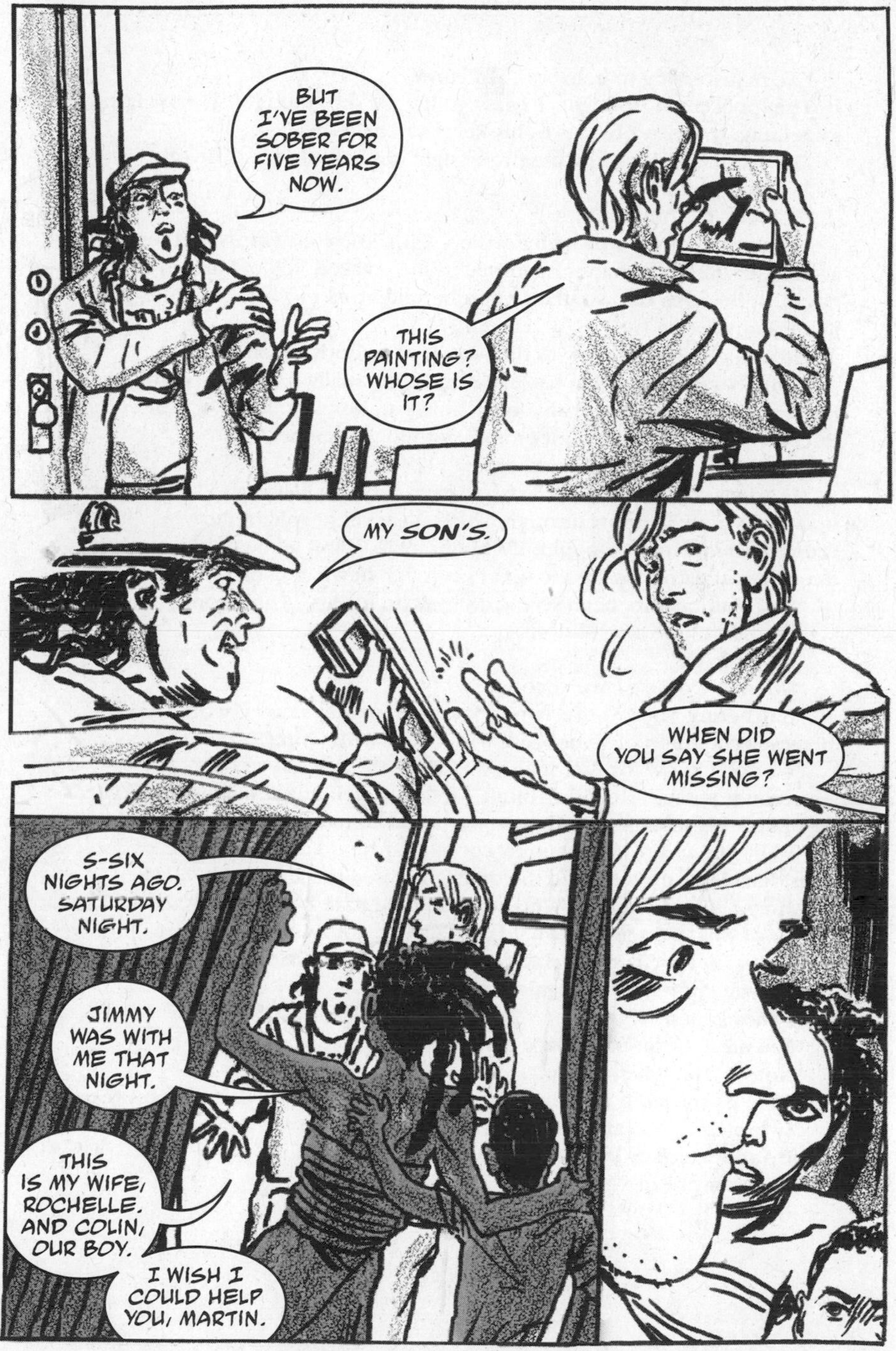
BUT I'VE BEEN SOBER FOR FIVE YEARS NOW.
THIS PAINTING? WHOSE IS IT?
MY SON'S.
WHEN DID YOU SAY SHE WENT MISSING?
S-SIX NIGHTS AGO. SATURDAY NIGHT.
JIMMY WAS WITH ME THAT NIGHT.
THIS IS MY WIFE, ROCHELLE. AND COLIN, OUR BOY.
I WISH I COULD HELP YOU, MARTIN.

"We're just trying to help you, Mr. Furey."

The policeman thought I was guilty. Or he thought I was hiding something. It was as obvious as his Kerry accent.

"Try harder. Is there anything you might not have told us?" he said.

"I don't...think so."

"You don't...think so?"

He repeated my words with derision. Oh, I knew his type. I had seen him around, in different shapes or forms, in the cracked lips of a much-loathed priest, in the eyes of my father when he caught us in some small lie, some minor indiscretion.

He was a bully. A bully with the weight of authority behind him.

By the way he tugged at his collar and continually stretched out his right leg, I could tell that the Irish Constabulary uniform he wore was ill-fitting. But surely that didn't account entirely for his bad temper.

"I've told you everything I know."

He grimaced, tweaked a little fabric from between his buttocks and looked up at the square window through which whatever grey light there was in the room entered. God, I thought, it's hot here. No air at all. I could make out a film of sweat gathering on the tip of his rough-hewn crag of a snout.

"Had your brother been seeing a physician for his...condition?"

"He didn't have a condition."

"Didn't have?"

"Doesn't. Doesn't have. A condition."

"Butchering your entire family for no apparent reason would seem to suggest a condition of some kind, would it not, Mr. Furey?"

"We don't know for sure that it was Hugh though, do we?"

Seconds passed. He didn't blink. I found myself not blinking either. Then he smiled, his voice now taking on a strangely unctuous tone.

"Well, I'm afraid he was seen covered in blood and in a state of some considerable distress around the time you raised the alarm."

"Hugh?" I said stupidly. Who else could he have been talking about? The horror of what I'd seen, of what Hugh had obviously done, began to invade my senses for the first time since I'd stumbled upon that nightmare.

"Do you know where he might run to?"

My head spun.

"You mean—you don't have him?"

"Not yet. But when we do..."

I held up my hand for him to stop. I knew what they'd do to my brother. My brother. I had an image of his swollen face above a tightening rope.

"Do you have any idea why he might do such a thing?"

I shook my head.

But I did have an idea. I could almost see it. Hugh coming home late and wild-eyed from whatever adventure he'd been on or fancied he'd been on, without the trotters he'd been sent out to buy. My father's gaze fixing him like a hook. Papa's voice like a line snagging through his skin. Papa won't let go. He pulls. He tears. Finally Hugh can stand no more. Finally...

But why Mary-Ann? Why Eveline? Why that thing with the eyes?

"So you've no idea where your brother might have ran to?"

"No. No idea at all."

He studied me a while longer, then seemed to relax. Maybe he'd been considering roughing me up, and had weighed this pleasant notion against the possible consequences for his career.

"Very well, Mr. Furey. You're a free man."

"Then I'm the only Irishman who is."

I hardly knew why I said this. It was the kind of thing Papa would say. Would have said. His words, living through me.

Police Sergeant Creegan stood silently while I walked to the door. Only when I had it opened did he continue.

"What will you be doing now? Now you're a man of means?" If here was irony there I didn't hear it.

"A man of debts, mostly."

He cocked his head slightly, possibly not believing me. Was this the cause of the dislike I'd felt from him? Did he think I was truly wealthy?

At that moment, his sweaty face, his implacable eyes, his ill-fitting uniform and scarcely contained threat of brutality seemed to encompass everything I wanted to flee from.

"I was thinking of going to America. There's nothing to keep me here now."

His eyelids opened a fraction. I had his attention: No, I had the attention of whatever creature lived buried beneath that edifice that went by the name of Sergeant Creegan.

"America?"

I had said it on a whim, to say something, to make it seem as though I was the kind of man who had plans. Who was going places. But as the word settled into that dank horrid little police room among the stink of sweat and tobacco smoke, the idea took root, became something, something hard and real inside me.

America.

I turned and was leaving when he said, softly,

"I've known people who were headed for America. Some of them never made it past the quayside."

I looked at him. He was smiling gently. God, he hated me so much.

"I have every intention of making it beyond the quayside."

"Of those that got on board, a good number never saw dry land again," he said with relish.

"Sure, isn't that why they call them coffin ships, Mr. Furey?"

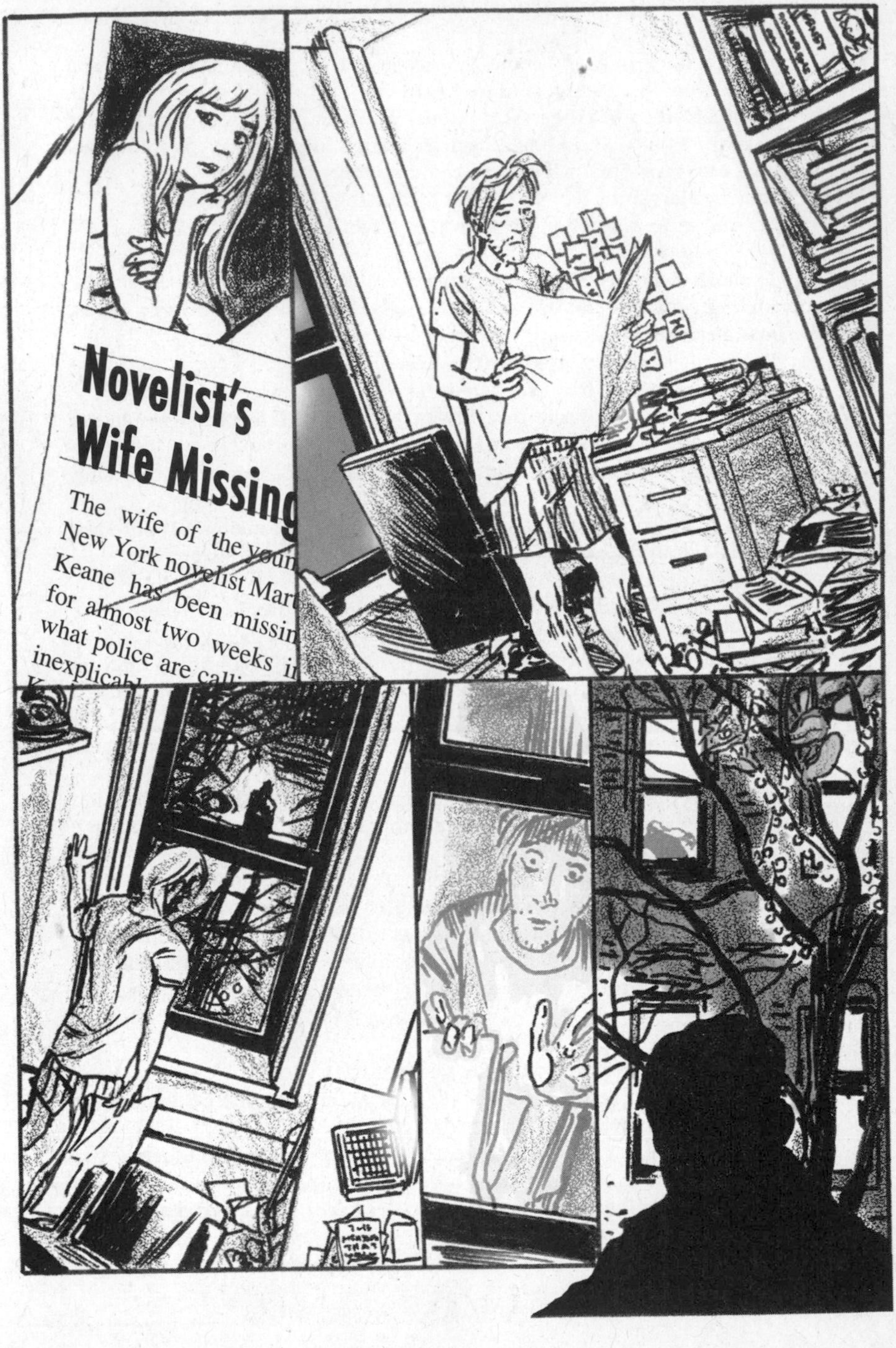

Novelist's Wife Missing
The wife of the youn
New York novelist Mart
Keane has been missin
for almost two weeks in
what police are calli
inexplicabl

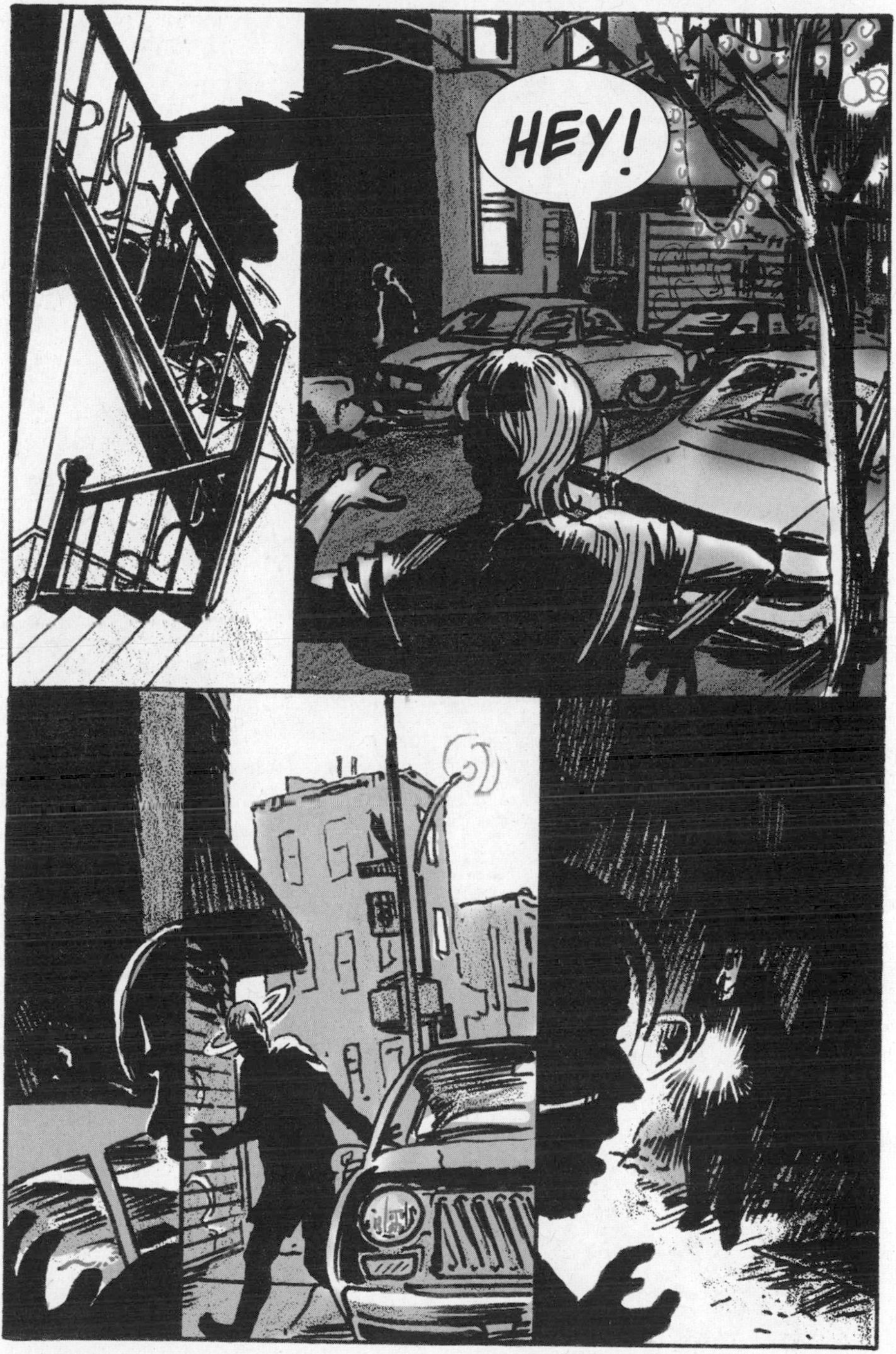
HEY!

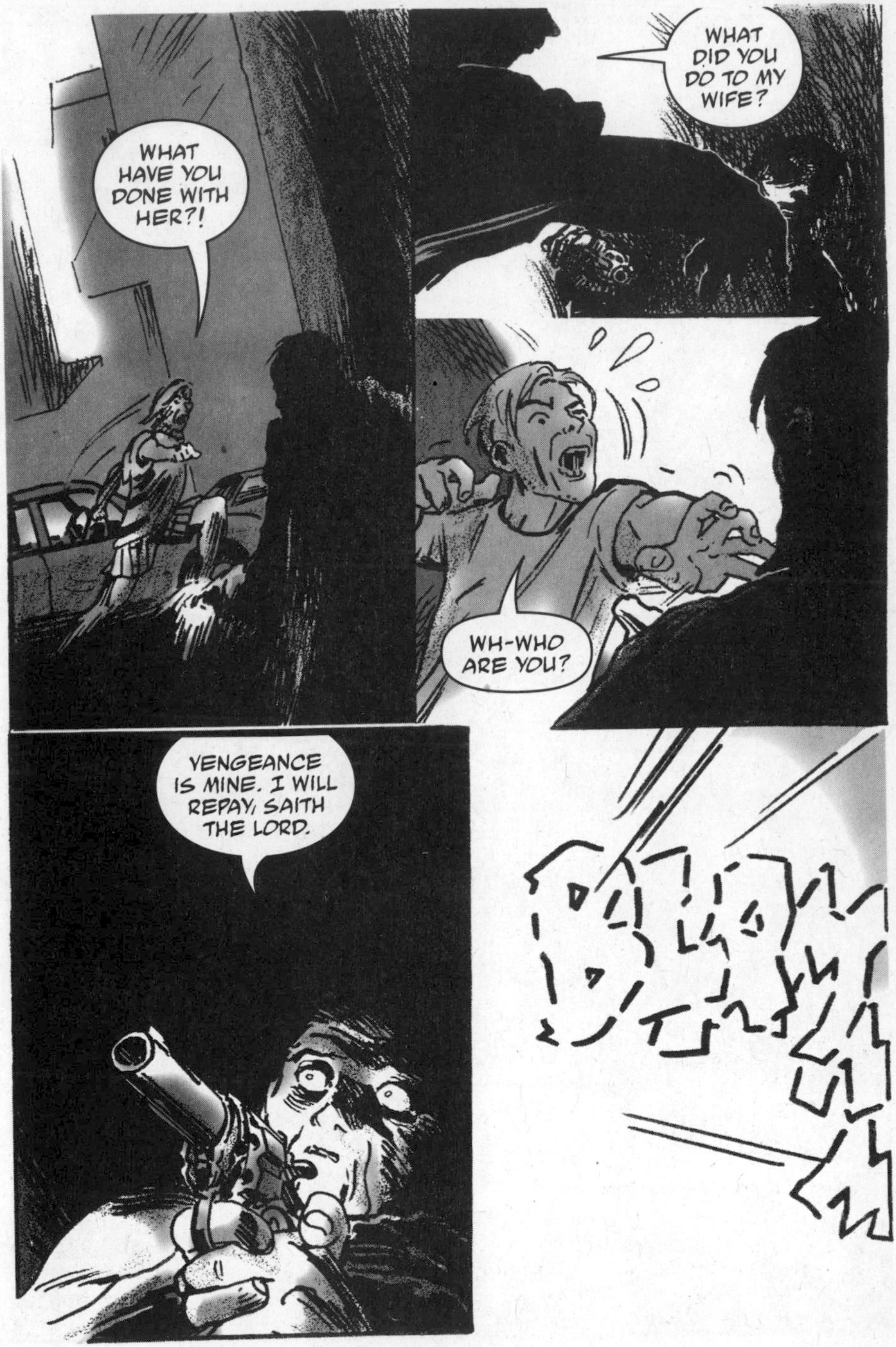
WHAT HAVE YOU DONE WITH HER?!
WHAT DID YOU DO TO MY WIFE?
WH-WHO ARE YOU?
VENGEANCE IS MINE. I WILL REPAY, SAITH THE LORD.

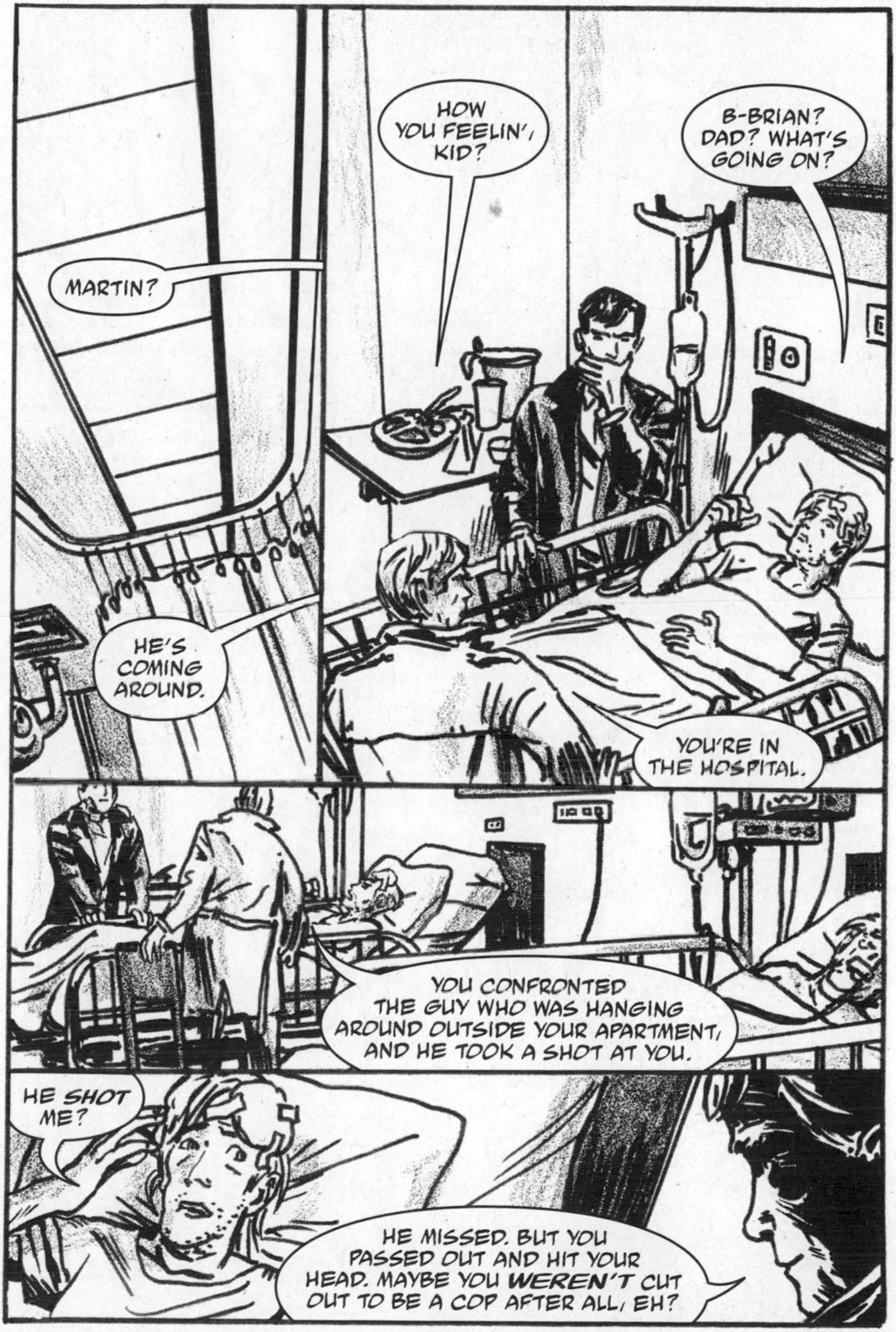
MARTIN?
HE'S COMING AROUND.
HOW YOU FEELIN', KID?
B-BRIAN? DAD? WHAT'S GOING ON?
YOU'RE IN THE HOSPITAL.
YOU CONFRONTED THE GUY WHO WAS HANGING AROUND OUTSIDE YOUR APARTMENT, AND HE TOOK A SHOT AT YOU.
HE SHOT ME?
HE MISSED. BUT YOU PASSED OUT AND HIT YOUR HEAD. MAYBE YOU WEREN'T CUT OUT TO BE A COP AFTER ALL, EH?

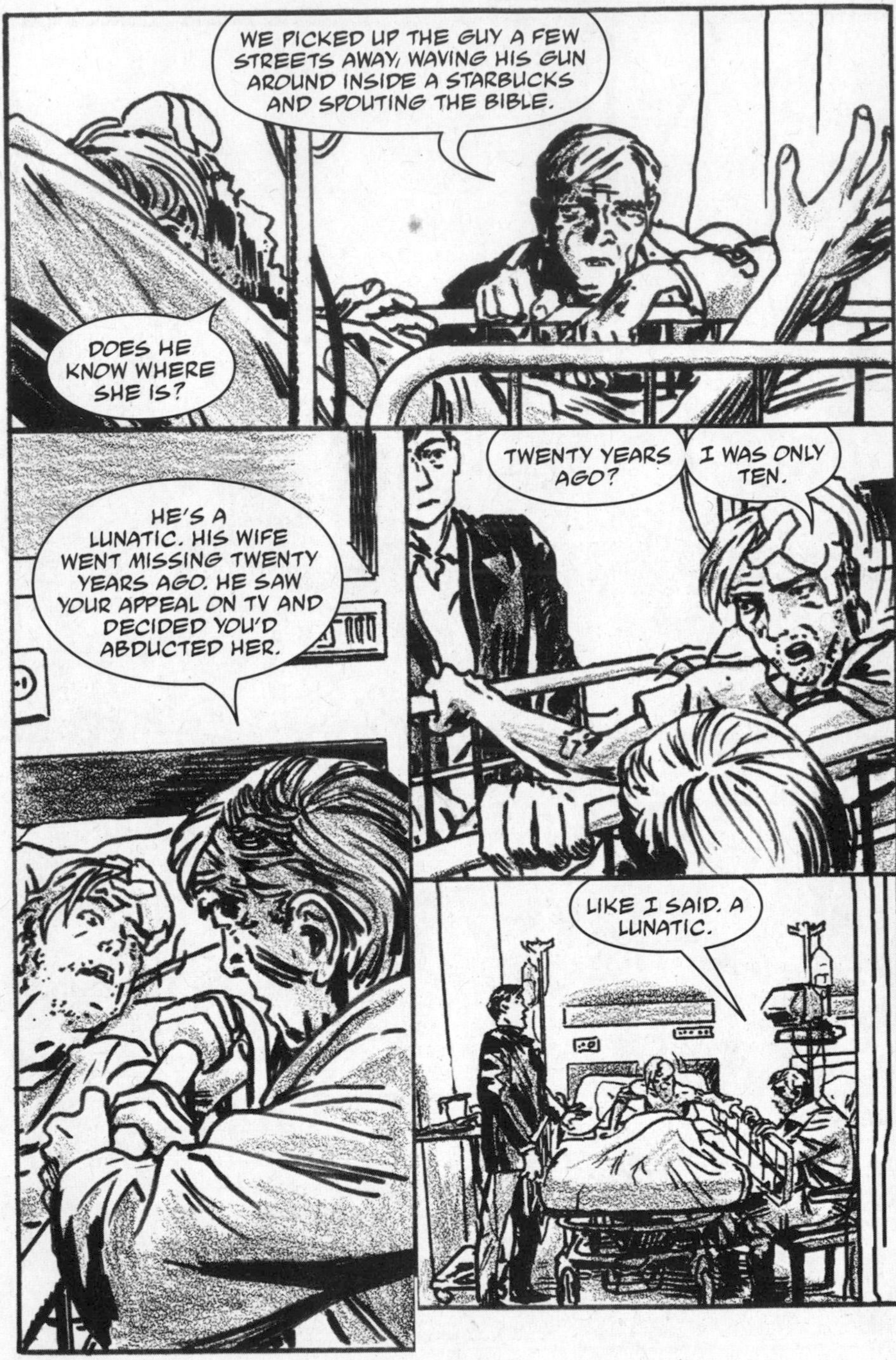
WE PICKED UP THE GUY A FEW STREETS AWAY, WAVING HIS GUN AROUND INSIDE A STARBUCKS AND SPOUTING THE BIBLE.
DOES HE KNOW WHERE SHE IS?
HE'S A LUNATIC. HIS WIFE WENT MISSING TWENTY YEARS AGO. HE SAW YOUR APPEAL ON TV AND DECIDED YOU'D ABDUCTED HER.
TWENTY YEARS AGO?
I WAS ONLY TEN.
LIKE I SAID. A LUNATIC.

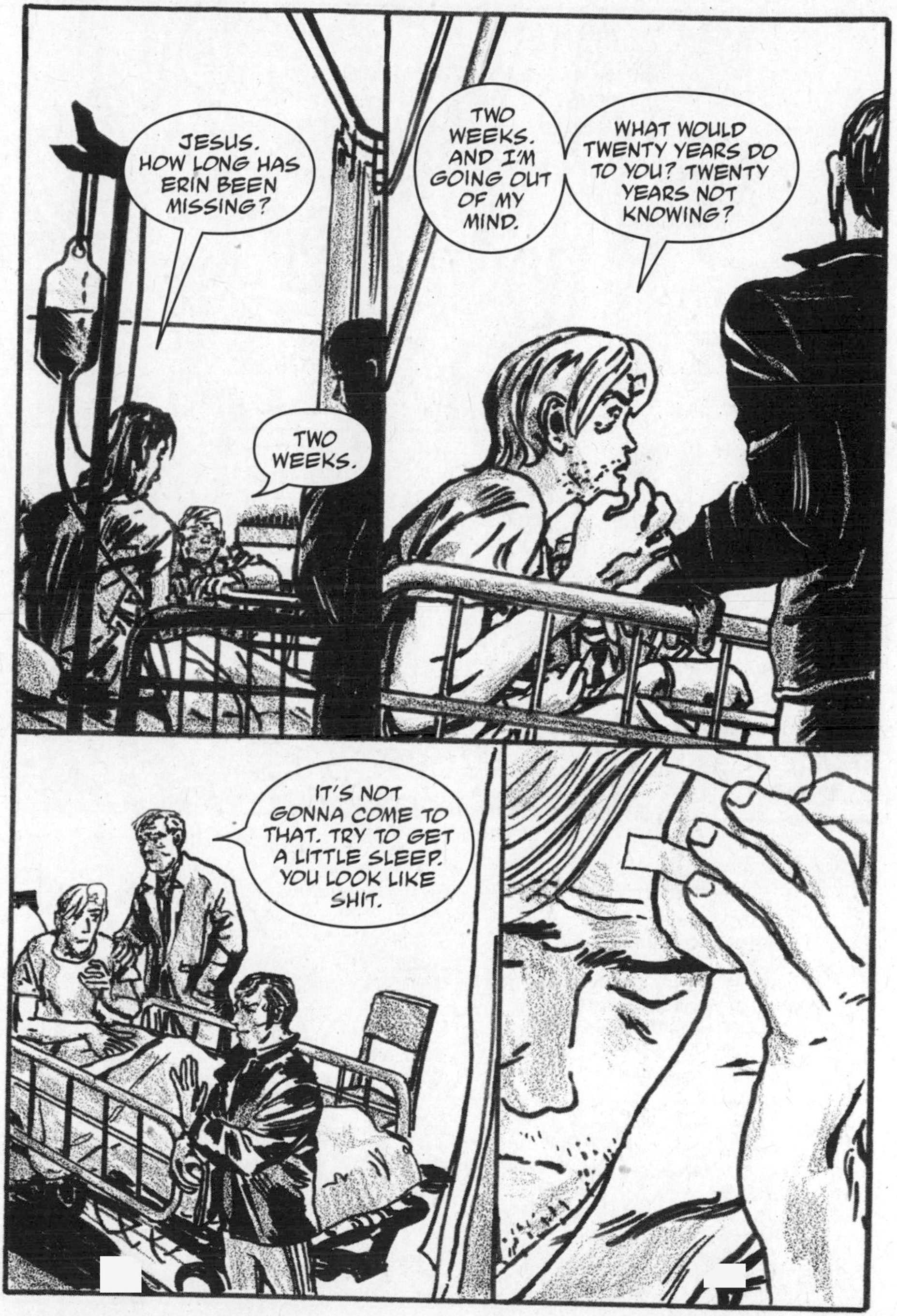
JESUS. HOW LONG HAS ERIN BEEN MISSING?
TWO WEEKS.
TWO WEEKS. AND I'M GOING OUT OF MY MIND.
WHAT WOULD TWENTY YEARS DO TO YOU? TWENTY YEARS NOT KNOWING?
IT'S NOT GONNA COME TO THAT. TRY TO GET A LITTLE SLEEP. YOU LOOK LIKE SHIT.

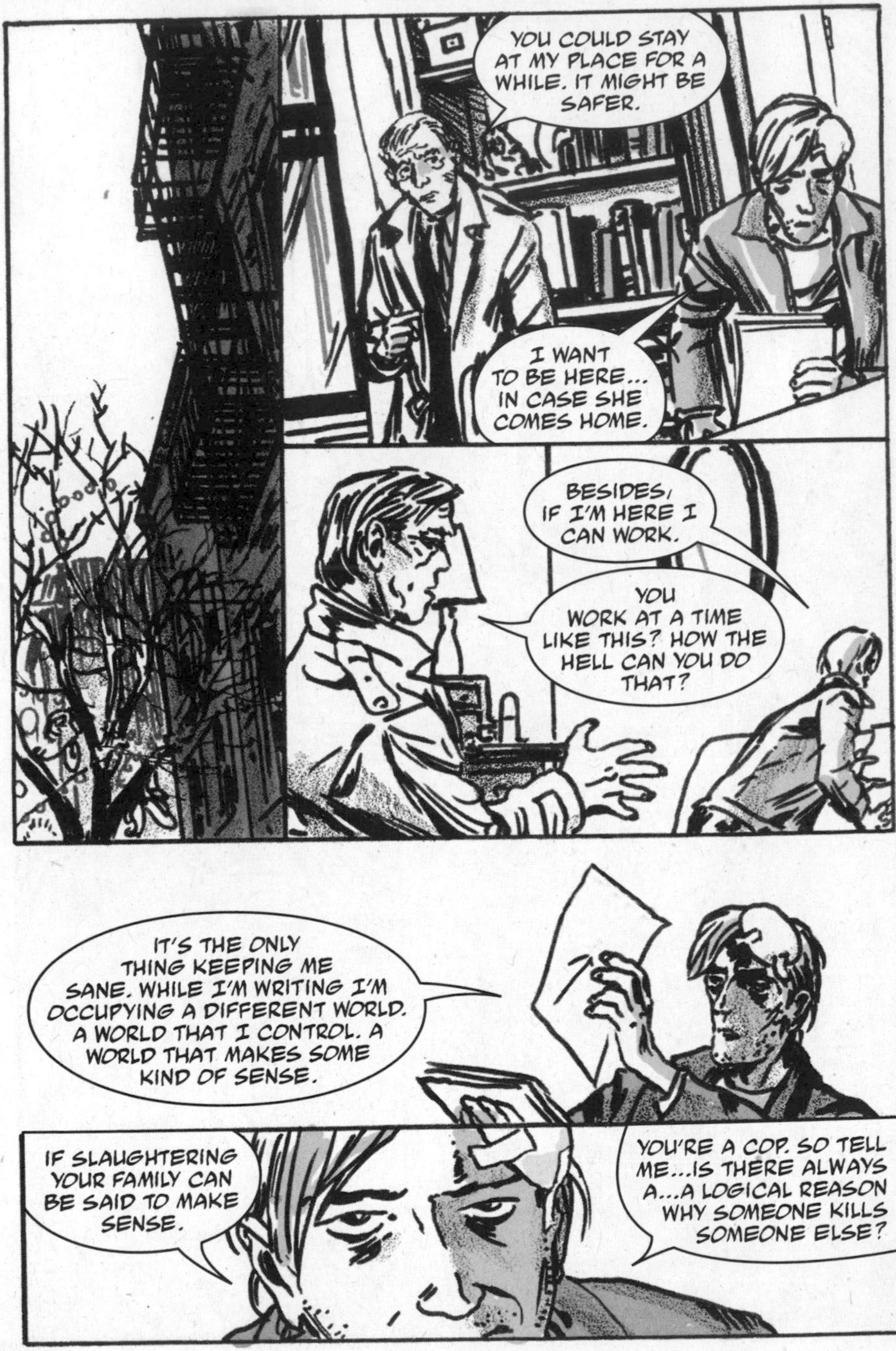
YOU COULD STAY AT MY PLACE FOR A WHILE. IT MIGHT BE SAFER.
I WANT TO BE HERE... IN CASE SHE COMES HOME.
BESIDES, IF I'M HERE I CAN WORK.
YOU WORK AT A TIME LIKE THIS? HOW THE HELL CAN YOU DO THAT?
IT'S THE ONLY THING KEEPING ME SANE. WHILE I'M WRITING I'M OCCUPYING A DIFFERENT WORLD. A WORLD THAT I CONTROL. A WORLD THAT MAKES SOME KIND OF SENSE.
IF SLAUGHTERING YOUR FAMILY CAN BE SAID TO MAKE SENSE.
YOU'RE A COP. SO TELL ME...IS THERE ALWAYS A...A LOGICAL REASON WHY SOMEONE KILLS SOMEONE ELSE?

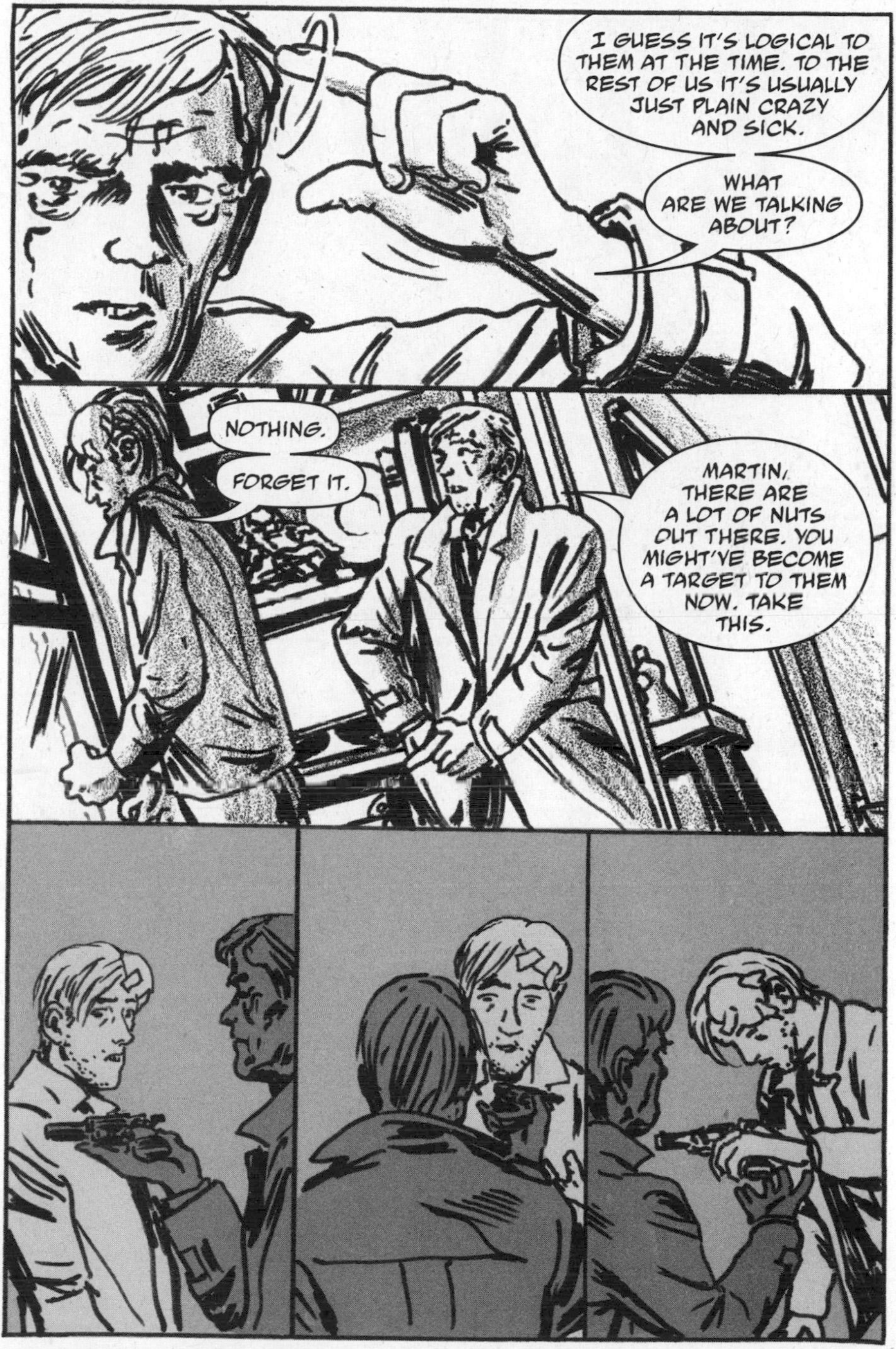
I GUESS IT'S LOGICAL TO THEM AT THE TIME. TO THE REST OF US IT'S USUALLY JUST PLAIN CRAZY AND SICK.
WHAT ARE WE TALKING ABOUT?
NOTHING.
FORGET IT.
MARTIN, THERE ARE A LOT OF NUTS OUT THERE. YOU MIGHT'VE BECOME A TARGET TO THEM NOW. TAKE THIS.

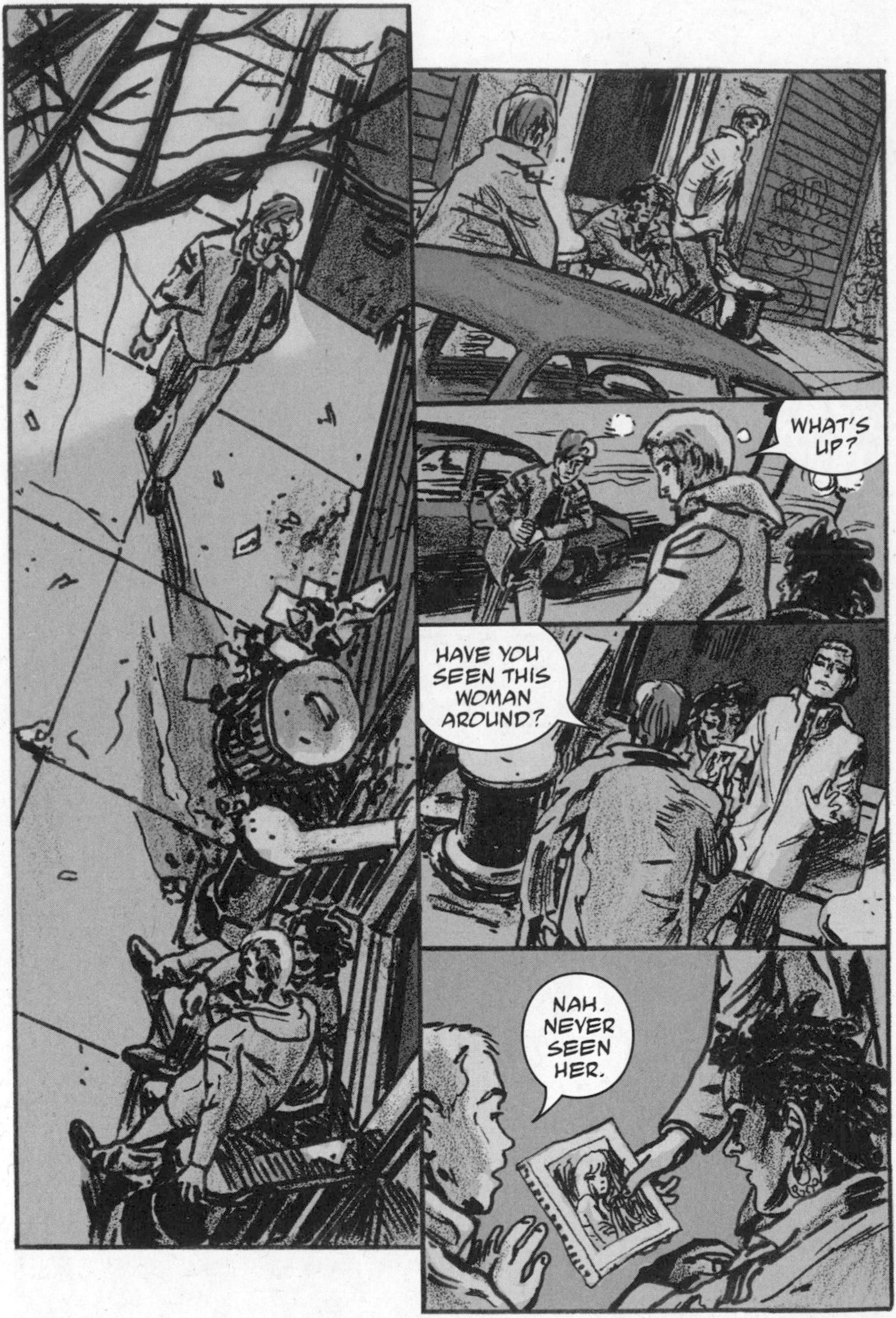
WHAT'S UP?
HAVE YOU SEEN THIS WOMAN AROUND?
NAH. NEVER SEEN HER.

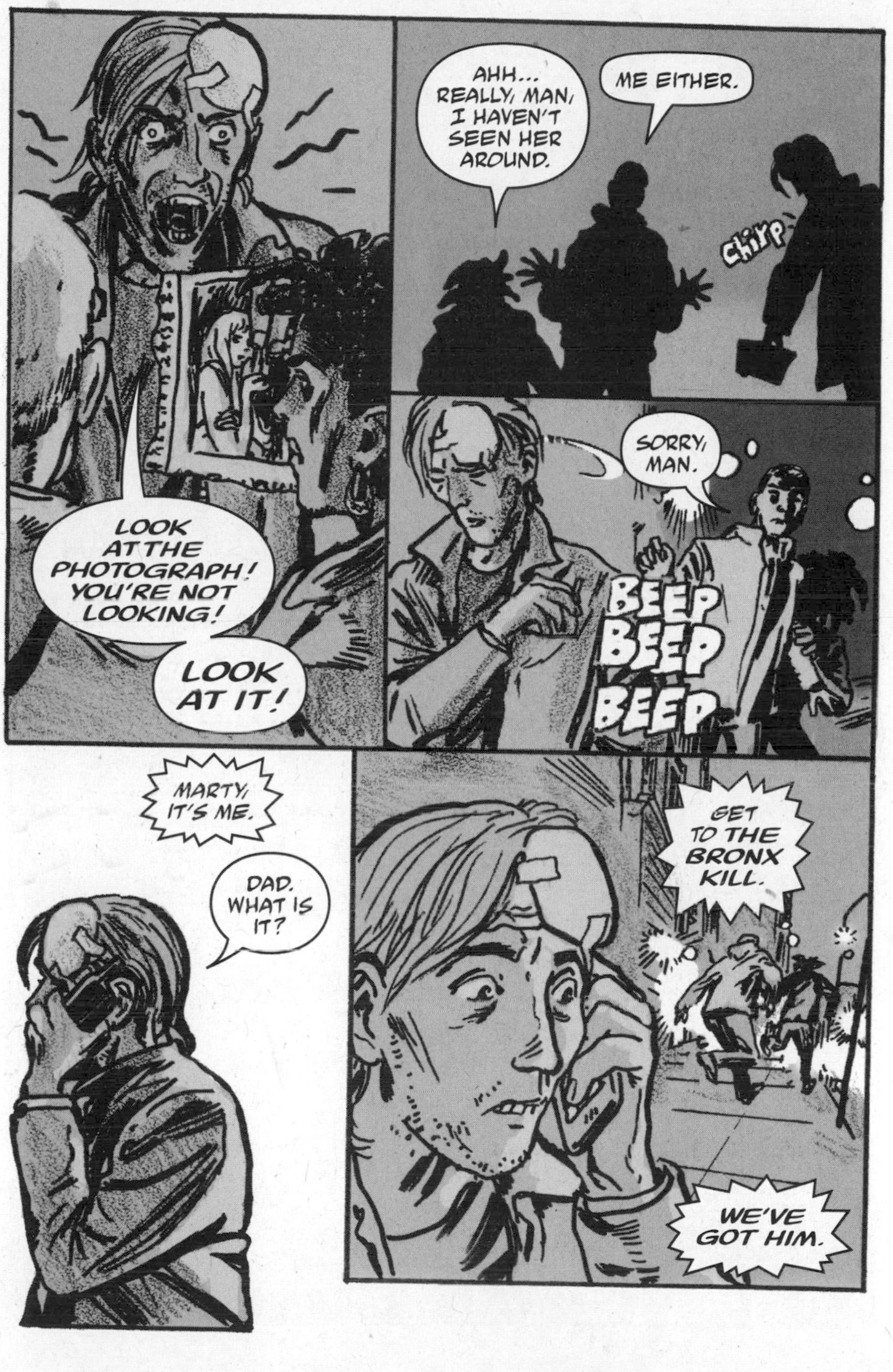
LOOK AT THE PHOTOGRAPH! YOU'RE NOT LOOKING!
LOOK AT IT!
AHH... REALLY, MAN, I HAVEN'T SEEN HER AROUND.
ME EITHER.
CHIRP
SORRY, MAN.
BEEP BEEP BEEP
MARTY, IT'S ME.
DAD. WHAT IS IT?
GET TO THE BRONX KILL.
WE'VE GOT HIM.

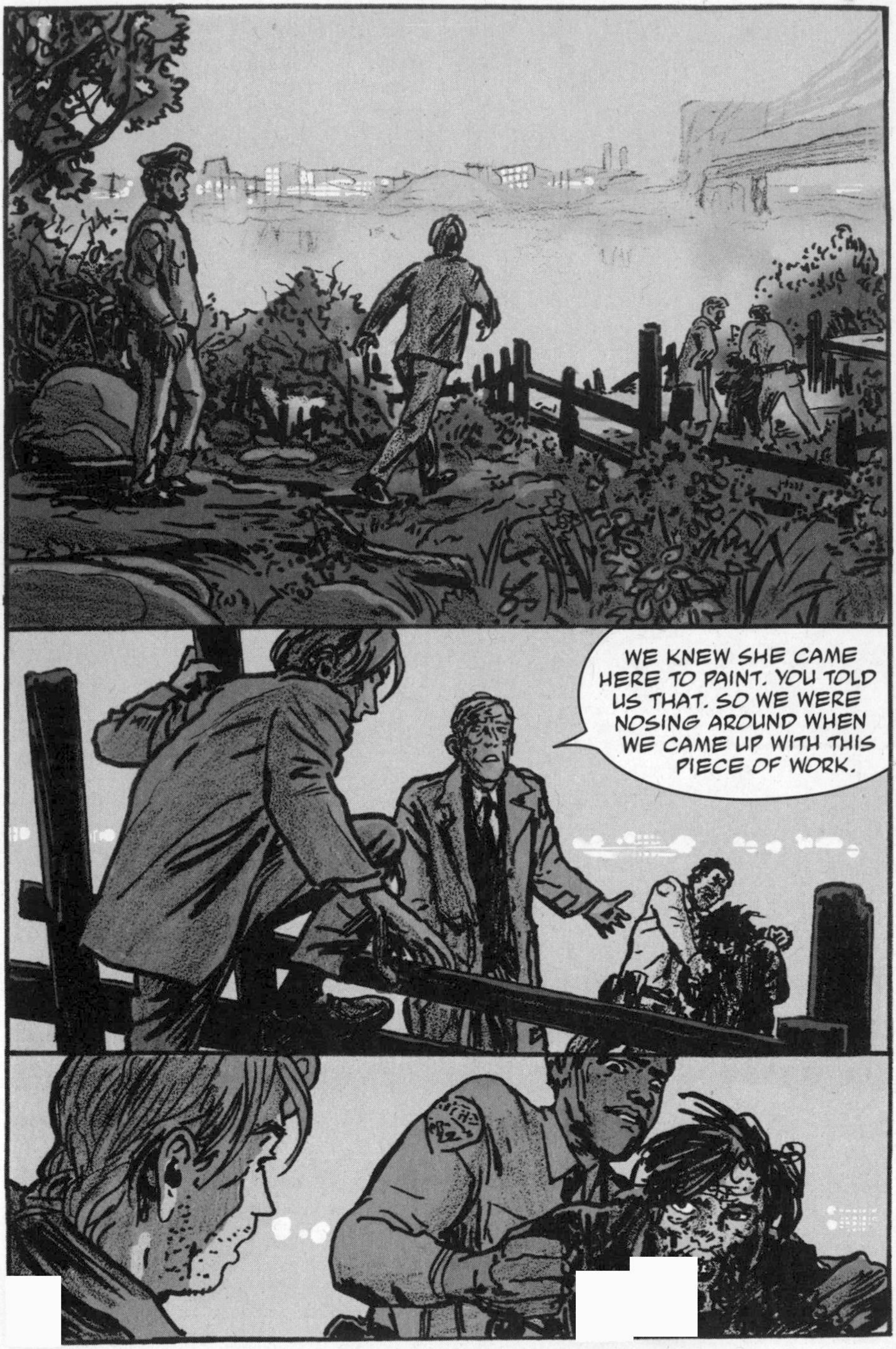
WE KNEW SHE CAME HERE TO PAINT. YOU TOLD US THAT. SO WE WERE NOSING AROUND WHEN WE CAME UP WITH THIS PIECE OF WORK.

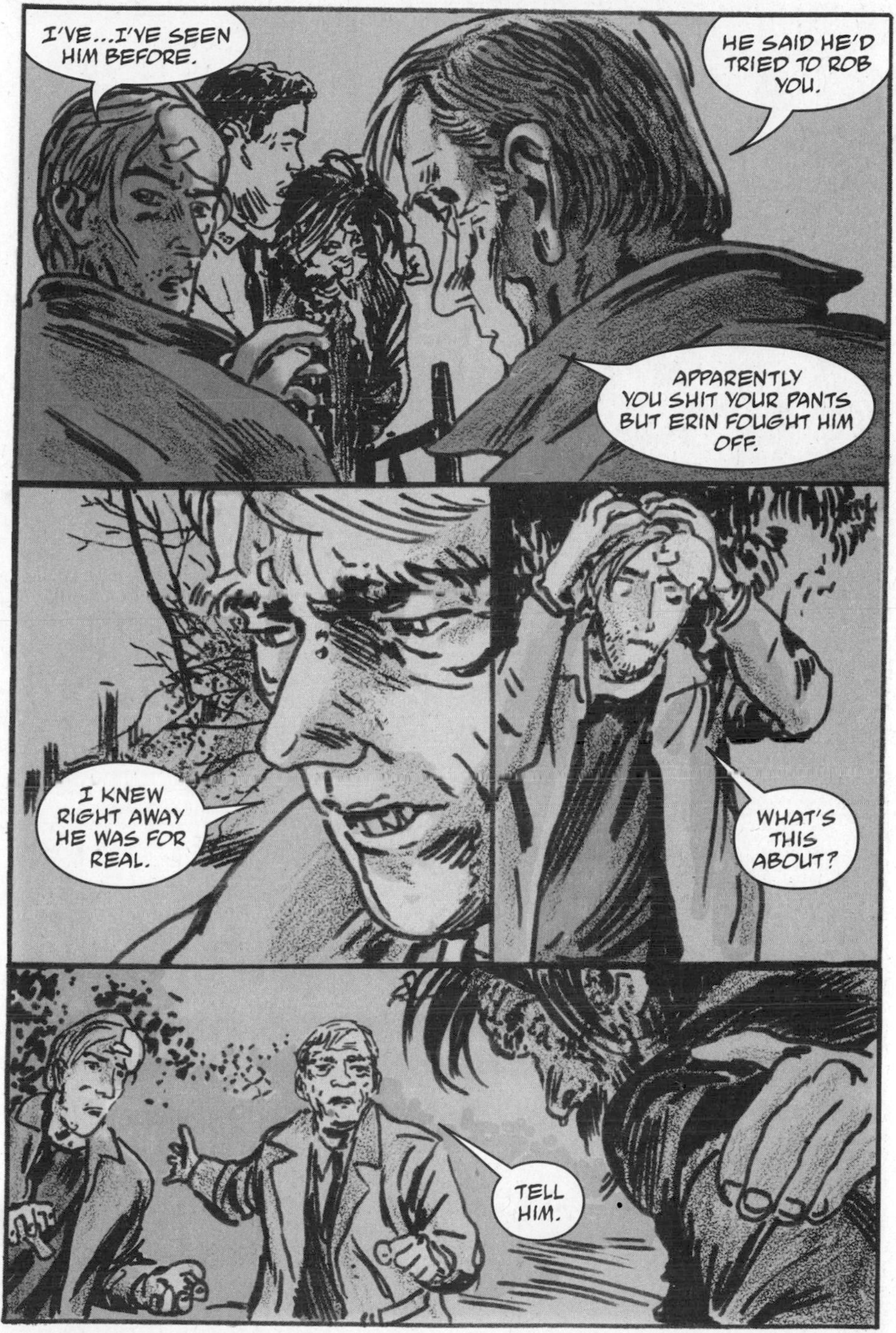
I'VE...I'VE SEEN HIM BEFORE.
HE SAID HE'D TRIED TO ROB YOU.
APPARENTLY YOU SHIT YOUR PANTS BUT ERIN FOUGHT HIM OFF.
I KNEW RIGHT AWAY HE WAS FOR REAL.
WHAT'S THIS ABOUT?
TELL HIM.

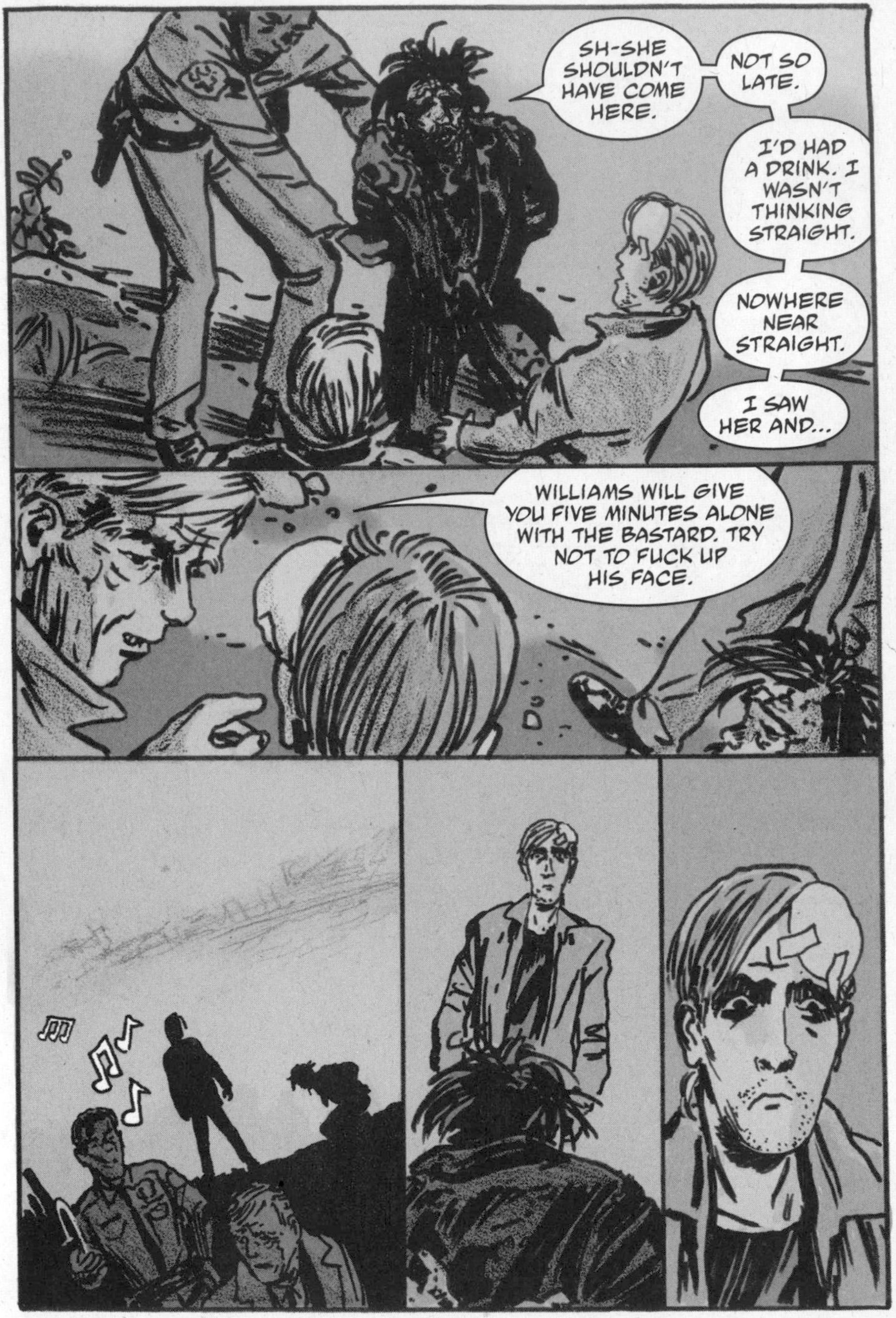
SH-SHE SHOULDN'T HAVE COME HERE.
NOT SO LATE.
I'D HAD A DRINK. I WASN'T THINKING STRAIGHT.
NOWHERE NEAR STRAIGHT.
I SAW HER AND...
WILLIAMS WILL GIVE YOU FIVE MINUTES ALONE WITH THE BASTARD. TRY NOT TO FUCK UP HIS FACE.

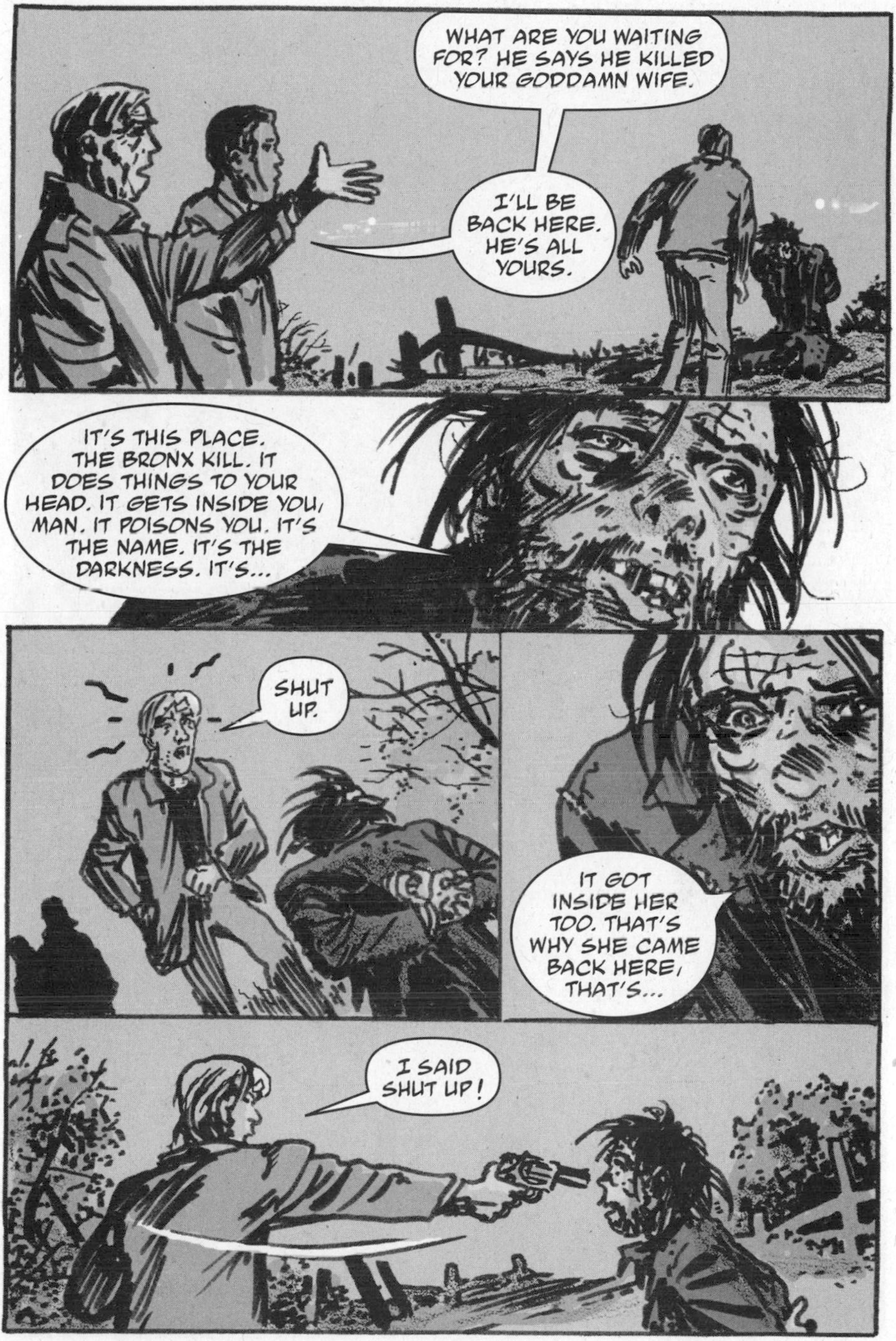
WHAT ARE YOU WAITING FOR? HE SAYS HE KILLED YOUR GODDAMN WIFE.
I'LL BE BACK HERE. HE'S ALL YOURS.
IT'S THIS PLACE. THE BRONX KILL. IT DOES THINGS TO YOUR HEAD. IT GETS INSIDE YOU, MAN. IT POISONS YOU. IT'S THE NAME. IT'S THE DARKNESS. IT'S...
SHUT UP.
IT GOT INSIDE HER TOO. THAT'S WHY SHE CAME BACK HERE, THAT'S...
I SAID SHUT UP!

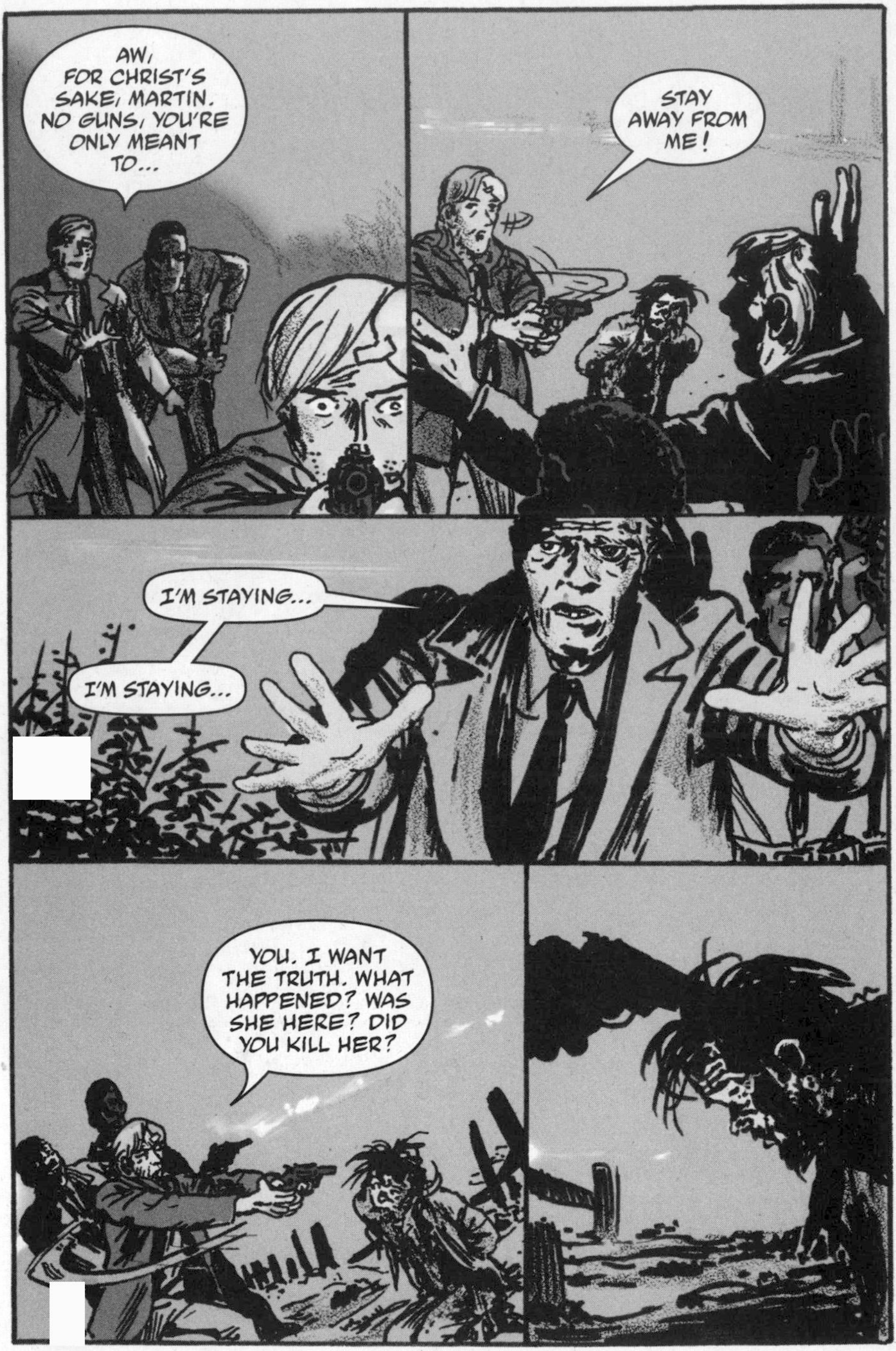
AW, FOR CHRIST'S SAKE, MARTIN. NO GUNS, YOU'RE ONLY MEANT TO...
STAY AWAY FROM ME!
I'M STAYING...
I'M STAYING...
YOU. I WANT THE TRUTH. WHAT HAPPENED? WAS SHE HERE? DID YOU KILL HER?

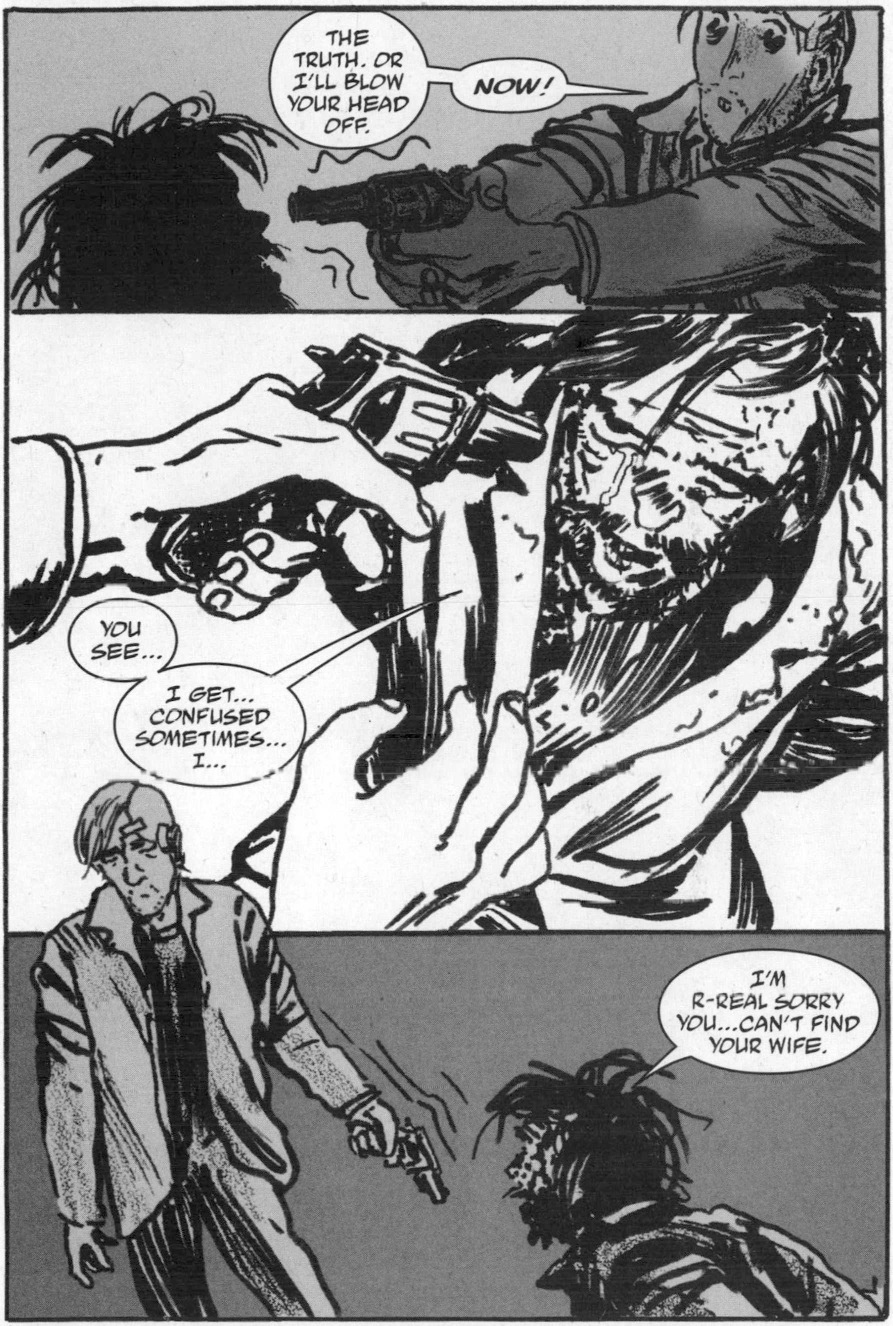
THE TRUTH. OR I'LL BLOW YOUR HEAD OFF.
NOW!
YOU SEE...
I GET... CONFUSED SOMETIMES... I...
I'M R-REAL SORRY YOU...CAN'T FIND YOUR WIFE.

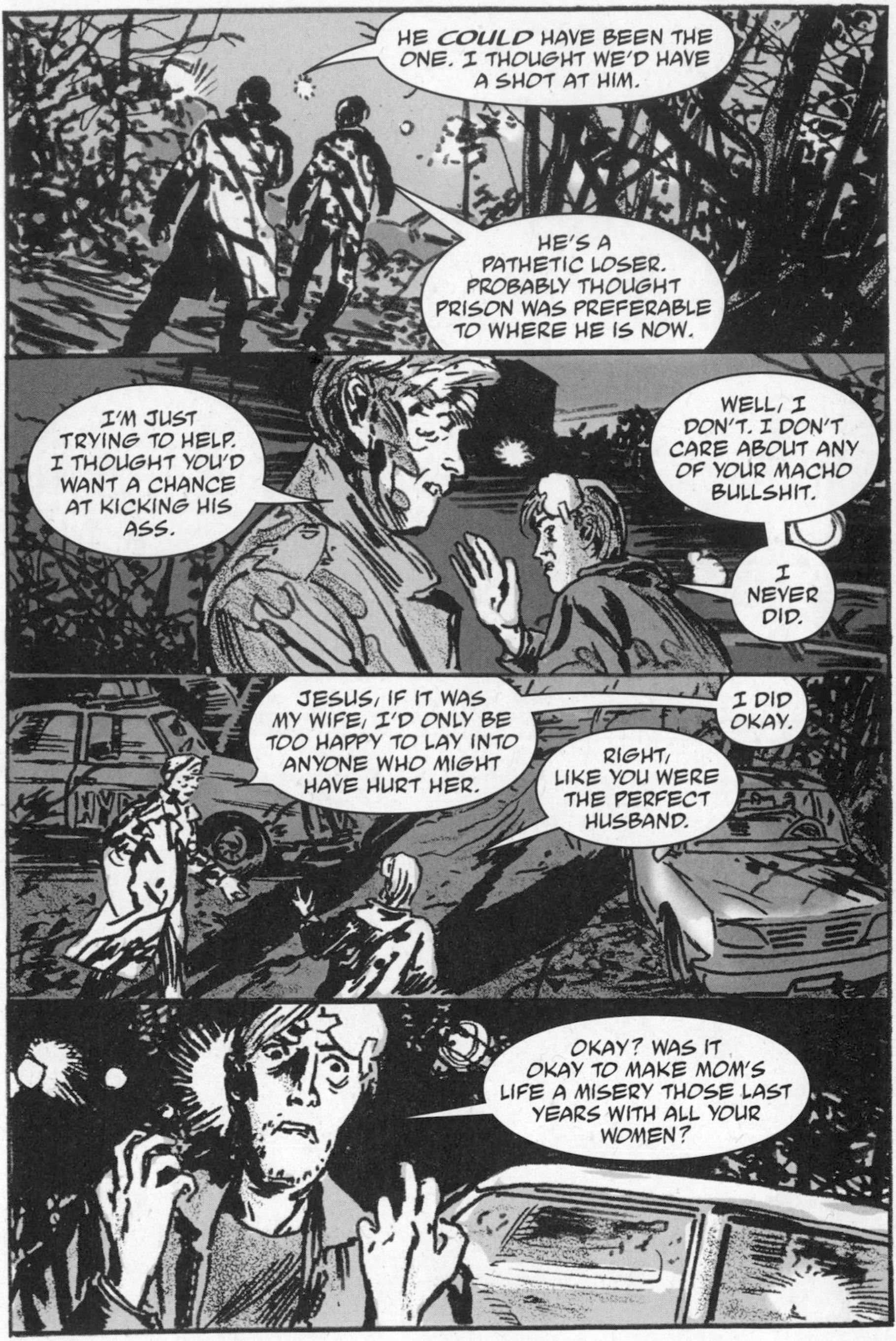
HE *COULD* HAVE BEEN THE ONE. I THOUGHT WE'D HAVE A SHOT AT HIM.
HE'S A PATHETIC LOSER. PROBABLY THOUGHT PRISON WAS PREFERABLE TO WHERE HE IS NOW.
I'M JUST TRYING TO HELP. I THOUGHT YOU'D WANT A CHANCE AT KICKING HIS ASS.
WELL, I DON'T. I DON'T CARE ABOUT ANY OF YOUR MACHO BULLSHIT.
I NEVER DID.
JESUS, IF IT WAS MY WIFE, I'D ONLY BE TOO HAPPY TO LAY INTO ANYONE WHO MIGHT HAVE HURT HER.
I DID OKAY.
RIGHT, LIKE YOU WERE THE PERFECT HUSBAND.
OKAY? WAS IT OKAY TO MAKE MOM'S LIFE A MISERY THOSE LAST YEARS WITH ALL YOUR WOMEN?

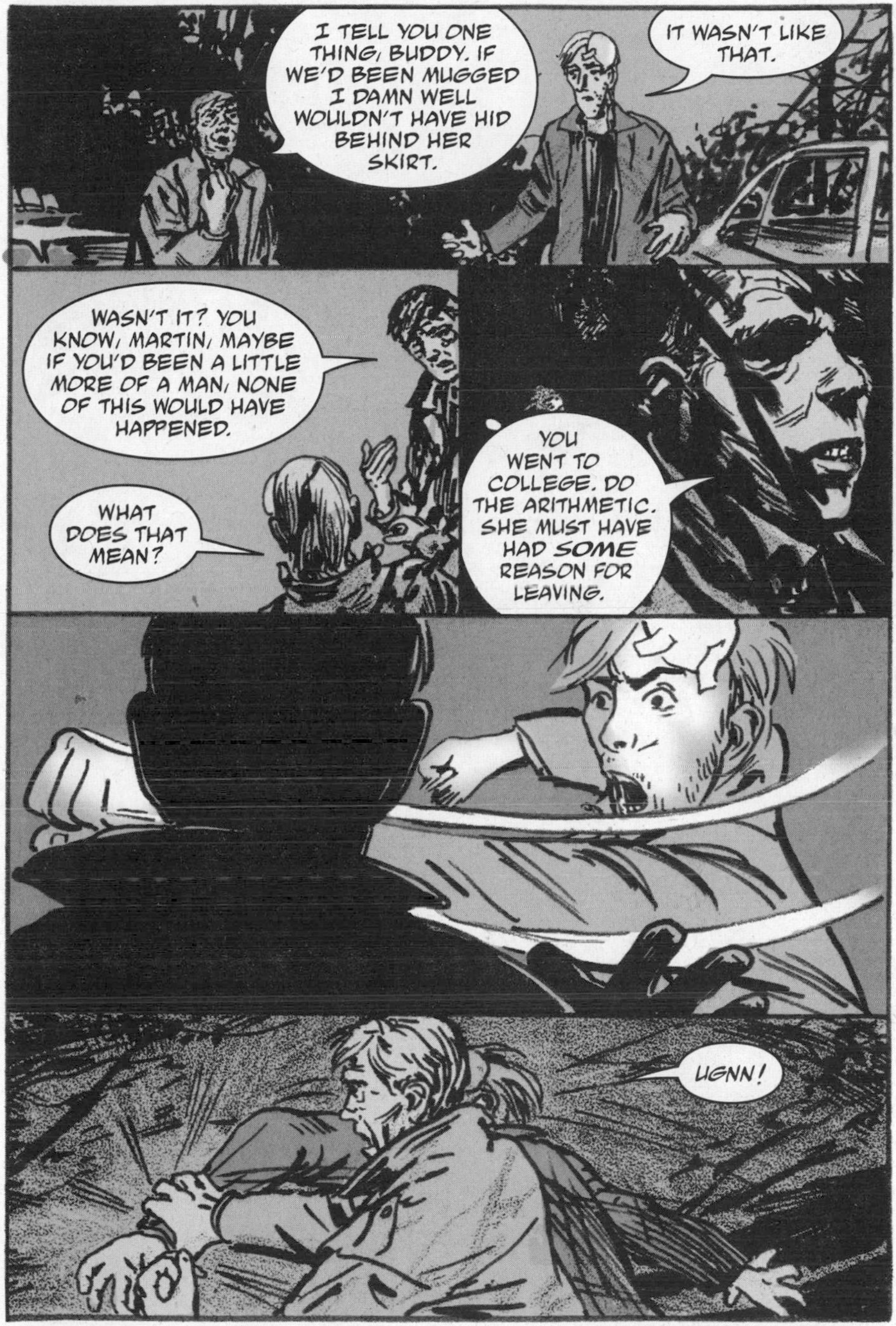
I TELL YOU ONE THING, BUDDY. IF WE'D BEEN MUGGED I DAMN WELL WOULDN'T HAVE HID BEHIND HER SKIRT.
IT WASN'T LIKE THAT.
WASN'T IT? YOU KNOW, MARTIN, MAYBE IF YOU'D BEEN A LITTLE MORE OF A MAN, NONE OF THIS WOULD HAVE HAPPENED.
WHAT DOES THAT MEAN?
YOU WENT TO COLLEGE. DO THE ARITHMETIC. SHE MUST HAVE HAD *SOME* REASON FOR LEAVING.
UGNN!

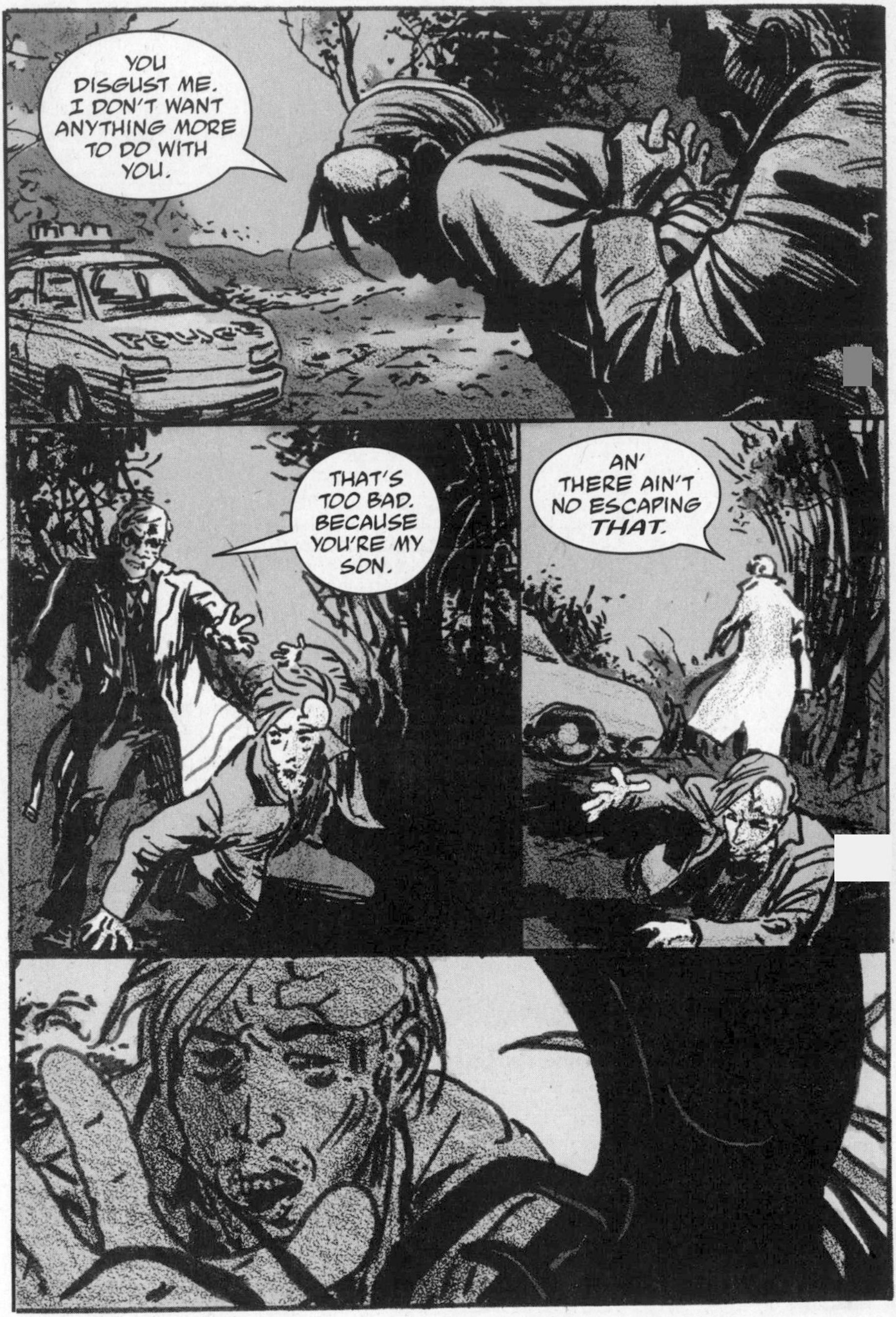
YOU DISGUST ME. I DON'T WANT ANYTHING MORE TO DO WITH YOU.
THAT'S TOO BAD. BECAUSE YOU'RE MY SON.
AN' THERE AIN'T NO ESCAPING *THAT*.

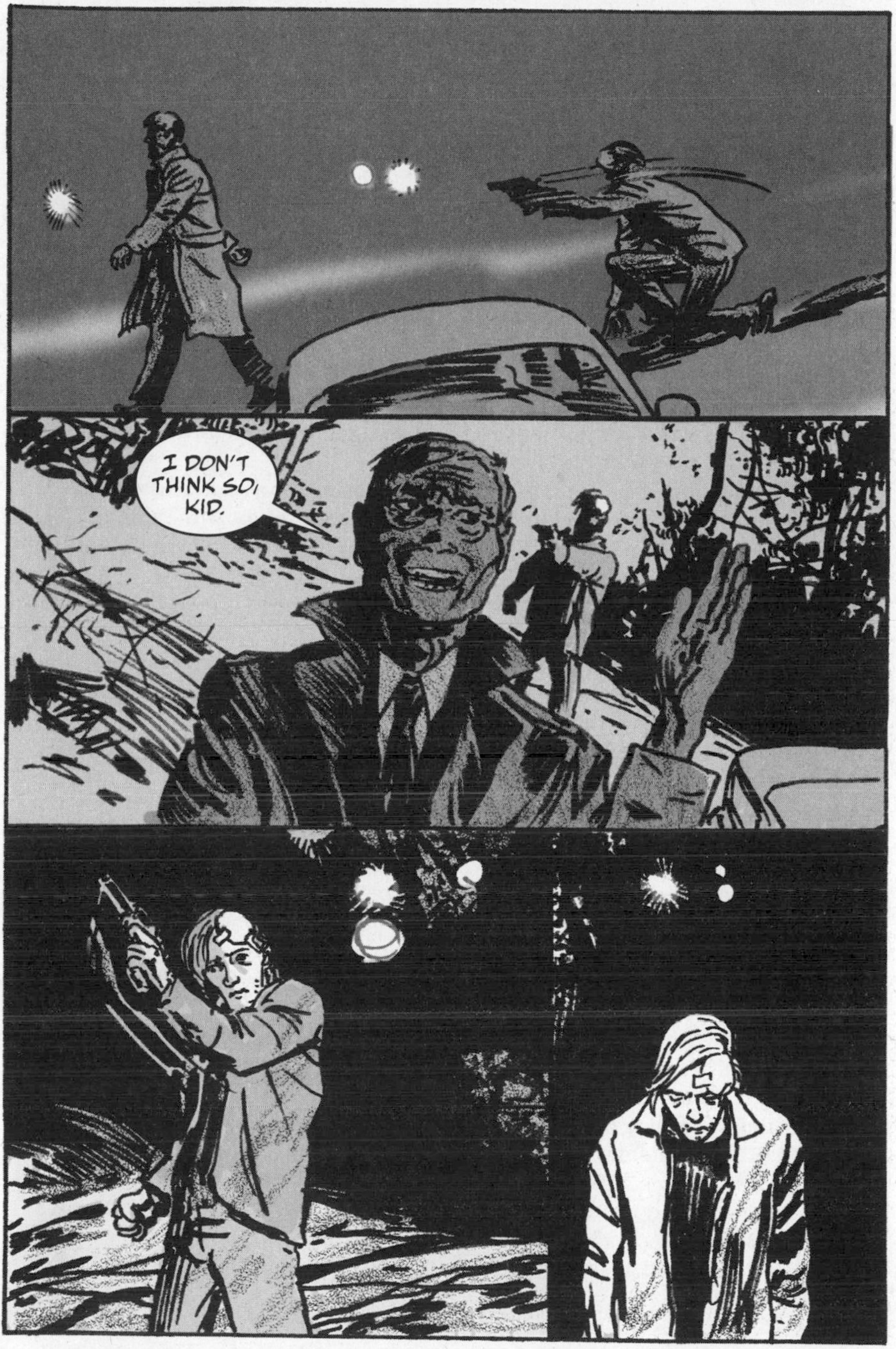
I DON'T THINK SO, KID.

You can run. You can change your landscape. But you cannot escape from that inner landscape that waits for you at night.

It had now been four years since I'd travelled thousands of miles across a deadly sea and made a home in this even deadlier sea of men called New York. And I had worked hard to leave my memories behind. This is a town that makes new memories fast. It's a town forever inventing itself, and is surely the perfect place for a man who wants to fashion himself anew. After four years, I almost felt like a New Yorker.

I almost felt like Michael Drury.

But that night Eveline came to me again. We met on a brickfield. This was in itself disconcerting. I had never met or associated my sister with that place bought and squeezed into dusty life by my grandfather, where our family's meager fortune was to be blended and baked into hard clay nuggets.

As she approached me, I heard a piano playing. For some reason that piano put the fear of God into me. Suddenly I couldn't bear the thought of Eveline getting any closer. It became, as these things do in dreams, the most urgent and important thing imaginable that Eveline kept her distance.

"Why, Michael? Why?" she moaned.

"Stay away! For God's sake…"

There was a moment, a small fraction of a moment, when the realization that I was suddenly, jarringly, shockingly awake occurred to me. But by then it was too late, the words were out, in a scream.

"Stay away!"

I was sitting up in bed. I'd shouted out, my hair was sticking to my scalp, and I had awoken the sickly child next door, who was adding his own angry sobs to my own.

For a moment I swore I heard a piano playing.

My wife thrashed out of her own sleep.

"Wh…what…Michael, what is it?"

I remained seated upright, sheet wrapped around moist legs, trying to clear my head, looking around at the room. Our bed. Chair. Desk. Closet.

Normal everyday things. But right then, my mind still wedged someplace in that weird warm kiln between sleep and wakefulness, the room and everything in it seemed as strange to me as any dream.

"Michael?" said Ann, sitting up beside me. "Are you unwell?"

My breathing was becoming normal. The room was becoming a solid box that I believed in again.

"I'm fine, Ann. Go back to sleep. Just a dream."

"I wish I could go back to sleep," she said, yawning. "But it's morning already."

Pale dawn light was entering the room through the threadbare drapes. Soon the temperature would start to rise. Ann ran her hand down the back of my head.

"What were you dreaming about? You're soaked."

"I dreamt I swam all the way from Ireland to America, and I picked a fight with a mermaid on the way," I lied, not wishing to discuss the real nature of my dream.

She laughed and pushed my head softly.

"Michael," she said. "Why did you desert your poor brother?"

Had I heard correctly?

"I did not desert..."

I had turned to face her. But that's as far as I got. For what I saw froze my tongue.

Ann had two black coins over her eyes.

Of course, I screamed. Who wouldn't scream? If I screamed loud enough maybe this would end, this world would shatter, vanish. But my tongue was still frozen. I couldn't feel it. I couldn't hear myself screaming. I did, though, hear the sound of a piano.

Her black coin eyes came closer. So close I could see the dark face of the King. I had another go at screaming.

"Michael. Michael. Wake up! It's all right. "

I opened my eyes.

She was shaking me. Her face above me. I turned my own burning face away. I dared not look at her.

"What is it, darling? What's wrong? Look at me!"

Slowly, my heart beating like hooves against my ribs, I turned. I turned and looked up at her. The firm outline of her jaw. The lips, pursed in concern. The nose, with its sprinkling of freckles.

The eyes.

The dream remained with me the better part of the morning. It was still there as I waited in the small room to where I'd been summoned by the telegram that had arrived at our boarding house. There were only two others with me. A young lady in a bonnet who stayed standing, swaying gently to a tune only she could hear. She kept her face turned to the window.

An actress, I wondered? The mistress of some rich and powerful man, who doesn't want to be seen or recognized?

I was aware that the trade I was trying to ply had inculcated in me a tendency to see the flashy story, the intriguing perspective behind every bland situation. The lady more likely took an interest in the architecture of downtown New York and was enjoying the view. More likely still she was shy and didn't want to meet our gazes. Knowing the salacious reputation of the Herald, she might presume any gentleman she met in here would be similarly disreputable.

My other companion was a large bearded man whose coal-black eyes watched me from beneath a tangled thicket of eyebrow. I had known some of the worst scoundrels in this city, yet none of them had made me feel quite as uneasy as the steady surgical gaze he fixed me with.

The door opened with a bang, and a dapper little man with brilliantined hair blew busily in. The bearded man began to rise. Brilliantine almost bowed to him.

"Mr. Bennett apologizes for the delay, Herr Marx."

Then Brilliantine turned to me.

"Mr. Drury."

As I followed—Brilliantine was already sweeping out of the room—I glanced back at my bearded friend, who was seating himself again, clearly irritated at being kept waiting. The young lady in the bonnet had finally turned from the window.

I noticed that she too had a beard.

The famous, the infamous, James Gordon Bennett, proprietor of the "Herald" and scourge of the finer New York sensibilities, was engaged in several large sheets of paper as I was shown into the office.

"Mr. Drury, sir," he said.

Bennett looked up from his cluttered desk. But it was clear I only had one small part of his attention. The rest never quite left the other tasks in which he was engaged. The sound of telegraph machines kept up a constant rap rap rap from other rooms.

Bennett had a long face, quick eyes, thin mouth, and hair that was almost white. I knew he had once studied for the priesthood. He would have looked the part, I thought. ~~Though his movements were too quick, altogether too energized, for the slow drawn-out tortures of the mass.~~

"Mr. Drury. Yes. I liked your article on The Dead Rabbits. Very…colorful."

So that was it. No formalities. Straight to business.

"Thank you, sir."

'They tell me you lived with those rogues for nigh-on three months to get their confidence."

"That's correct, sir."

As I spoke, the door opened and a young man, red-faced and breathless, tore in and pushed what looked like a telegram in front of the great newspaperman. He studied it quickly, scribbled a note on it, and gave it back to the boy. Who fled with it, giving me the briefest nod as he passed me.

"Excuse me, Mr. Drury. My critics, and they are legion, suggest I have an unwillingness or an inability to delegate."

"Maybe you just never found the people you can trust, sir."

More work on Bennett. His relationship w/ Lincoln.
Set at outbreak of Civil War? America's dark past: Slavery. Weight of past!

I almost swallowed my fat tongue. There I was, five seconds in the office of one of New York's most powerful men, and I was telling him he was surrounded by traitors.

"Maybe so," he said, watching me. "What were we discussing?"

"My article, sir," I said quickly, glad to get the subject back to me and my great talent. "You were saying you enjoyed my article on The Dead Rabbits."

"Yes. Exactly. Tell me now...living alongside them for the time that you did...were you ever concerned that you would get too close to your subject?"

"No, sir. Though I was occasionally concerned that I'd be *killed* by my subject."

Bennett laughed a laugh that was somewhere between a laugh and a dry cough. Then the door flew open again and another young man—a different one—skidded in carrying another telegram, which Bennett read, scribbled on, and dispatched in double quick time. And then he looked at me again. This time with something like suspicion.

"Drury. That's not an Irish name. But your accent belongs most definitely to a Hibernanian."

I was ready for this. I had changed my name. I had tried to change my past. But an accent tempered in the long fire of your childhood is a hard thing to erase, even in this city of changes.

"To paraphrase Swift...just because I was born in a pigsty, does not make me a pig."

God, I could almost feel my father pushing himself out of his grave, could hear his voice condemning me as a traitor to my people.

"Swift? I'm not after Swift, Mr. Drury. The people in the street, the semi-literate rabble who make up the majority of our readership do not, I think, want Swift. They want something more...more..."

"Colorful, sir?"

"Exactly. I have a commission for you, Furey. I mean...Drury."

Our eyes met for a second. Was this a slip of the tongue? Or had he had me investigated? He certainly had the means, if he had the inclination.

"There has been a murder. Several murders, of the most heinous kind."

"How terrible, sir."

"No, Drury. How wonderful. I want you to take a look at where the bodies were discovered. Gather details. Set the scene. Use all your colorful talents. Give me Dickens, but gutter Dickens, if you get my meaning."

"I think so, sir."

"A carriage will take you to the scene of the murder. Have you been to the Bronx before, Mr. Durey?"

Erin's latest obsessions... The Bronx.
Grandmother abandoning a baby.
EVERYTHING COMES BACK TO MY FAMILY!!

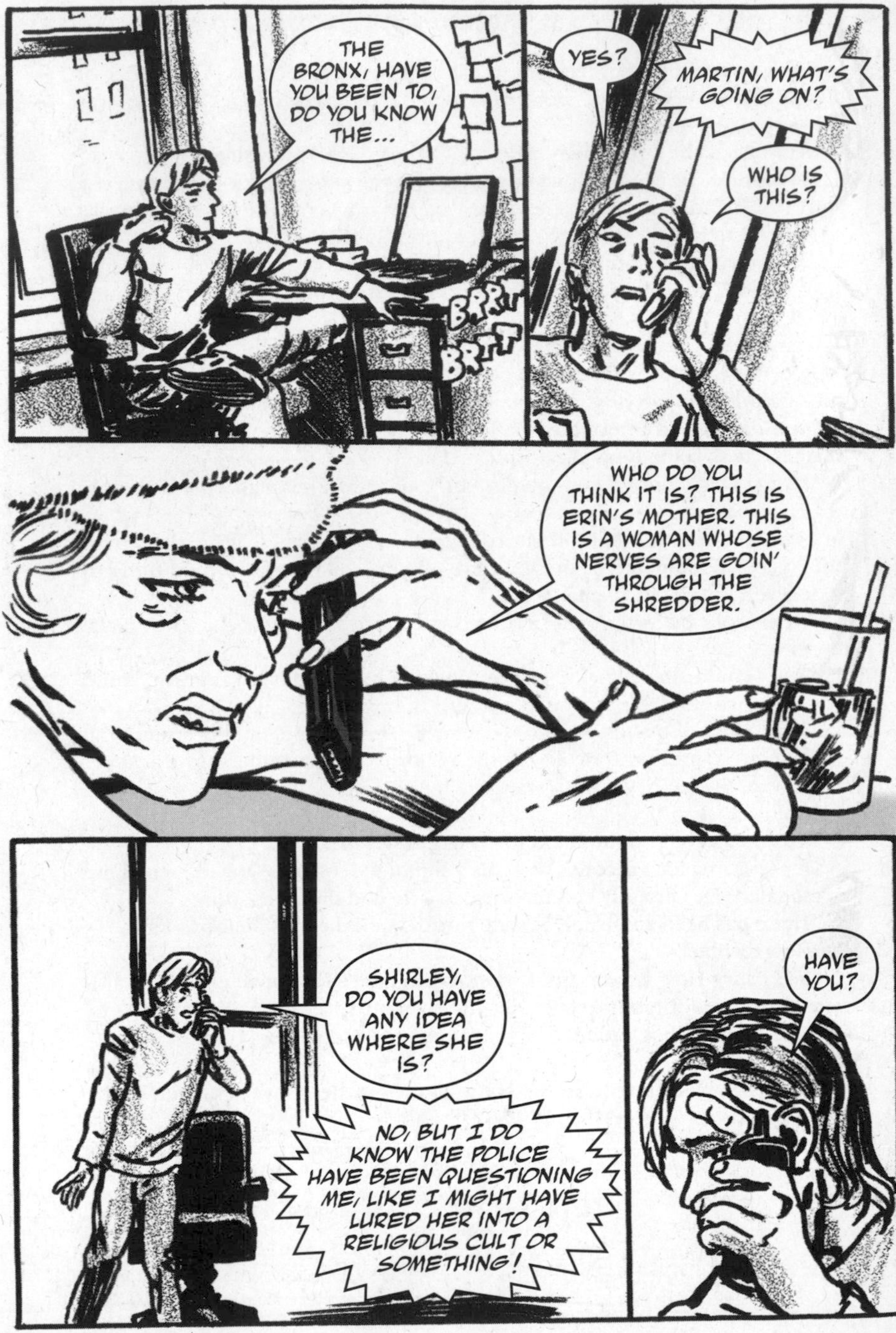
THE BRONX, HAVE YOU BEEN TO, DO YOU KNOW THE...
BRRT BRTT
YES?
MARTIN, WHAT'S GOING ON?
WHO IS THIS?
WHO DO YOU THINK IT IS? THIS IS ERIN'S MOTHER. THIS IS A WOMAN WHOSE NERVES ARE GOIN' THROUGH THE SHREDDER.
SHIRLEY, DO YOU HAVE ANY IDEA WHERE SHE IS?
NO, BUT I DO KNOW THE POLICE HAVE BEEN QUESTIONING ME, LIKE I MIGHT HAVE LURED HER INTO A RELIGIOUS CULT OR SOMETHING!
HAVE YOU?

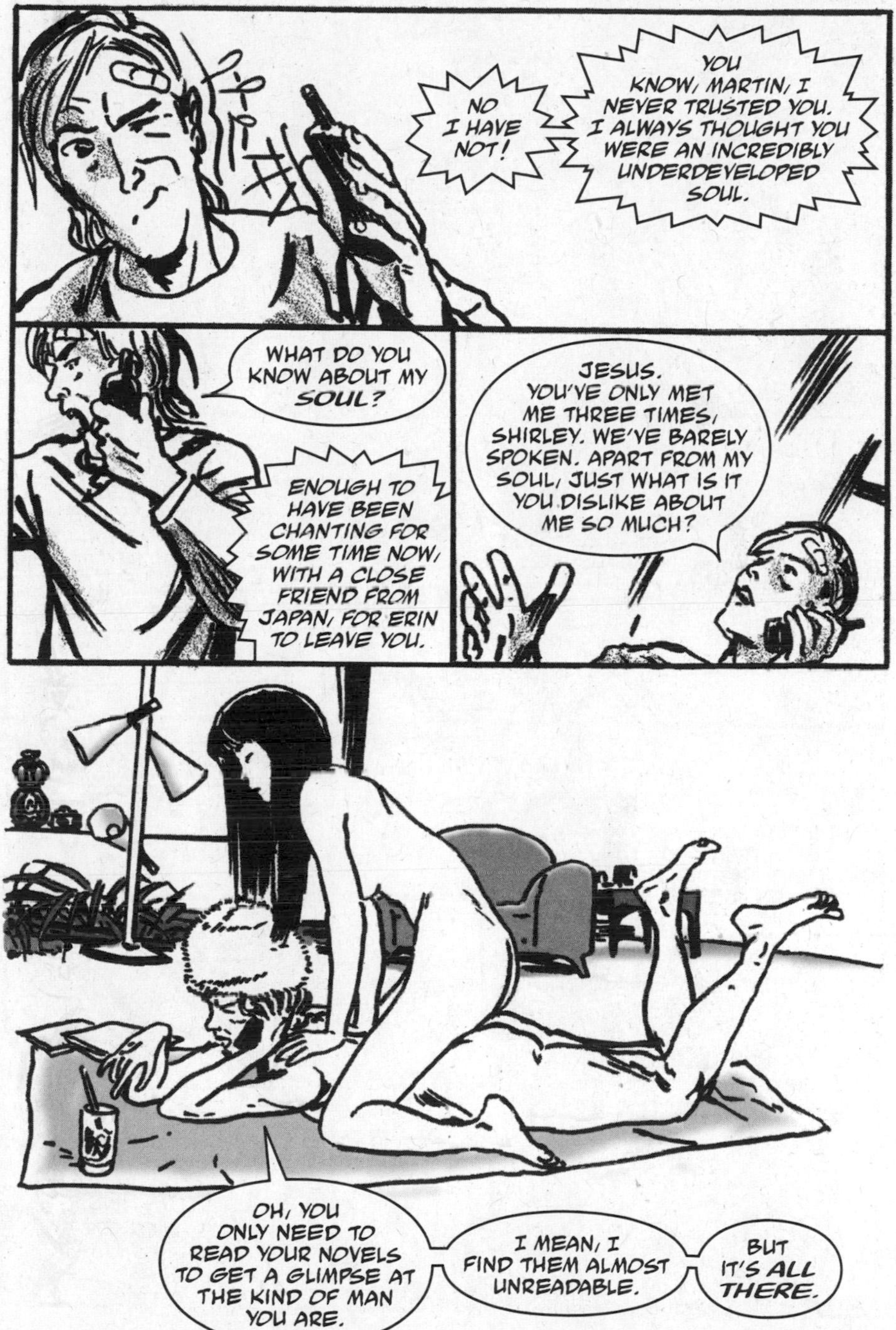
NO I HAVE NOT!
YOU KNOW, MARTIN, I NEVER TRUSTED YOU. I ALWAYS THOUGHT YOU WERE AN INCREDIBLY UNDERDEVELOPED SOUL.
WHAT DO YOU KNOW ABOUT MY SOUL?
ENOUGH TO HAVE BEEN CHANTING FOR SOME TIME NOW, WITH A CLOSE FRIEND FROM JAPAN, FOR ERIN TO LEAVE YOU.
JESUS. YOU'VE ONLY MET ME THREE TIMES, SHIRLEY. WE'VE BARELY SPOKEN. APART FROM MY SOUL, JUST WHAT IS IT YOU DISLIKE ABOUT ME SO MUCH?
OH, YOU ONLY NEED TO READ YOUR NOVELS TO GET A GLIMPSE AT THE KIND OF MAN YOU ARE.
I MEAN, I FIND THEM ALMOST UNREADABLE.
BUT IT'S ALL THERE.

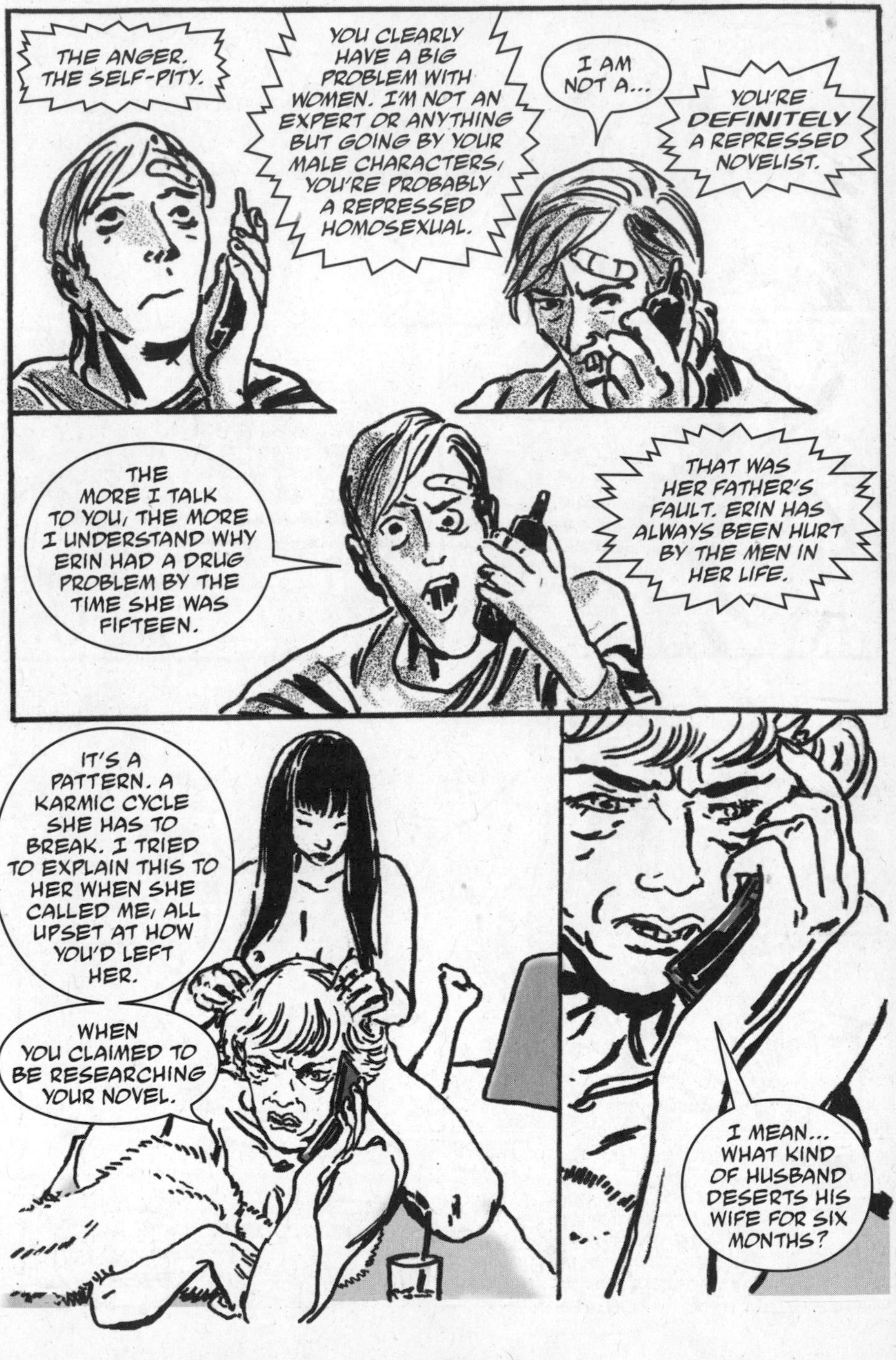
THE ANGER. THE SELF-PITY.
YOU CLEARLY HAVE A BIG PROBLEM WITH WOMEN. I'M NOT AN EXPERT OR ANYTHING BUT GOING BY YOUR MALE CHARACTERS, YOU'RE PROBABLY A REPRESSED HOMOSEXUAL.
I AM NOT A...
YOU'RE DEFINITELY A REPRESSED NOVELIST.
THE MORE I TALK TO YOU, THE MORE I UNDERSTAND WHY ERIN HAD A DRUG PROBLEM BY THE TIME SHE WAS FIFTEEN.
THAT WAS HER FATHER'S FAULT. ERIN HAS ALWAYS BEEN HURT BY THE MEN IN HER LIFE.
IT'S A PATTERN. A KARMIC CYCLE SHE HAS TO BREAK. I TRIED TO EXPLAIN THIS TO HER WHEN SHE CALLED ME, ALL UPSET AT HOW YOU'D LEFT HER.
WHEN YOU CLAIMED TO BE RESEARCHING YOUR NOVEL.
I MEAN... WHAT KIND OF HUSBAND DESERTS HIS WIFE FOR SIX MONTHS?

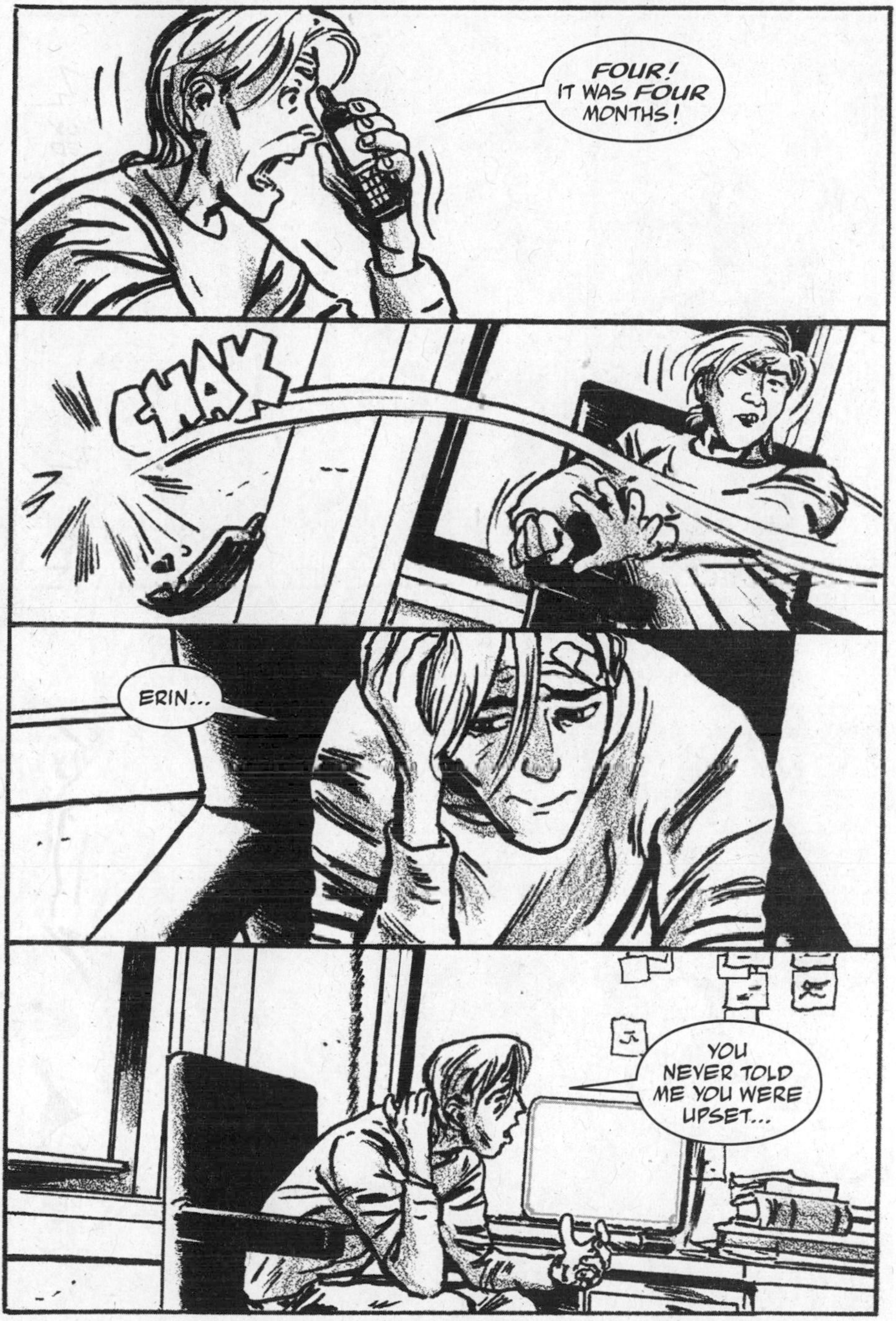
FOUR! IT WAS FOUR MONTHS!
CHAK
ERIN...
YOU NEVER TOLD ME YOU WERE UPSET...

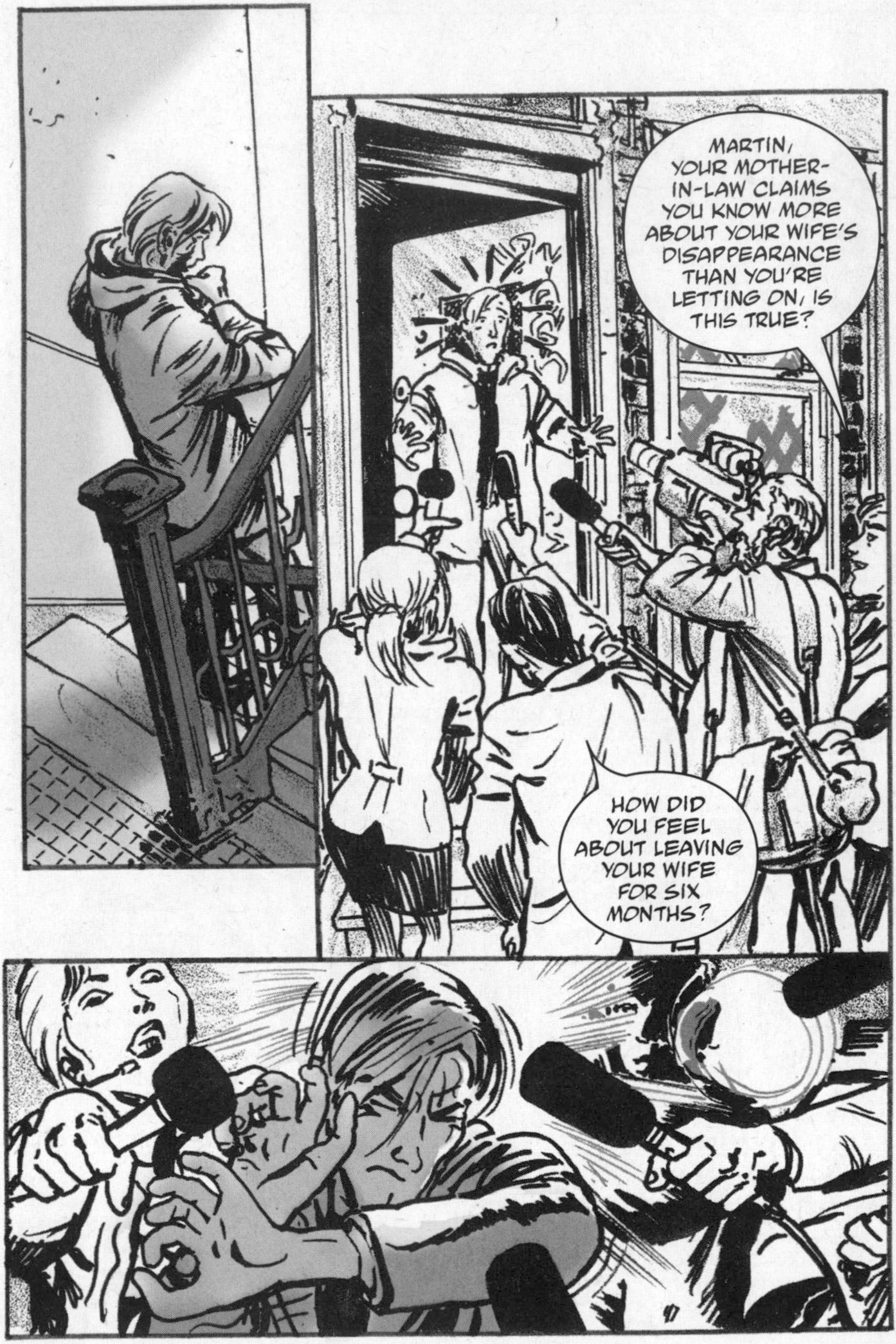
MARTIN, YOUR MOTHER-IN-LAW CLAIMS YOU KNOW MORE ABOUT YOUR WIFE'S DISAPPEARANCE THAN YOU'RE LETTING ON, IS THIS TRUE?
HOW DID YOU FEEL ABOUT LEAVING YOUR WIFE FOR SIX MONTHS?

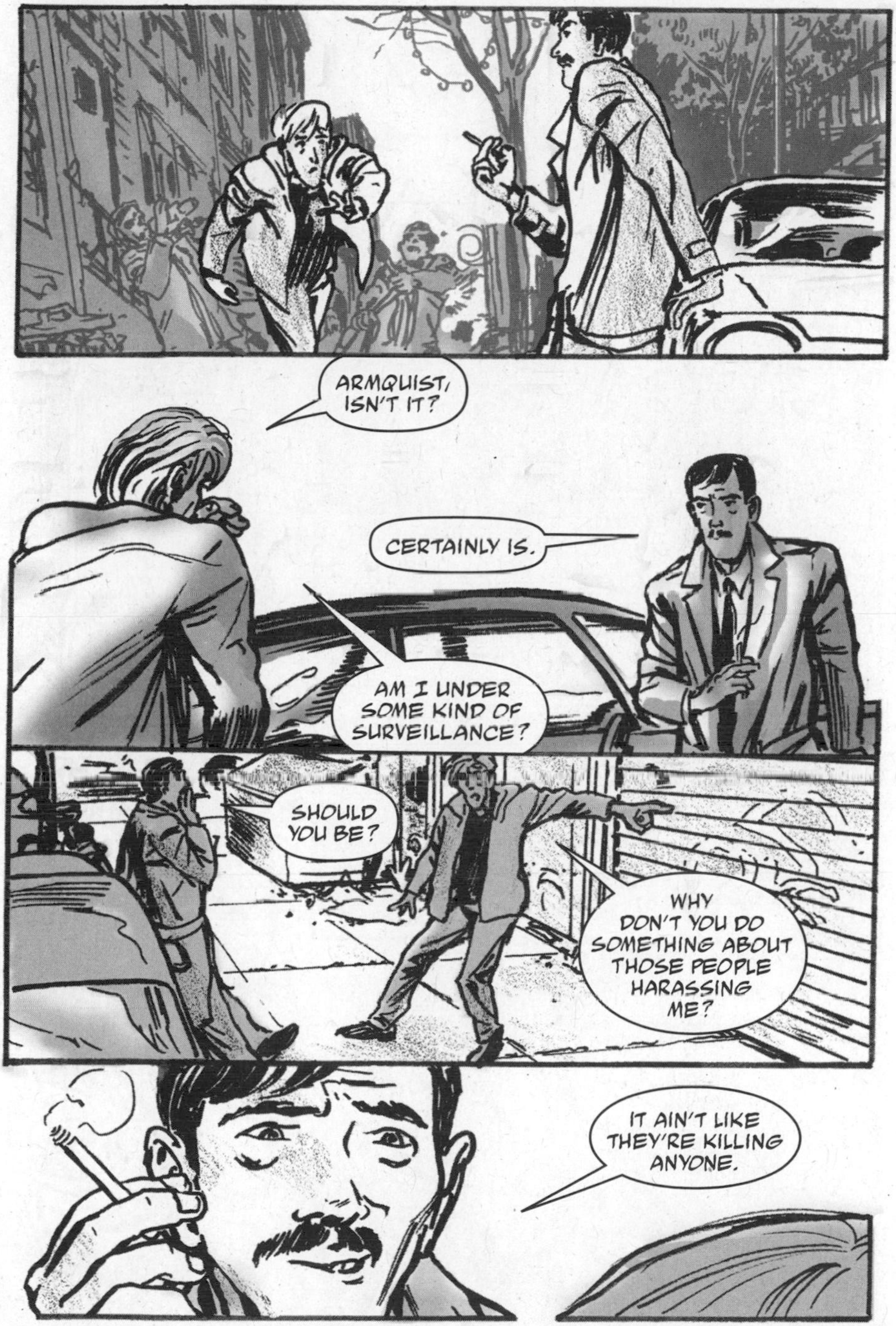
ARMQUIST, ISN'T IT?
CERTAINLY IS.
AM I UNDER SOME KIND OF SURVEILLANCE?
SHOULD YOU BE?
WHY DON'T YOU DO SOMETHING ABOUT THOSE PEOPLE HARASSING ME?
IT AIN'T LIKE THEY'RE KILLING ANYONE.

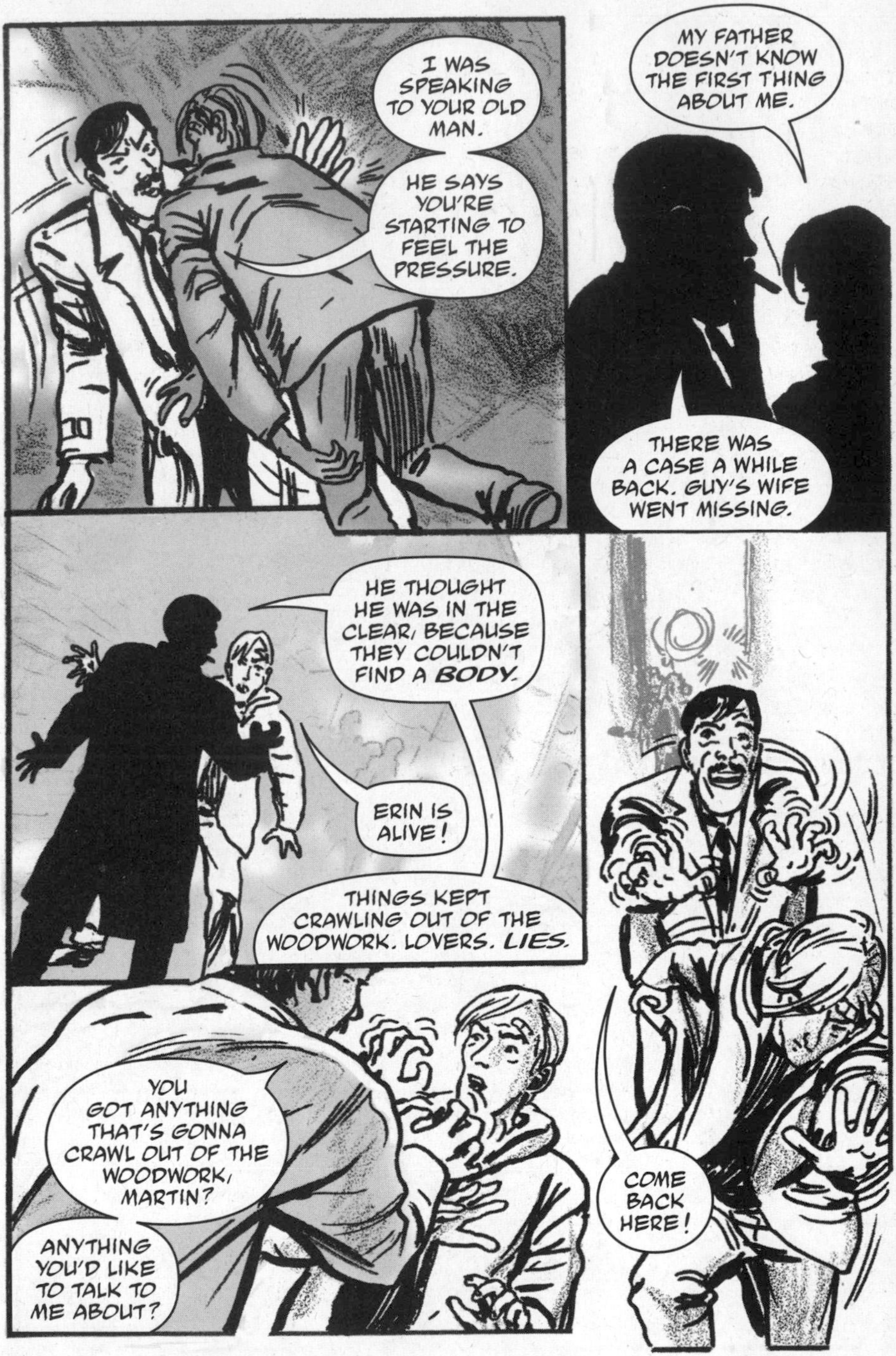
I WAS SPEAKING TO YOUR OLD MAN.
HE SAYS YOU'RE STARTING TO FEEL THE PRESSURE.
MY FATHER DOESN'T KNOW THE FIRST THING ABOUT ME.
THERE WAS A CASE A WHILE BACK. GUY'S WIFE WENT MISSING.
HE THOUGHT HE WAS IN THE CLEAR, BECAUSE THEY COULDN'T FIND A *BODY*.
ERIN IS ALIVE!
THINGS KEPT CRAWLING OUT OF THE WOODWORK. LOVERS. *LIES*.
YOU GOT ANYTHING THAT'S GONNA CRAWL OUT OF THE WOODWORK, MARTIN?
ANYTHING YOU'D LIKE TO TALK TO ME ABOUT?
COME BACK HERE!

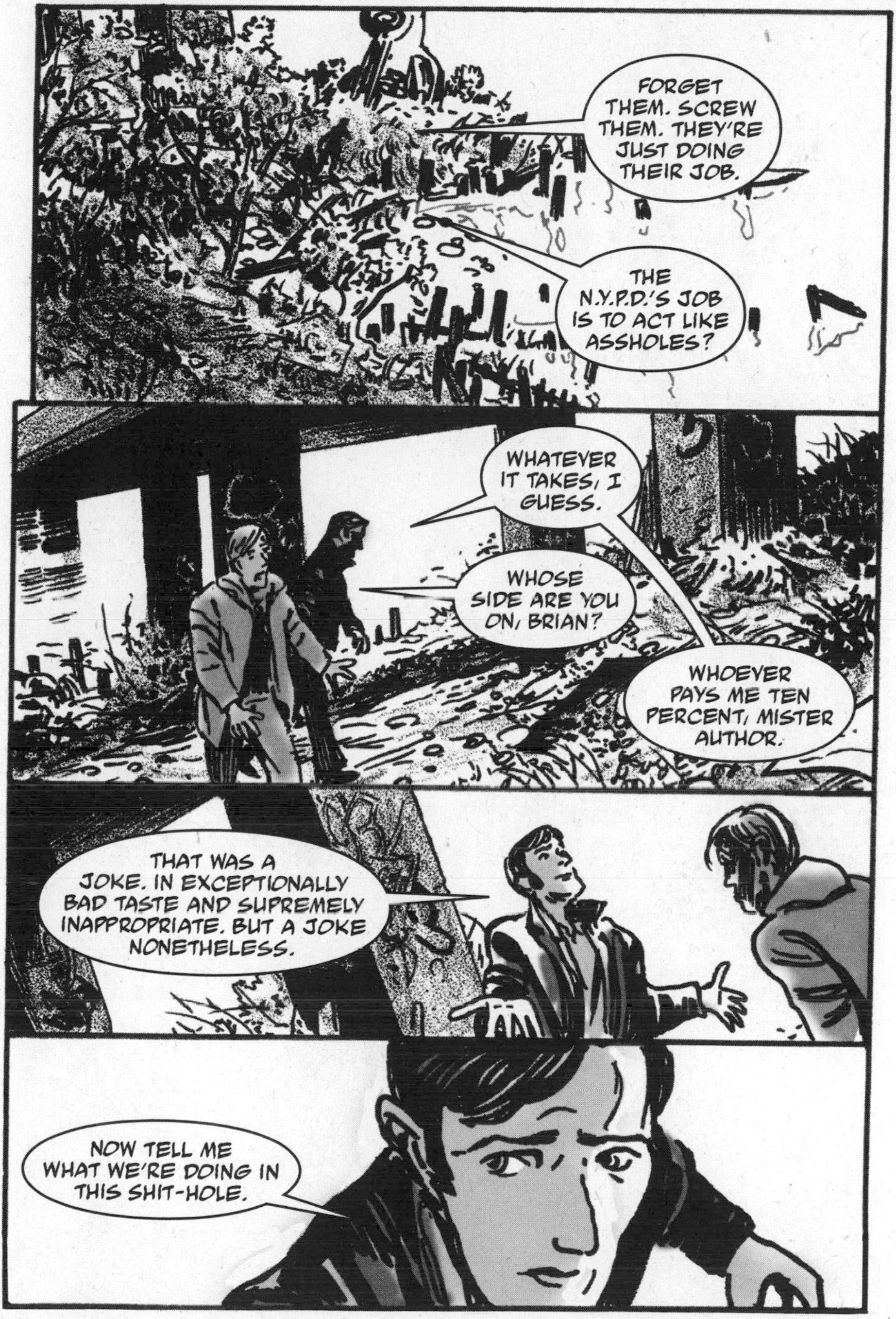
FORGET THEM. SCREW THEM. THEY'RE JUST DOING THEIR JOB.
THE N.Y.P.D.'S JOB IS TO ACT LIKE ASSHOLES?
WHATEVER IT TAKES, I GUESS.
WHOSE SIDE ARE YOU ON, BRIAN?
WHOEVER PAYS ME TEN PERCENT, MISTER AUTHOR.
THAT WAS A JOKE. IN EXCEPTIONALLY BAD TASTE AND SUPREMELY INAPPROPRIATE. BUT A JOKE NONETHELESS.
NOW TELL ME WHAT WE'RE DOING IN THIS SHIT-HOLE.

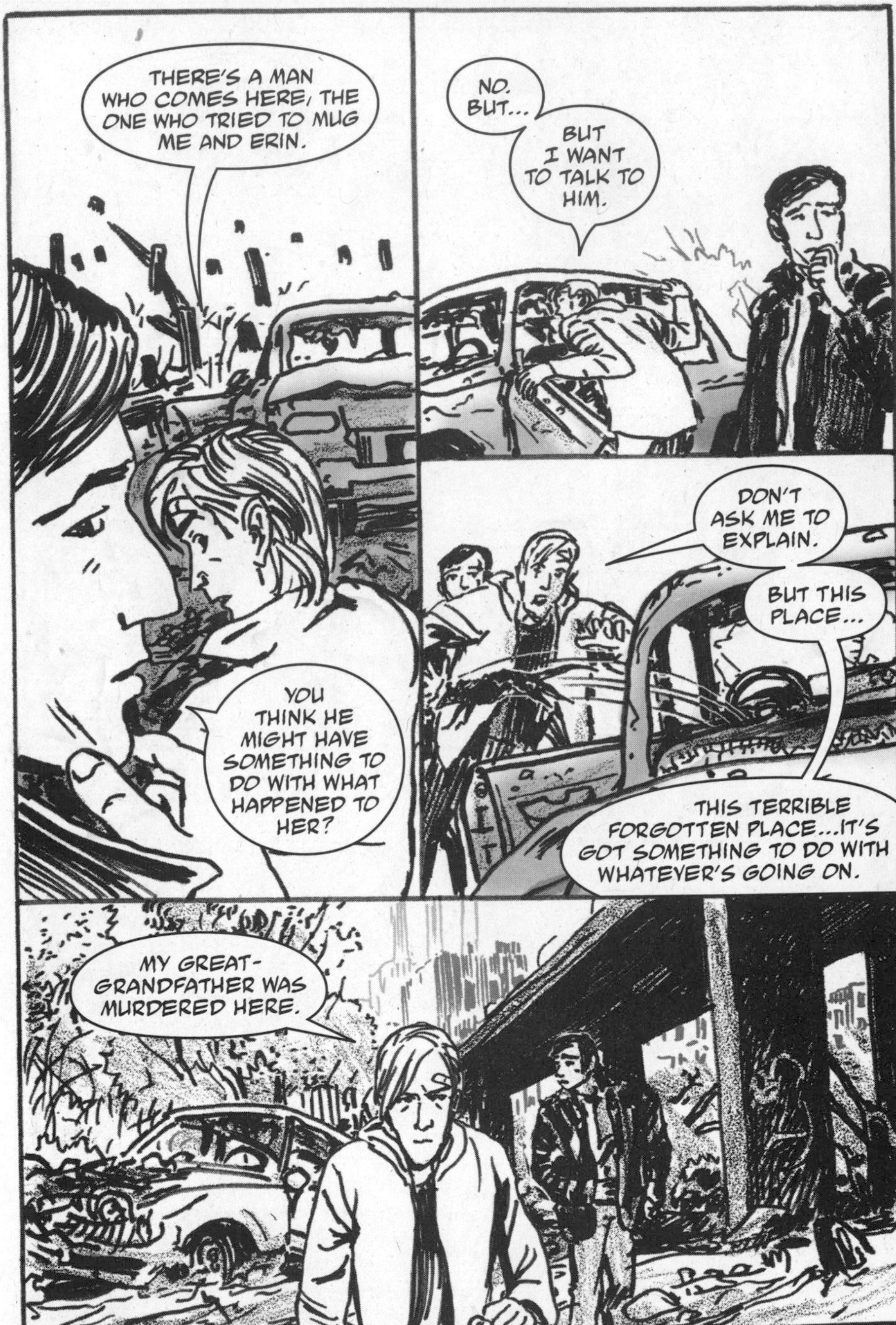
THERE'S A MAN WHO COMES HERE, THE ONE WHO TRIED TO MUG ME AND ERIN.
YOU THINK HE MIGHT HAVE SOMETHING TO DO WITH WHAT HAPPENED TO HER?
NO. BUT...
BUT I WANT TO TALK TO HIM.
DON'T ASK ME TO EXPLAIN.
BUT THIS PLACE...
THIS TERRIBLE FORGOTTEN PLACE...IT'S GOT SOMETHING TO DO WITH WHATEVER'S GOING ON.
MY GREAT-GRANDFATHER WAS MURDERED HERE.

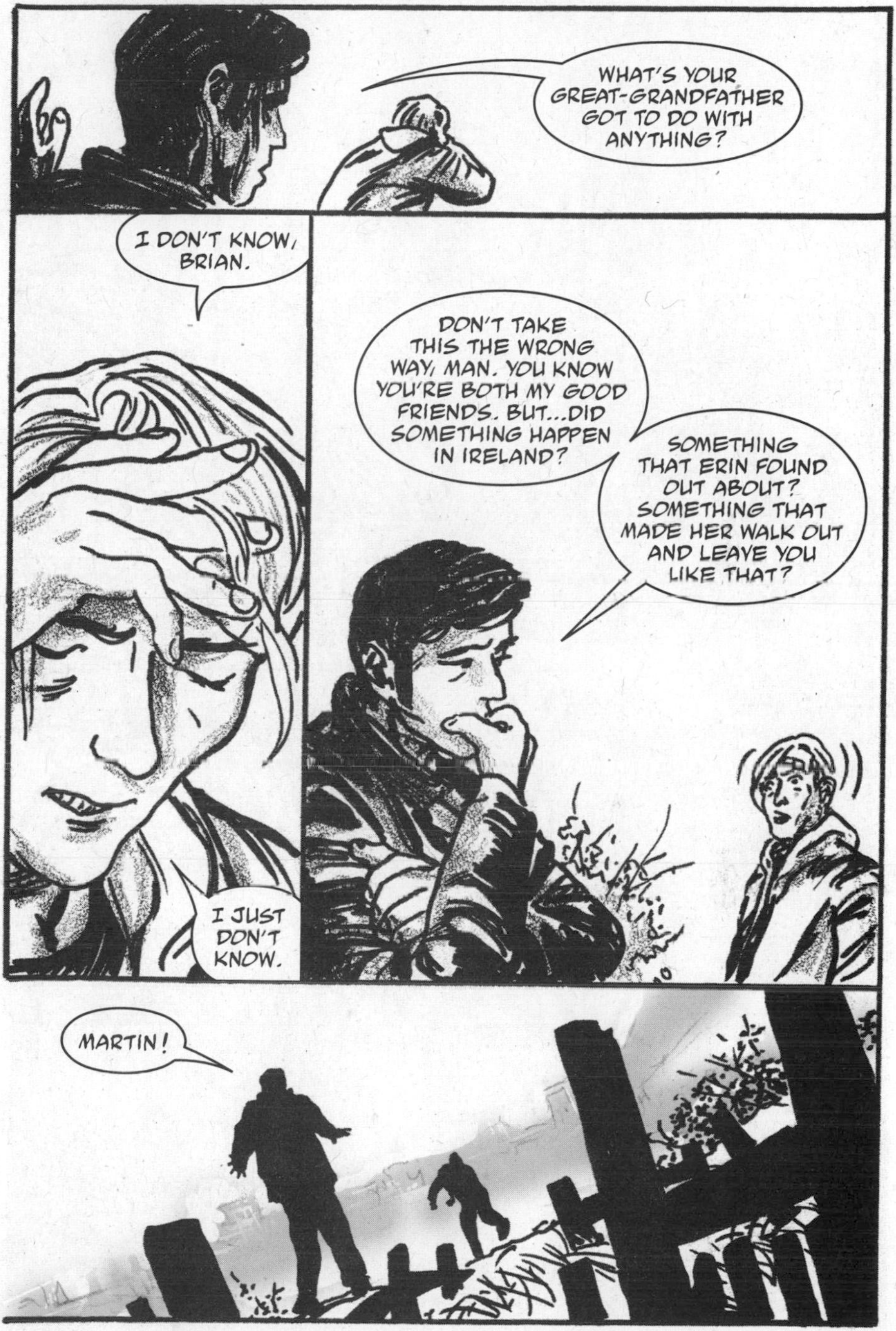
WHAT'S YOUR GREAT-GRANDFATHER GOT TO DO WITH ANYTHING?
I DON'T KNOW, BRIAN.
I JUST DON'T KNOW.
DON'T TAKE THIS THE WRONG WAY, MAN. YOU KNOW YOU'RE BOTH MY GOOD FRIENDS. BUT...DID SOMETHING HAPPEN IN IRELAND?
SOMETHING THAT ERIN FOUND OUT ABOUT? SOMETHING THAT MADE HER WALK OUT AND LEAVE YOU LIKE THAT?
MARTIN!

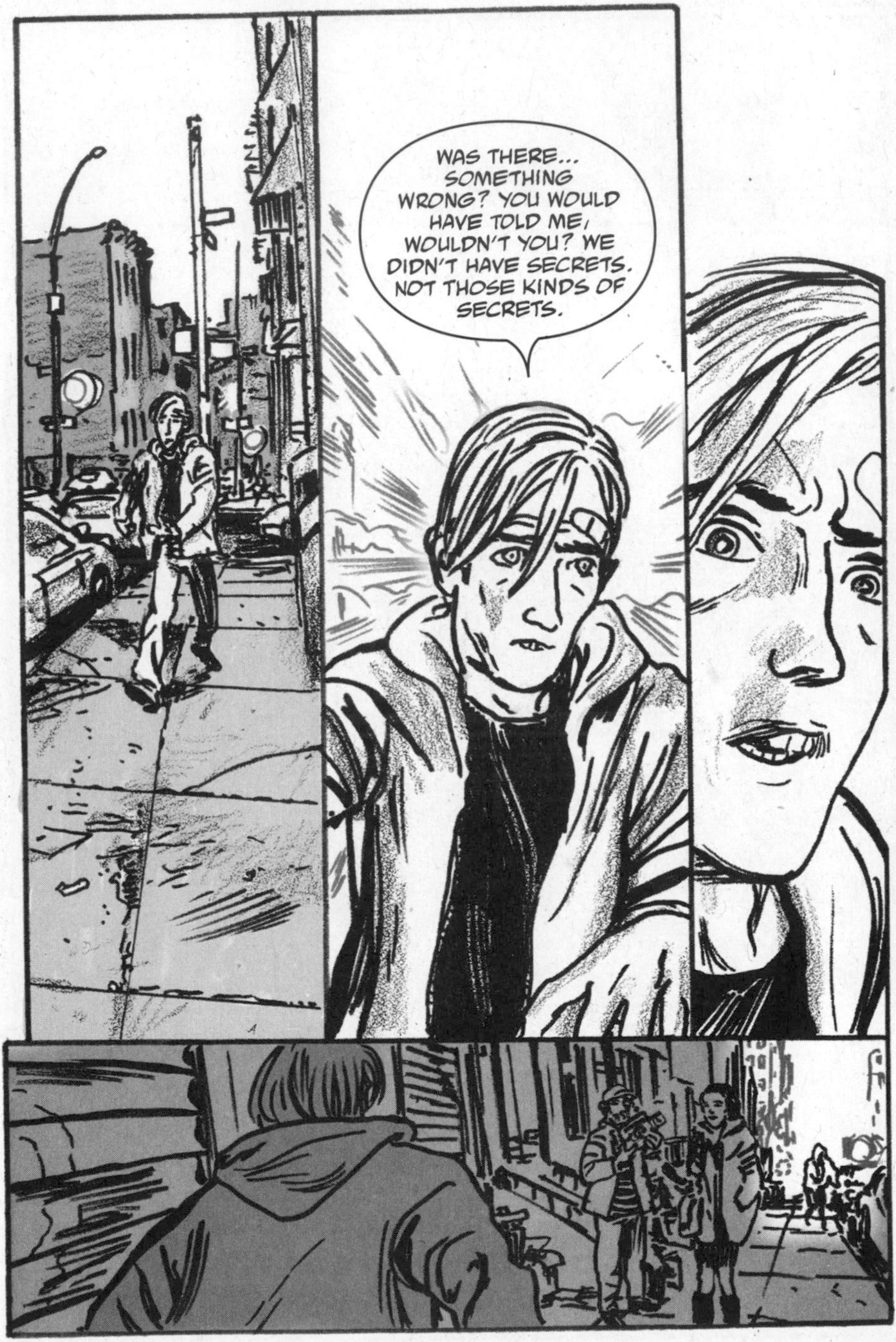
WAS THERE... SOMETHING WRONG? YOU WOULD HAVE TOLD ME, WOULDN'T YOU? WE DIDN'T HAVE SECRETS. NOT THOSE KINDS OF SECRETS.

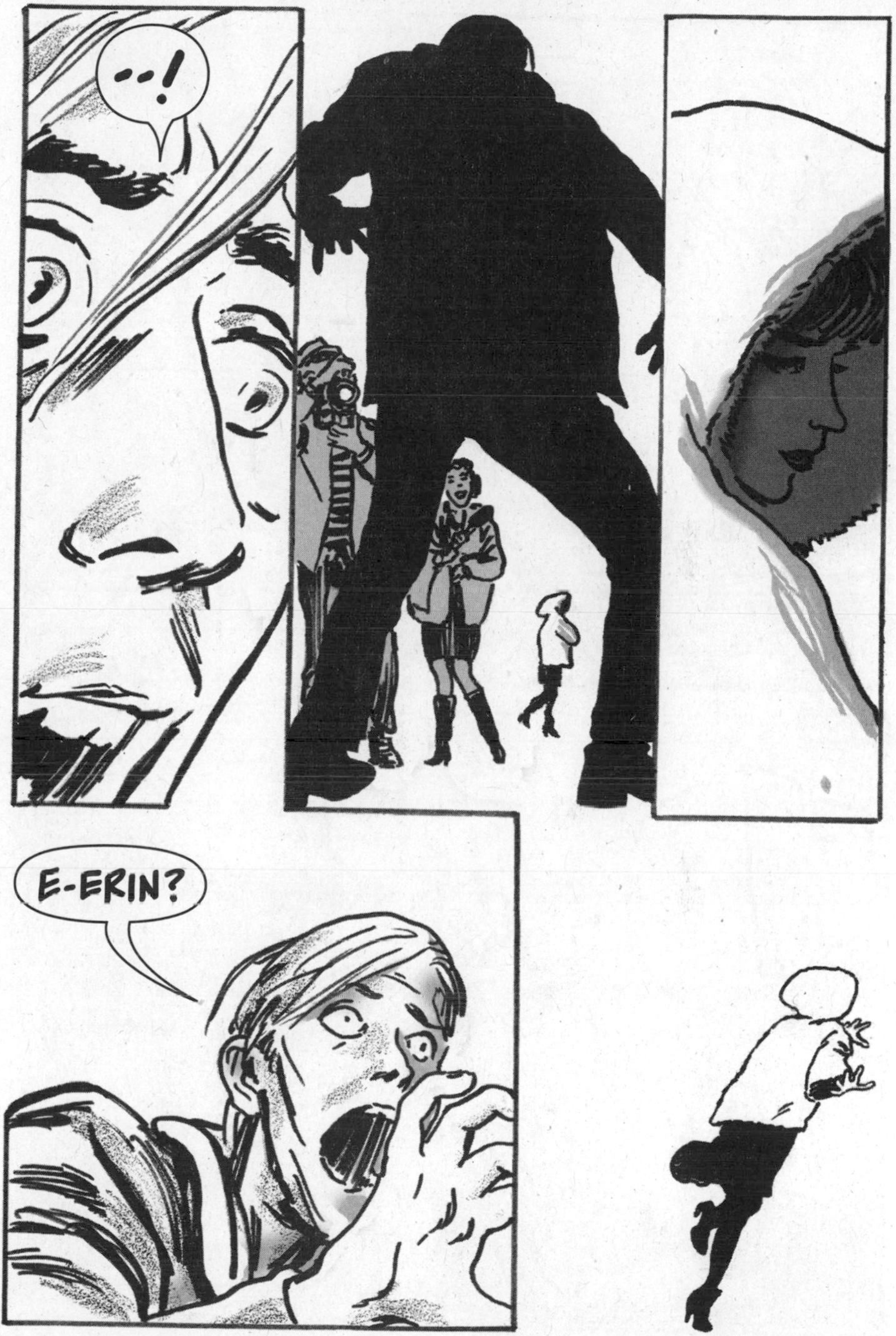

--!
E-ERIN?

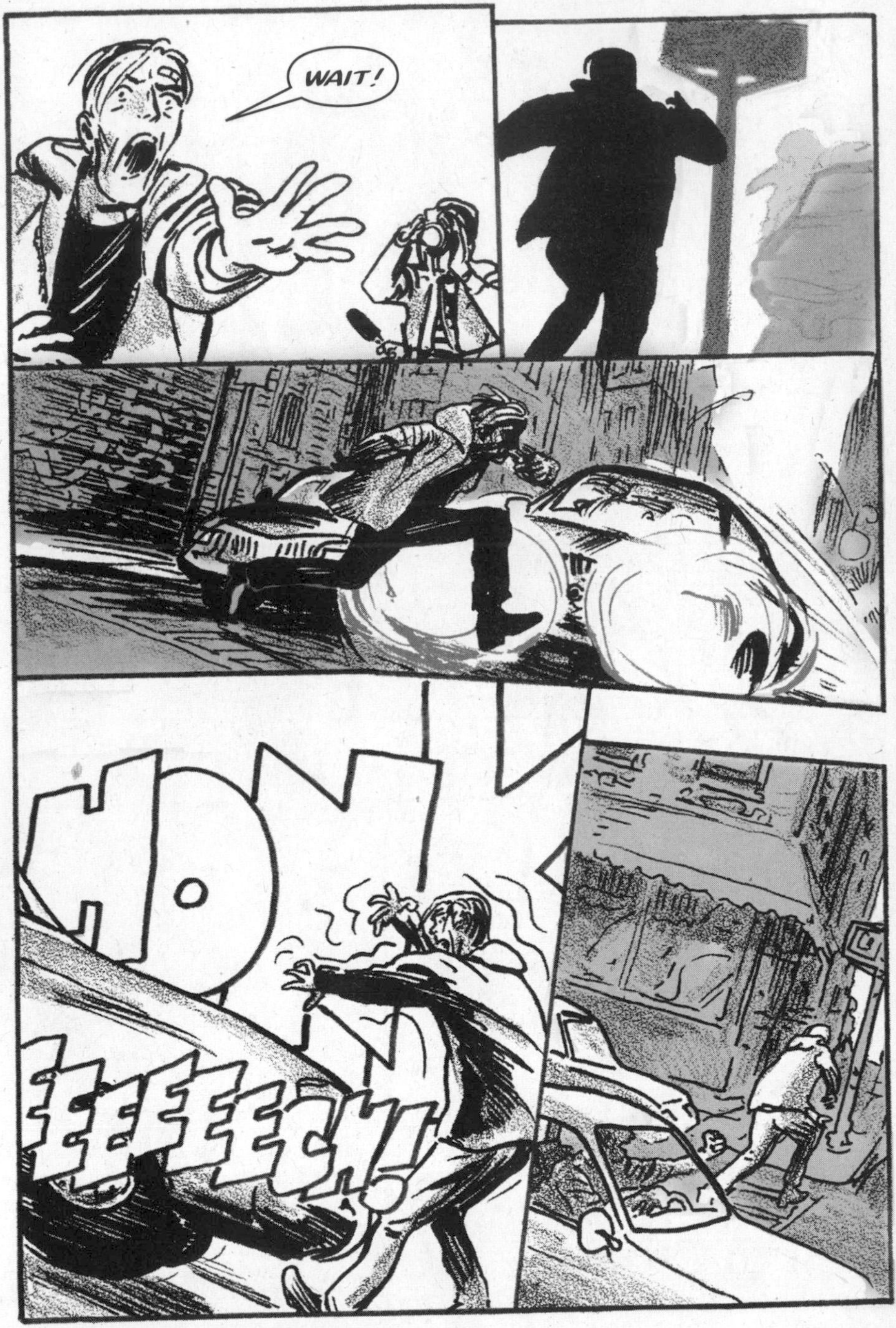
WAIT!
HONK
EEEEECH!!

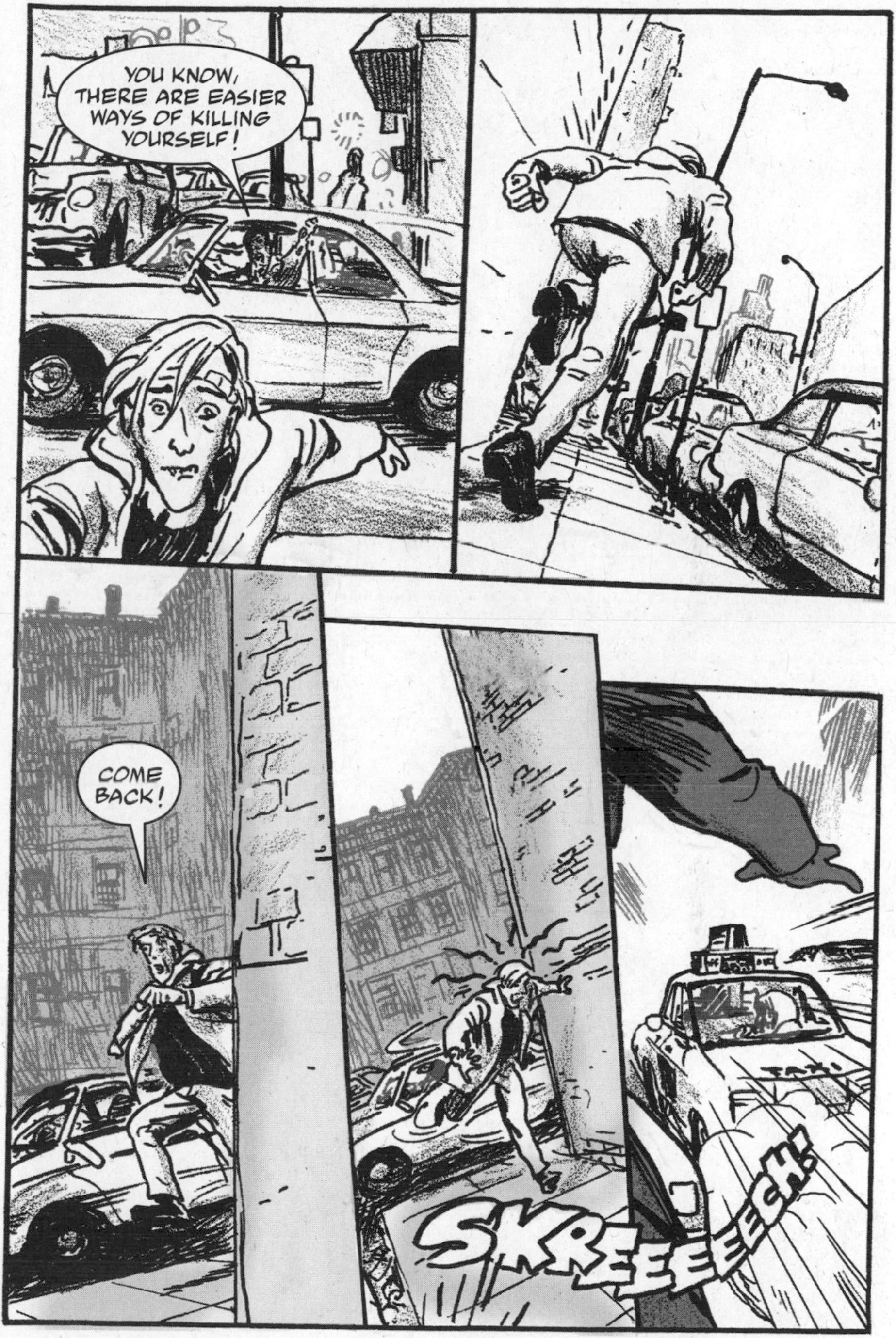
YOU KNOW, THERE ARE EASIER WAYS OF KILLING YOURSELF!
COME BACK!
SKREEEEEECH!

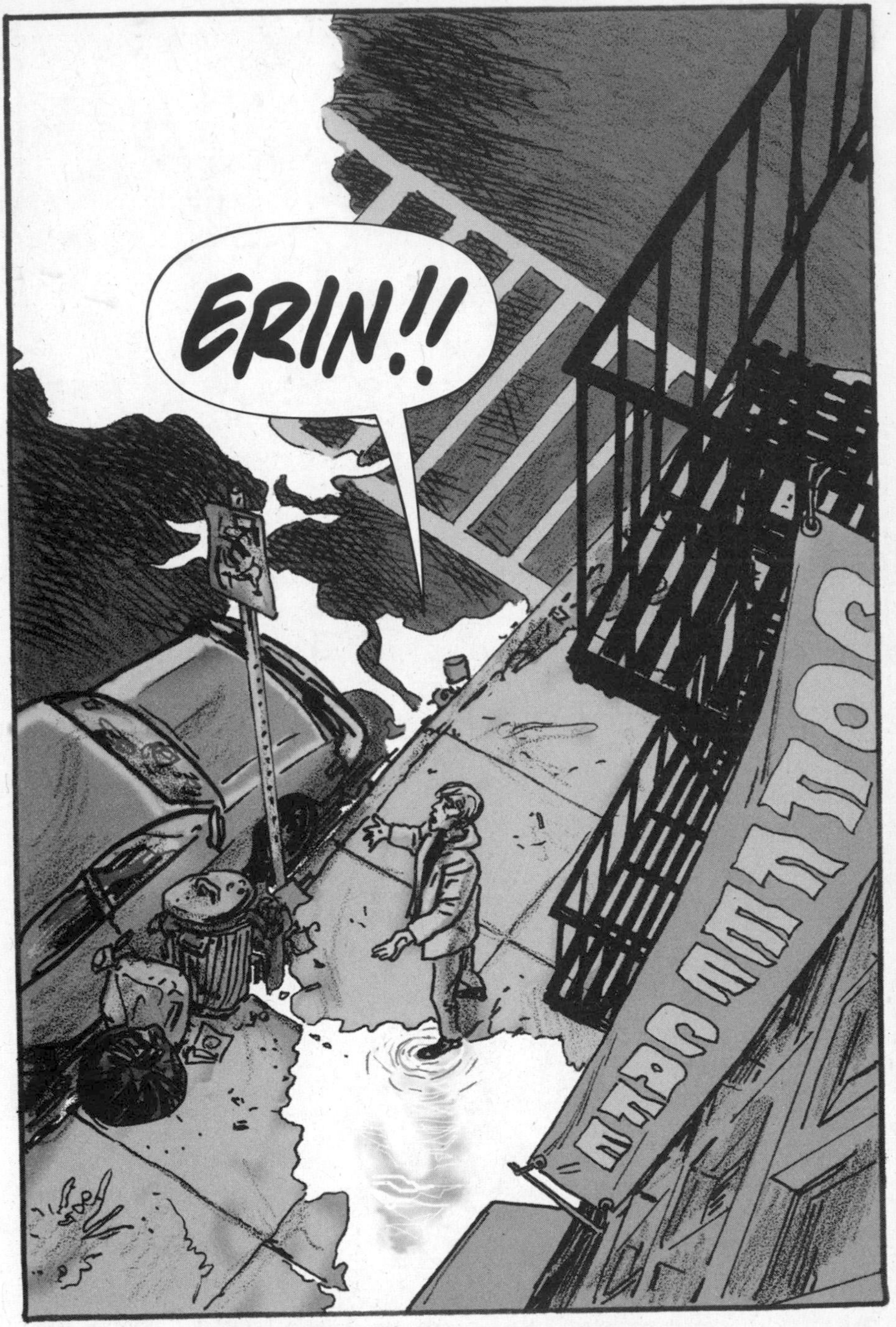
ERIN!!

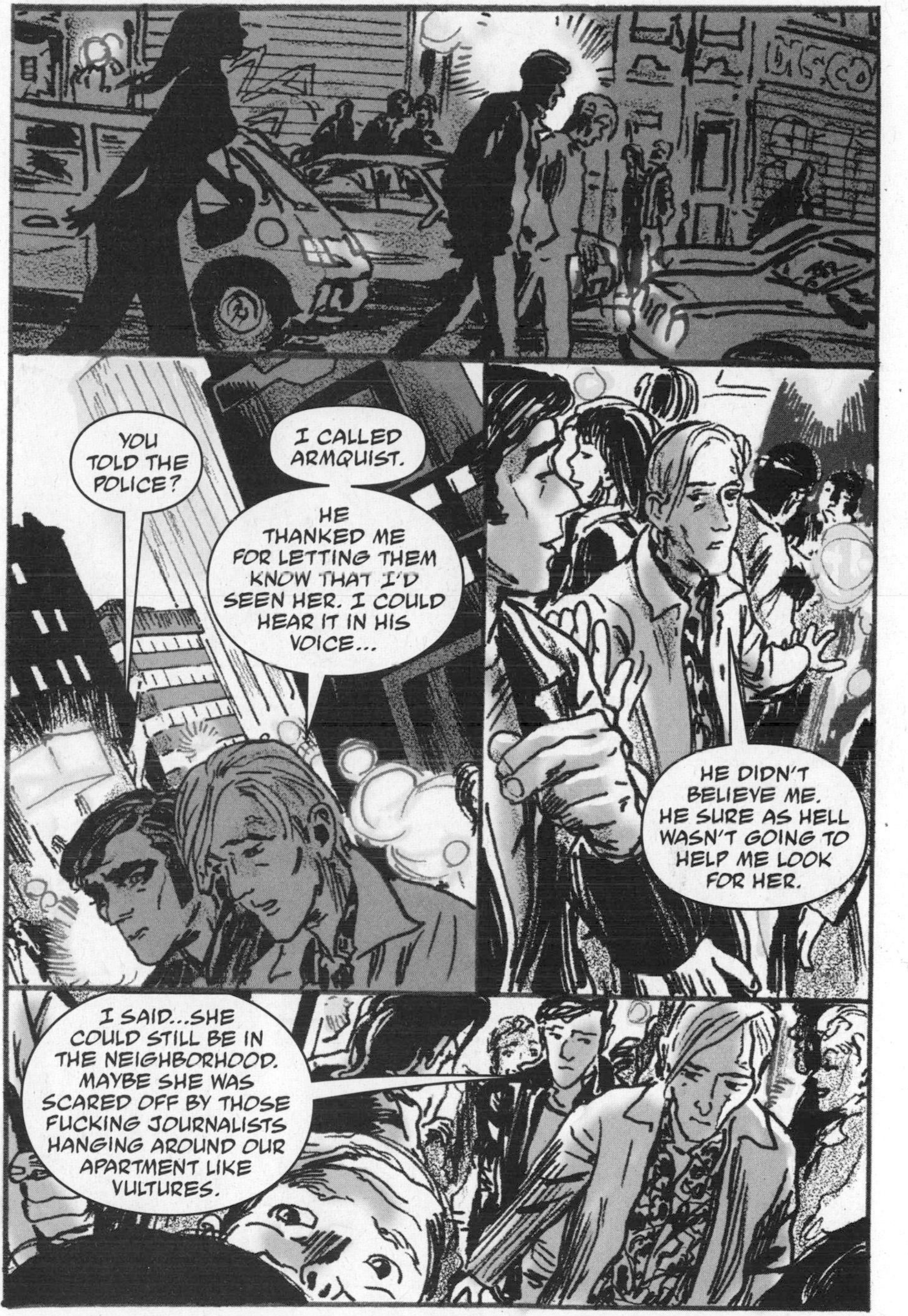
YOU TOLD THE POLICE?
I CALLED ARMQUIST.
HE THANKED ME FOR LETTING THEM KNOW THAT I'D SEEN HER. I COULD HEAR IT IN HIS VOICE...
HE DIDN'T BELIEVE ME. HE SURE AS HELL WASN'T GOING TO HELP ME LOOK FOR HER.
I SAID...SHE COULD STILL BE IN THE NEIGHBORHOOD. MAYBE SHE WAS SCARED OFF BY THOSE FUCKING JOURNALISTS HANGING AROUND OUR APARTMENT LIKE VULTURES.

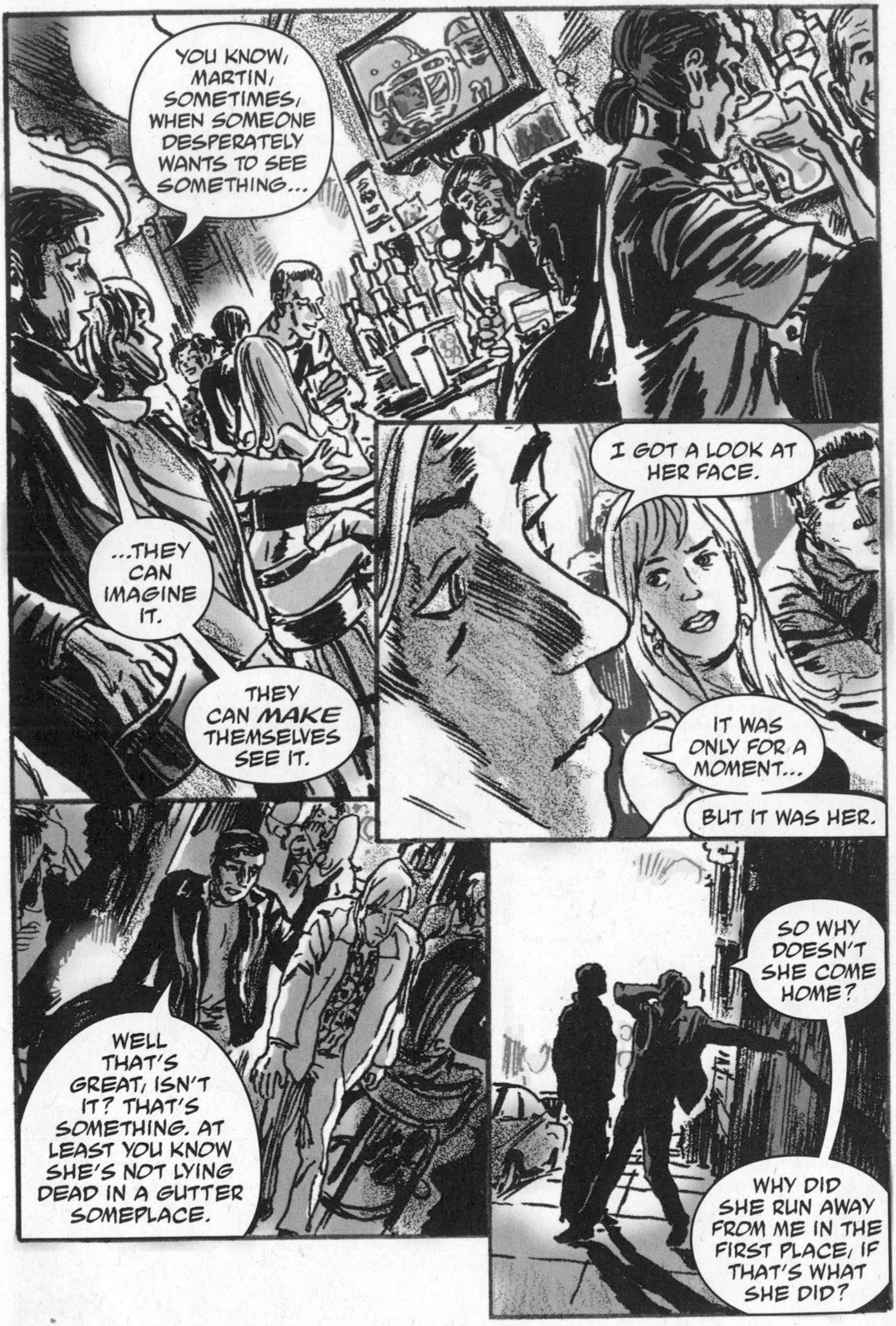
YOU KNOW, MARTIN, SOMETIMES, WHEN SOMEONE DESPERATELY WANTS TO SEE SOMETHING...
...THEY CAN IMAGINE IT.
THEY CAN *MAKE* THEMSELVES SEE IT.
I GOT A LOOK AT HER FACE.
IT WAS ONLY FOR A MOMENT...
BUT IT WAS HER.
WELL THAT'S GREAT, ISN'T IT? THAT'S SOMETHING. AT LEAST YOU KNOW SHE'S NOT LYING DEAD IN A GUTTER SOMEPLACE.
SO WHY DOESN'T SHE COME HOME?
WHY DID SHE RUN AWAY FROM ME IN THE FIRST PLACE, IF THAT'S WHAT SHE DID?

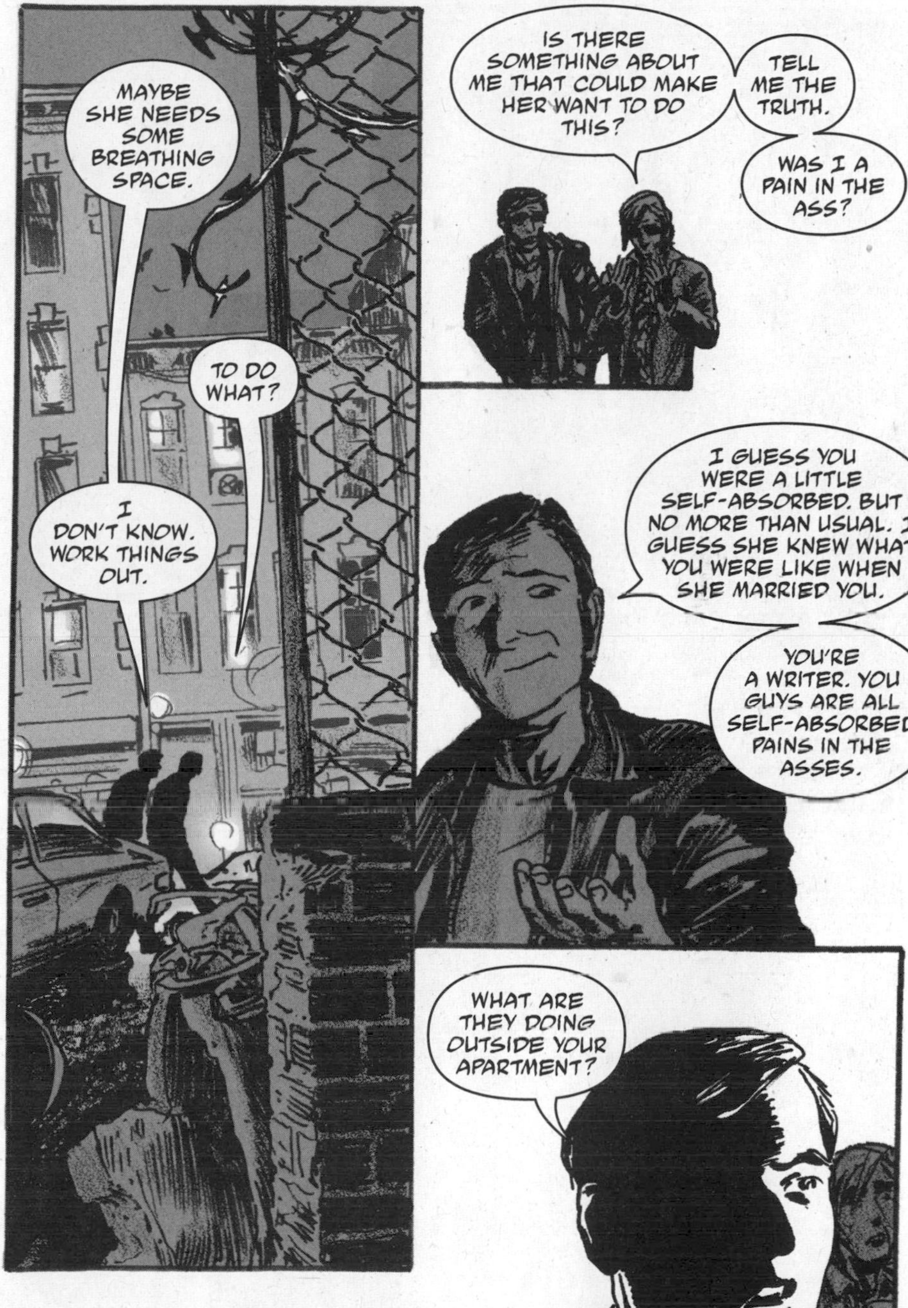
MAYBE SHE NEEDS SOME BREATHING SPACE.
TO DO WHAT?
I DON'T KNOW. WORK THINGS OUT.
IS THERE SOMETHING ABOUT ME THAT COULD MAKE HER WANT TO DO THIS?
TELL ME THE TRUTH.
WAS I A PAIN IN THE ASS?
I GUESS YOU WERE A LITTLE SELF-ABSORBED. BUT NO MORE THAN USUAL. I GUESS SHE KNEW WHAT YOU WERE LIKE WHEN SHE MARRIED YOU.
YOU'RE A WRITER. YOU GUYS ARE ALL SELF-ABSORBED PAINS IN THE ASSES.
WHAT ARE THEY DOING OUTSIDE YOUR APARTMENT?

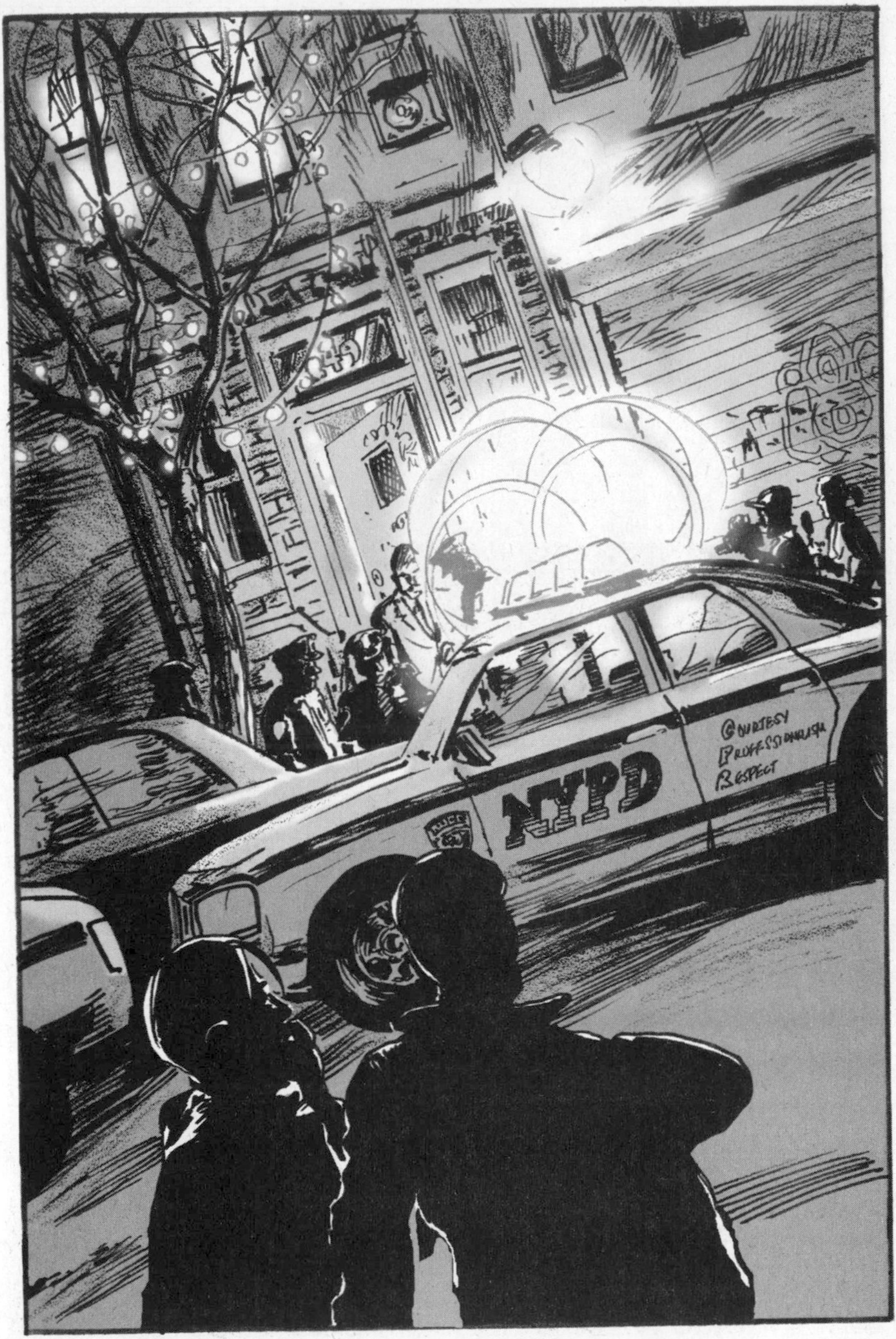
NYPD

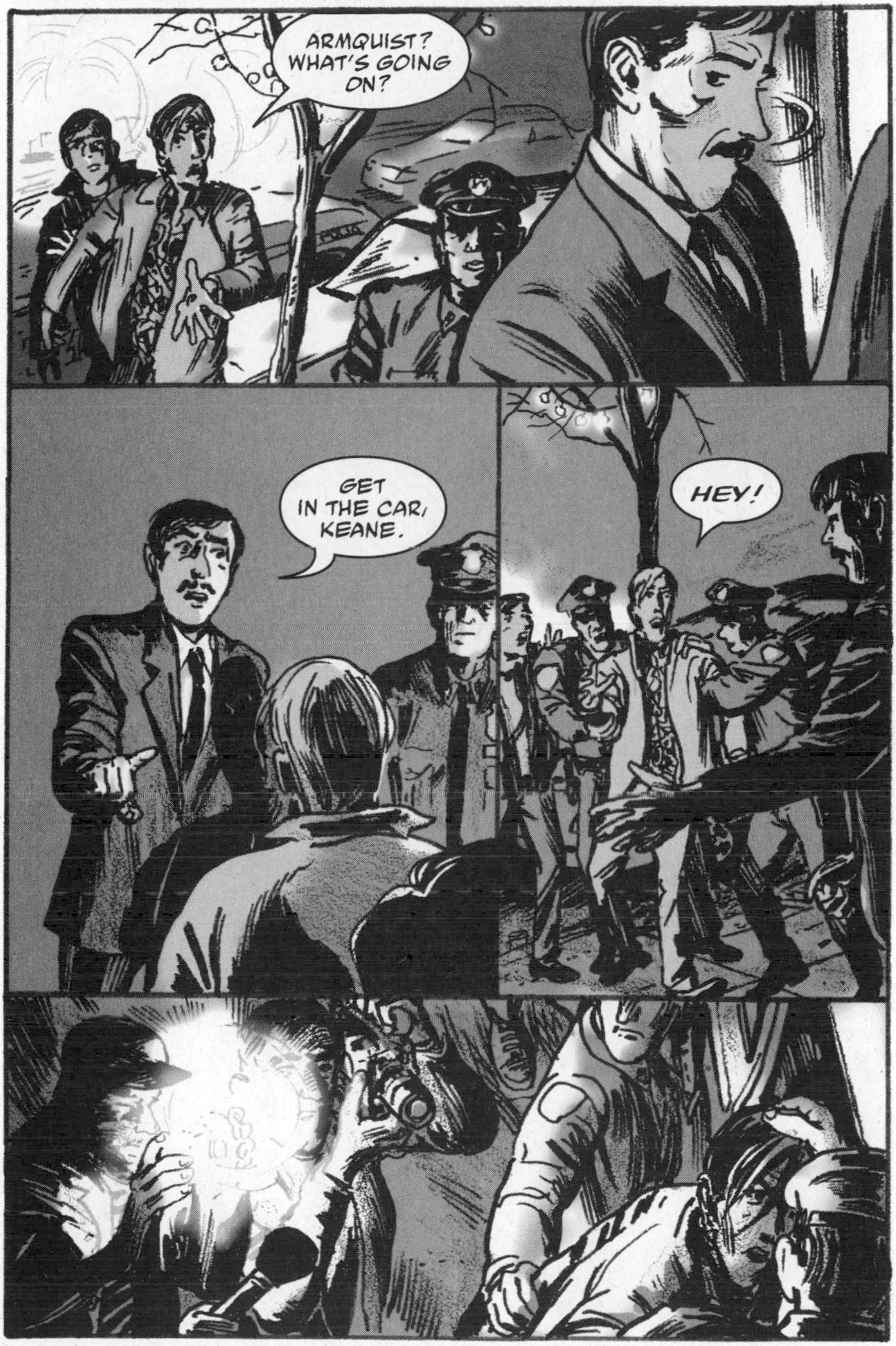
ARMQUIST? WHAT'S GOING ON?
GET IN THE CAR, KEANE.
HEY!

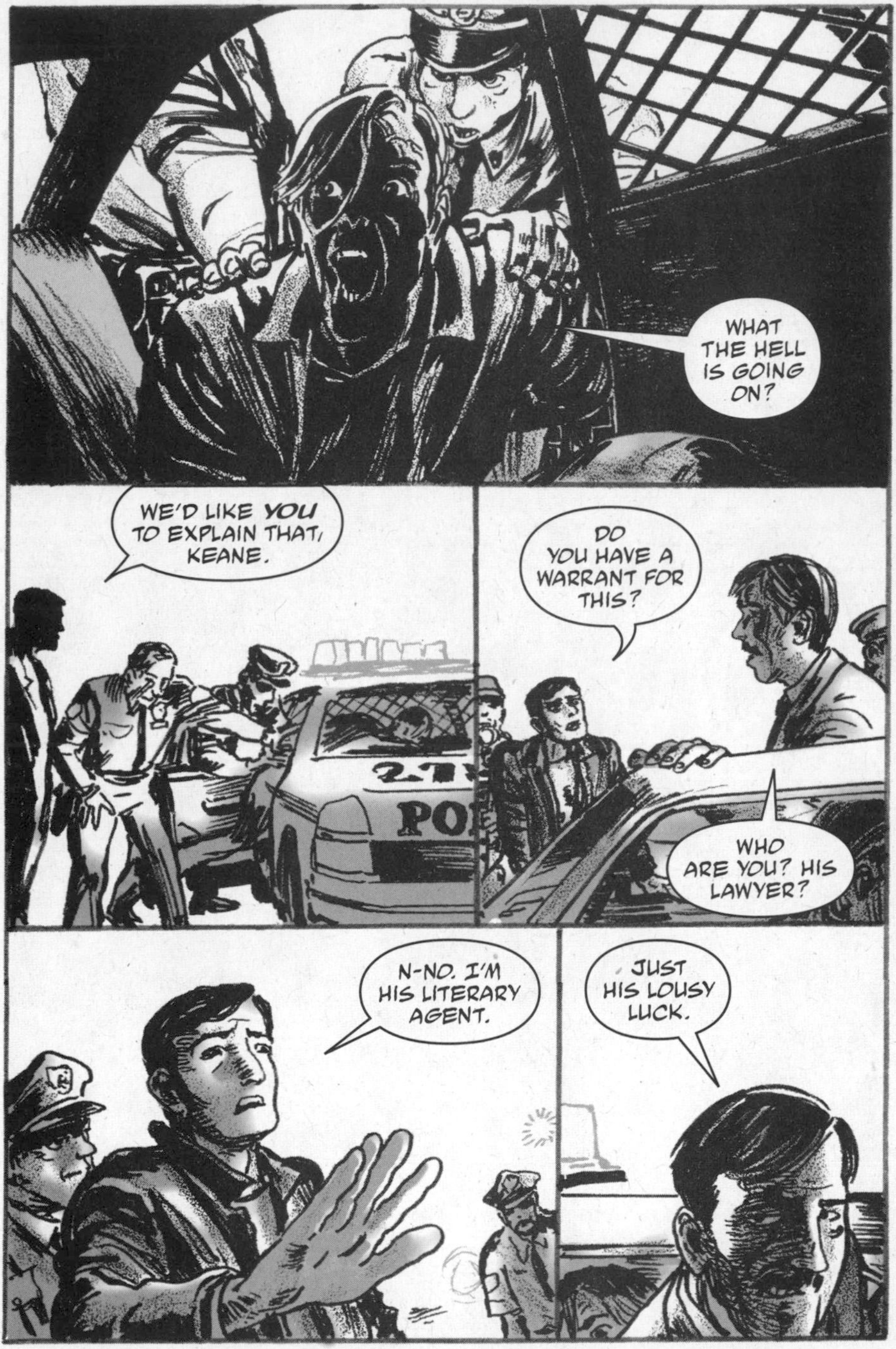
WHAT THE HELL IS GOING ON?
WE'D LIKE *YOU* TO EXPLAIN THAT, KEANE.
DO YOU HAVE A WARRANT FOR THIS?
WHO ARE YOU? HIS LAWYER?
N-NO. I'M HIS LITERARY AGENT.
JUST HIS LOUSY LUCK.

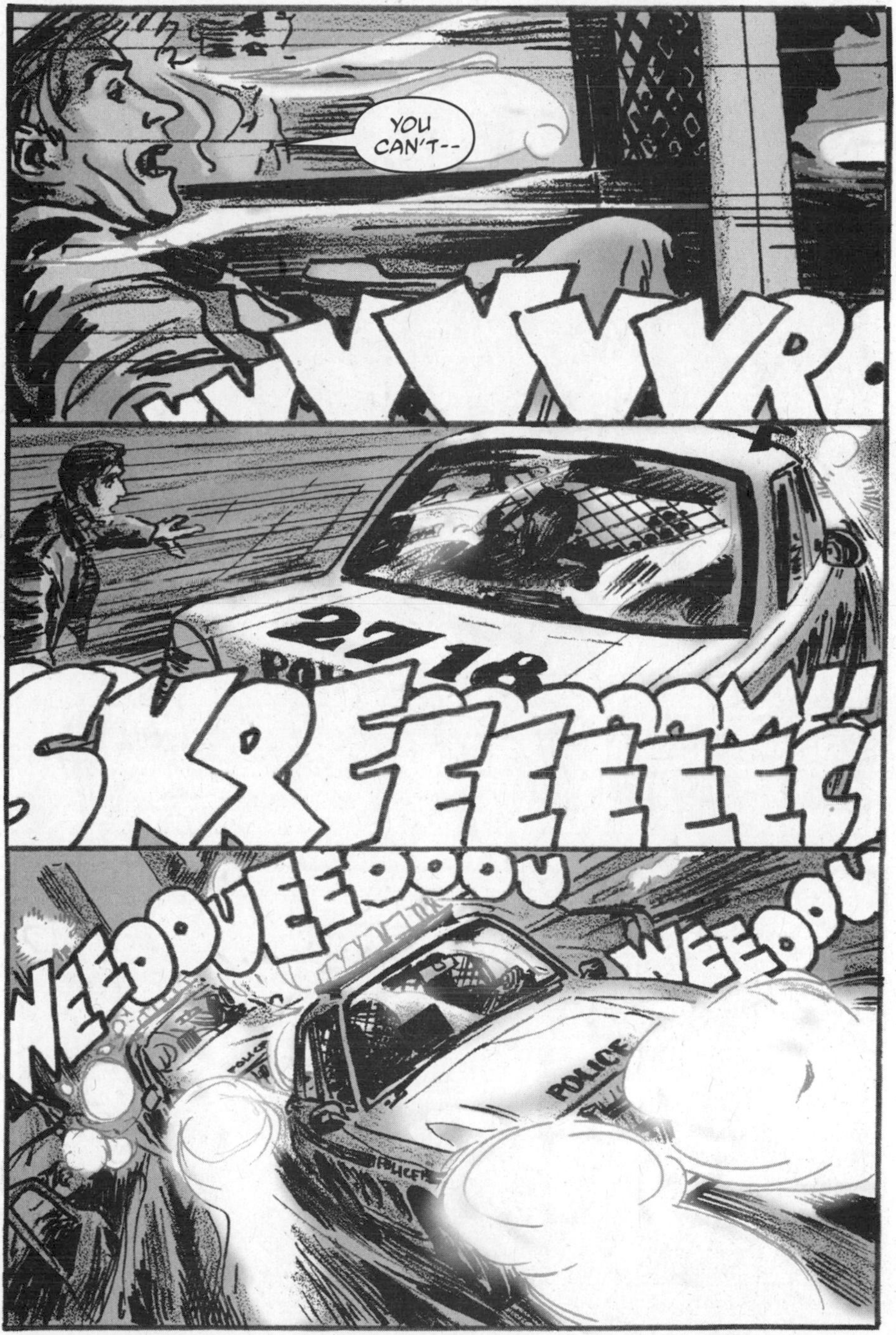
YOU CAN'T--

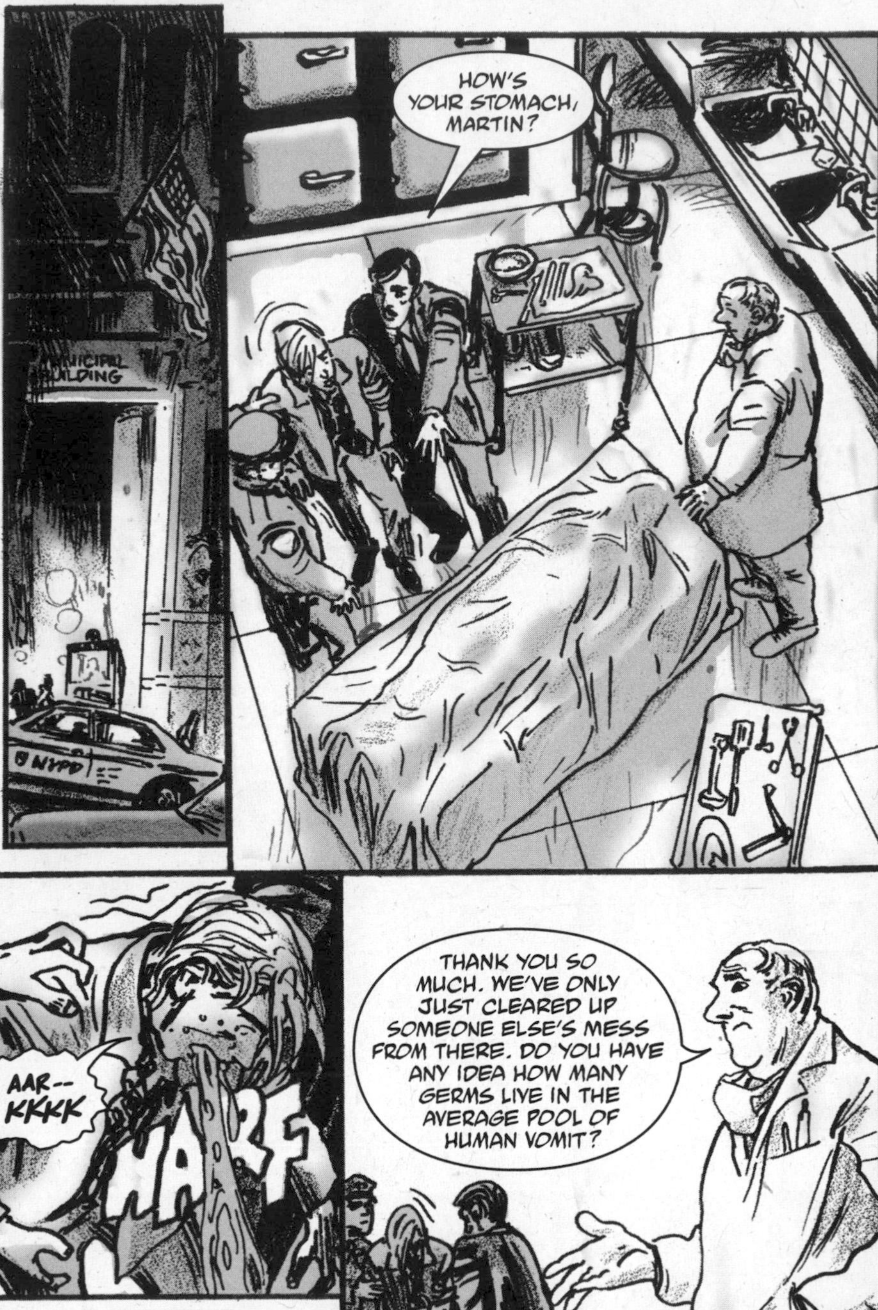
NYPD
HOW'S YOUR STOMACH, MARTIN?
AAR-- KKKK
THANK YOU SO MUCH. WE'VE ONLY JUST CLEARED UP SOMEONE ELSE'S MESS FROM THERE. DO YOU HAVE ANY IDEA HOW MANY GERMS LIVE IN THE AVERAGE POOL OF HUMAN VOMIT?

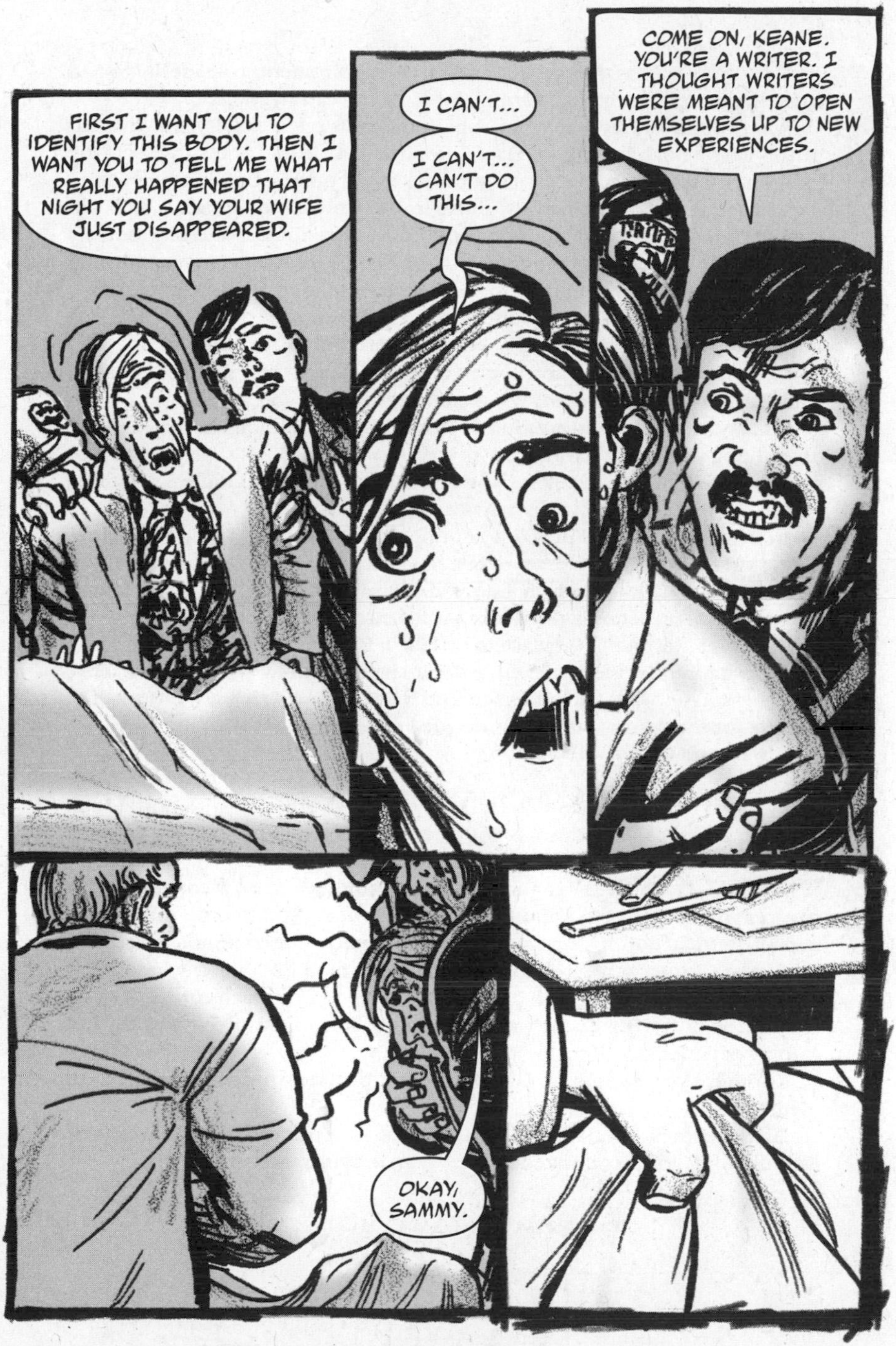
FIRST I WANT YOU TO IDENTIFY THIS BODY. THEN I WANT YOU TO TELL ME WHAT REALLY HAPPENED THAT NIGHT YOU SAY YOUR WIFE JUST DISAPPEARED.
I CAN'T...
I CAN'T... CAN'T DO THIS...
COME ON, KEANE. YOU'RE A WRITER. I THOUGHT WRITERS WERE MEANT TO OPEN THEMSELVES UP TO NEW EXPERIENCES.
OKAY, SAMMY.

The Bronx Kill, as they called it, was a disappointment, considering it had taken the better part of the morning for me to be carriaged here.

What could you say—or write—about this featureless watery scar that led to the East River? True, the very knowledge that it had recently been the location of a terrible crime leant it some frisson of infamy, but I had witnessed the consequences of barbarous, inexplicable violence in Ireland, and had then lived alongside some of New York's most disreputable and bloodthirsty villains when I researched my article on the Dead Rabbits, so it needed a little more than an imagined shudder to instill in me a sense of geographical dread.

Putting these doubts to one side, I told myself that this was my opportunity to become established as a contributor to the Herald, so I diligently pencilled in my notebook whatever details I thought I could use to whet the base appetites of my prospective readers.

What was there? No suggestion of a ghoul, or a crumbling medieval castle, or anything that might have found its way into one of Sir Horace Walpole's or Ann Radliffe's dark narratives. Nothing Gothic. Nothing Godless. Nothing ✗ cursed or conducive to bloody activities.

In truth, The Bronx Kill was a not-unpleasant location. The air was clean here, spumy and fragrant. Perhaps one day some enterprising soul might even build a promenade on which fine ladies and gentlemen will stroll about, watching the sun set over the unobstructed stretch of water.

There is surely no good place to be killed. But this kill was not such a bad place to have your life snatched away, if snatched away it had to be. This, though, was not what the readers of The Herald wanted to read, this was not the fare for that penny dreadful. I decided to head back to the city.

It was time to view the bodies.

"Let's forget God for a moment, Mr. Drury. Let us overlook the immortal soul. The human corpse is a carcass. With a predisposition to decay, rot, become noisome to the senses and harrowing to the emotions."

some time

It was several hours later and I was moving along a narrow corridor of the city morgue beneath the tumult of Manhattan, being lectured on the ways of human putrefaction by an employee of the medical examiner's office. His name was Cripps, and this happy soul now led me into a long, windowless, high-ceilinged dormitory with paltry lamps burning from each corner. A room of shadows and whispers, it was not unlike a hospital ward for wealthy but gloomy patients.

Though the patients in this ward were beyond the reach of modern medicine.

"If the corpses are not brought here in good time our task is made extremely difficult, of course," continued my very own ferryman across the Styx.

✗ Gothic, doomed. The Furey.
THE KEANES.
ABSALOM! ABSALOM!

114

Squat marble tables ran down each side of the ward, each occupied by a body covered with a sheet. A few of the bodies seemed to be swollen, as though, God forbid, they were pregnant. Pregnant with death, I thought with revulsion.

Cripps saw the wan look on my face.

"It's the gas that bloats the body. It turns the skin from green to purple and then to black. It's this that makes the tongue and eyes protrude…"

I coughed loudly. The noise seemed to travel all the way down the ward of death, passed the sleeping soulless carcasses, and echo back again, like a wave. My companion smiled.

"Of course, sir. You'll want to see your bodies."

"If I could. Please."

The room was chilled but beneath the smell of camphor, detergents and what I took to be some kind of embalming fluid I could discern an underlying odor of sweet-rank decay. I began to feel nauseated.

"This way, sir."

Cripps limped down the room, between the rows of corpse beds. ~~Did I tell you he limped?~~ Not simply a limp, it was an exaggerated motion whereby he first swung his right arm out, clasped an invisible rope, shifted his left leg out and around as though it were a dead weight, placed the heel of his left foot firmly on the ground and then, throwing his left shoulder forward, straightened. The whole grotesque performance made our passage through this necropolis unbearably long. All I could do was make my normal step behind him and then wait, and wait, until he had executed his complicated maneuver. Occasionally he'd look over his shoulder, smile, and—between cheerful descriptions of bloodstained fluids and swollen internal organs—say, *[handwritten margin note: Have I told you about his limp?]*

"Keep up there, Mr. Drury! Keep up!"

Finally, Cripps stopped in front of two tables. Or slabs, as he called them.

"A quick look is all I can give you, sir. Letting gentlemen of the press in here ain't exactly normal procedure."

I nodded, wondering just how Bennett had used his influence with the police or the medical examiner's office to get me access to the victims of the murder. I took out my notepad and pencil.

"When you're ready, " I said.

"I should warn you, sir. This ain't nice."

"Don't worry yourself. I've seen dead bodies before."

"Maybe. But you won't have seen anything like this."

With that he pulled away the sheets from two of the tables, revealing the bodies of the murder victims.

I took a deep breath. And then I could breathe no more. My collar seemed to tighten around my neck like a noose. Cripps was wrong. He was very wrong. I had seen something like this before.

Four years earlier. In Ireland.

[handwritten note across bottom: In Ireland. What happened when I was in Ireland? Did she meet someone? Abandoned me like my grandmother abandoned her child?]

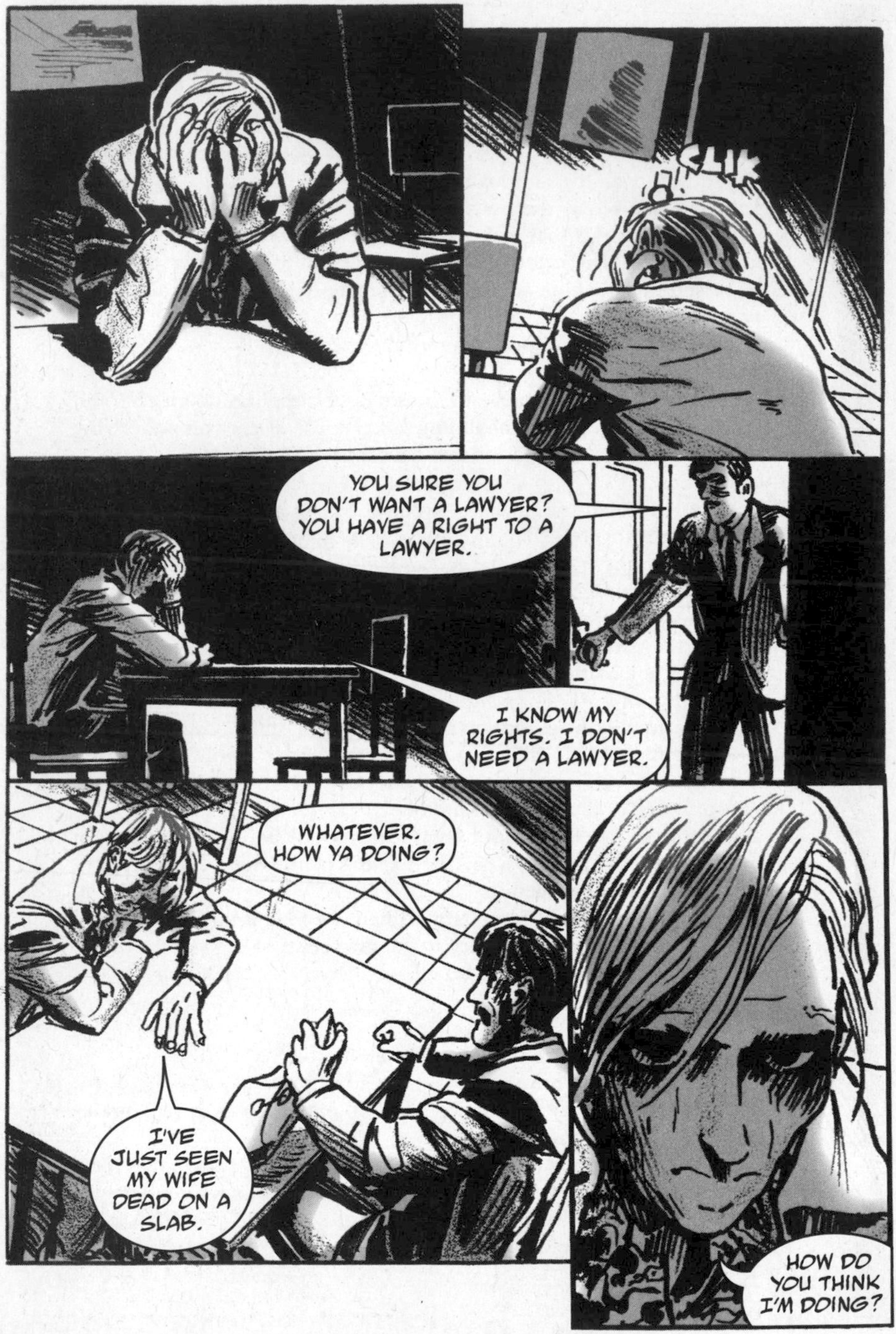
CLIK
YOU SURE YOU DON'T WANT A LAWYER? YOU HAVE A RIGHT TO A LAWYER.
I KNOW MY RIGHTS. I DON'T NEED A LAWYER.
WHATEVER. HOW YA DOING?
I'VE JUST SEEN MY WIFE DEAD ON A SLAB.
HOW DO YOU THINK I'M DOING?

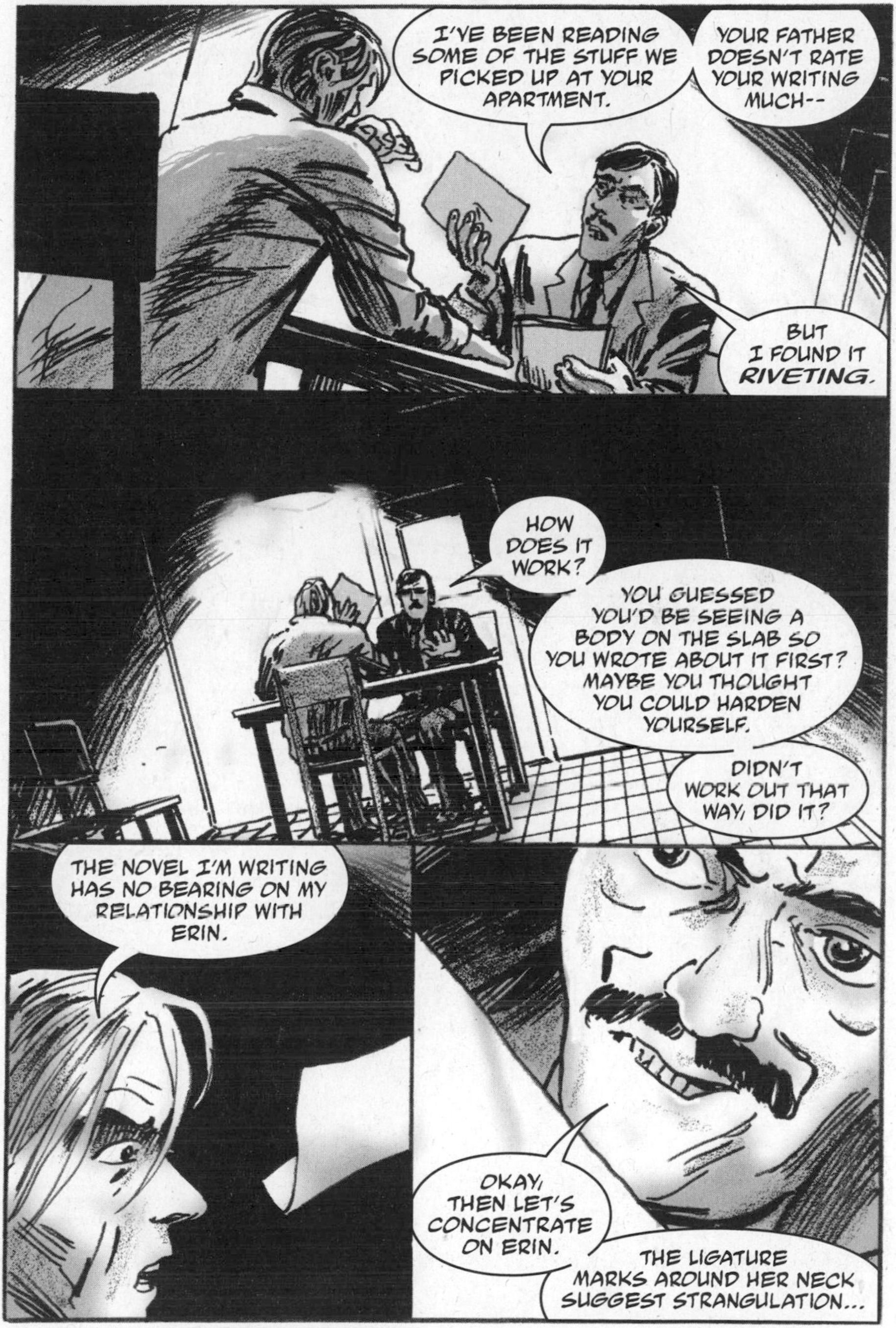
I'VE BEEN READING SOME OF THE STUFF WE PICKED UP AT YOUR APARTMENT.
YOUR FATHER DOESN'T RATE YOUR WRITING MUCH--
BUT I FOUND IT *RIVETING*.
HOW DOES IT WORK?
YOU GUESSED YOU'D BE SEEING A BODY ON THE SLAB SO YOU WROTE ABOUT IT FIRST? MAYBE YOU THOUGHT YOU COULD HARDEN YOURSELF.
DIDN'T WORK OUT THAT WAY, DID IT?
THE NOVEL I'M WRITING HAS NO BEARING ON MY RELATIONSHIP WITH ERIN.
OKAY, THEN LET'S CONCENTRATE ON ERIN.
THE LIGATURE MARKS AROUND HER NECK SUGGEST STRANGULATION...

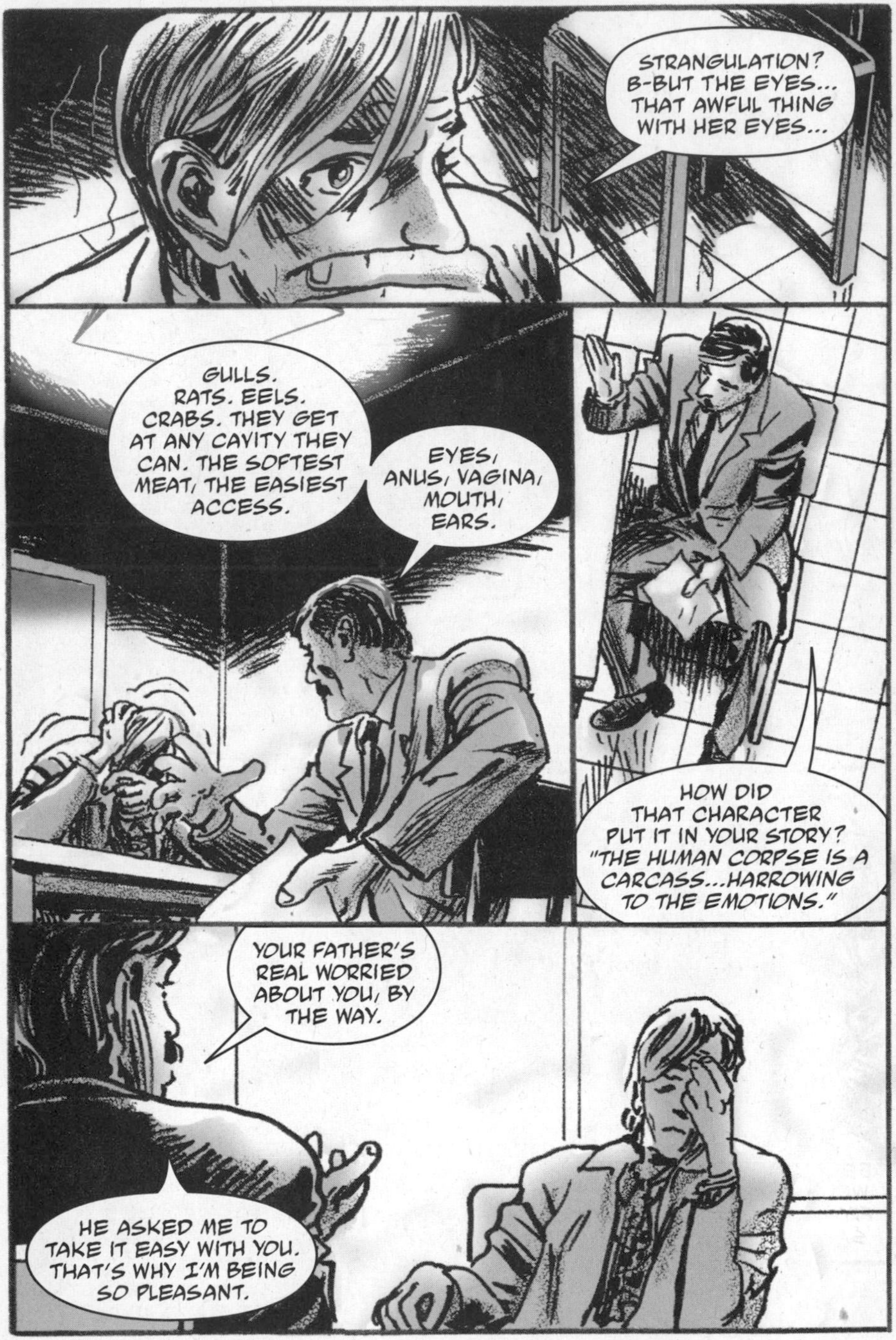
STRANGULATION? B-BUT THE EYES... THAT AWFUL THING WITH HER EYES...
GULLS. RATS. EELS. CRABS. THEY GET AT ANY CAVITY THEY CAN. THE SOFTEST MEAT, THE EASIEST ACCESS.
EYES, ANUS, VAGINA, MOUTH, EARS.
HOW DID THAT CHARACTER PUT IT IN YOUR STORY? "THE HUMAN CORPSE IS A CARCASS...HARROWING TO THE EMOTIONS."
YOUR FATHER'S REAL WORRIED ABOUT YOU, BY THE WAY.
HE ASKED ME TO TAKE IT EASY WITH YOU. THAT'S WHY I'M BEING SO PLEASANT.

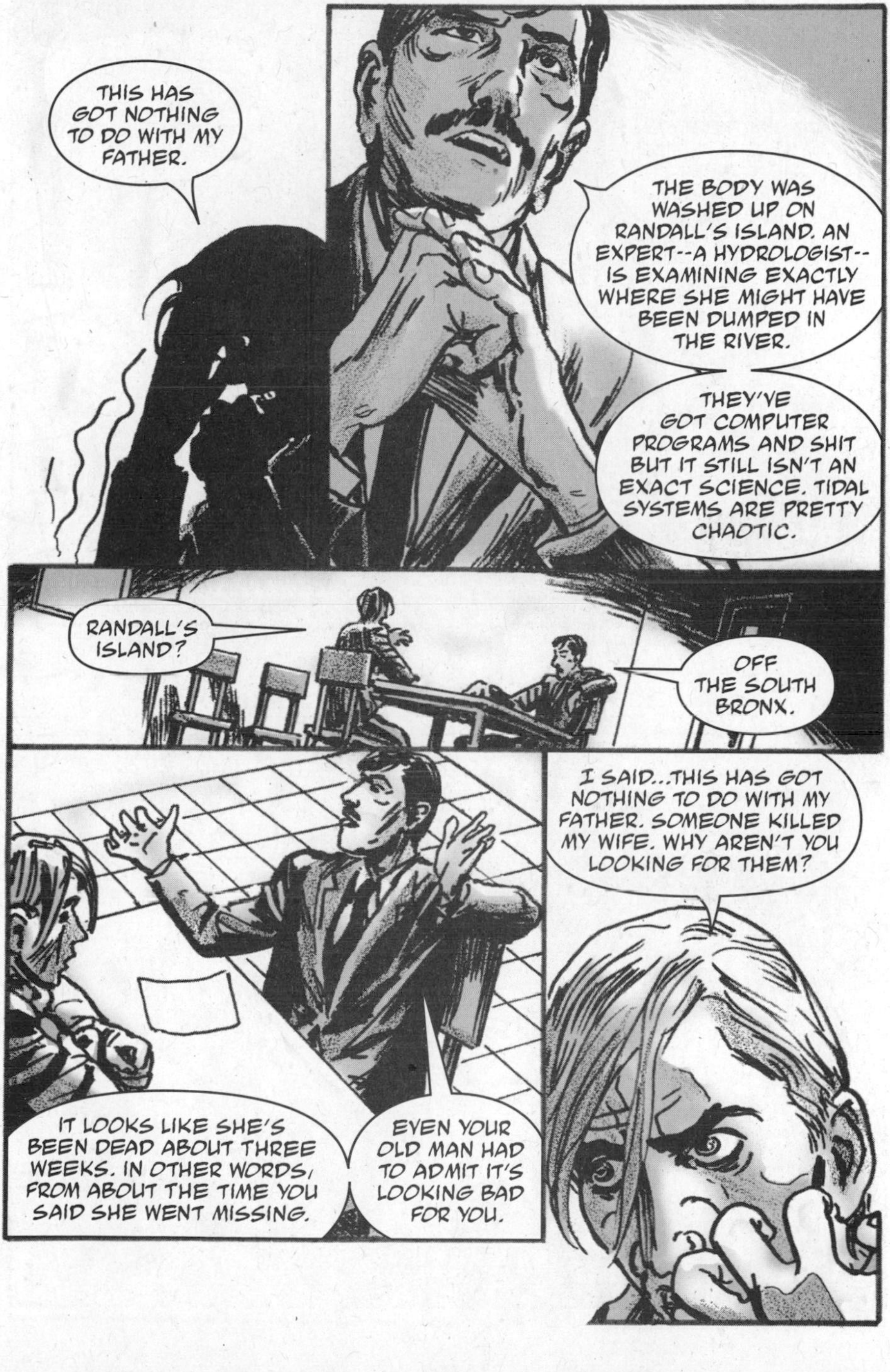
THIS HAS GOT NOTHING TO DO WITH MY FATHER.
THE BODY WAS WASHED UP ON RANDALL'S ISLAND. AN EXPERT--A HYDROLOGIST--IS EXAMINING EXACTLY WHERE SHE MIGHT HAVE BEEN DUMPED IN THE RIVER.
THEY'VE GOT COMPUTER PROGRAMS AND SHIT BUT IT STILL ISN'T AN EXACT SCIENCE. TIDAL SYSTEMS ARE PRETTY CHAOTIC.
RANDALL'S ISLAND?
OFF THE SOUTH BRONX.
IT LOOKS LIKE SHE'S BEEN DEAD ABOUT THREE WEEKS. IN OTHER WORDS, FROM ABOUT THE TIME YOU SAID SHE WENT MISSING.
EVEN YOUR OLD MAN HAD TO ADMIT IT'S LOOKING BAD FOR YOU.
I SAID...THIS HAS GOT NOTHING TO DO WITH MY FATHER. SOMEONE KILLED MY WIFE. WHY AREN'T YOU LOOKING FOR THEM?

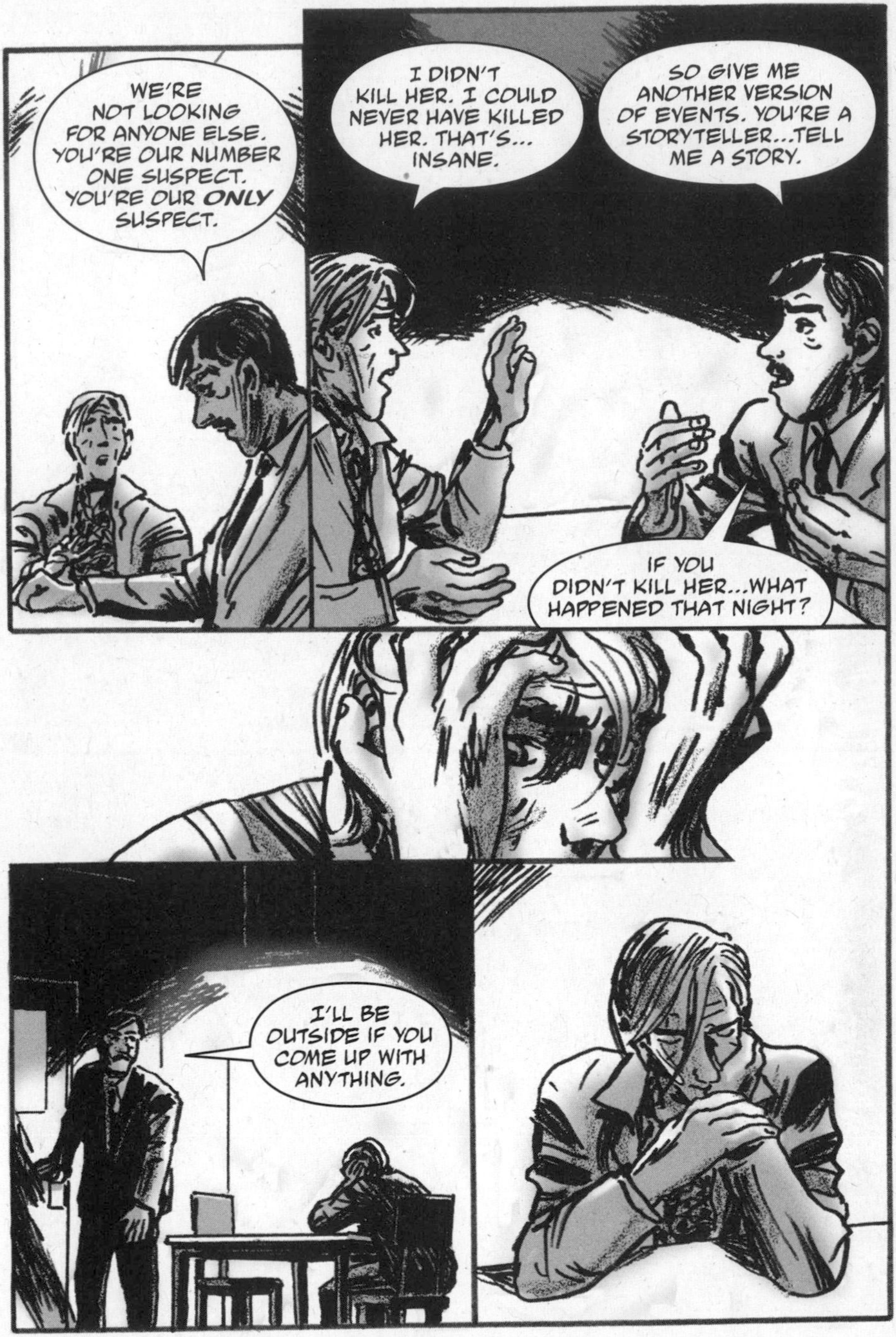
WE'RE NOT LOOKING FOR ANYONE ELSE. YOU'RE OUR NUMBER ONE SUSPECT. YOU'RE OUR ONLY SUSPECT.
I DIDN'T KILL HER. I COULD NEVER HAVE KILLED HER. THAT'S... INSANE.
SO GIVE ME ANOTHER VERSION OF EVENTS. YOU'RE A STORYTELLER...TELL ME A STORY.
IF YOU DIDN'T KILL HER...WHAT HAPPENED THAT NIGHT?
I'LL BE OUTSIDE IF YOU COME UP WITH ANYTHING.

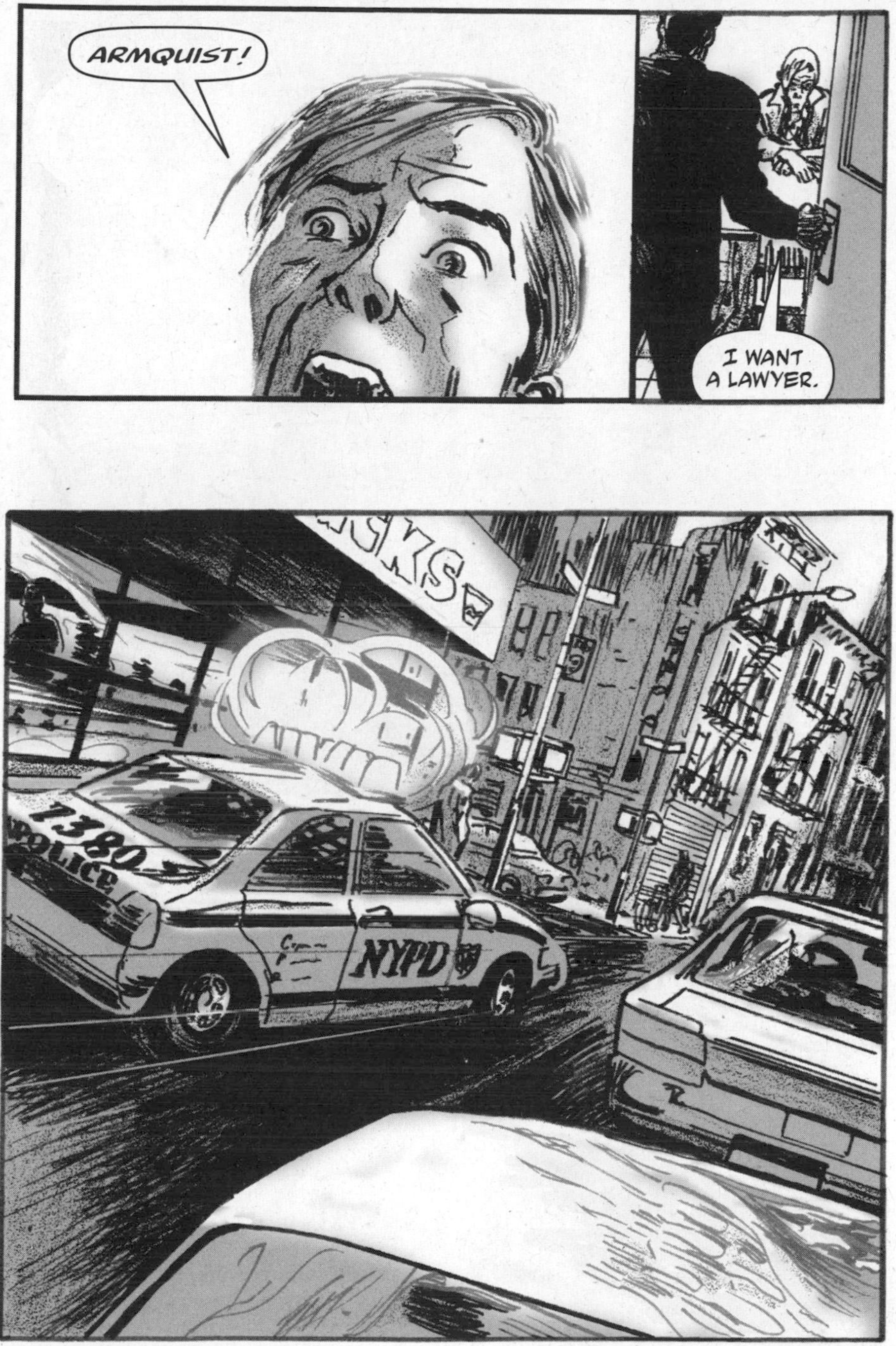
ARMQUIST!
I WANT A LAWYER.
1380
NYPD

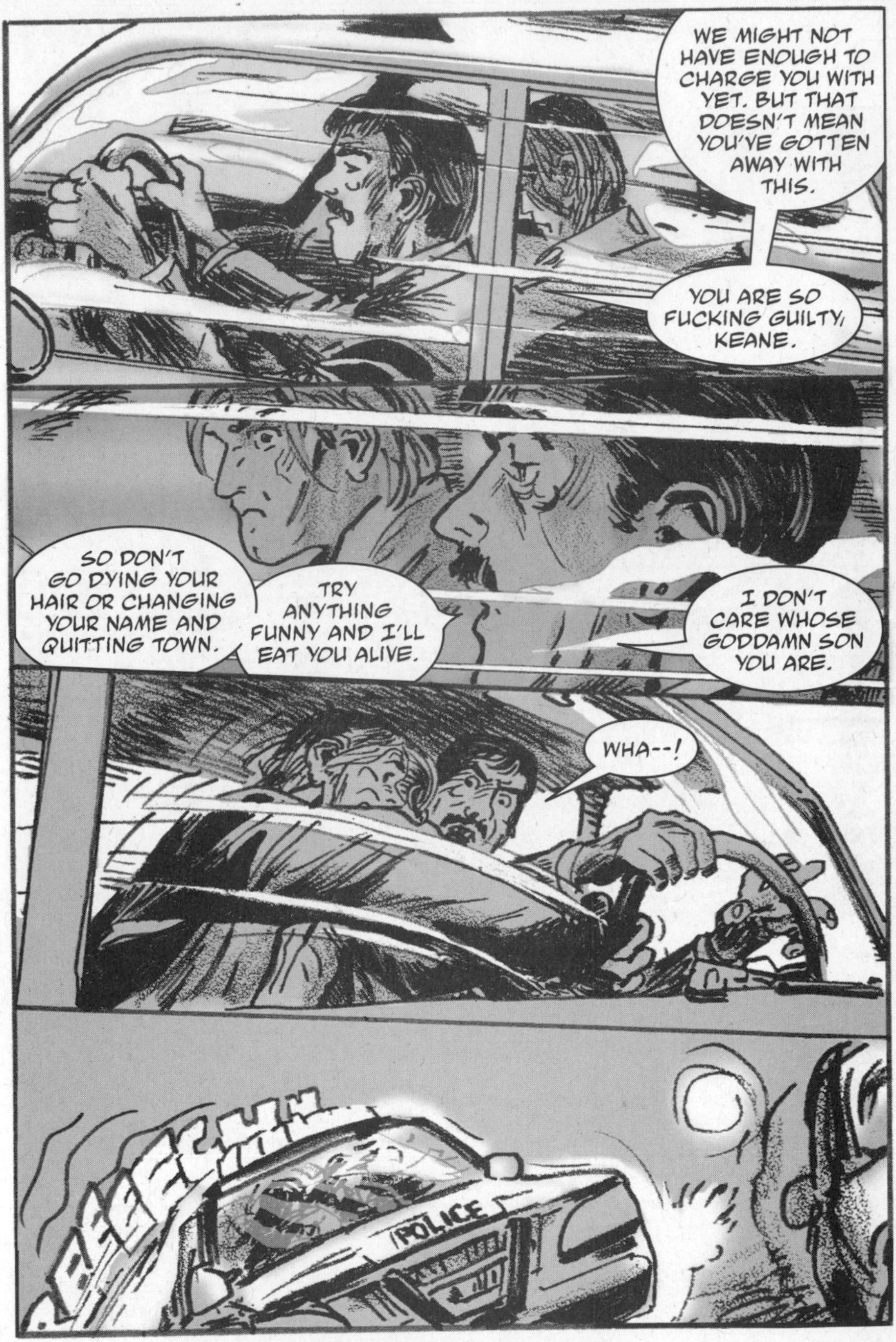
WE MIGHT NOT HAVE ENOUGH TO CHARGE YOU WITH YET. BUT THAT DOESN'T MEAN YOU'VE GOTTEN AWAY WITH THIS.
YOU ARE SO FUCKING GUILTY, KEANE.
SO DON'T GO DYING YOUR HAIR OR CHANGING YOUR NAME AND QUITTING TOWN.
TRY ANYTHING FUNNY AND I'LL EAT YOU ALIVE.
I DON'T CARE WHOSE GODDAMN SON YOU ARE.
WHA--!
POLICE

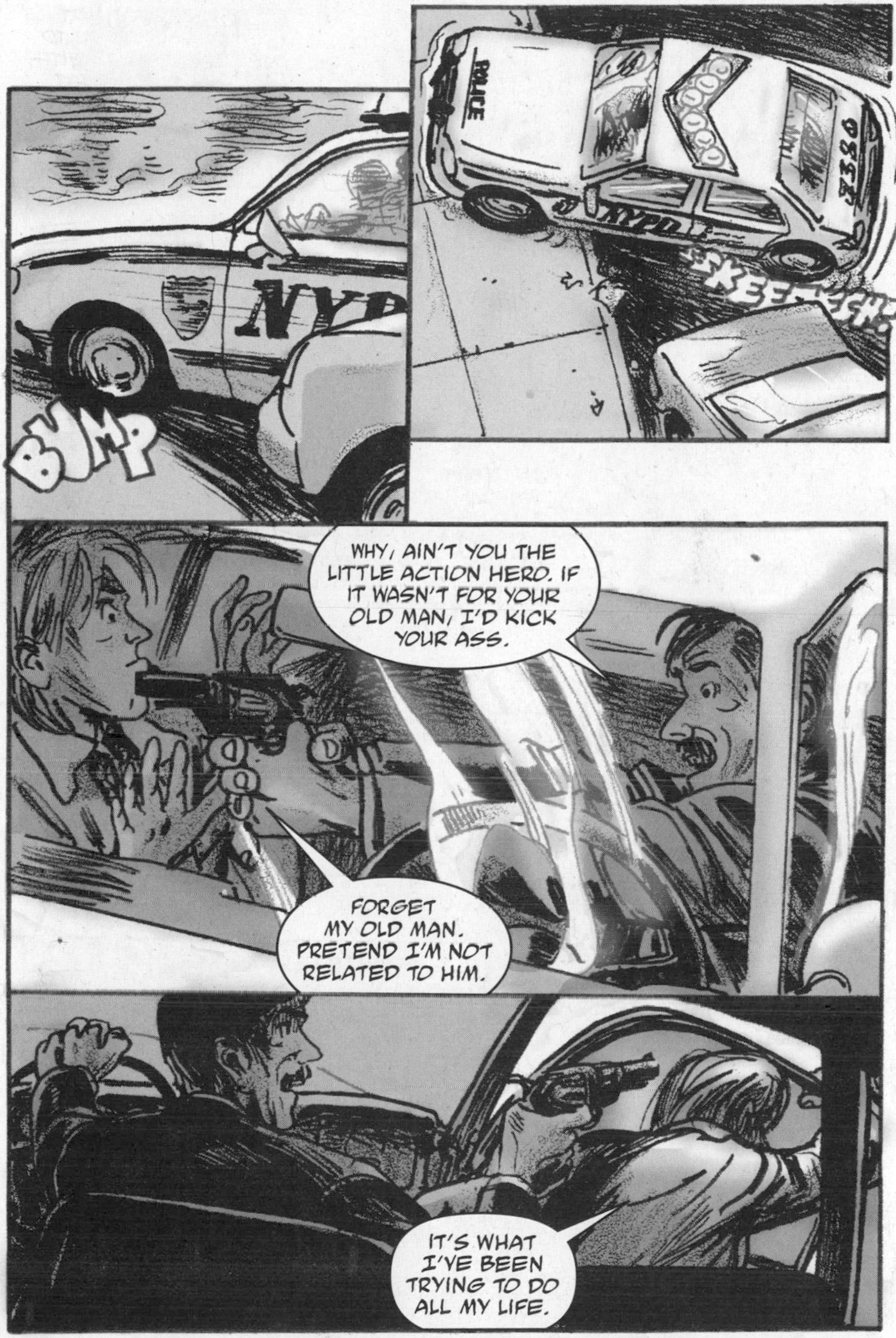
BUMP
NYPD
POLICE
NYPD
SKEEEESH!
WHY, AIN'T YOU THE LITTLE ACTION HERO. IF IT WASN'T FOR YOUR OLD MAN, I'D KICK YOUR ASS.
FORGET MY OLD MAN. PRETEND I'M NOT RELATED TO HIM.
IT'S WHAT I'VE BEEN TRYING TO DO ALL MY LIFE.

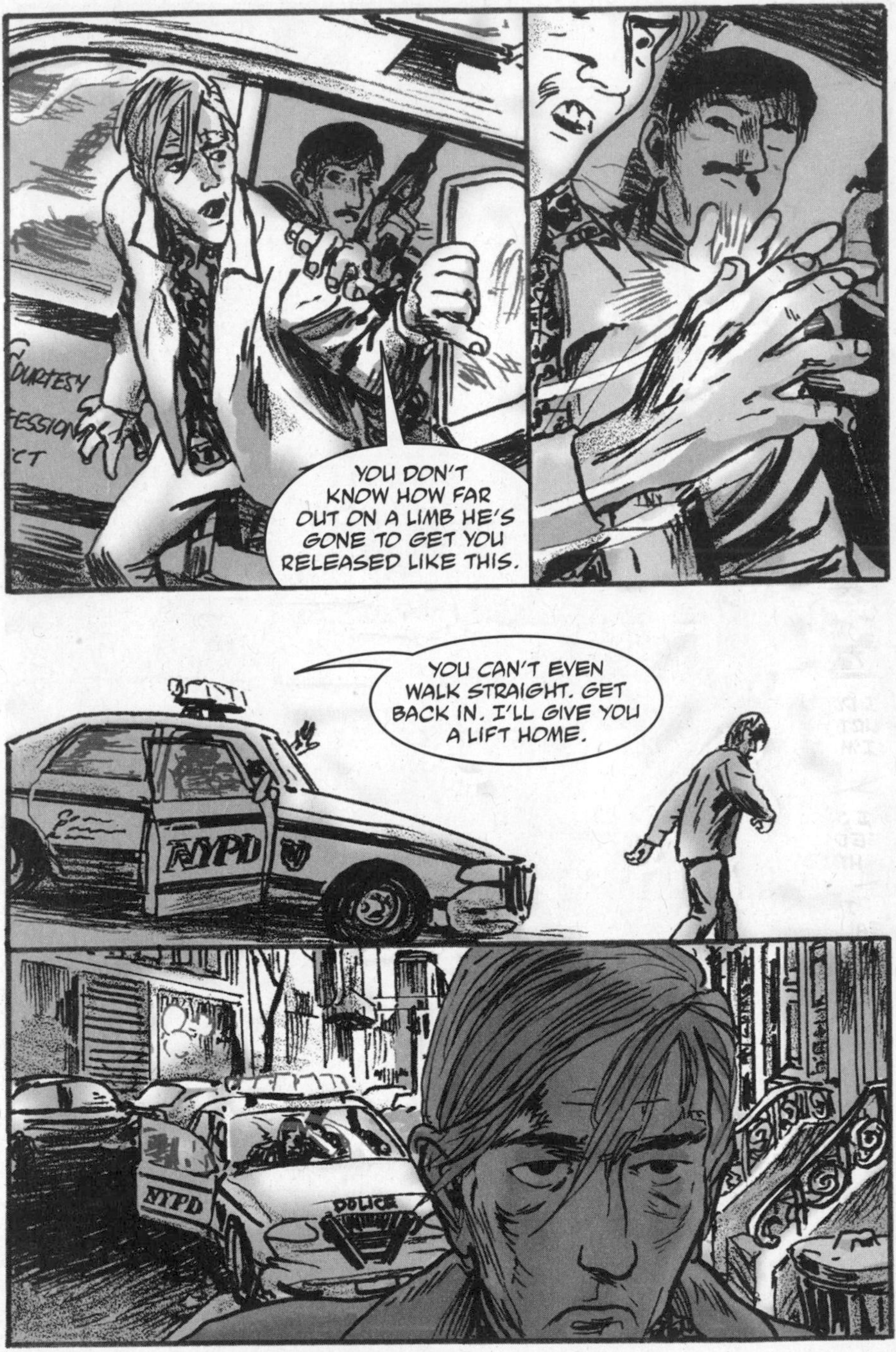
YOU DON'T KNOW HOW FAR OUT ON A LIMB HE'S GONE TO GET YOU RELEASED LIKE THIS.
YOU CAN'T EVEN WALK STRAIGHT. GET BACK IN. I'LL GIVE YOU A LIFT HOME.
NYPD
NYPD

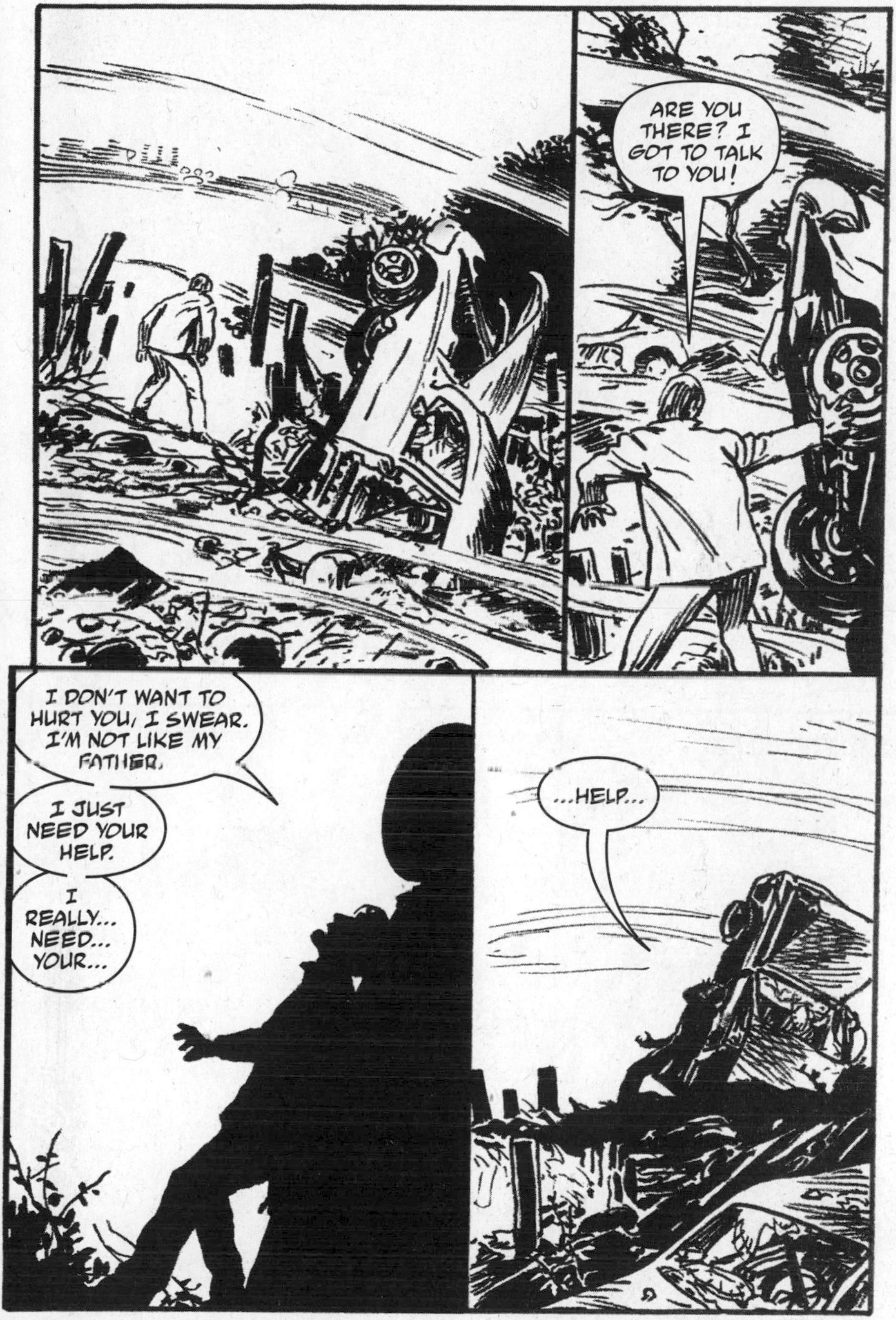
ARE YOU THERE? I GOT TO TALK TO YOU!
I DON'T WANT TO HURT YOU, I SWEAR. I'M NOT LIKE MY FATHER.
I JUST NEED YOUR HELP.
I REALLY... NEED... YOUR...
...HELP...

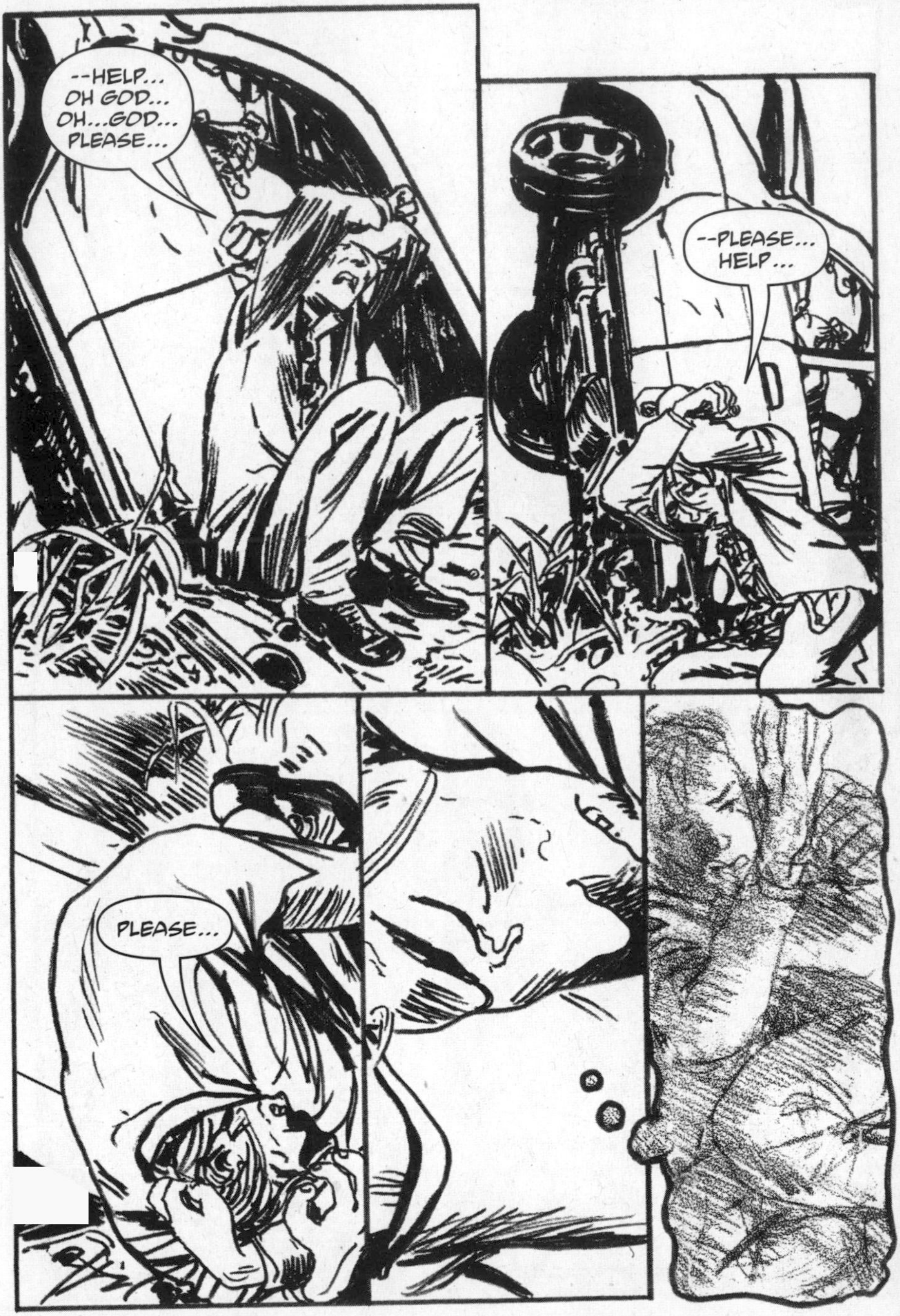
--HELP... OH GOD... OH...GOD... PLEASE...
--PLEASE... HELP...
PLEASE...

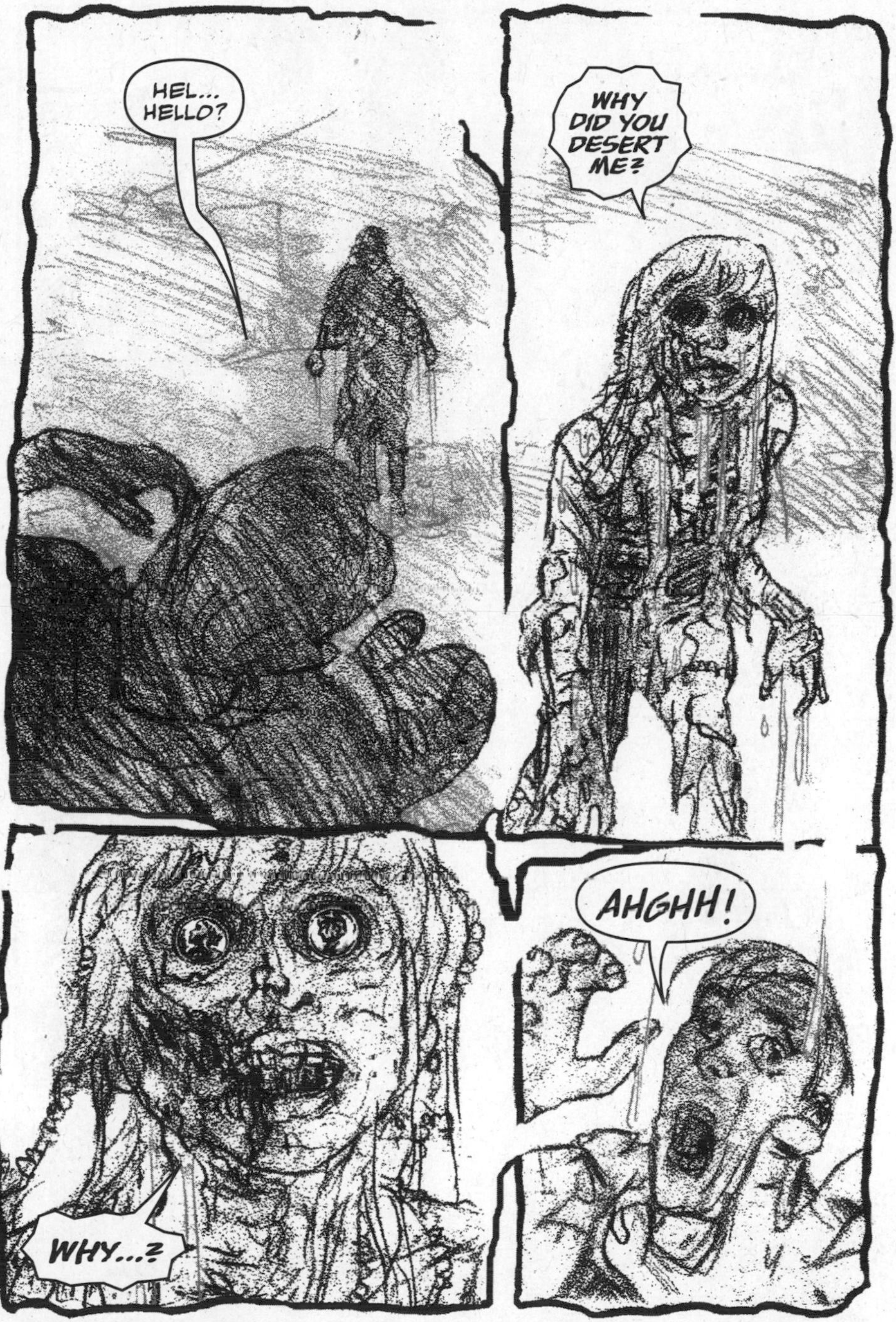
HEL... HELLO?
WHY DID YOU DESERT ME?
WHY...?
AHGHH!

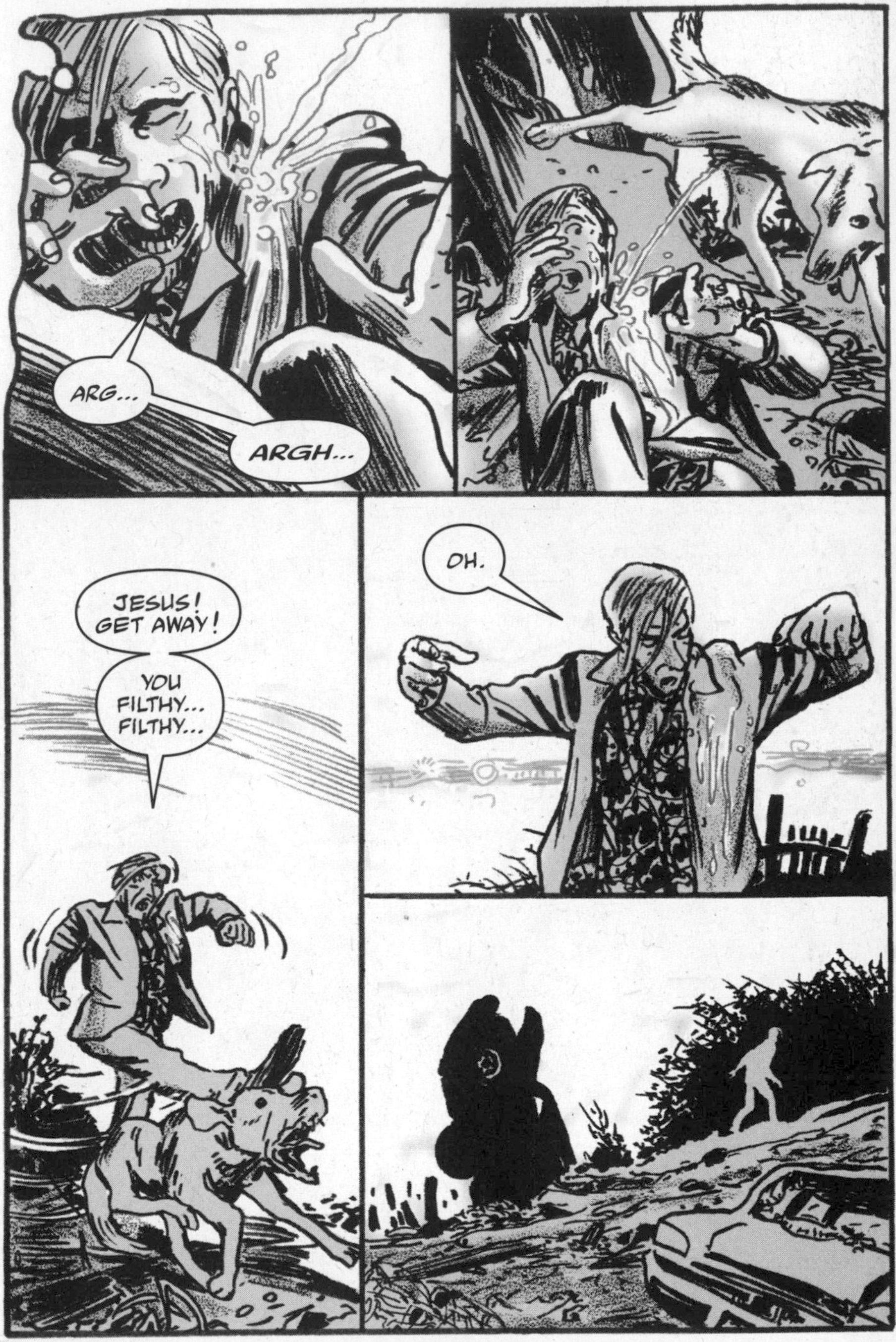
ARG...
ARGH...
JESUS! GET AWAY!
YOU FILTHY... FILTHY...
OH.

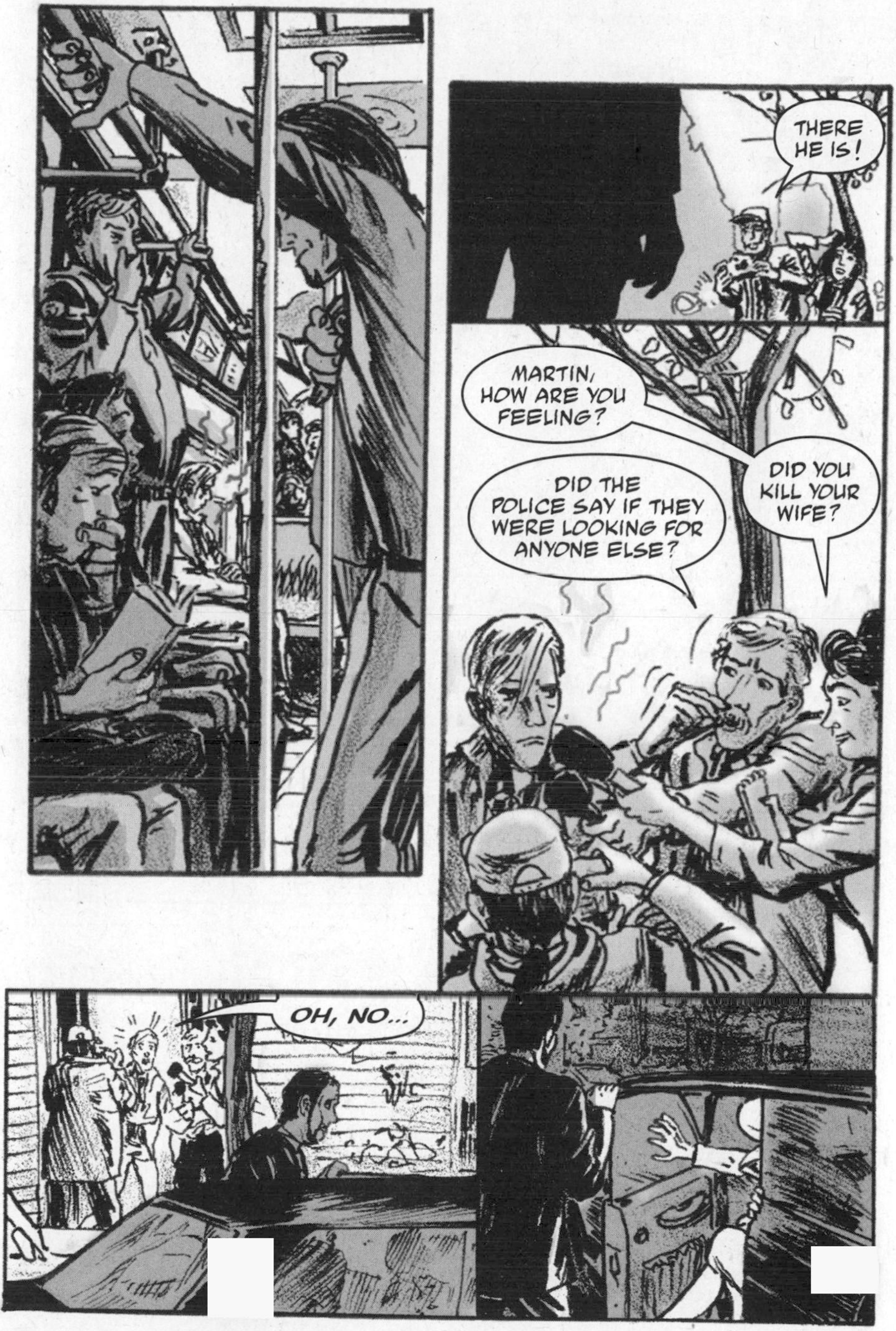
THERE HE IS!
MARTIN, HOW ARE YOU FEELING?
DID YOU KILL YOUR WIFE?
DID THE POLICE SAY IF THEY WERE LOOKING FOR ANYONE ELSE?
OH, NO...

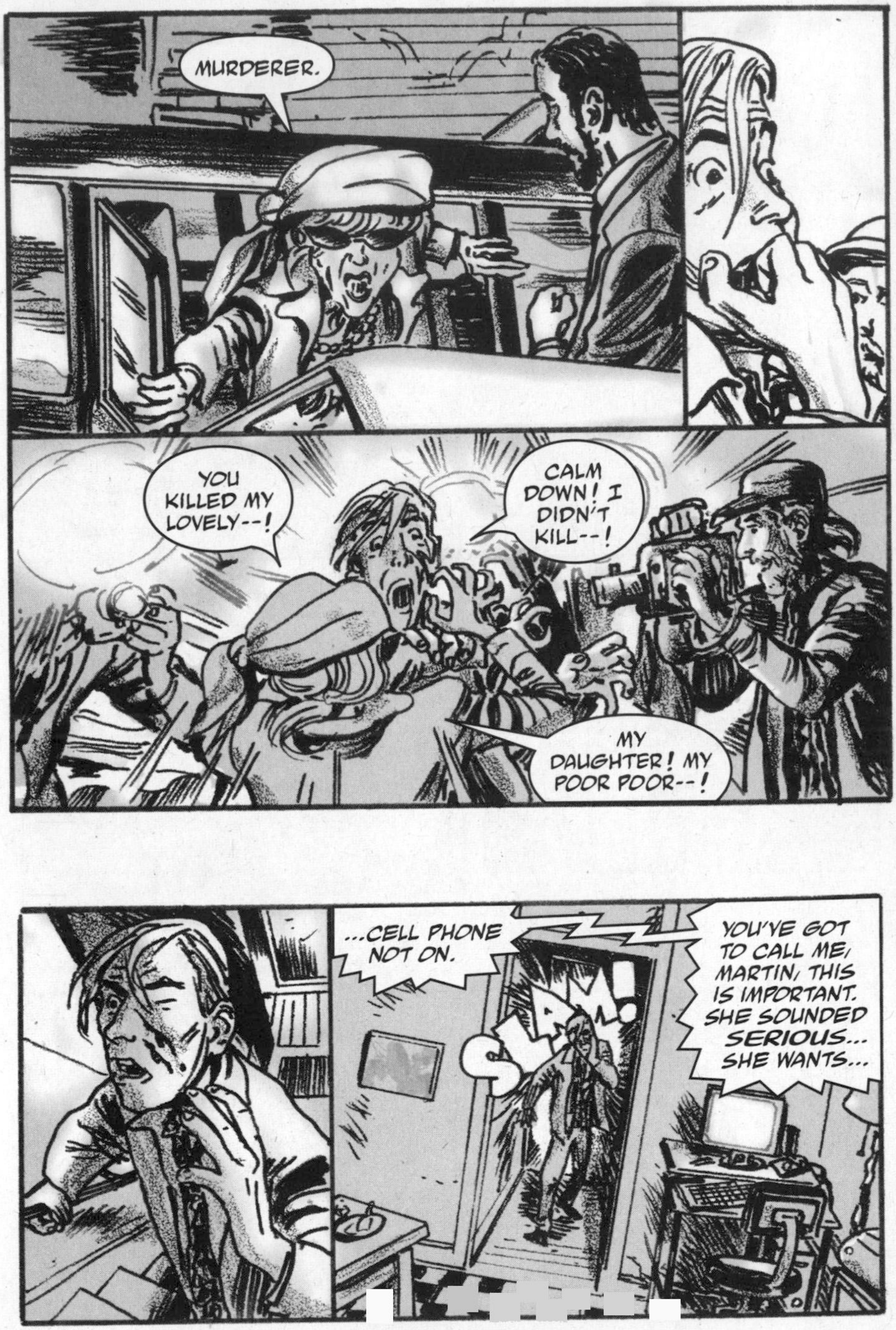
MURDERER.
YOU KILLED MY LOVELY--!
CALM DOWN! I DIDN'T KILL--!
MY DAUGHTER! MY POOR POOR--!
...CELL PHONE NOT ON.
YOU'VE GOT TO CALL ME, MARTIN, THIS IS IMPORTANT. SHE SOUNDED SERIOUS... SHE WANTS...
SLAM!

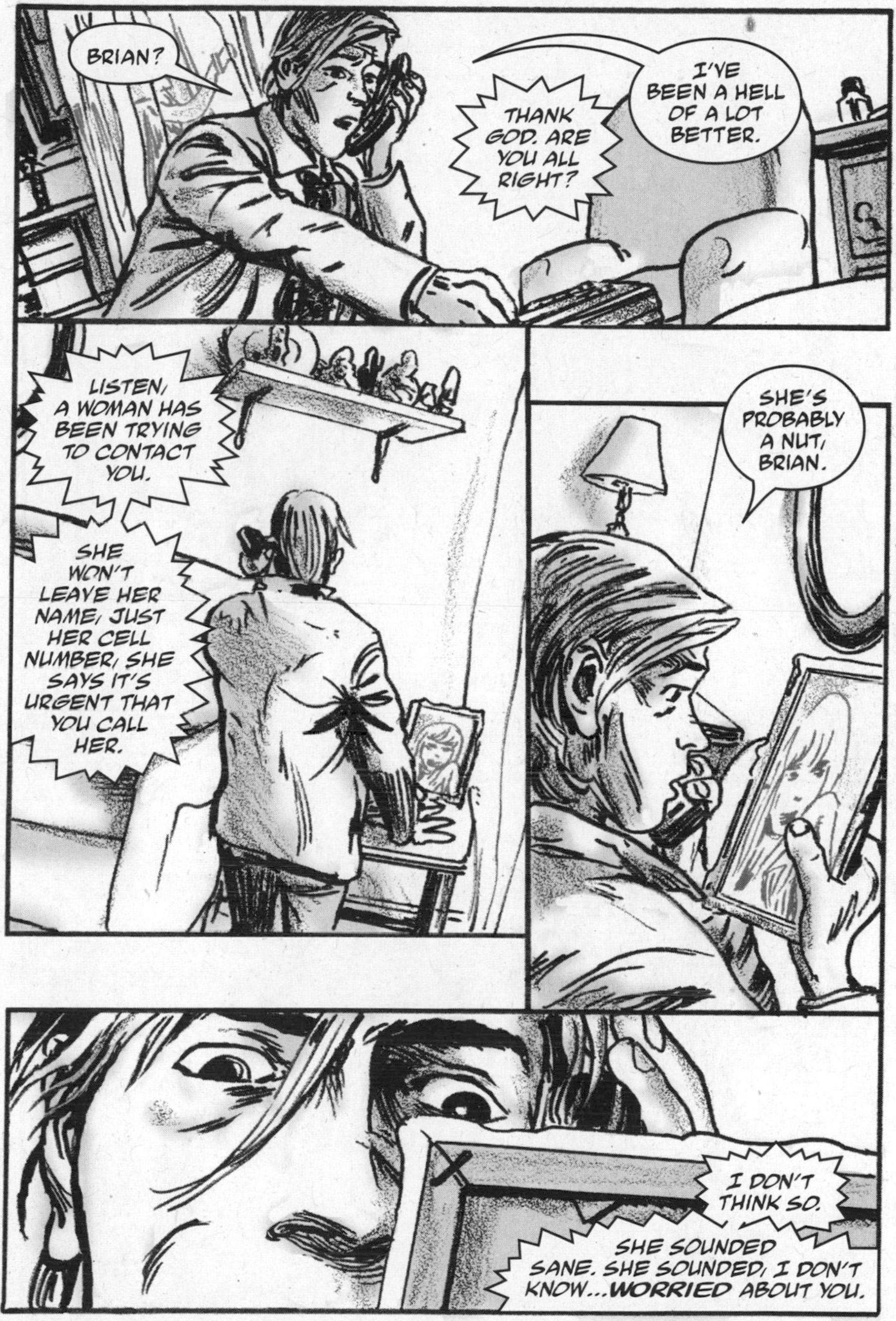
BRIAN?
THANK GOD. ARE YOU ALL RIGHT?
I'VE BEEN A HELL OF A LOT BETTER.
LISTEN, A WOMAN HAS BEEN TRYING TO CONTACT YOU.
SHE WON'T LEAVE HER NAME, JUST HER CELL NUMBER, SHE SAYS IT'S URGENT THAT YOU CALL HER.
SHE'S PROBABLY A NUT, BRIAN.
I DON'T THINK SO.
SHE SOUNDED SANE. SHE SOUNDED, I DON'T KNOW...**WORRIED** ABOUT YOU.

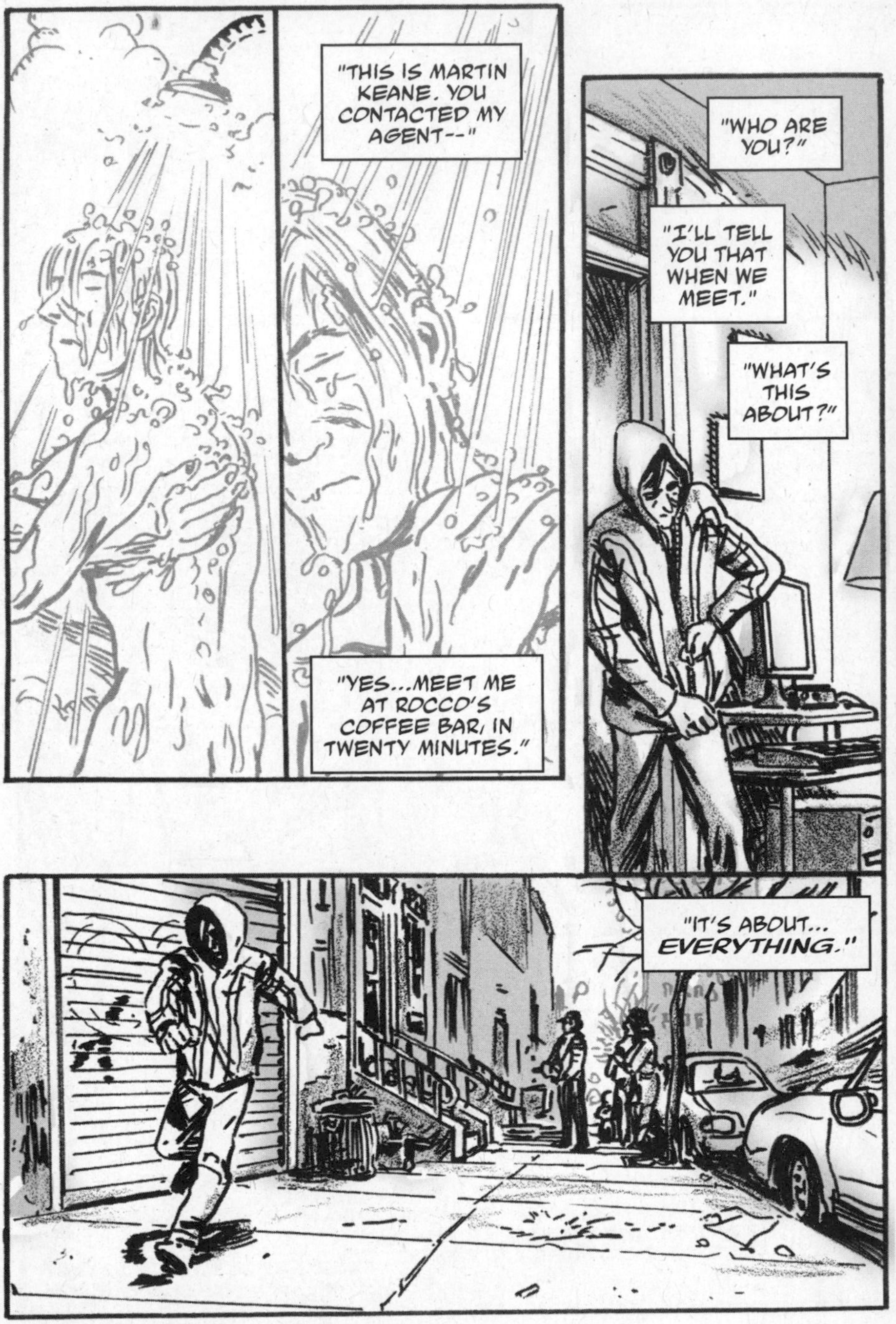
"THIS IS MARTIN KEANE. YOU CONTACTED MY AGENT--"
"YES...MEET ME AT ROCCO'S COFFEE BAR, IN TWENTY MINUTES."
"WHO ARE YOU?"
"I'LL TELL YOU THAT WHEN WE MEET."
"WHAT'S THIS ABOUT?"
"IT'S ABOUT... *EVERYTHING.*"

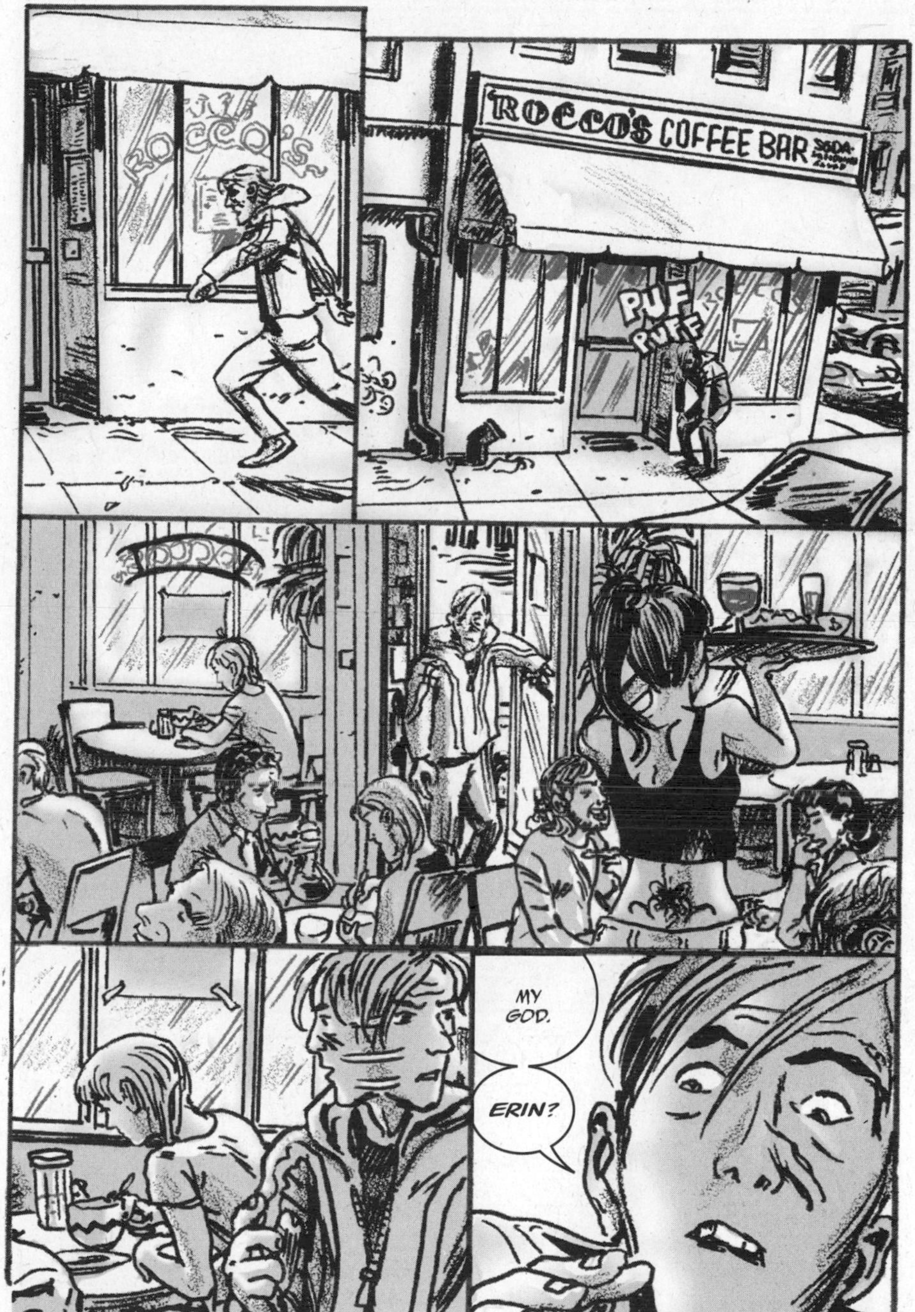
ROCCO'S COFFEE BAR
PUF
PUFF
MY GOD.
ERIN?

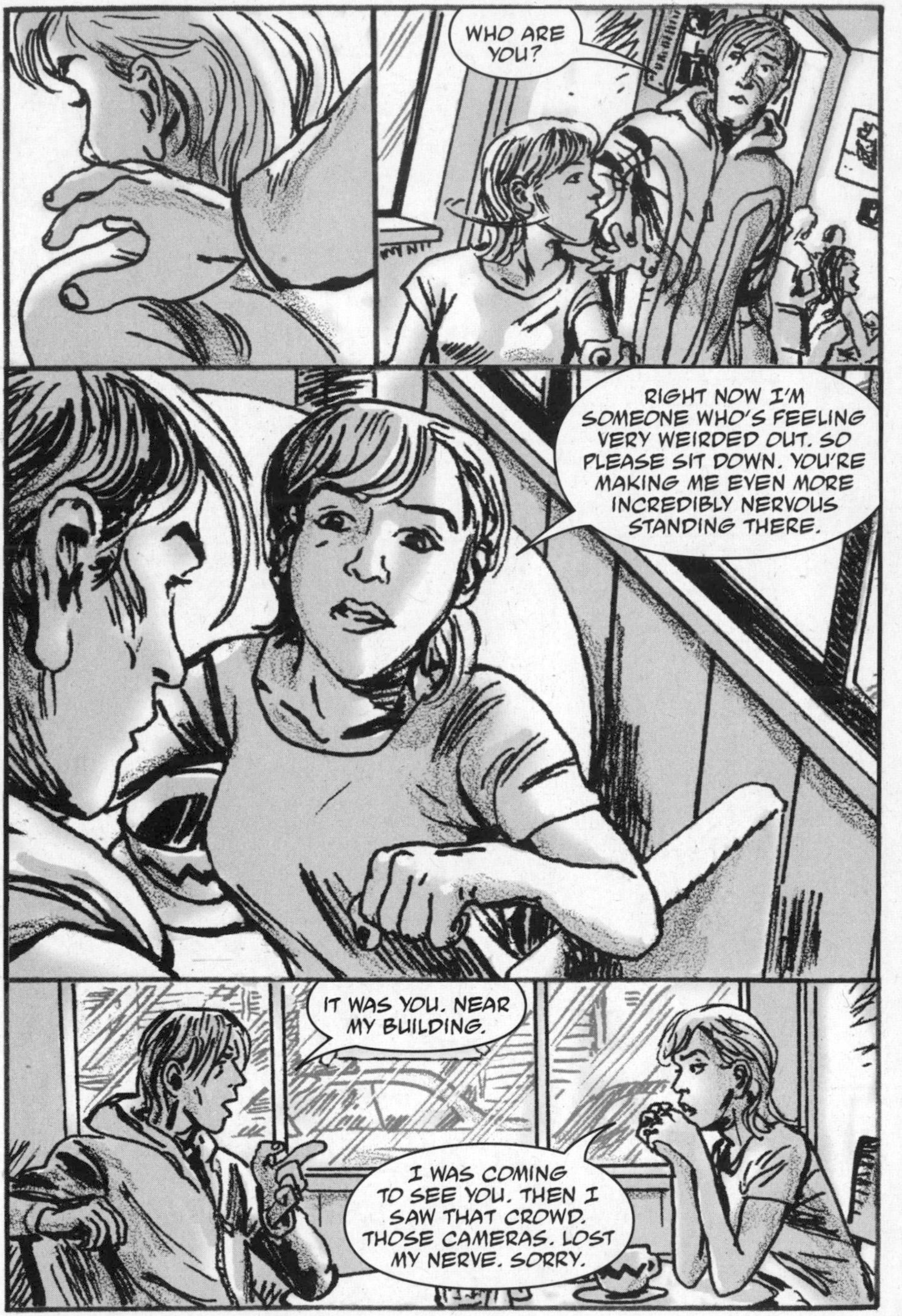
WHO ARE YOU?
RIGHT NOW I'M SOMEONE WHO'S FEELING VERY WEIRDED OUT. SO PLEASE SIT DOWN. YOU'RE MAKING ME EVEN MORE INCREDIBLY NERVOUS STANDING THERE.
IT WAS YOU. NEAR MY BUILDING.
I WAS COMING TO SEE YOU. THEN I SAW THAT CROWD. THOSE CAMERAS. LOST MY NERVE. SORRY.

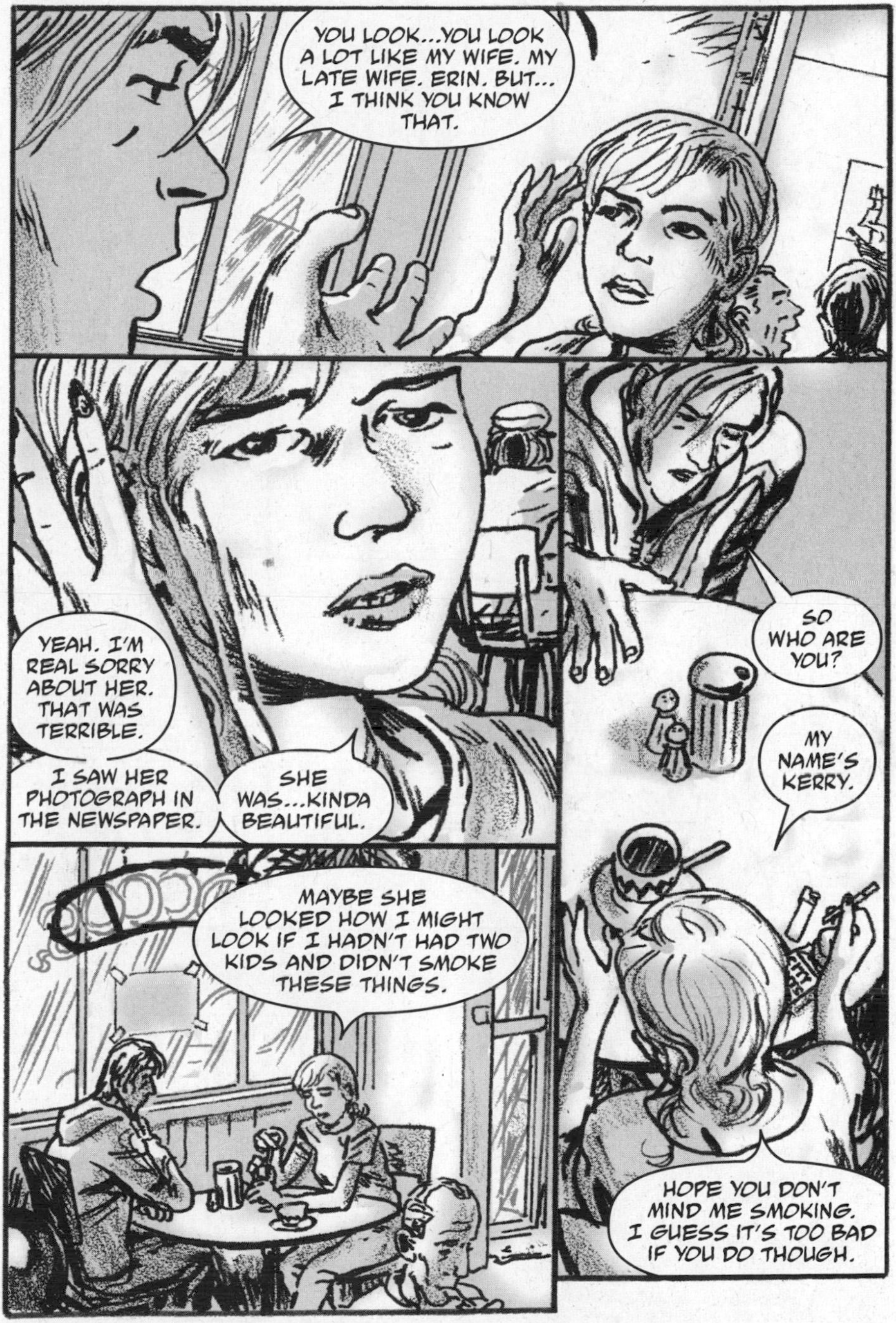
YOU LOOK...YOU LOOK A LOT LIKE MY WIFE. MY LATE WIFE. ERIN. BUT... I THINK YOU KNOW THAT.
YEAH. I'M REAL SORRY ABOUT HER. THAT WAS TERRIBLE.
I SAW HER PHOTOGRAPH IN THE NEWSPAPER.
SHE WAS...KINDA BEAUTIFUL.
SO WHO ARE YOU?
MY NAME'S KERRY.
MAYBE SHE LOOKED HOW I MIGHT LOOK IF I HADN'T HAD TWO KIDS AND DIDN'T SMOKE THESE THINGS.
HOPE YOU DON'T MIND ME SMOKING. I GUESS IT'S TOO BAD IF YOU DO THOUGH.

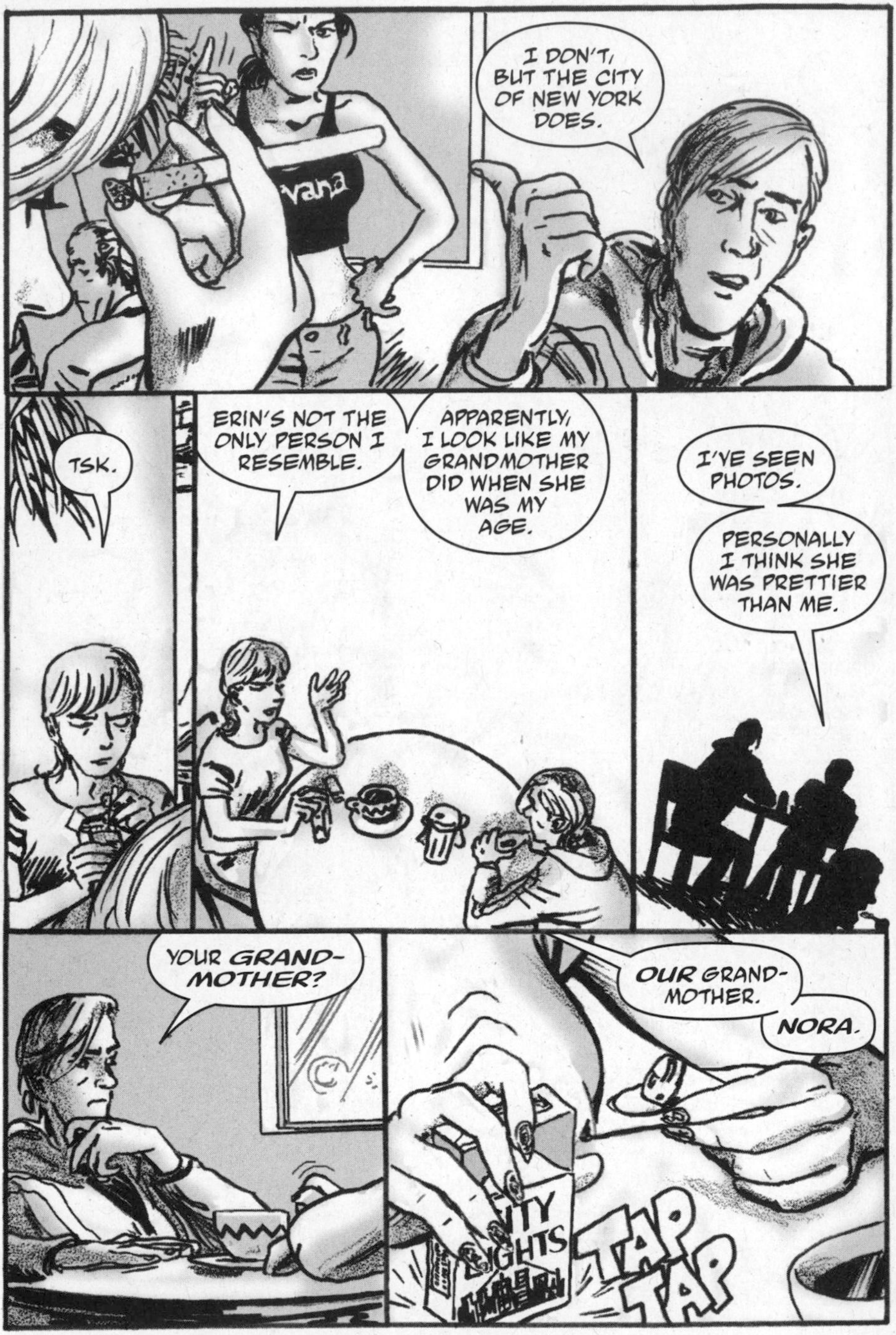

I DON'T, BUT THE CITY OF NEW YORK DOES.
TSK.
ERIN'S NOT THE ONLY PERSON I RESEMBLE.
APPARENTLY, I LOOK LIKE MY GRANDMOTHER DID WHEN SHE WAS MY AGE.
I'VE SEEN PHOTOS.
PERSONALLY I THINK SHE WAS PRETTIER THAN ME.
YOUR GRAND-MOTHER?
OUR GRAND-MOTHER.
NORA.
TAP TAP

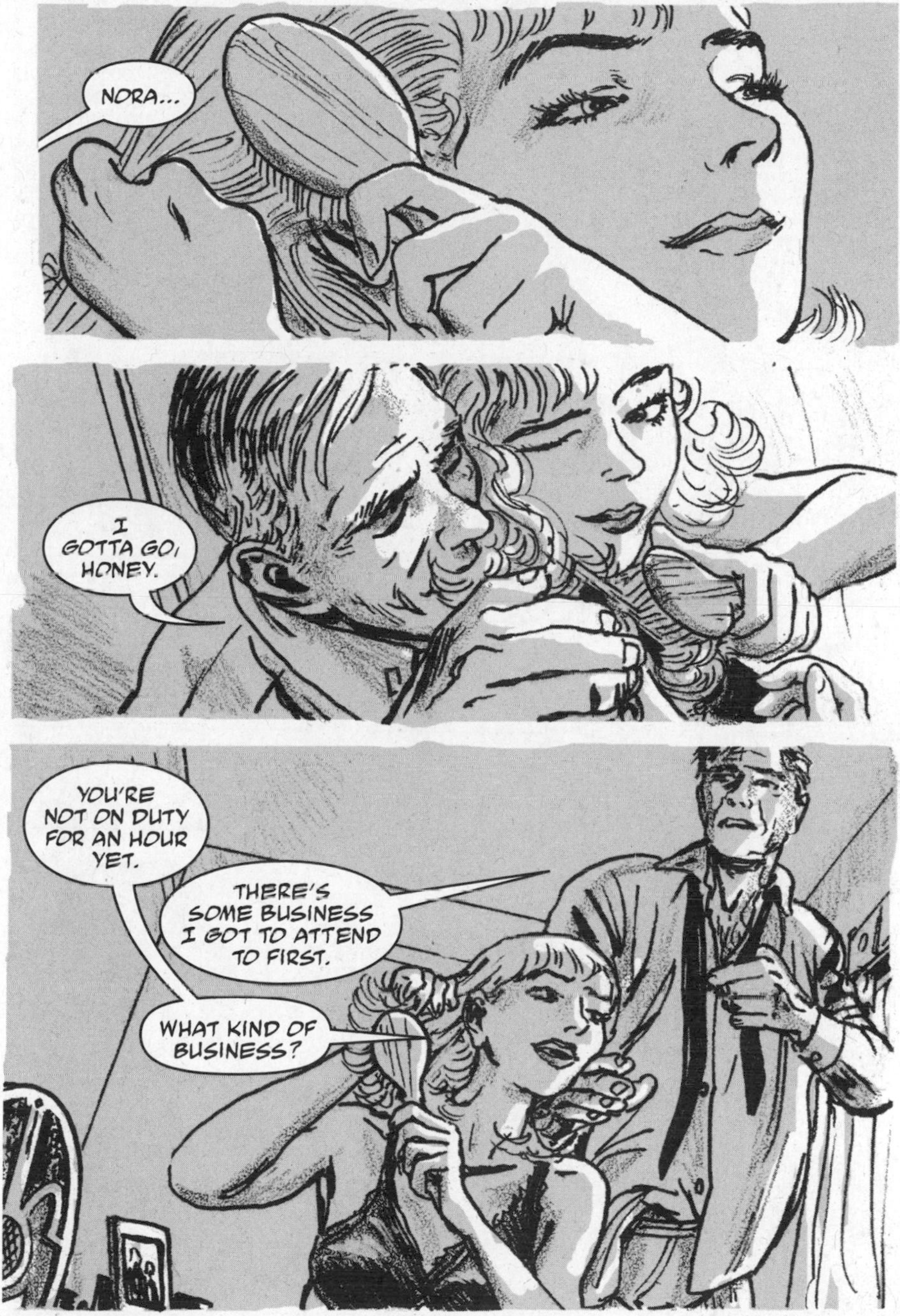
NORA...
I GOTTA GO, HONEY.
YOU'RE NOT ON DUTY FOR AN HOUR YET.
THERE'S SOME BUSINESS I GOT TO ATTEND TO FIRST.
WHAT KIND OF BUSINESS?

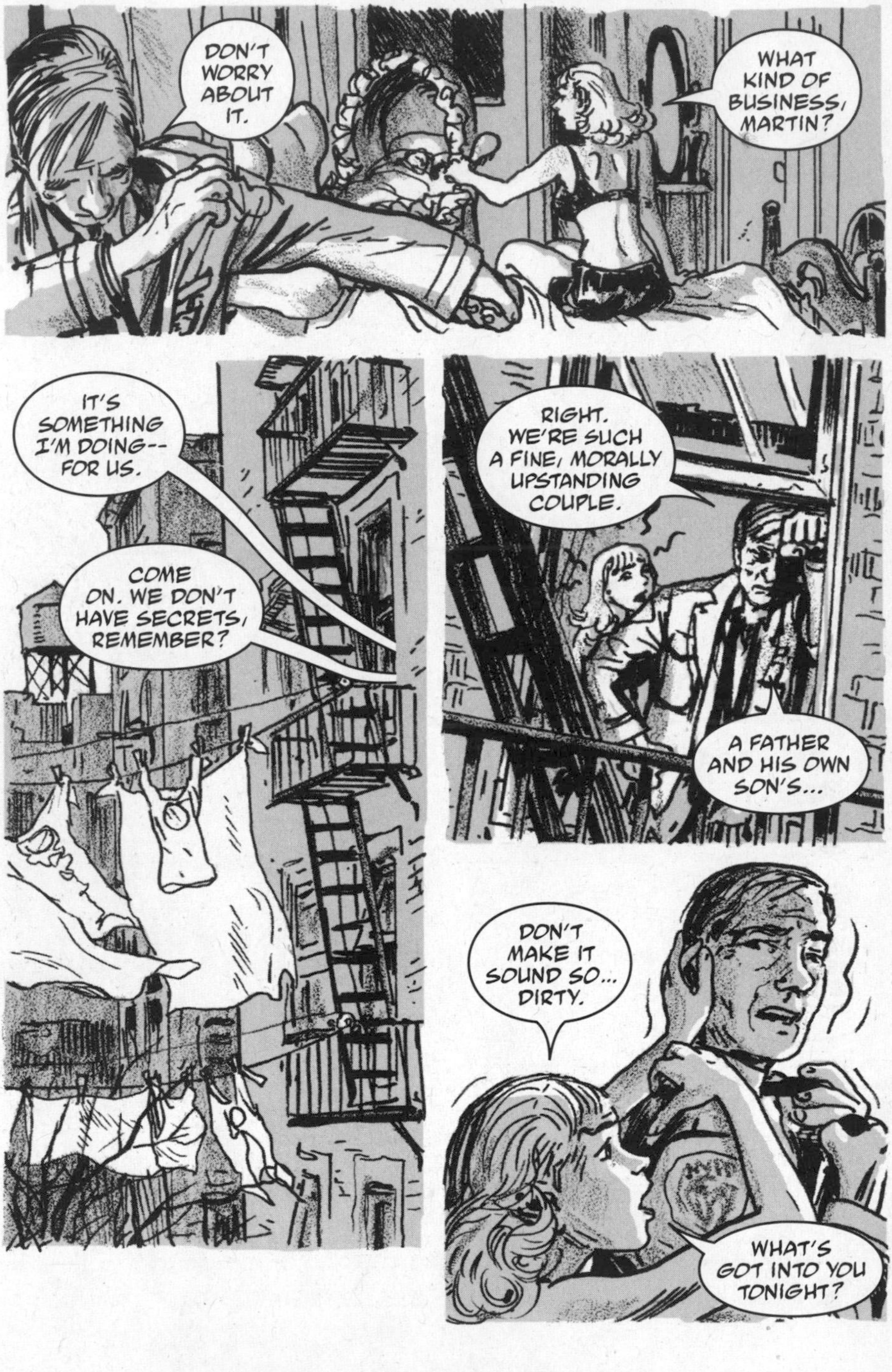
DON'T WORRY ABOUT IT.
WHAT KIND OF BUSINESS, MARTIN?
IT'S SOMETHING I'M DOING-- FOR US.
COME ON. WE DON'T HAVE SECRETS, REMEMBER?
RIGHT. WE'RE SUCH A FINE, MORALLY UPSTANDING COUPLE.
A FATHER AND HIS OWN SON'S...
DON'T MAKE IT SOUND SO... DIRTY.
WHAT'S GOT INTO YOU TONIGHT?

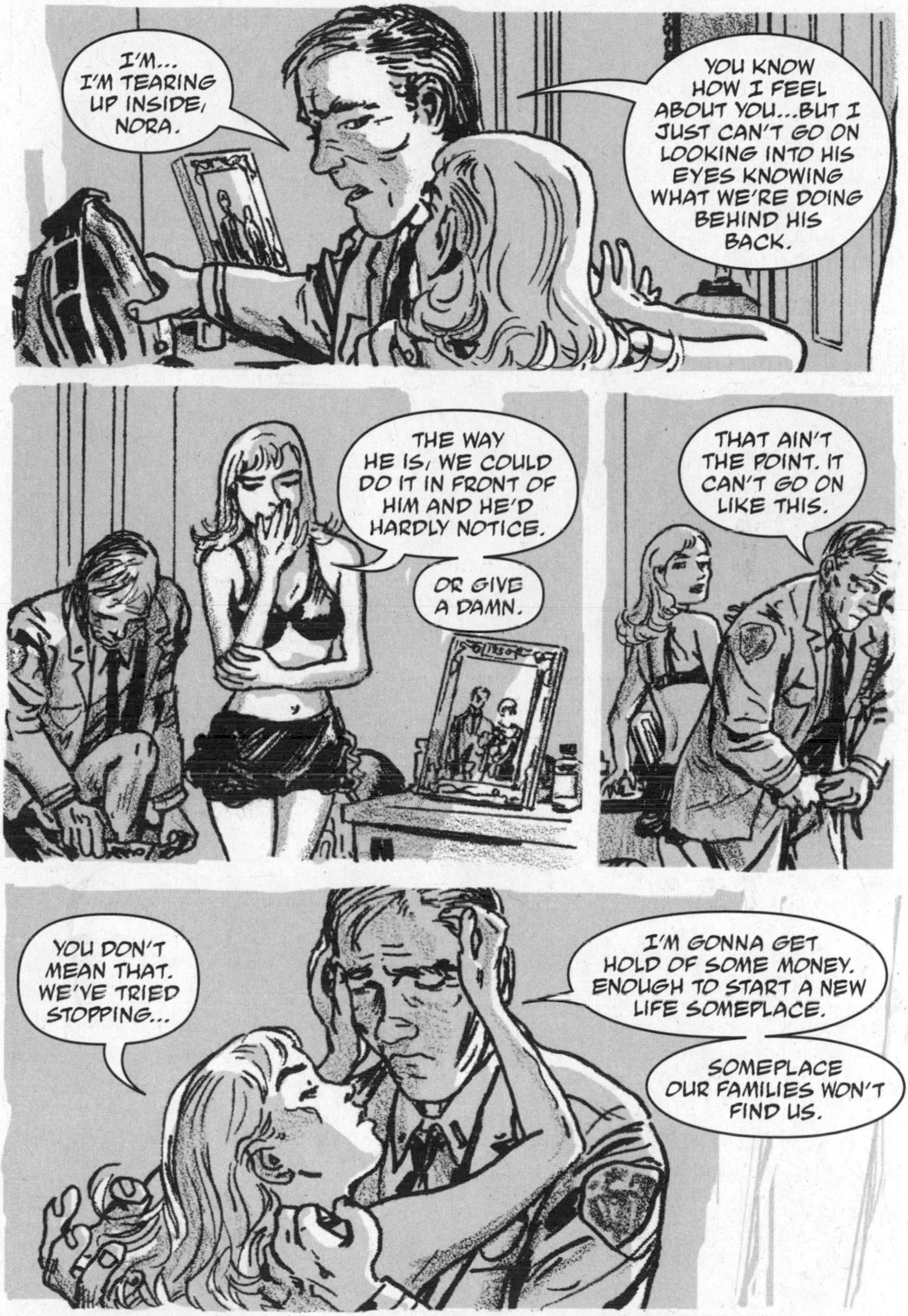
I'M... I'M TEARING UP INSIDE, NORA.
YOU KNOW HOW I FEEL ABOUT YOU...BUT I JUST CAN'T GO ON LOOKING INTO HIS EYES KNOWING WHAT WE'RE DOING BEHIND HIS BACK.
THE WAY HE IS, WE COULD DO IT IN FRONT OF HIM AND HE'D HARDLY NOTICE.
OR GIVE A DAMN.
THAT AIN'T THE POINT. IT CAN'T GO ON LIKE THIS.
YOU DON'T MEAN THAT. WE'VE TRIED STOPPING...
I'M GONNA GET HOLD OF SOME MONEY. ENOUGH TO START A NEW LIFE SOMEPLACE.
SOMEPLACE OUR FAMILIES WON'T FIND US.

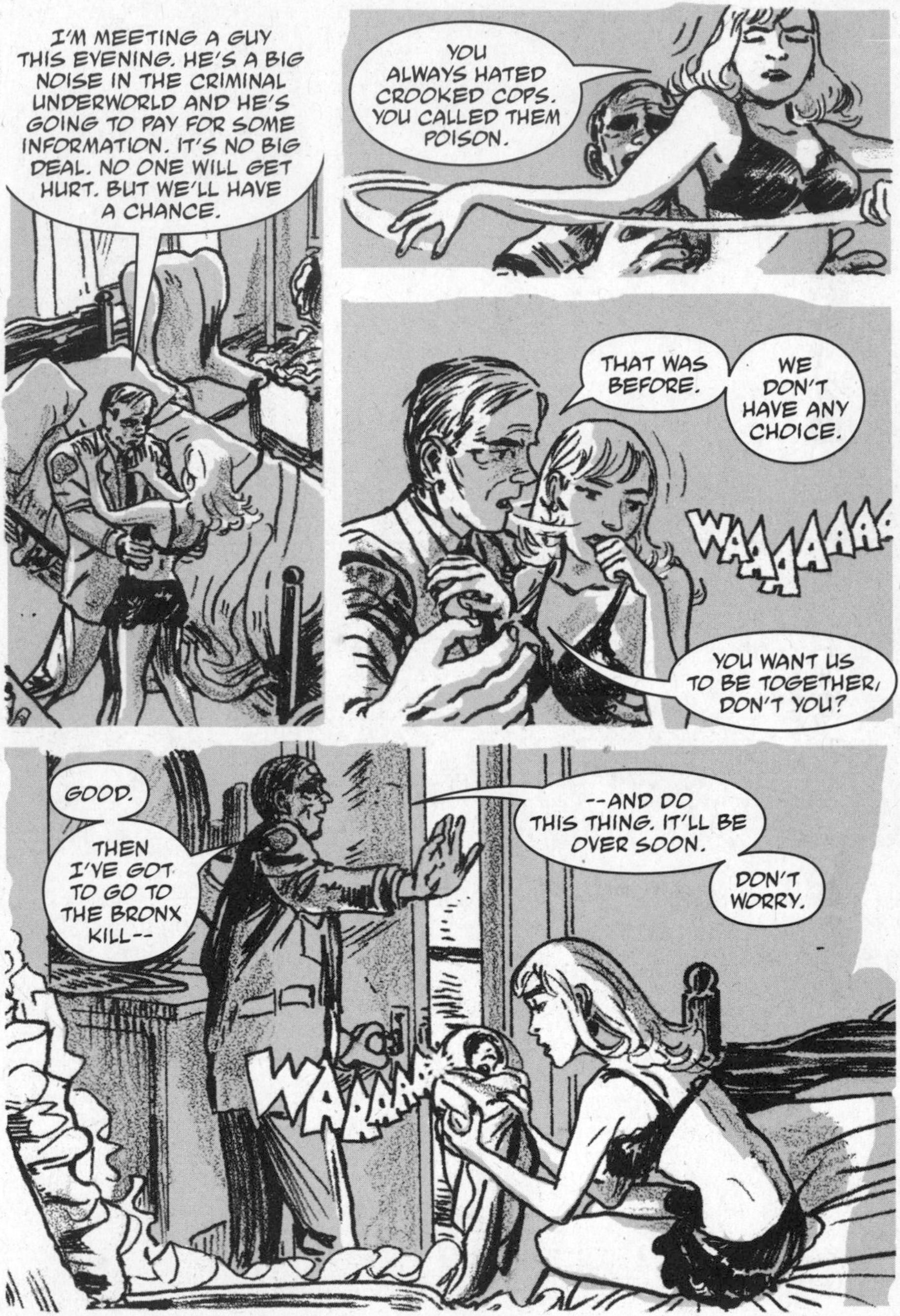
I'M MEETING A GUY THIS EVENING. HE'S A BIG NOISE IN THE CRIMINAL UNDERWORLD AND HE'S GOING TO PAY FOR SOME INFORMATION. IT'S NO BIG DEAL. NO ONE WILL GET HURT. BUT WE'LL HAVE A CHANCE.
YOU ALWAYS HATED CROOKED COPS. YOU CALLED THEM POISON.
THAT WAS BEFORE.
WE DON'T HAVE ANY CHOICE.
WAAAAAA
YOU WANT US TO BE TOGETHER, DON'T YOU?
GOOD.
THEN I'VE GOT TO GO TO THE BRONX KILL--
--AND DO THIS THING. IT'LL BE OVER SOON.
DON'T WORRY.
WAAAA

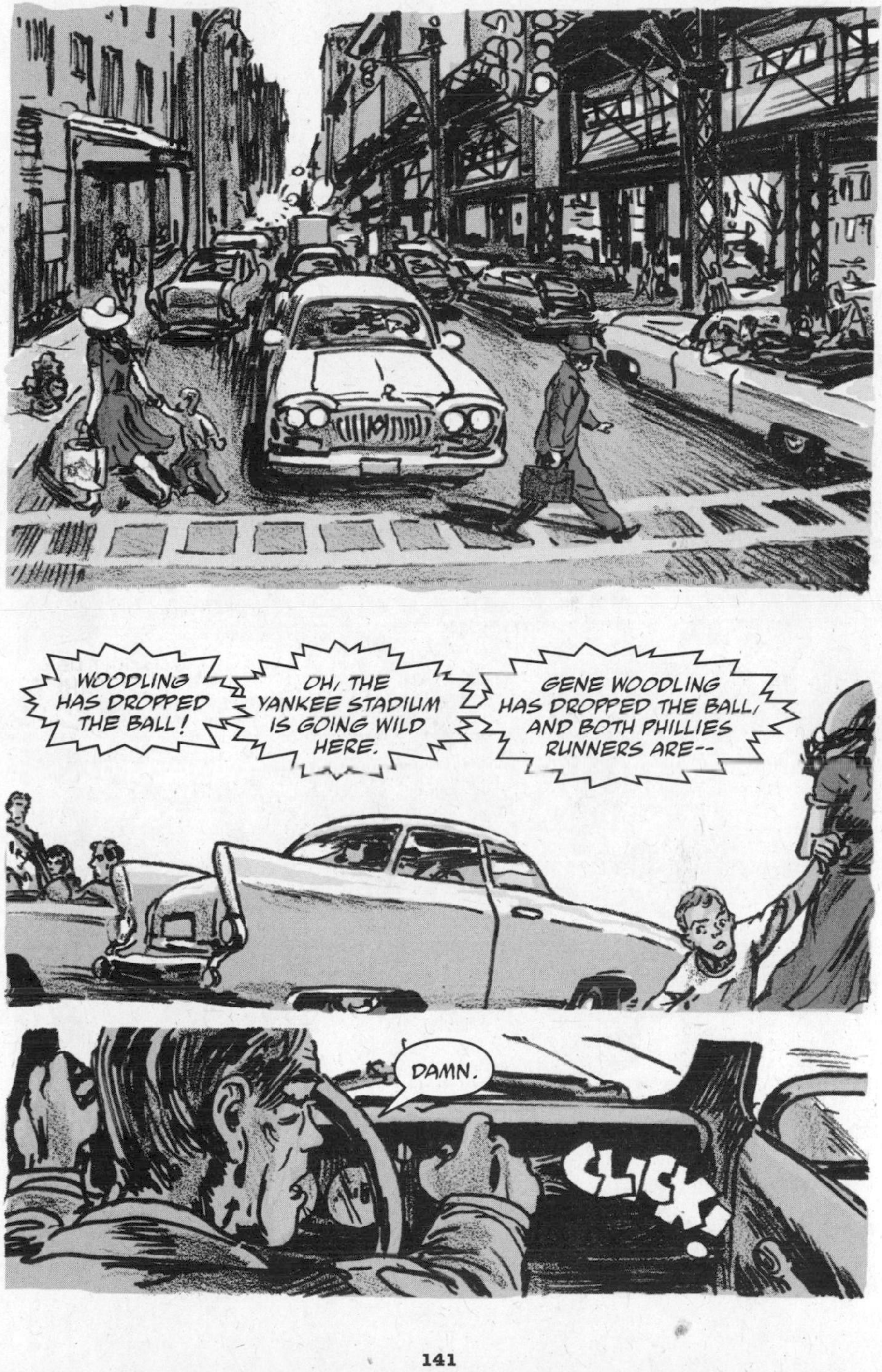
WOODLING HAS DROPPED THE BALL!
OH, THE YANKEE STADIUM IS GOING WILD HERE.
GENE WOODLING HAS DROPPED THE BALL, AND BOTH PHILLIES RUNNERS ARE--
DAMN.
CLICK!

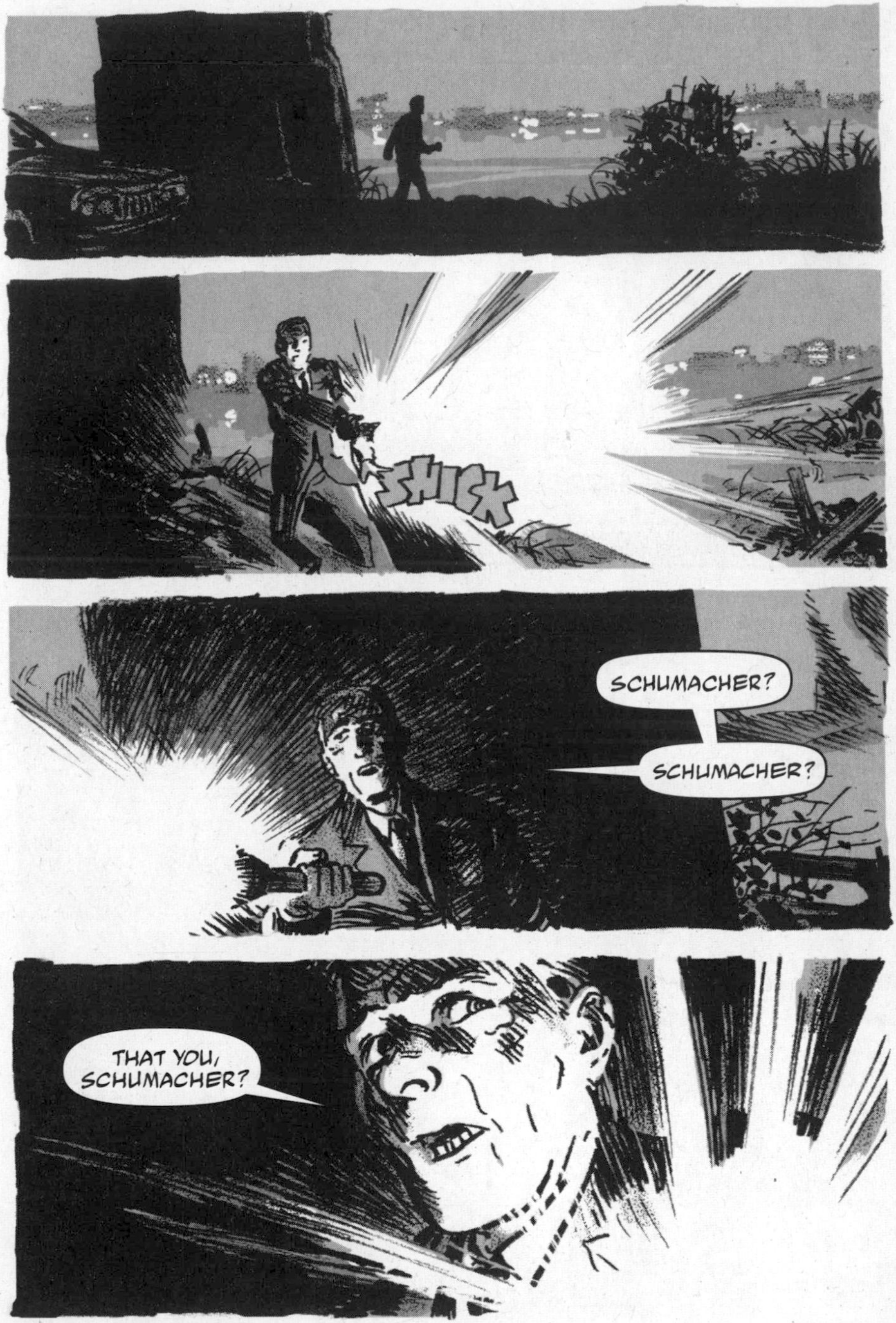
SHICK
SCHUMACHER?
SCHUMACHER?
THAT YOU, SCHUMACHER?

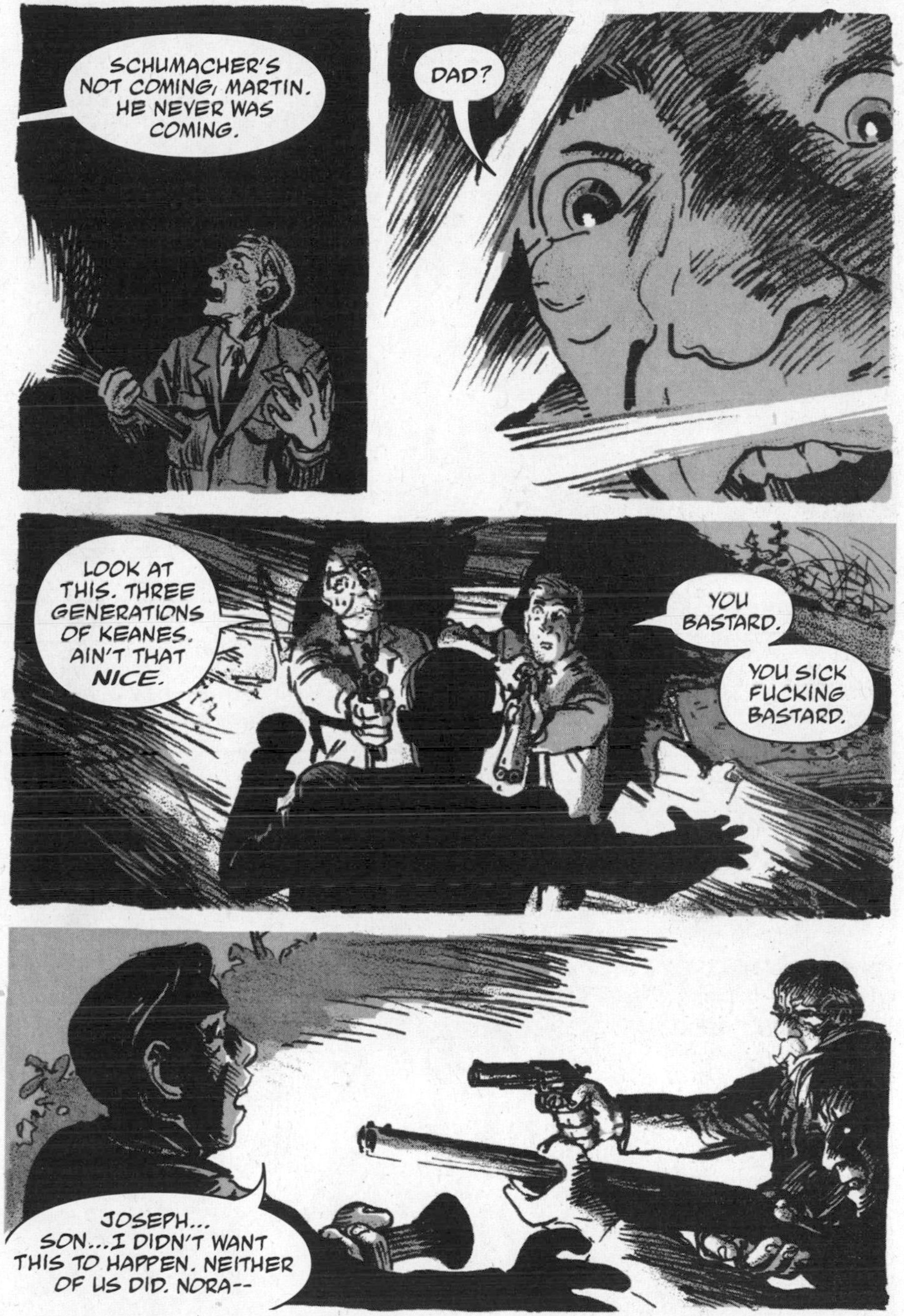
SCHUMACHER'S NOT COMING, MARTIN. HE NEVER WAS COMING.
DAD?
LOOK AT THIS. THREE GENERATIONS OF KEANES. AIN'T THAT NICE.
YOU BASTARD.
YOU SICK FUCKING BASTARD.
JOSEPH... SON...I DIDN'T WANT THIS TO HAPPEN. NEITHER OF US DID. NORA--

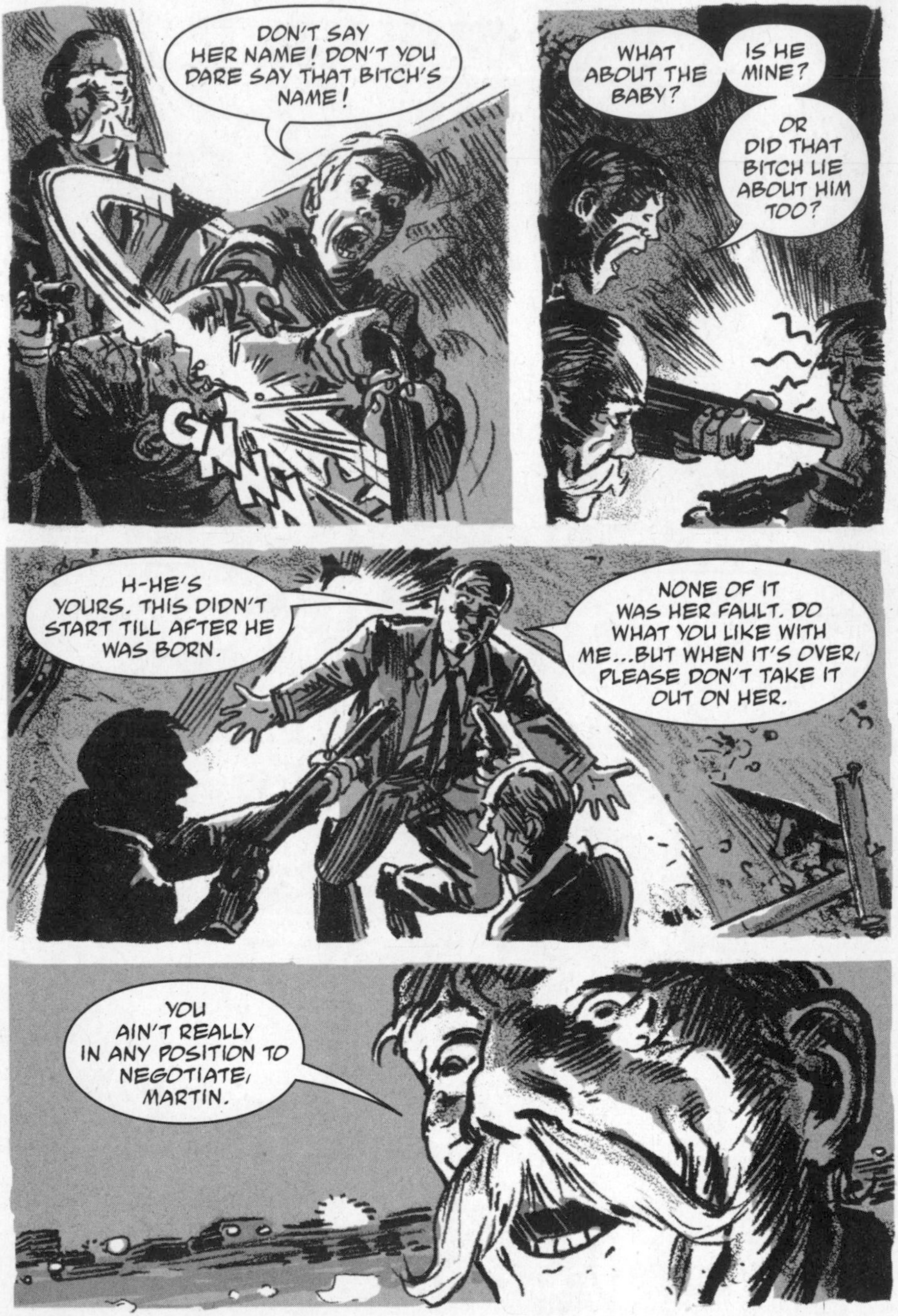
DON'T SAY HER NAME! DON'T YOU DARE SAY THAT BITCH'S NAME!
WHAT ABOUT THE BABY?
IS HE MINE?
OR DID THAT BITCH LIE ABOUT HIM TOO?
H-HE'S YOURS. THIS DIDN'T START TILL AFTER HE WAS BORN.
NONE OF IT WAS HER FAULT. DO WHAT YOU LIKE WITH ME...BUT WHEN IT'S OVER, PLEASE DON'T TAKE IT OUT ON HER.
YOU AIN'T REALLY IN ANY POSITION TO NEGOTIATE, MARTIN.

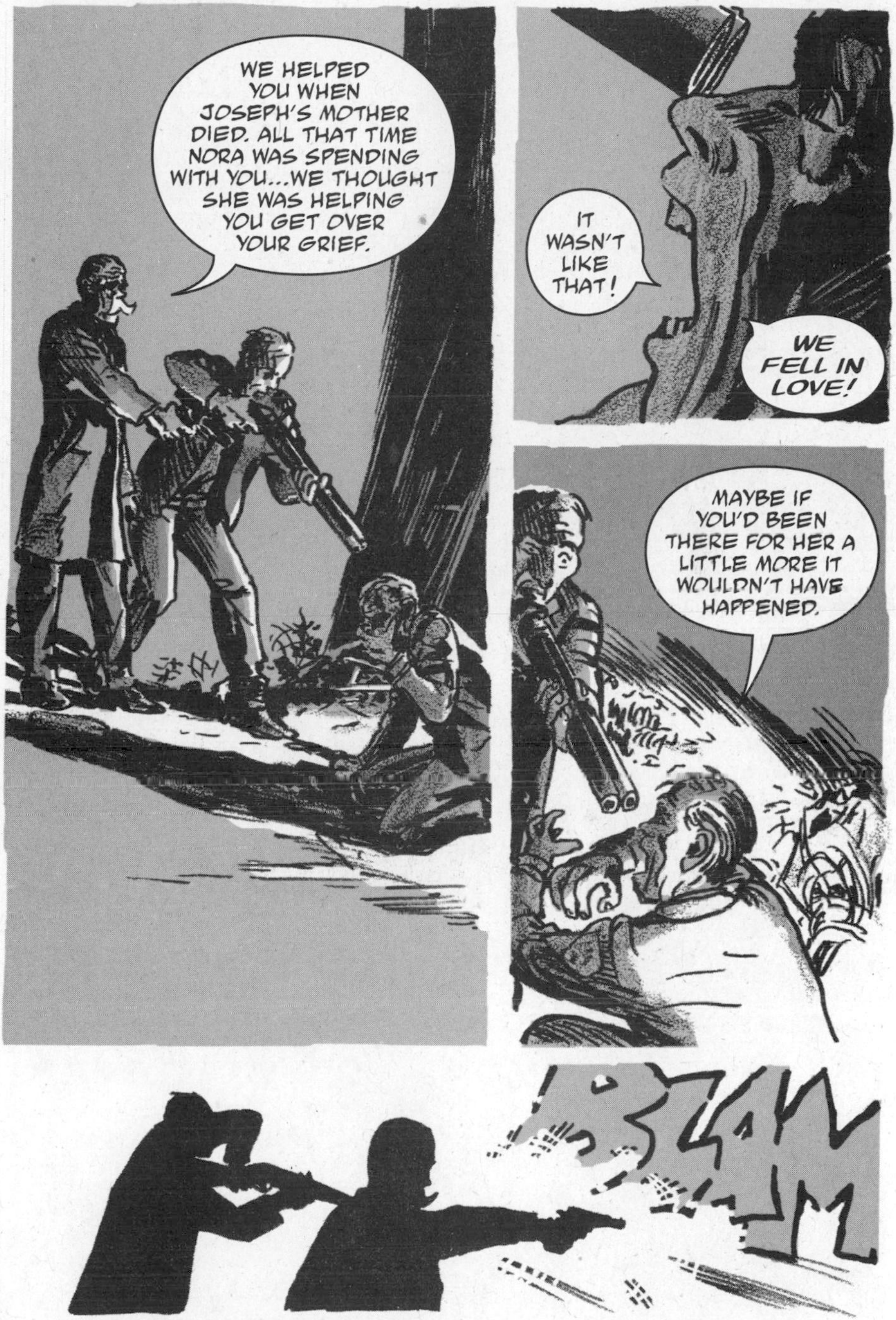
WE HELPED YOU WHEN JOSEPH'S MOTHER DIED. ALL THAT TIME NORA WAS SPENDING WITH YOU...WE THOUGHT SHE WAS HELPING YOU GET OVER YOUR GRIEF.
IT WASN'T LIKE THAT!
WE FELL IN LOVE!
MAYBE IF YOU'D BEEN THERE FOR HER A LITTLE MORE IT WOULDN'T HAVE HAPPENED.
BLAM

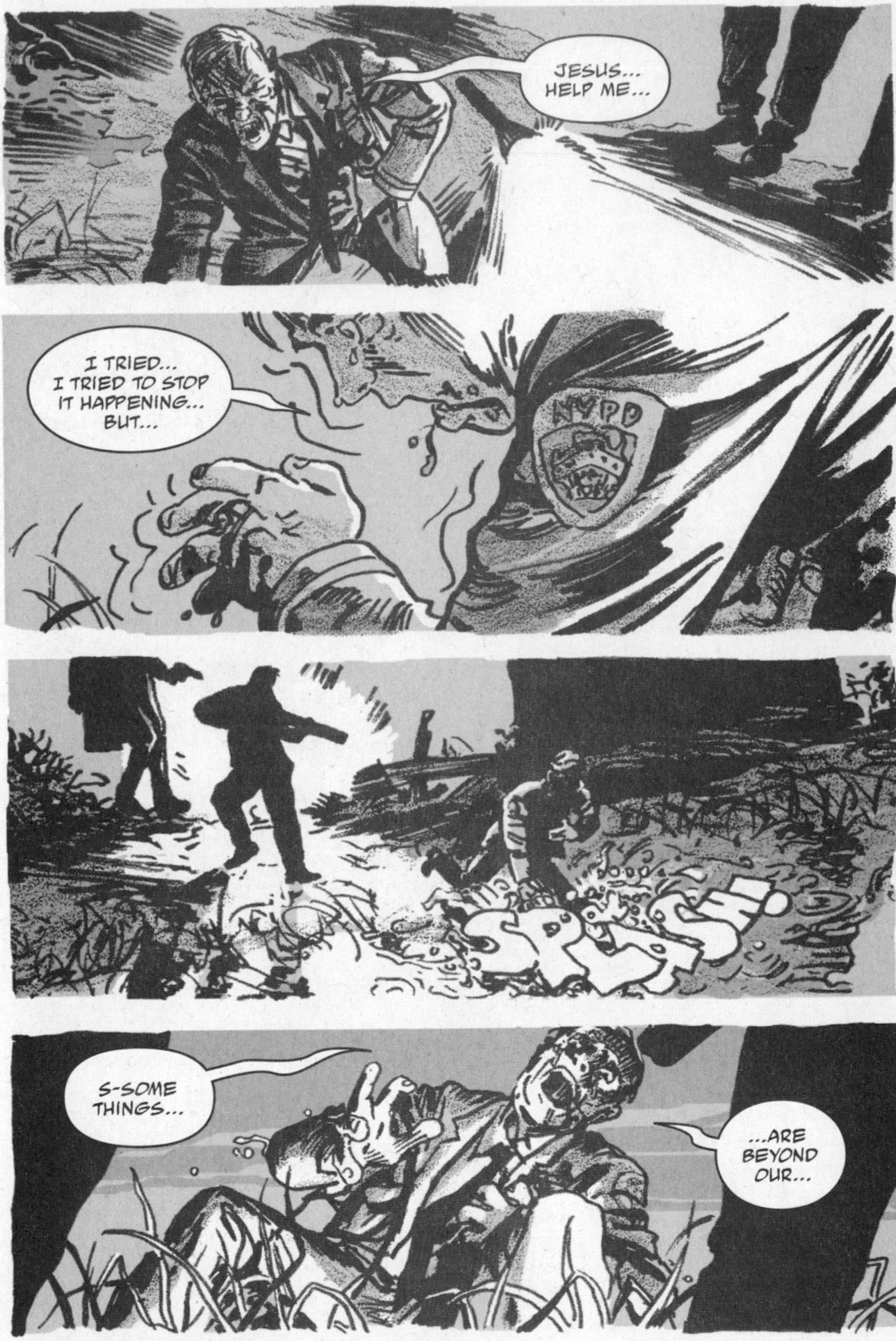
JESUS... HELP ME...
I TRIED... I TRIED TO STOP IT HAPPENING... BUT...
S-SOME THINGS...
...ARE BEYOND OUR...

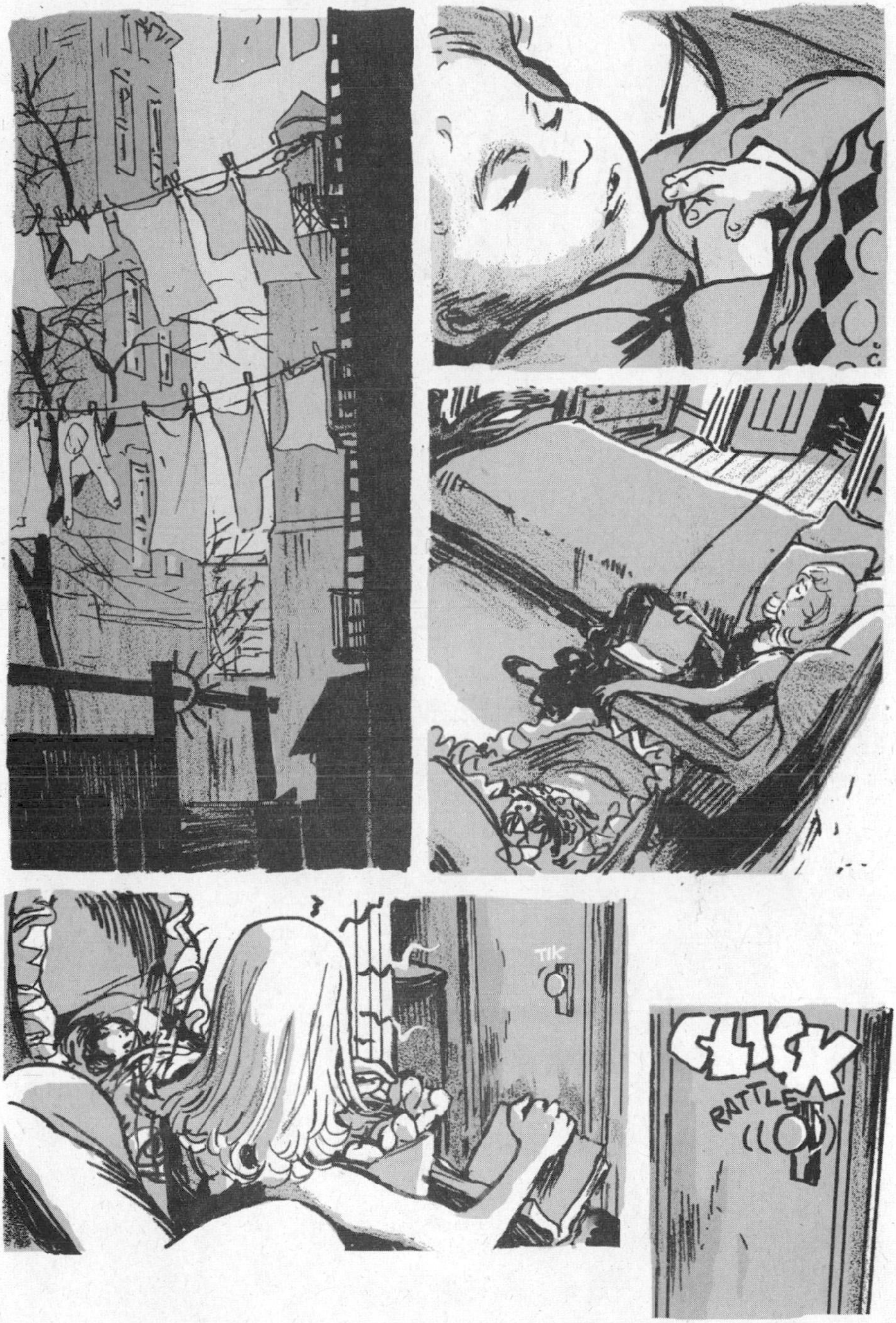
TIK
CLICK
RATTLE

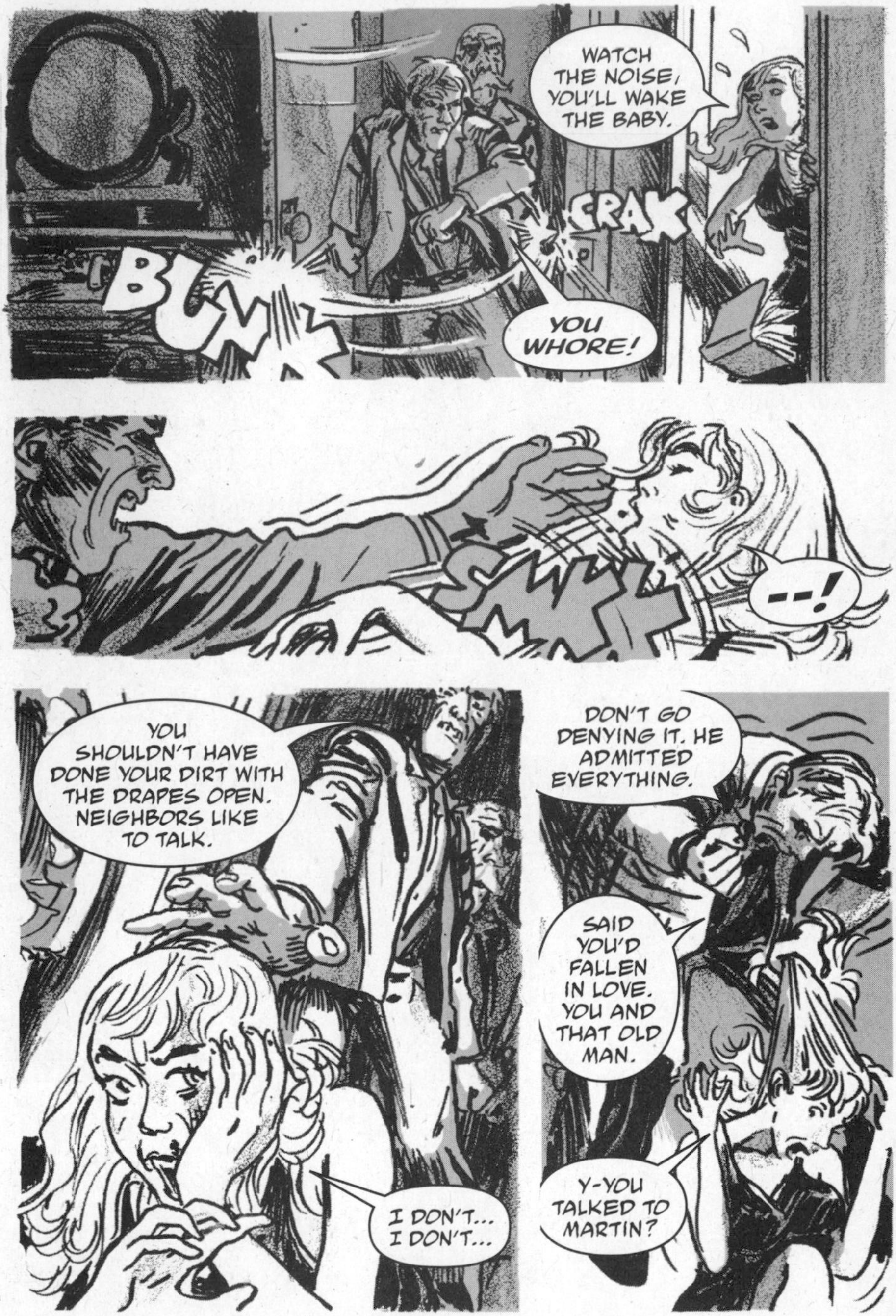
WATCH THE NOISE, YOU'LL WAKE THE BABY.
BUM
CRAK
YOU WHORE!
SMAK
--!
YOU SHOULDN'T HAVE DONE YOUR DIRT WITH THE DRAPES OPEN. NEIGHBORS LIKE TO TALK.
I DON'T... I DON'T...
DON'T GO DENYING IT. HE ADMITTED EVERYTHING.
SAID YOU'D FALLEN IN LOVE. YOU AND THAT OLD MAN.
Y-YOU TALKED TO MARTIN?

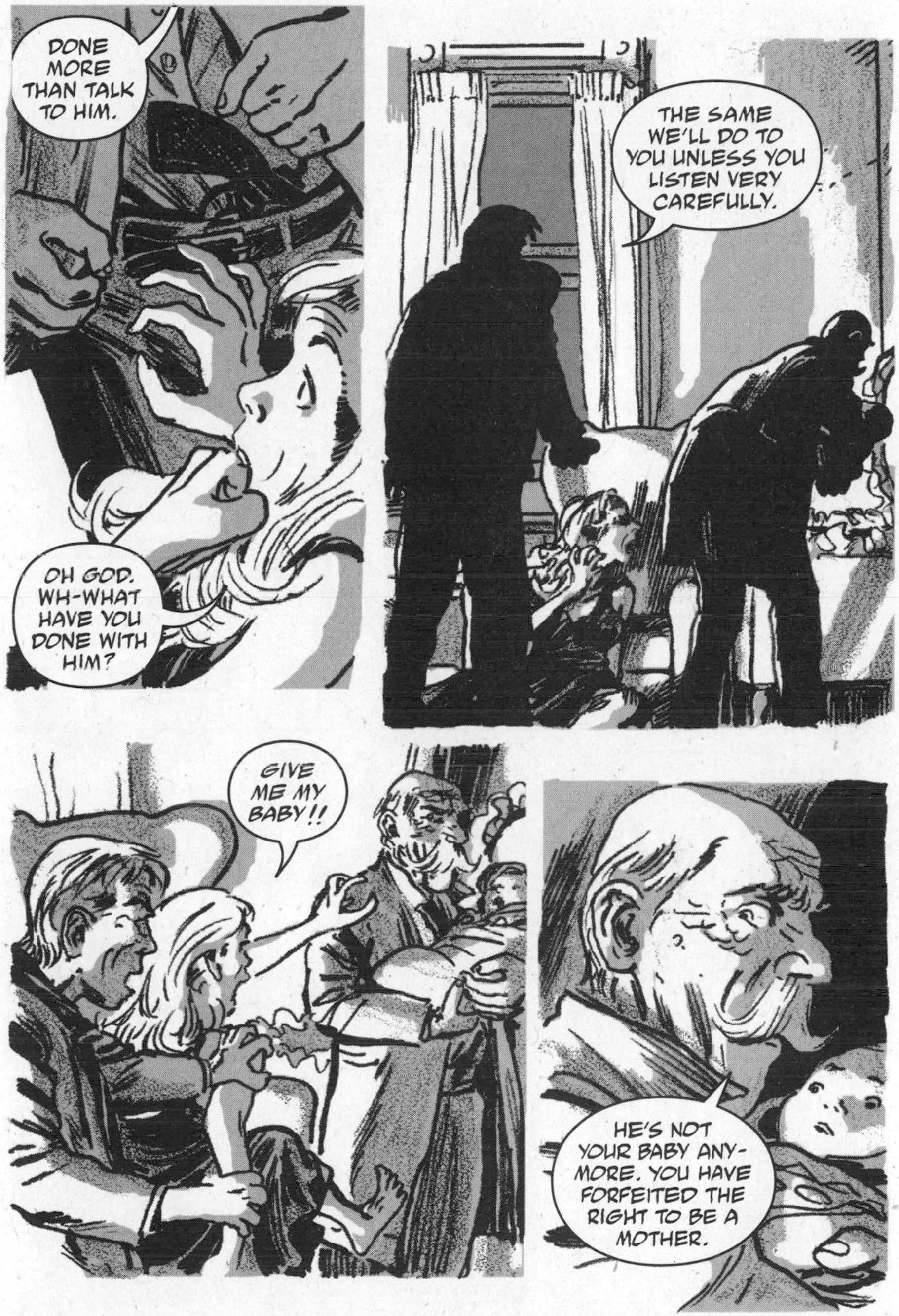
DONE MORE THAN TALK TO HIM.
OH GOD. WH-WHAT HAVE YOU DONE WITH HIM?
THE SAME WE'LL DO TO YOU UNLESS YOU LISTEN VERY CAREFULLY.
GIVE ME MY BABY!!
HE'S NOT YOUR BABY ANY-MORE. YOU HAVE FORFEITED THE RIGHT TO BE A MOTHER.

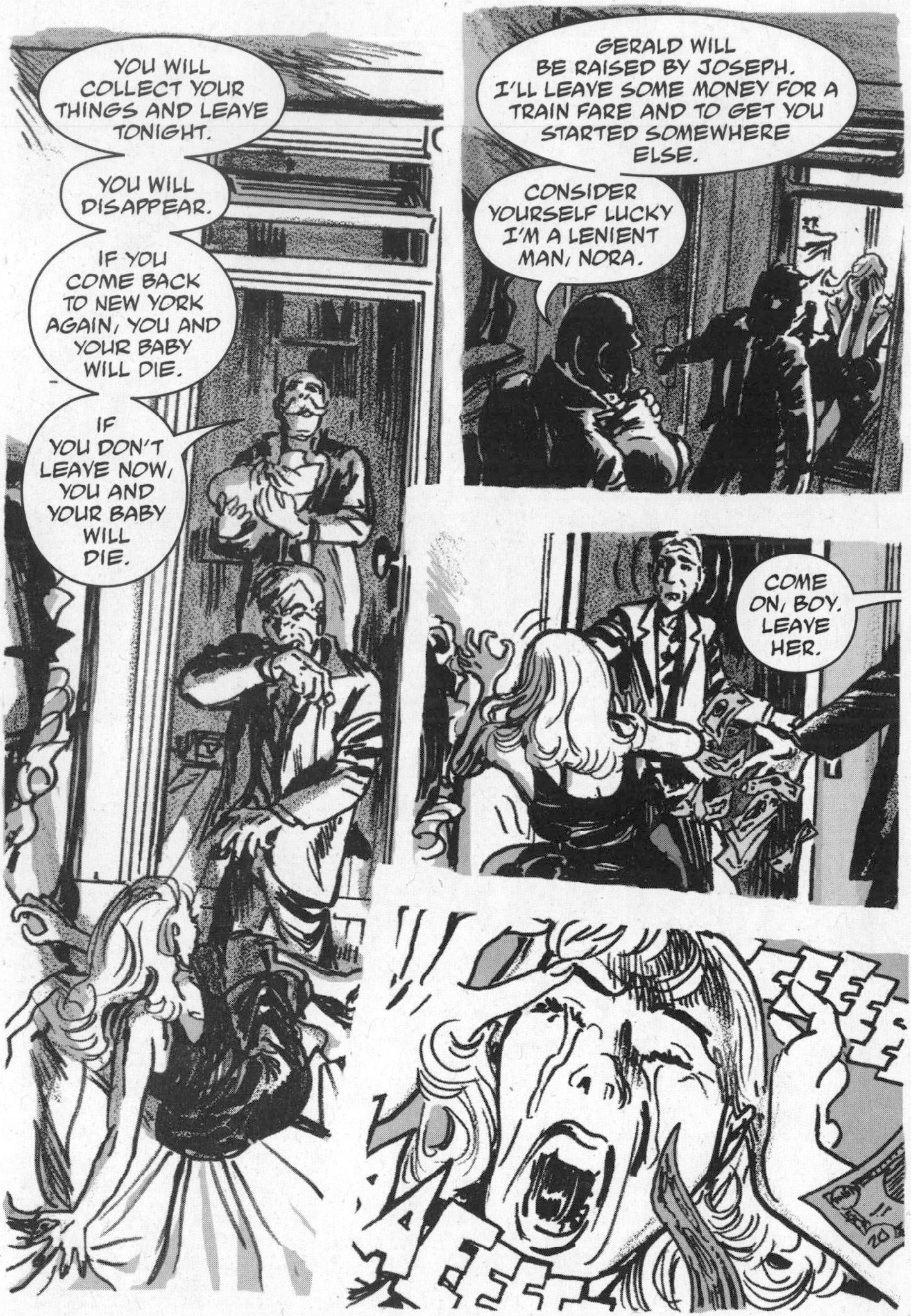
YOU WILL COLLECT YOUR THINGS AND LEAVE TONIGHT.
YOU WILL DISAPPEAR.
IF YOU COME BACK TO NEW YORK AGAIN, YOU AND YOUR BABY WILL DIE.
IF YOU DON'T LEAVE NOW, YOU AND YOUR BABY WILL DIE.
GERALD WILL BE RAISED BY JOSEPH. I'LL LEAVE SOME MONEY FOR A TRAIN FARE AND TO GET YOU STARTED SOMEWHERE ELSE.
CONSIDER YOURSELF LUCKY I'M A LENIENT MAN, NORA.
COME ON, BOY. LEAVE HER.

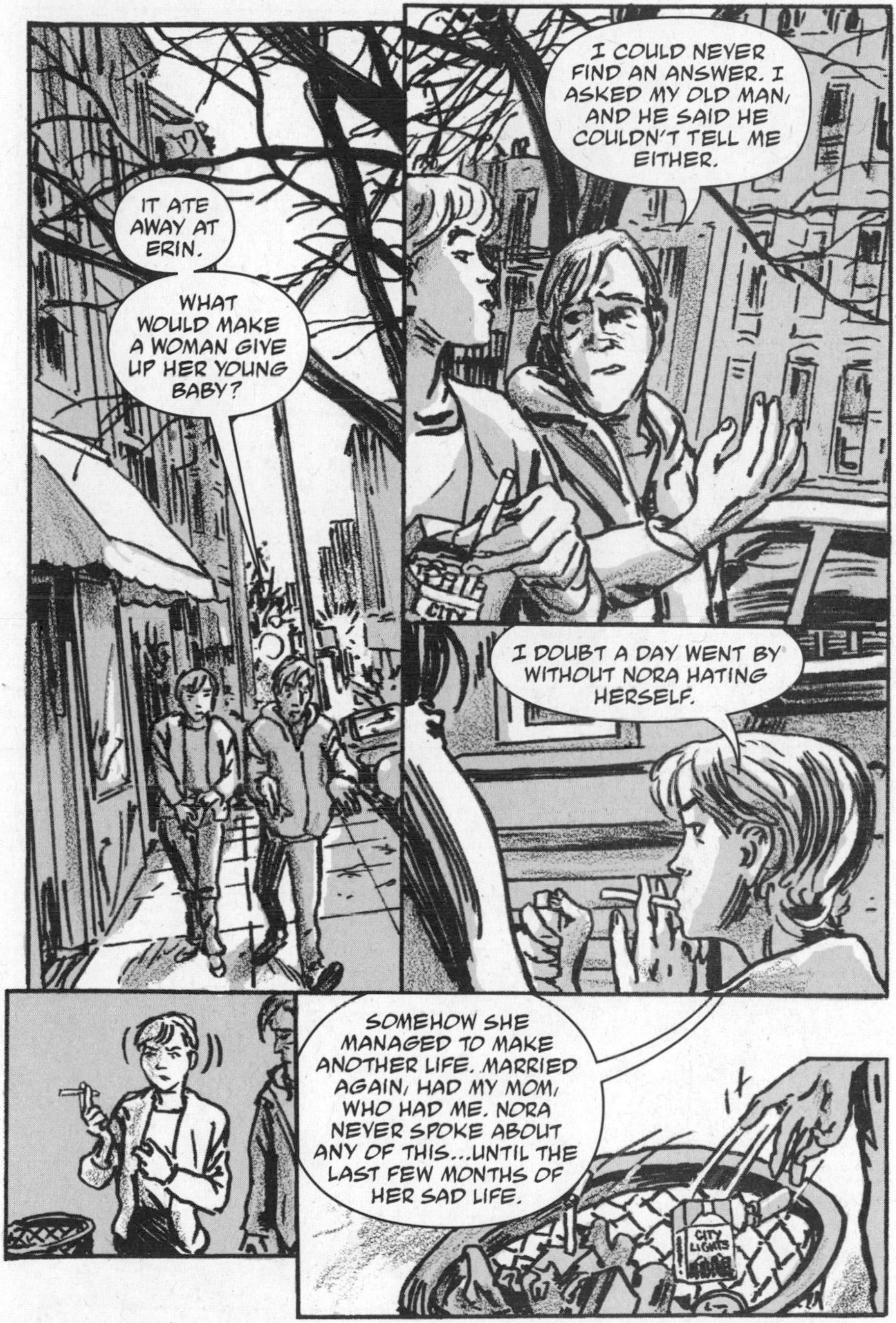
IT ATE AWAY AT ERIN.
WHAT WOULD MAKE A WOMAN GIVE UP HER YOUNG BABY?
I COULD NEVER FIND AN ANSWER. I ASKED MY OLD MAN, AND HE SAID HE COULDN'T TELL ME EITHER.
I DOUBT A DAY WENT BY WITHOUT NORA HATING HERSELF.
SOMEHOW SHE MANAGED TO MAKE ANOTHER LIFE. MARRIED AGAIN, HAD MY MOM, WHO HAD ME. NORA NEVER SPOKE ABOUT ANY OF THIS...UNTIL THE LAST FEW MONTHS OF HER SAD LIFE.
CITY LIGHTS

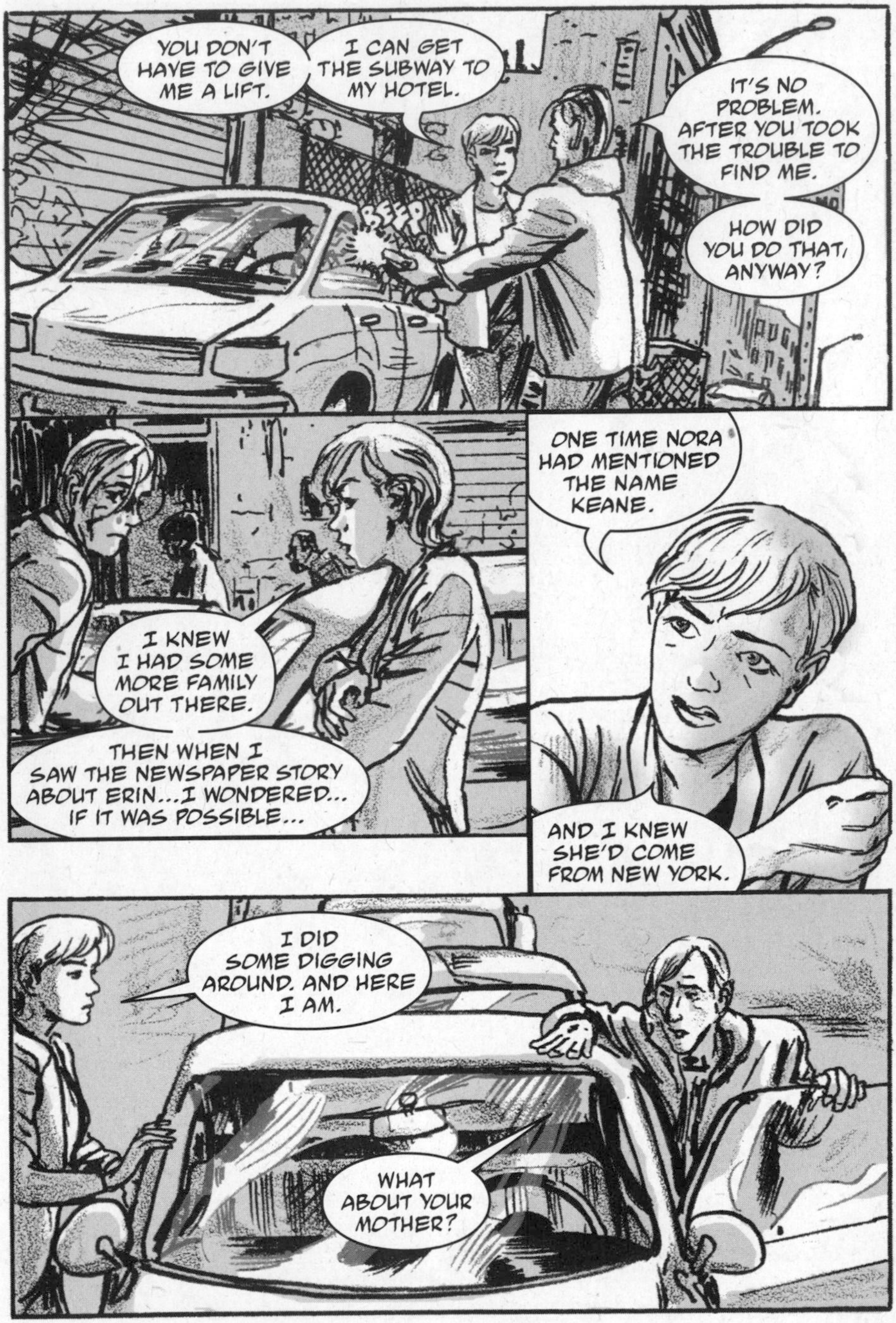
YOU DON'T HAVE TO GIVE ME A LIFT.
I CAN GET THE SUBWAY TO MY HOTEL.
IT'S NO PROBLEM. AFTER YOU TOOK THE TROUBLE TO FIND ME.
HOW DID YOU DO THAT, ANYWAY?
BEEP
I KNEW I HAD SOME MORE FAMILY OUT THERE.
THEN WHEN I SAW THE NEWSPAPER STORY ABOUT ERIN...I WONDERED... IF IT WAS POSSIBLE...
ONE TIME NORA HAD MENTIONED THE NAME KEANE.
AND I KNEW SHE'D COME FROM NEW YORK.
I DID SOME DIGGING AROUND. AND HERE I AM.
WHAT ABOUT YOUR MOTHER?

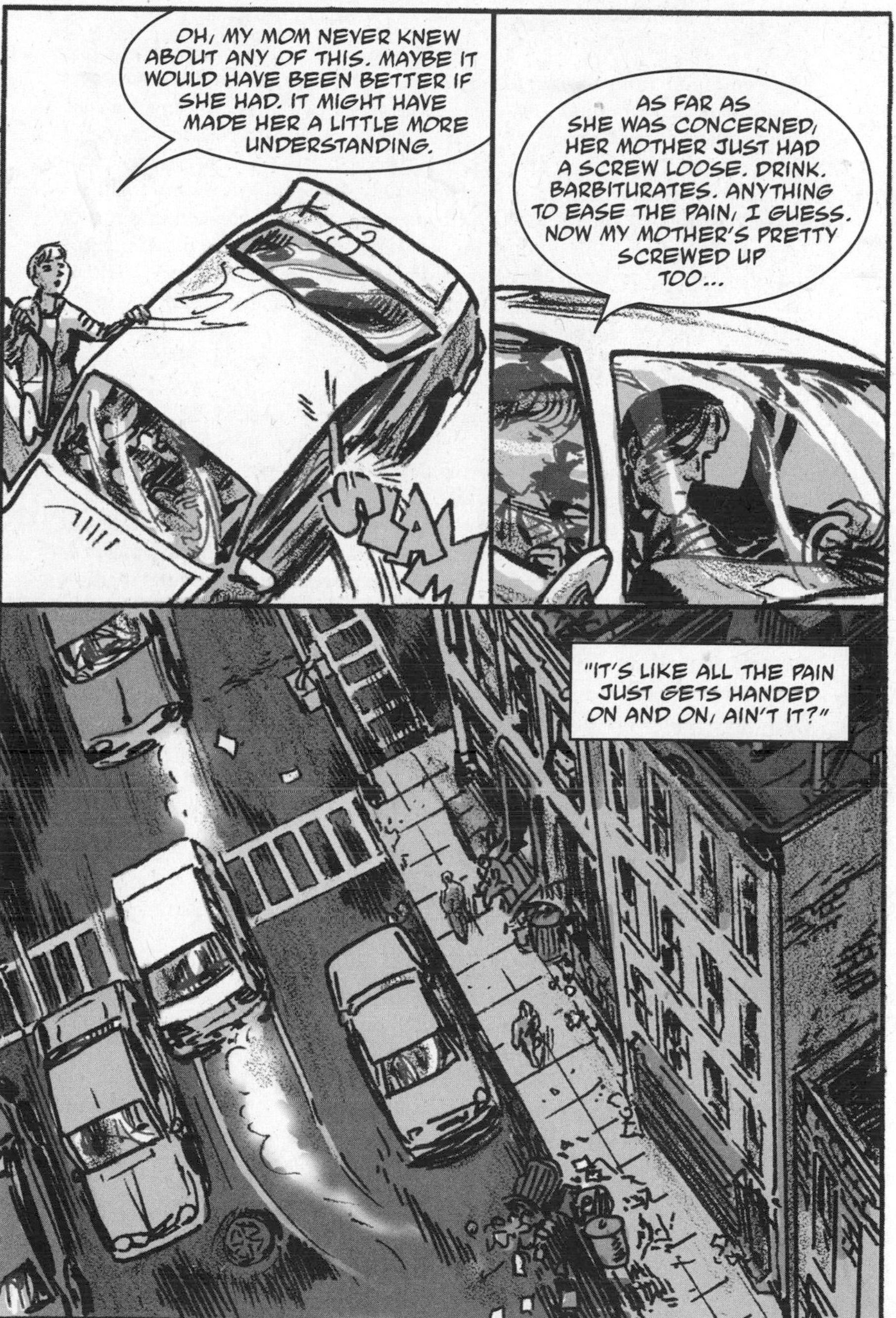
OH, MY MOM NEVER KNEW ABOUT ANY OF THIS. MAYBE IT WOULD HAVE BEEN BETTER IF SHE HAD. IT MIGHT HAVE MADE HER A LITTLE MORE UNDERSTANDING.
SLAM
AS FAR AS SHE WAS CONCERNED, HER MOTHER JUST HAD A SCREW LOOSE. DRINK. BARBITURATES. ANYTHING TO EASE THE PAIN, I GUESS. NOW MY MOTHER'S PRETTY SCREWED UP TOO...
"IT'S LIKE ALL THE PAIN JUST GETS HANDED ON AND ON, AIN'T IT?"

As I emerged from the wretched shock of the city morgue, the sun was beginning to drop behind the great buildings of Manhattan. I, who had fearlessly encountered the more infamous saloons and gambling houses of the Bowery, had a sudden, all-consuming dread of the coming dark. I ran across town, across avenue, down lawless alley. I stopped to fill my tortured lungs in Washington Square, perhaps hoping that its rarefied air might fortify me a little. It did not. If anything, the nausea I had felt in the pit of my gut while in the morgue intensified. My stomach churned; I sweated. I felt as though the yellow fever that occasionally ravaged this town had me in its sickly grasp. I kept seeing those bodies, those faces.

Those eyes.

Cut some of Sister Helga's stuff?

Sister Helga's eyes disappeared beneath folds of well-scrubbed, well-fed, malevolent yet pious American fat. I had almost fallen into the hall of her boarding house, crashing the front door back on its hinges.

"We're in a dreadful hurry today, Mr. Drury."

Sister Helga did not like her boarders running about. Sister Helga, it seemed to me, only barely managed to countenance our having the temerity to breathe. I sensed she'd rather her boarders remain inanimate in their rooms the entire time, like the corpses on Cripps's marble tables, moving only, slowly, and with due and proper warning, to dispense her the rent money.

Could start section here

Ann looked around in alarm when I threw open the door and ran into our room.

"Michael, what in God's name is it?"

"Hugh," I said, as though this one name, this blurted syllable, would explain everything.

"What about him? Have they caught him?"

Breathlessness and agitation combined to prevent me from speaking. Ann, my sweet Ann, took my inability to articulate as a sign of profound distress.

"Michael, you knew they'd catch him sooner or later. He's been running wild in those hills for years now. It's a wonder he's remained at large for as long as..."

I put my hand on her mouth, quietening her. I shook my head.

"He's here."

Silence seemed to invade the room. Though in truth, it was never silent in this room. We lived too close to the main street, where life and noise never completely died away. My fingers were still on her mouth. She took hold of my wrist. Her fingers slowly massaging my arm.

Without warning, without instruction, I felt my penis engorge, harden. The body is a fugitive to the emotions. It makes its own wild life in the untamed hills. Ann moved my hand from her mouth.

cock? lose?

"You've seen him?" she asked, quietly, as though he might be listening from outside the door.

The thought occurred to me suddenly that he *might* be listening from outside the door. As a child on the streets of Cork, Hugh was a great one for following me around, hidden, nipping into shop fronts and behind carts when I looked behind, only to leap out with the devil's own roar when I least expected it. Arghhh! Had he been waiting outside the morgue? Had he followed me here? Hugh was insane, of this there was no doubt. Therefore no insane action was beyond him.

"Michael? Have you seen him?"

"No. But I saw what he *did*."

So I told her about the city morgue. I even mentioned Cripps's lamentable limp to lend my story a degree of grotesque color. And then I described the murder victims. The way the eyes had been hollowed out of their faces. The exact way that papa and my poor sisters' eyes had been removed. I felt lightheaded talking about it.

"Couldn't it have been someone else? There are a lot of cutthroats and degenerates in New York."

"These wounds weren't simply similar. They were perfect copies. It was…it was as though those missing eyes were a message… *some kind of*

"A message?"

"From Hugh to me. A Furey telegram."

"And what…what did this message say?"

I looked at her. She looked at me. The floorboards creaked in the hall outside. That would be Sister Helga, I told myself.

"He's here. And there is only one reason why he'd be here."

"The same reason you're here. To flee Ireland and make a new life."

I shook my head, as though she were a simple child.

"To find me. To do to me what he did to the rest of my family."

I stood quickly, now that my thickening sex had subsided.

"You don't know that for sure," said Ann.

"I know it sure enough. I know it enough not to risk our staying here."

I got on my knees and reached for the travelling case we kept under the bed.

"What's the use changing boarding houses?"

"We're not changing boarding houses. We're changing cities."

I drew out the case, placed it on the bed, and faced Ann.

"I thought if I put an entire ocean between me and the past — that I'd be free of it forever. But the past has found me. The past is right here. In New York." *The past has found me!*

"The future is in New York too."

"I know a man at the Herald who has property in Chicago. It's a good city, I hear."

"And what if Hugh follows us to Chicago? People like us, we're always running, Michael. From poverty or persecution. But there comes a time when you must stop running. There comes a time when you must face the past." *too much?!*

"So I must face Hugh?"

"If need be. Where did the murders take place?"

"The Bronx Kill."

"The Bronx Kill? Where or what is the Bronx Kill?"

Everything comes down to the Bronx Kill.

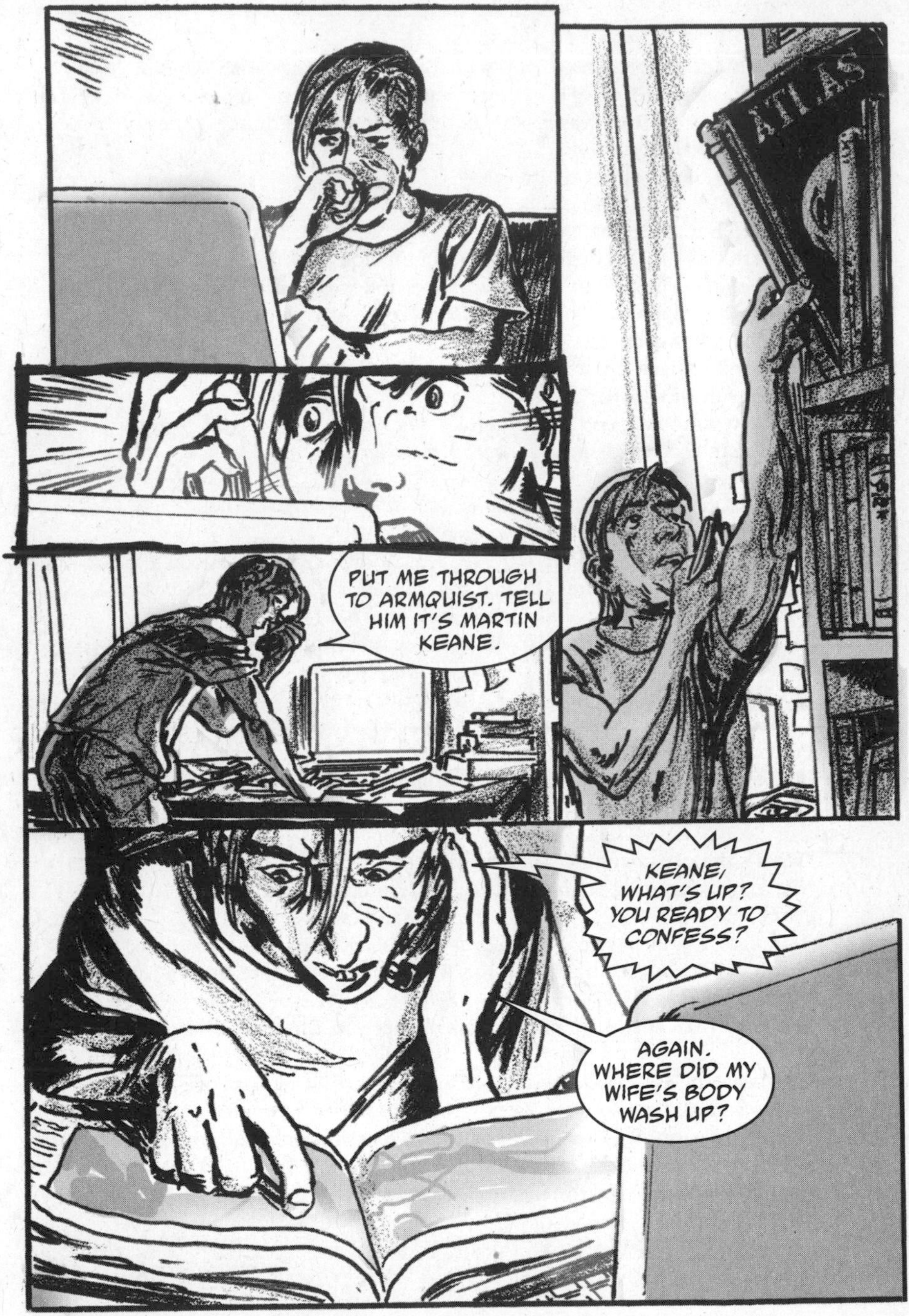
ATLAS
PUT ME THROUGH TO ARMQUIST. TELL HIM IT'S MARTIN KEANE.
KEANE, WHAT'S UP? YOU READY TO CONFESS?
AGAIN. WHERE DID MY WIFE'S BODY WASH UP?

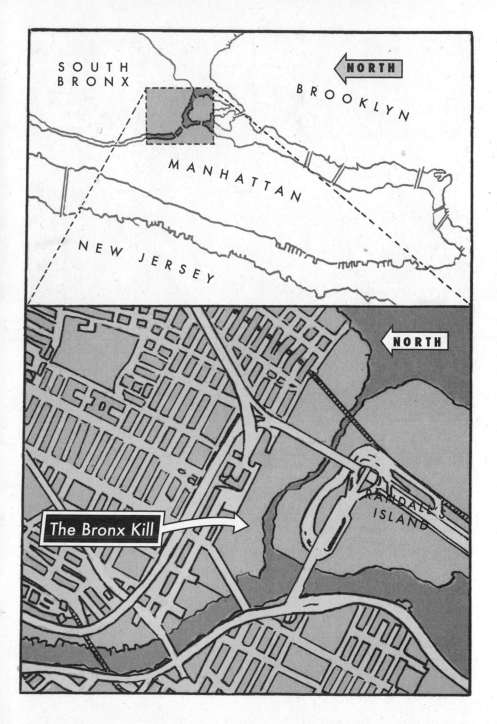

SOUTH BRONX

NORTH

BROOKLYN

MANHATTAN

NEW JERSEY

NORTH

The Bronx Kill

RANDALL'S ISLAND

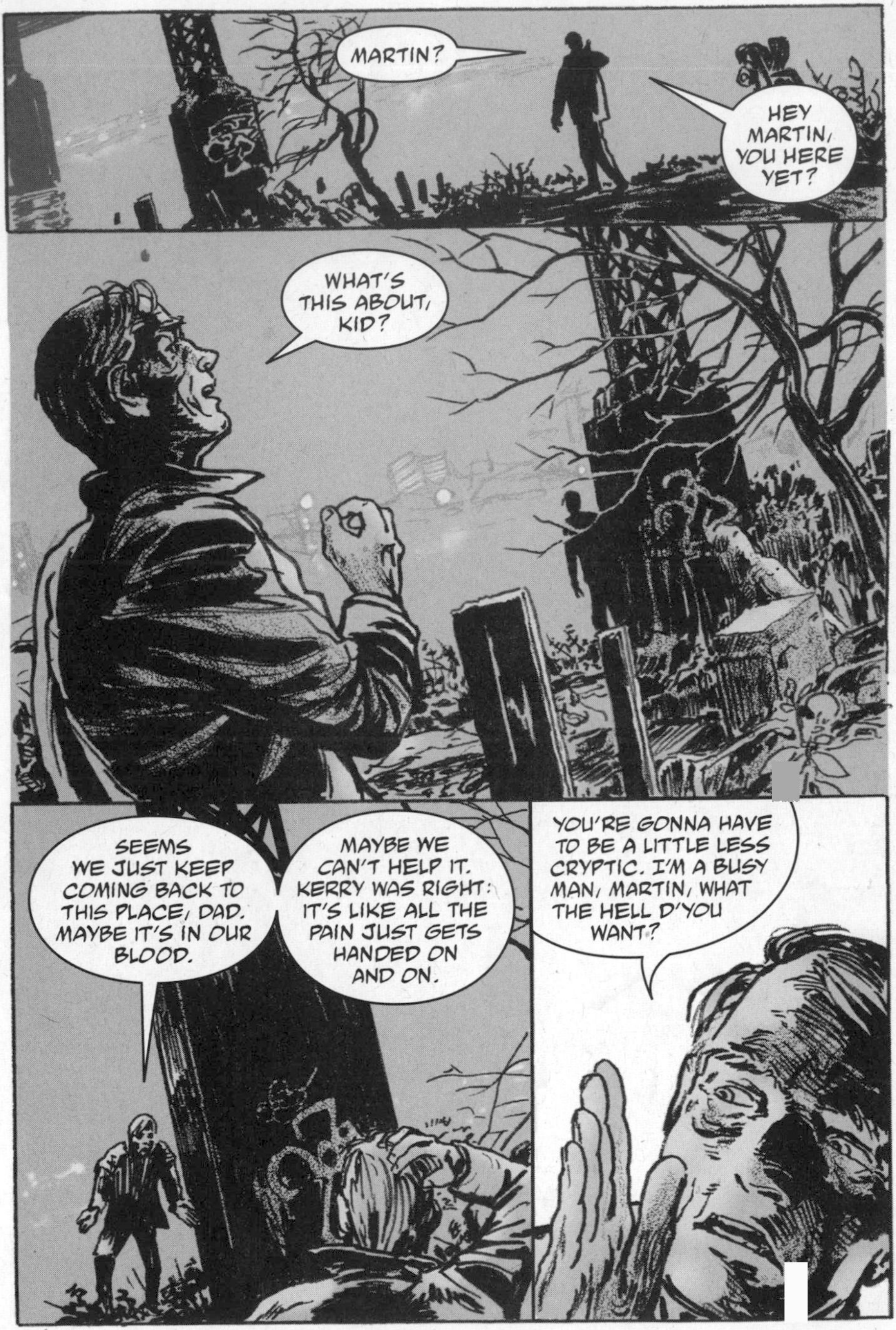
MARTIN?
HEY MARTIN, YOU HERE YET?
WHAT'S THIS ABOUT, KID?
SEEMS WE JUST KEEP COMING BACK TO THIS PLACE, DAD. MAYBE IT'S IN OUR BLOOD.
MAYBE WE CAN'T HELP IT. KERRY WAS RIGHT: IT'S LIKE ALL THE PAIN JUST GETS HANDED ON AND ON.
YOU'RE GONNA HAVE TO BE A LITTLE LESS CRYPTIC. I'M A BUSY MAN, MARTIN, WHAT THE HELL D'YOU WANT?

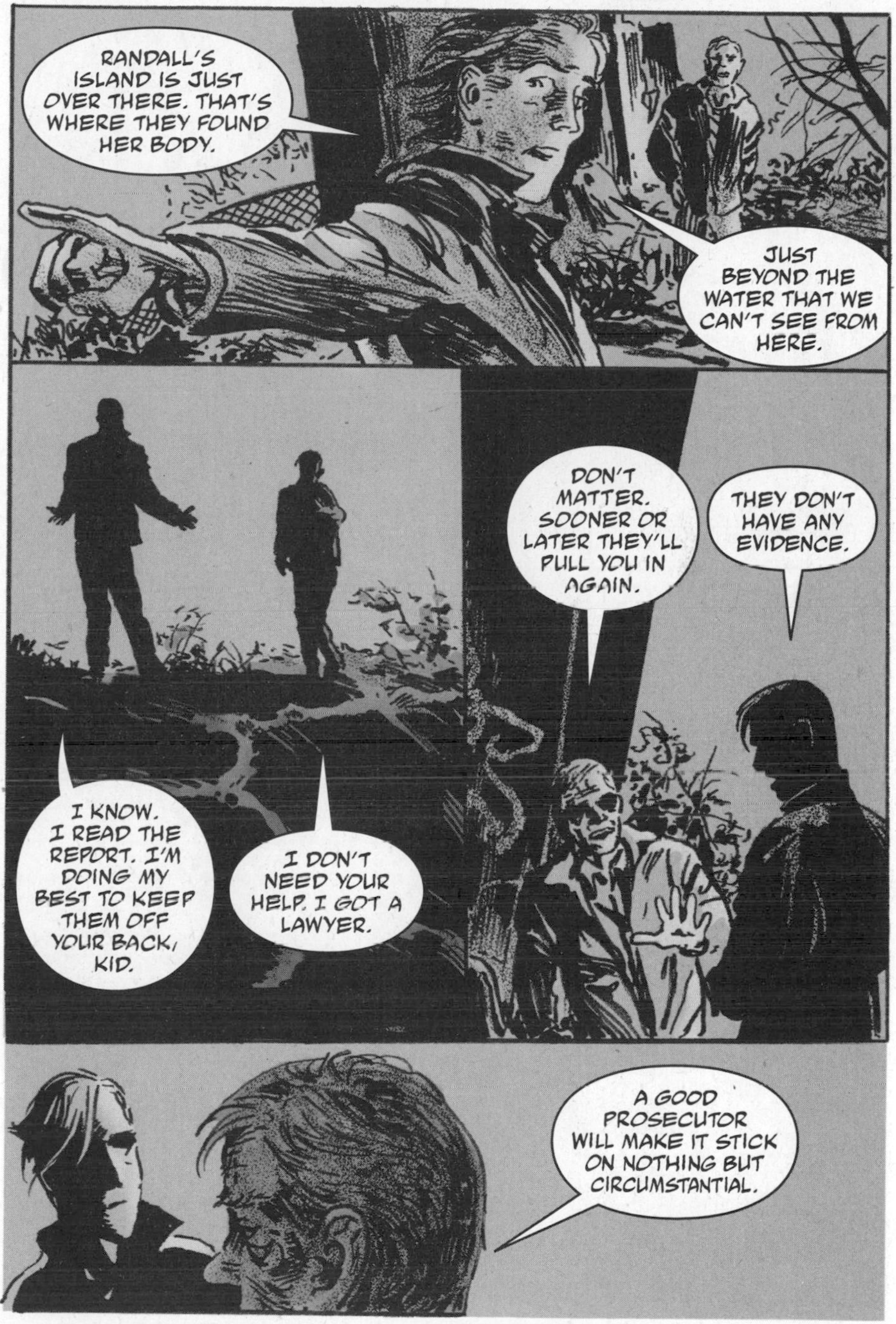
RANDALL'S ISLAND IS JUST OVER THERE. THAT'S WHERE THEY FOUND HER BODY.
JUST BEYOND THE WATER THAT WE CAN'T SEE FROM HERE.
THEY DON'T HAVE ANY EVIDENCE.
DON'T MATTER. SOONER OR LATER THEY'LL PULL YOU IN AGAIN.
I KNOW. I READ THE REPORT. I'M DOING MY BEST TO KEEP THEM OFF YOUR BACK, KID.
I DON'T NEED YOUR HELP. I GOT A LAWYER.
A GOOD PROSECUTOR WILL MAKE IT STICK ON NOTHING BUT CIRCUMSTANTIAL.

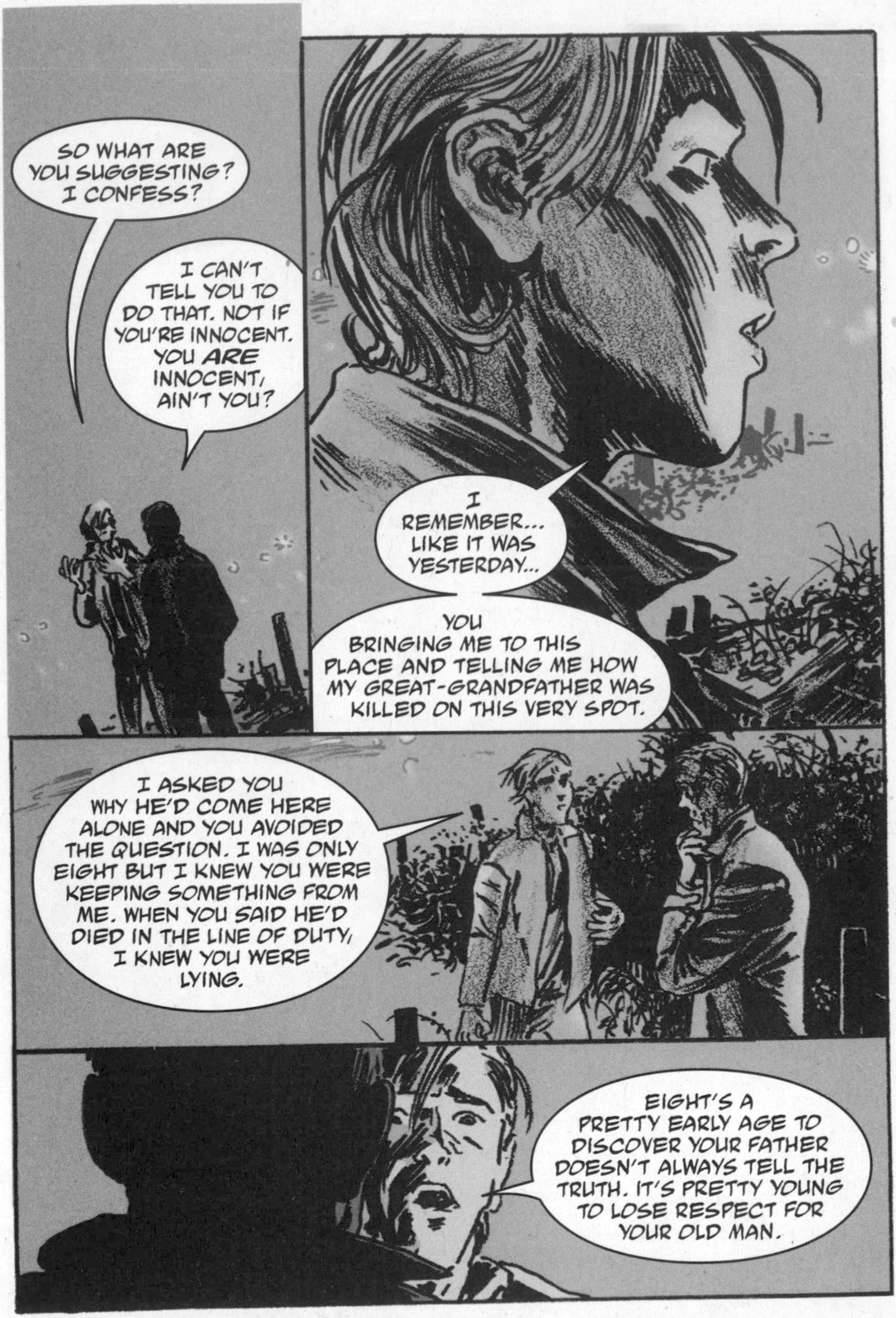
SO WHAT ARE YOU SUGGESTING? I CONFESS?
I CAN'T TELL YOU TO DO THAT. NOT IF YOU'RE INNOCENT. YOU *ARE* INNOCENT, AIN'T YOU?
I REMEMBER... LIKE IT WAS YESTERDAY...
YOU BRINGING ME TO THIS PLACE AND TELLING ME HOW MY GREAT-GRANDFATHER WAS KILLED ON THIS VERY SPOT.
I ASKED YOU WHY HE'D COME HERE ALONE AND YOU AVOIDED THE QUESTION. I WAS ONLY EIGHT BUT I KNEW YOU WERE KEEPING SOMETHING FROM ME. WHEN YOU SAID HE'D DIED IN THE LINE OF DUTY, I KNEW YOU WERE LYING.
EIGHT'S A PRETTY EARLY AGE TO DISCOVER YOUR FATHER DOESN'T ALWAYS TELL THE TRUTH. IT'S PRETTY YOUNG TO LOSE RESPECT FOR YOUR OLD MAN.

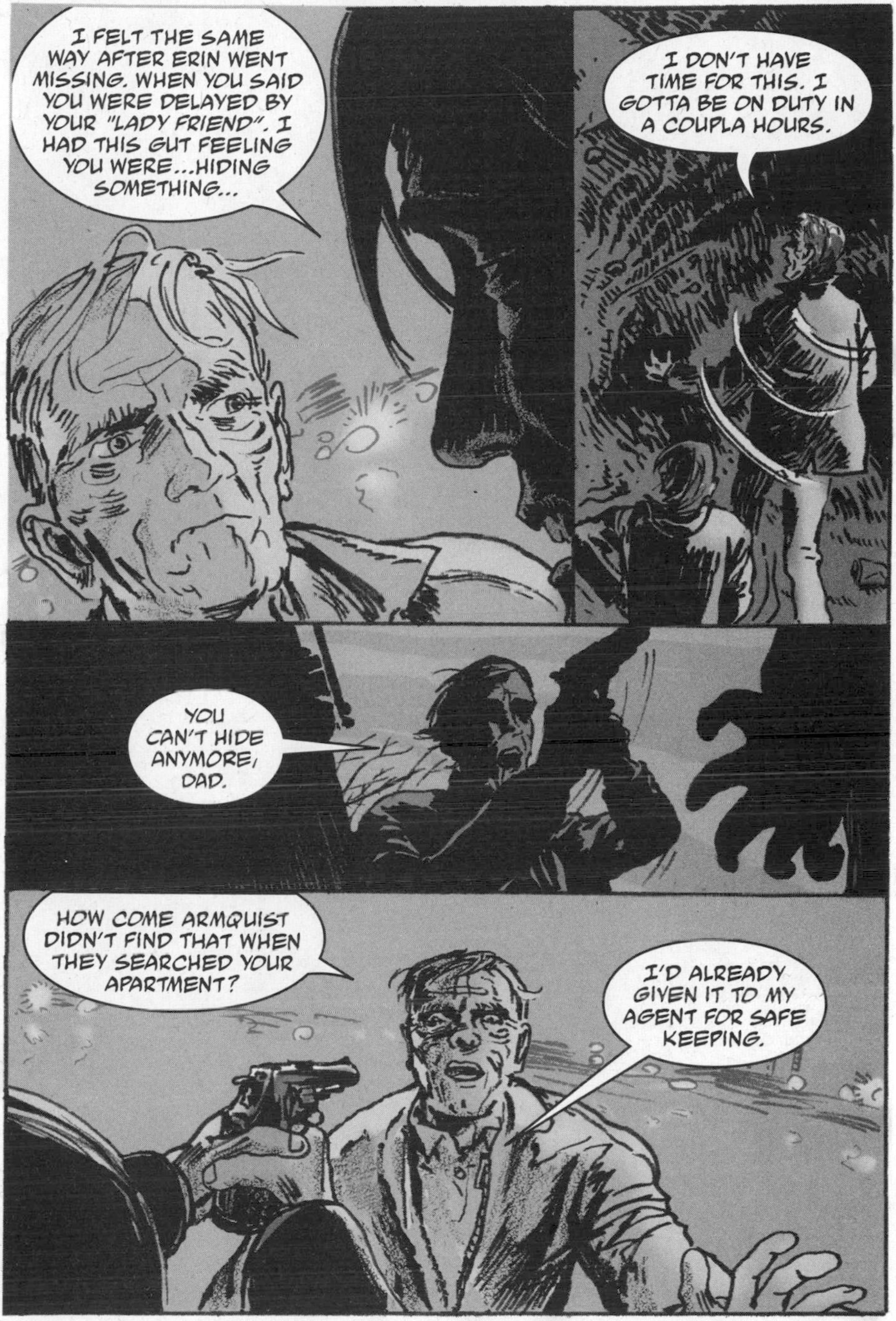

I FELT THE SAME WAY AFTER ERIN WENT MISSING. WHEN YOU SAID YOU WERE DELAYED BY YOUR "LADY FRIEND". I HAD THIS GUT FEELING YOU WERE...HIDING SOMETHING...
I DON'T HAVE TIME FOR THIS. I GOTTA BE ON DUTY IN A COUPLA HOURS.
YOU CAN'T HIDE ANYMORE, DAD.
HOW COME ARMQUIST DIDN'T FIND THAT WHEN THEY SEARCHED YOUR APARTMENT?
I'D ALREADY GIVEN IT TO MY AGENT FOR SAFE KEEPING.

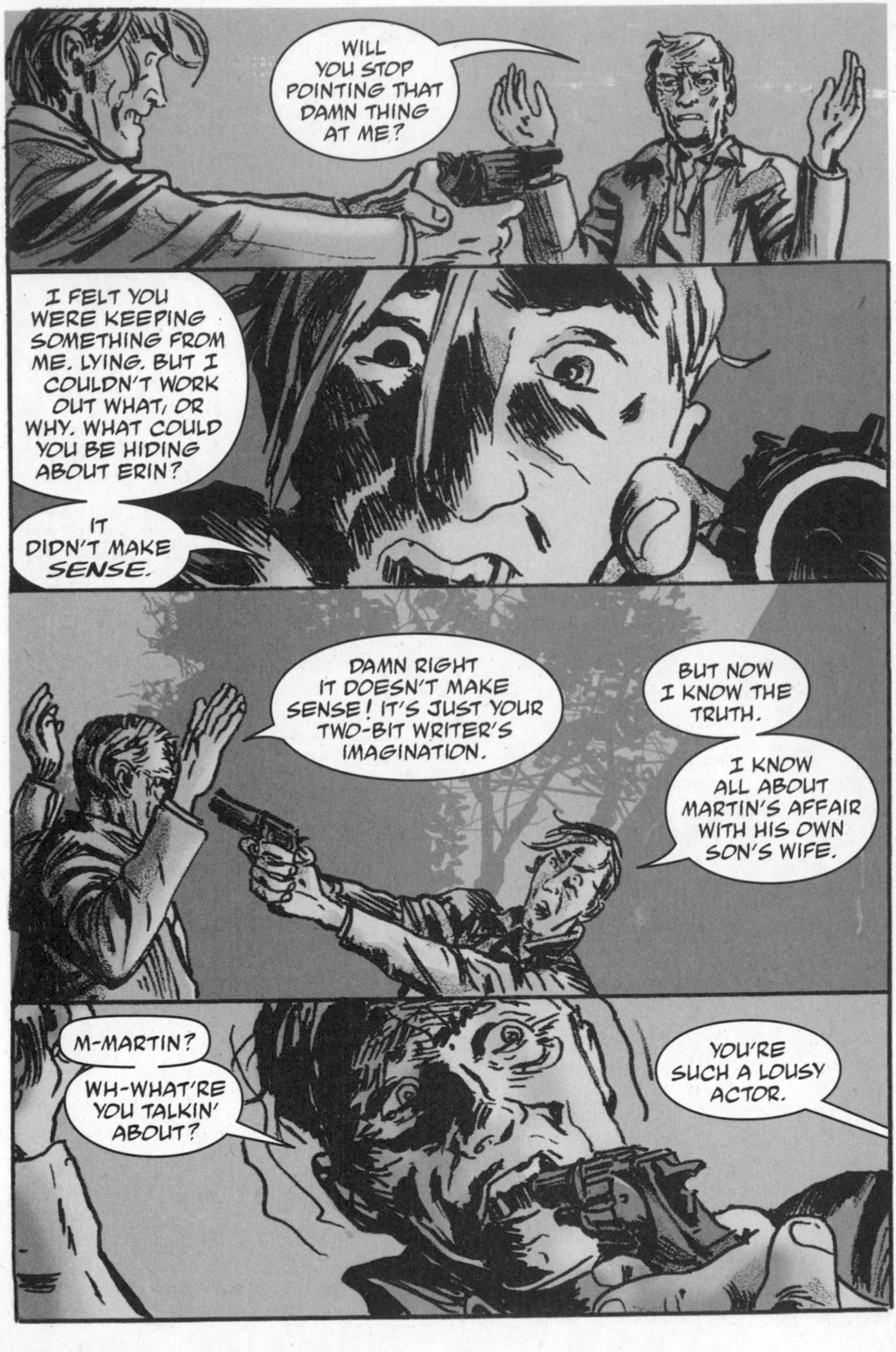

WILL YOU STOP POINTING THAT DAMN THING AT ME?
I FELT YOU WERE KEEPING SOMETHING FROM ME. LYING. BUT I COULDN'T WORK OUT WHAT, OR WHY. WHAT COULD YOU BE HIDING ABOUT ERIN?
IT DIDN'T MAKE SENSE.
DAMN RIGHT IT DOESN'T MAKE SENSE! IT'S JUST YOUR TWO-BIT WRITER'S IMAGINATION.
BUT NOW I KNOW THE TRUTH.
I KNOW ALL ABOUT MARTIN'S AFFAIR WITH HIS OWN SON'S WIFE.
M-MARTIN?
WH-WHAT'RE YOU TALKIN' ABOUT?
YOU'RE SUCH A LOUSY ACTOR.

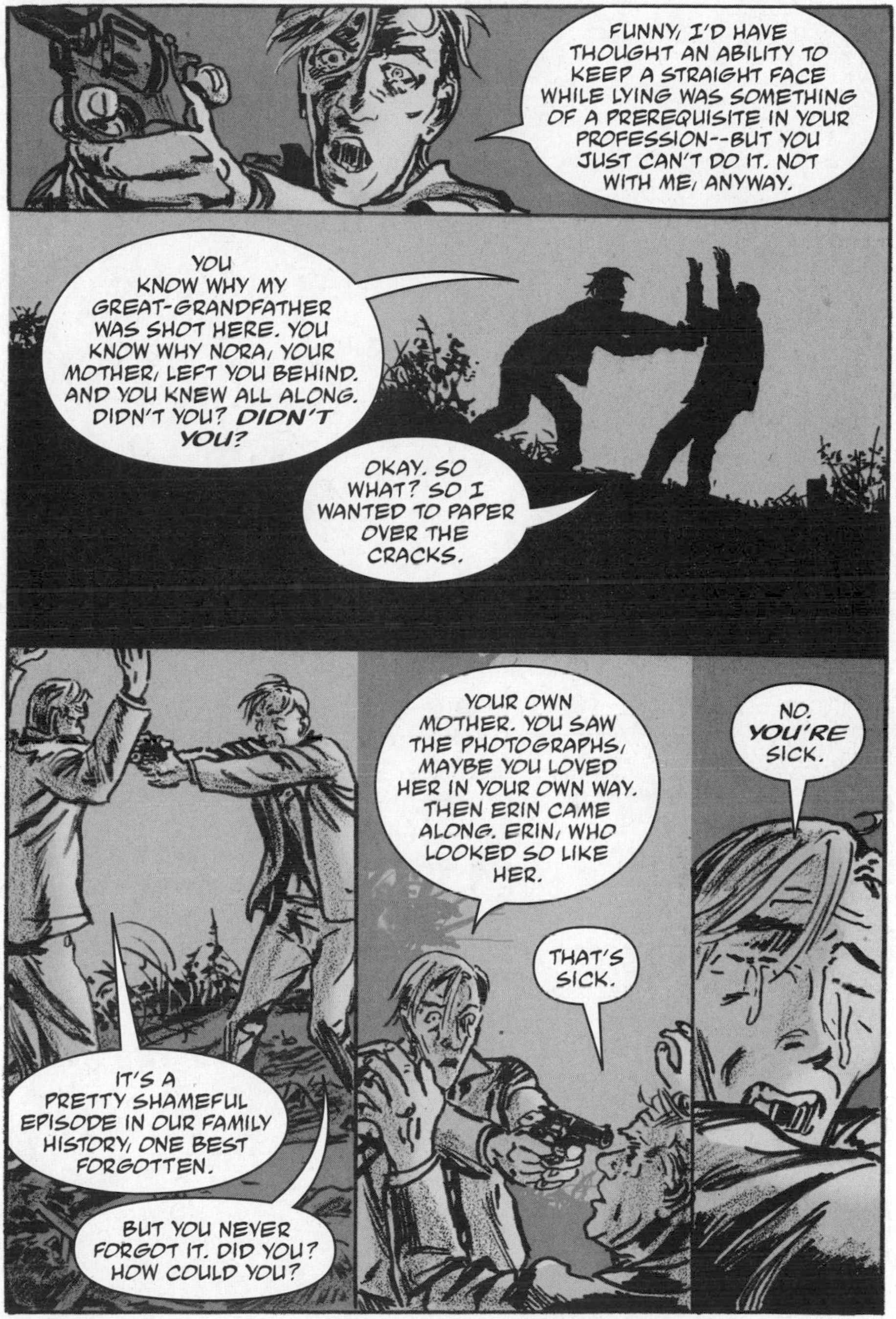
FUNNY, I'D HAVE THOUGHT AN ABILITY TO KEEP A STRAIGHT FACE WHILE LYING WAS SOMETHING OF A PREREQUISITE IN YOUR PROFESSION--BUT YOU JUST CAN'T DO IT. NOT WITH ME, ANYWAY.
YOU KNOW WHY MY GREAT-GRANDFATHER WAS SHOT HERE. YOU KNOW WHY NORA, YOUR MOTHER, LEFT YOU BEHIND. AND YOU KNEW ALL ALONG. DIDN'T YOU? DIDN'T YOU?
OKAY. SO WHAT? SO I WANTED TO PAPER OVER THE CRACKS.
IT'S A PRETTY SHAMEFUL EPISODE IN OUR FAMILY HISTORY, ONE BEST FORGOTTEN.
BUT YOU NEVER FORGOT IT. DID YOU? HOW COULD YOU?
YOUR OWN MOTHER. YOU SAW THE PHOTOGRAPHS, MAYBE YOU LOVED HER IN YOUR OWN WAY. THEN ERIN CAME ALONG. ERIN, WHO LOOKED SO LIKE HER.
THAT'S SICK.
NO. YOU'RE SICK.

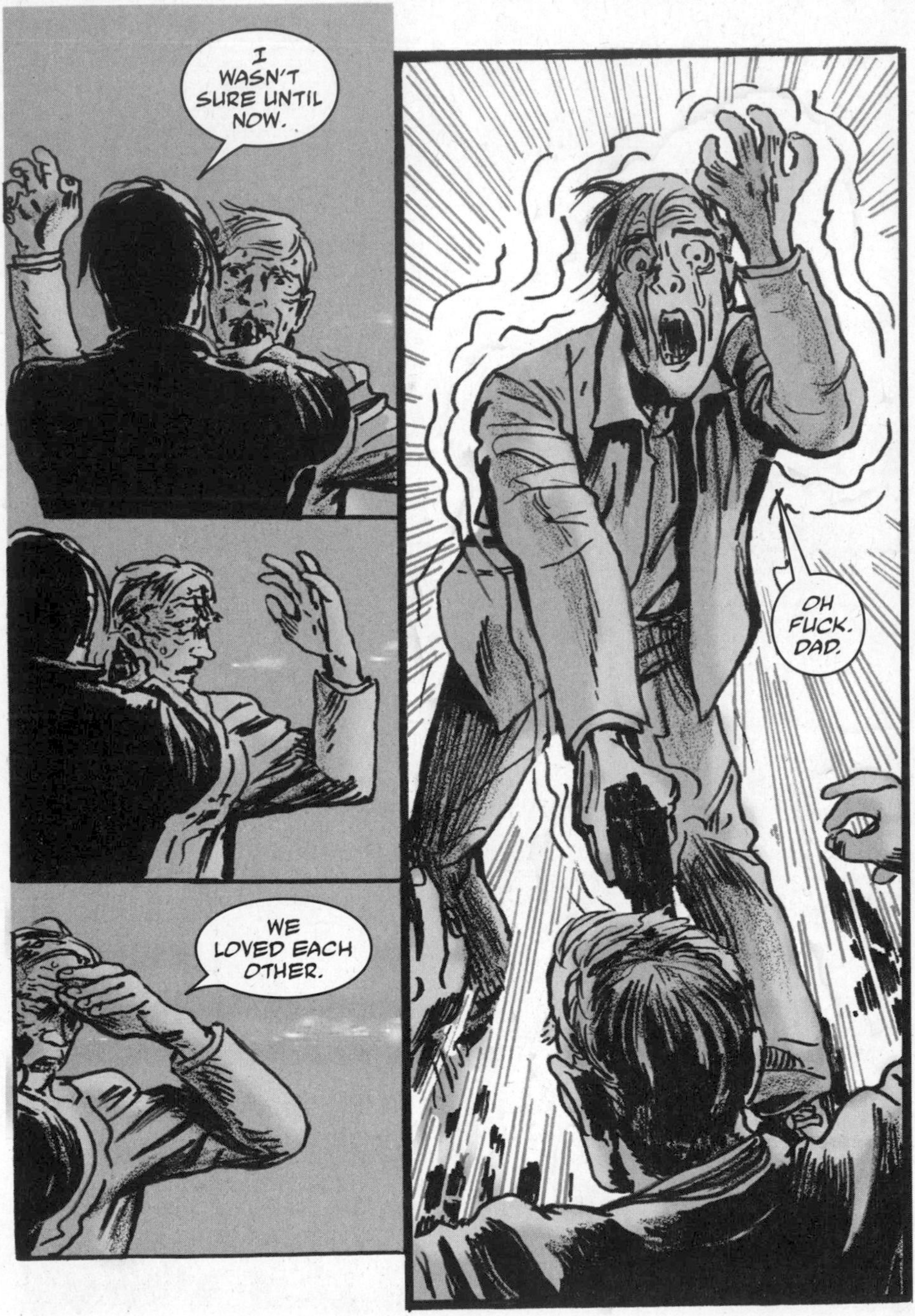
I WASN'T SURE UNTIL NOW.
WE LOVED EACH OTHER.
OH FUCK. DAD.

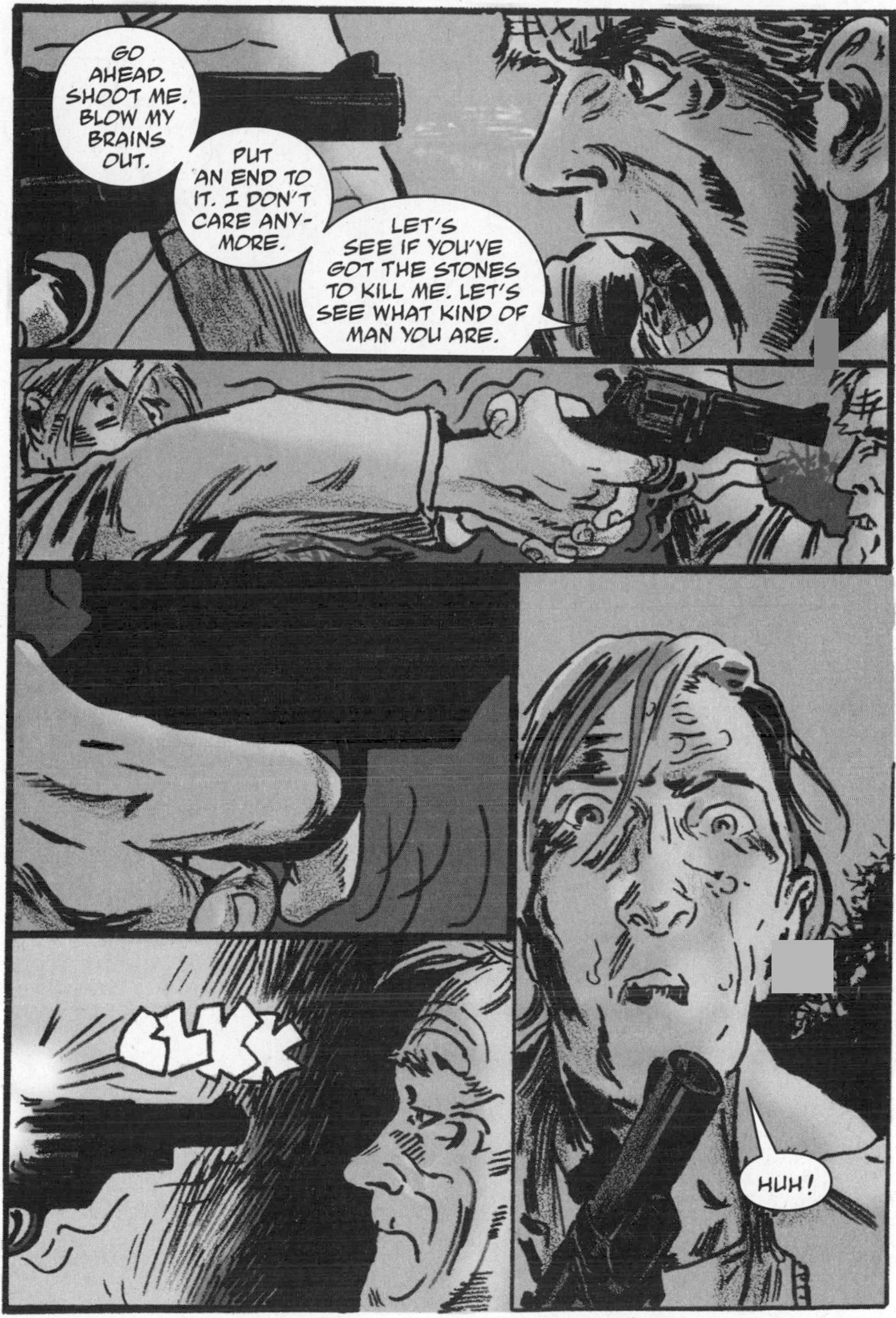

GO AHEAD. SHOOT ME. BLOW MY BRAINS OUT.
PUT AN END TO IT. I DON'T CARE ANY-MORE.
LET'S SEE IF YOU'VE GOT THE STONES TO KILL ME. LET'S SEE WHAT KIND OF MAN YOU ARE.
CLIK
HUH!

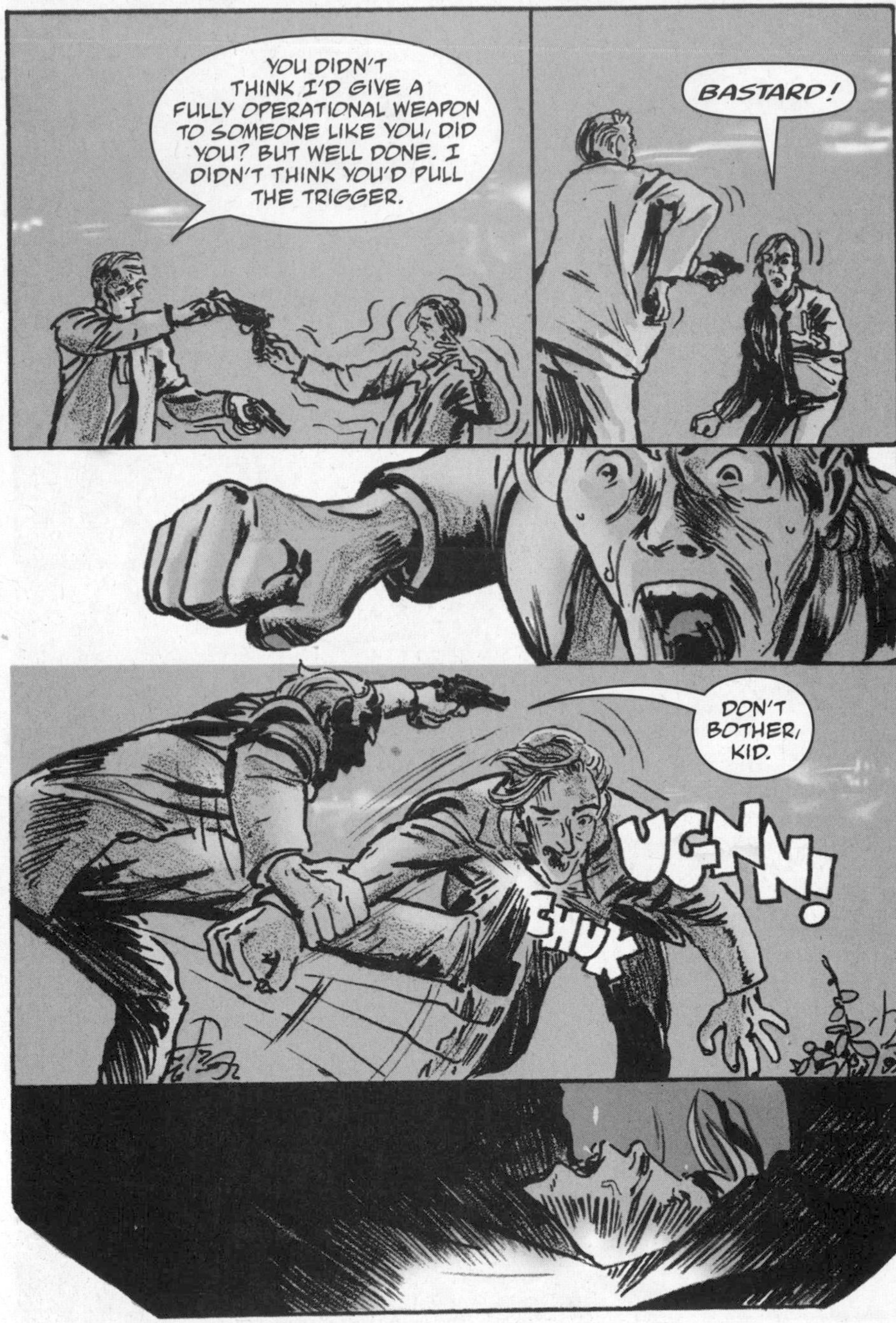
YOU DIDN'T THINK I'D GIVE A FULLY OPERATIONAL WEAPON TO SOMEONE LIKE YOU, DID YOU? BUT WELL DONE. I DIDN'T THINK YOU'D PULL THE TRIGGER.
BASTARD!
DON'T BOTHER, KID.
UGNN!
CHUK

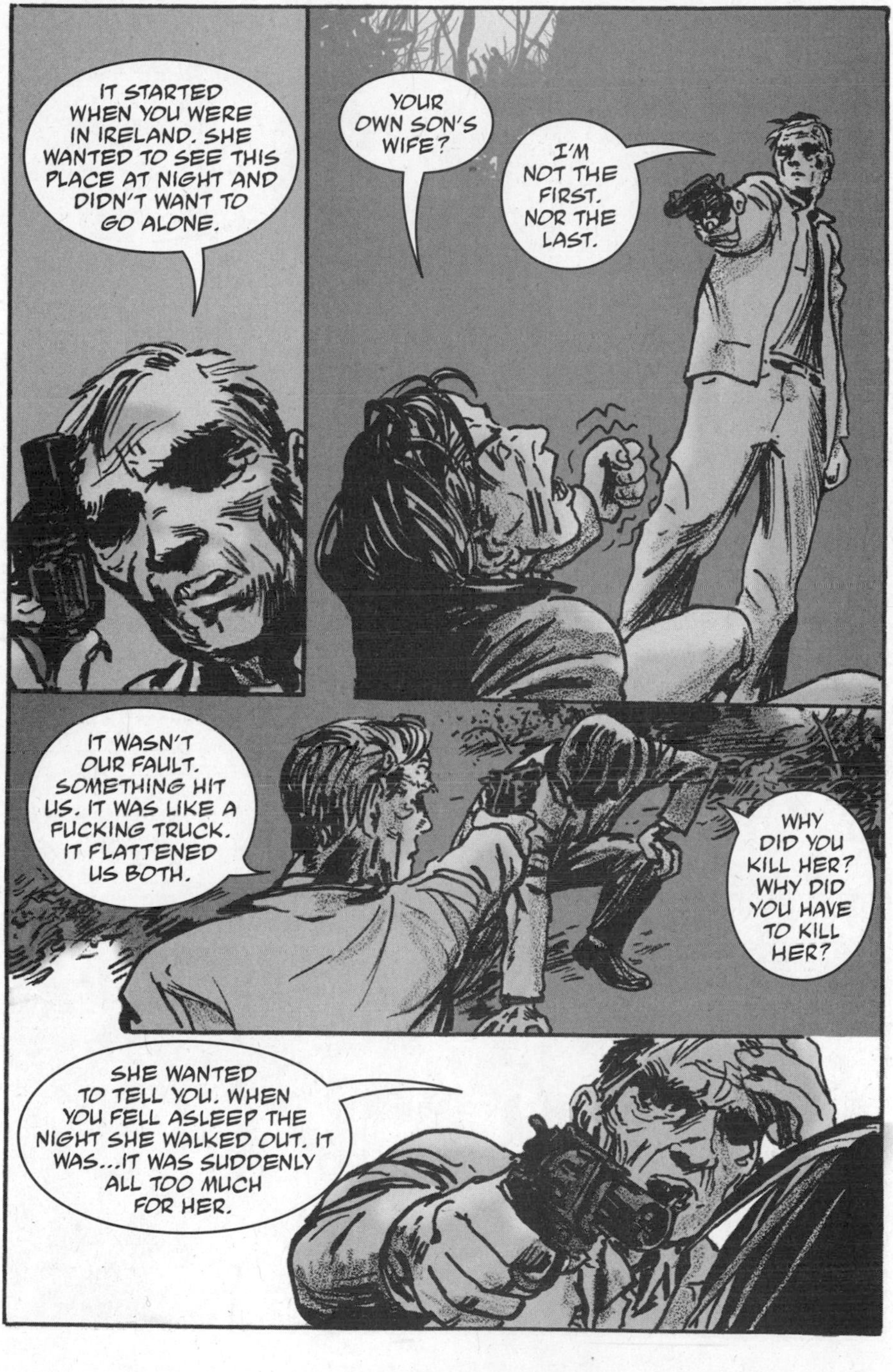
IT STARTED WHEN YOU WERE IN IRELAND. SHE WANTED TO SEE THIS PLACE AT NIGHT AND DIDN'T WANT TO GO ALONE.
YOUR OWN SON'S WIFE?
I'M NOT THE FIRST. NOR THE LAST.
IT WASN'T OUR FAULT. SOMETHING HIT US. IT WAS LIKE A FUCKING TRUCK. IT FLATTENED US BOTH.
WHY DID YOU KILL HER? WHY DID YOU HAVE TO KILL HER?
SHE WANTED TO TELL YOU. WHEN YOU FELL ASLEEP THE NIGHT SHE WALKED OUT. IT WAS...IT WAS SUDDENLY ALL TOO MUCH FOR HER.

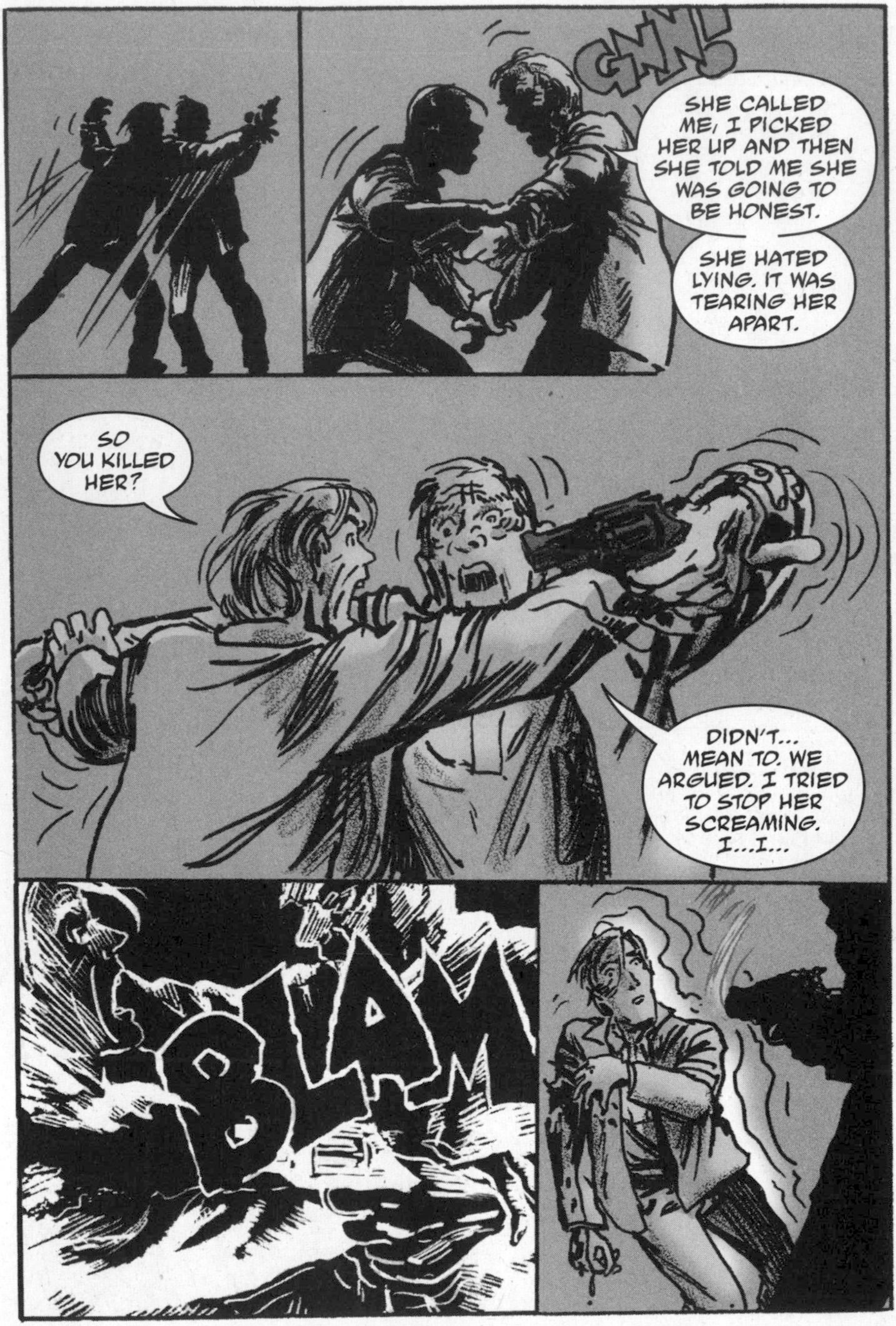
GNN!
SHE CALLED ME, I PICKED HER UP AND THEN SHE TOLD ME SHE WAS GOING TO BE HONEST.
SHE HATED LYING. IT WAS TEARING HER APART.
SO YOU KILLED HER?
DIDN'T... MEAN TO. WE ARGUED. I TRIED TO STOP HER SCREAMING. I...I...
BLAM

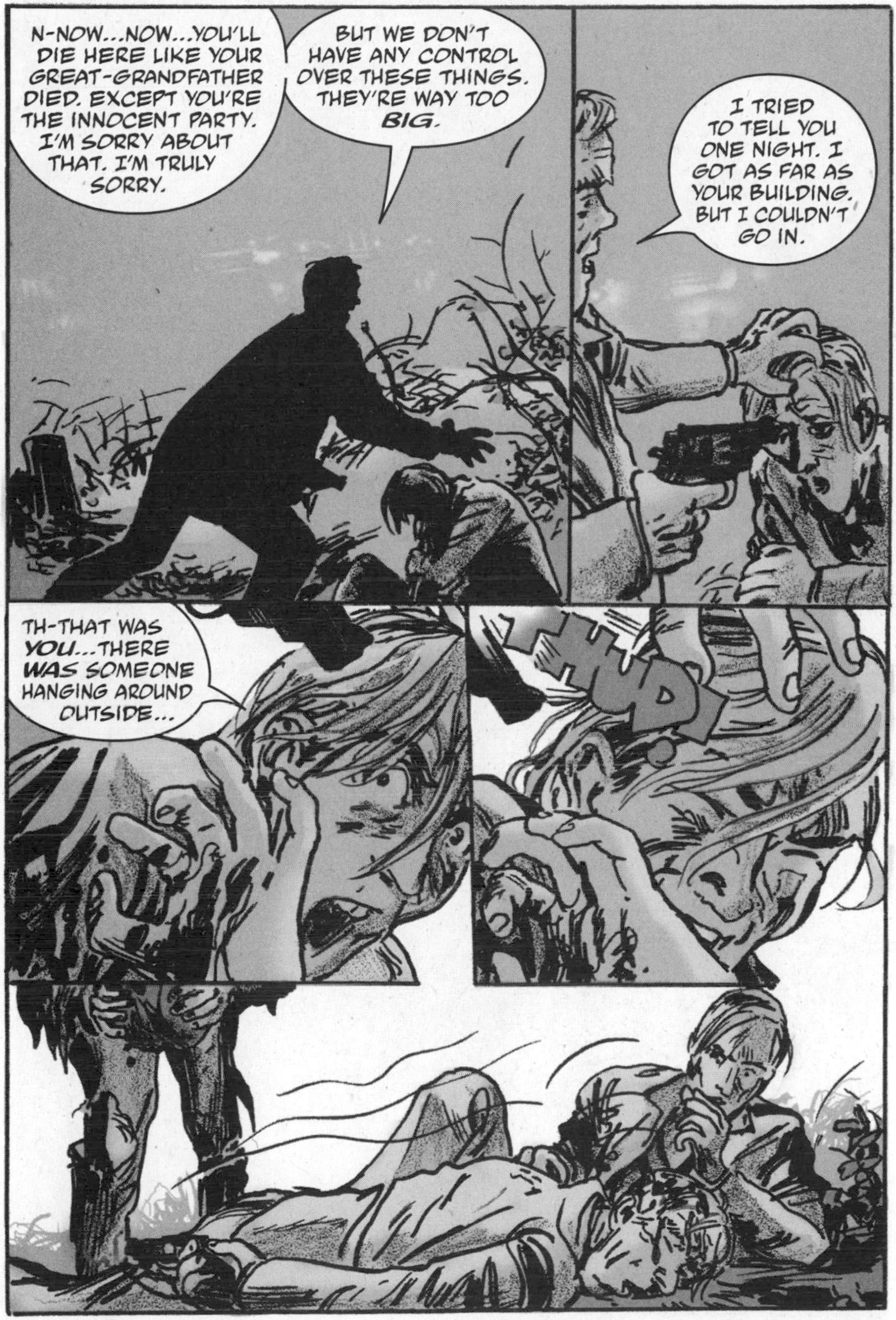
N-NOW...NOW...YOU'LL DIE HERE LIKE YOUR GREAT-GRANDFATHER DIED. EXCEPT YOU'RE THE INNOCENT PARTY. I'M SORRY ABOUT THAT. I'M TRULY SORRY.
BUT WE DON'T HAVE ANY CONTROL OVER THESE THINGS. THEY'RE WAY TOO *BIG*.
I TRIED TO TELL YOU ONE NIGHT. I GOT AS FAR AS YOUR BUILDING. BUT I COULDN'T GO IN.
TH-THAT WAS *YOU*...THERE *WAS* SOMEONE HANGING AROUND OUTSIDE...
THUD

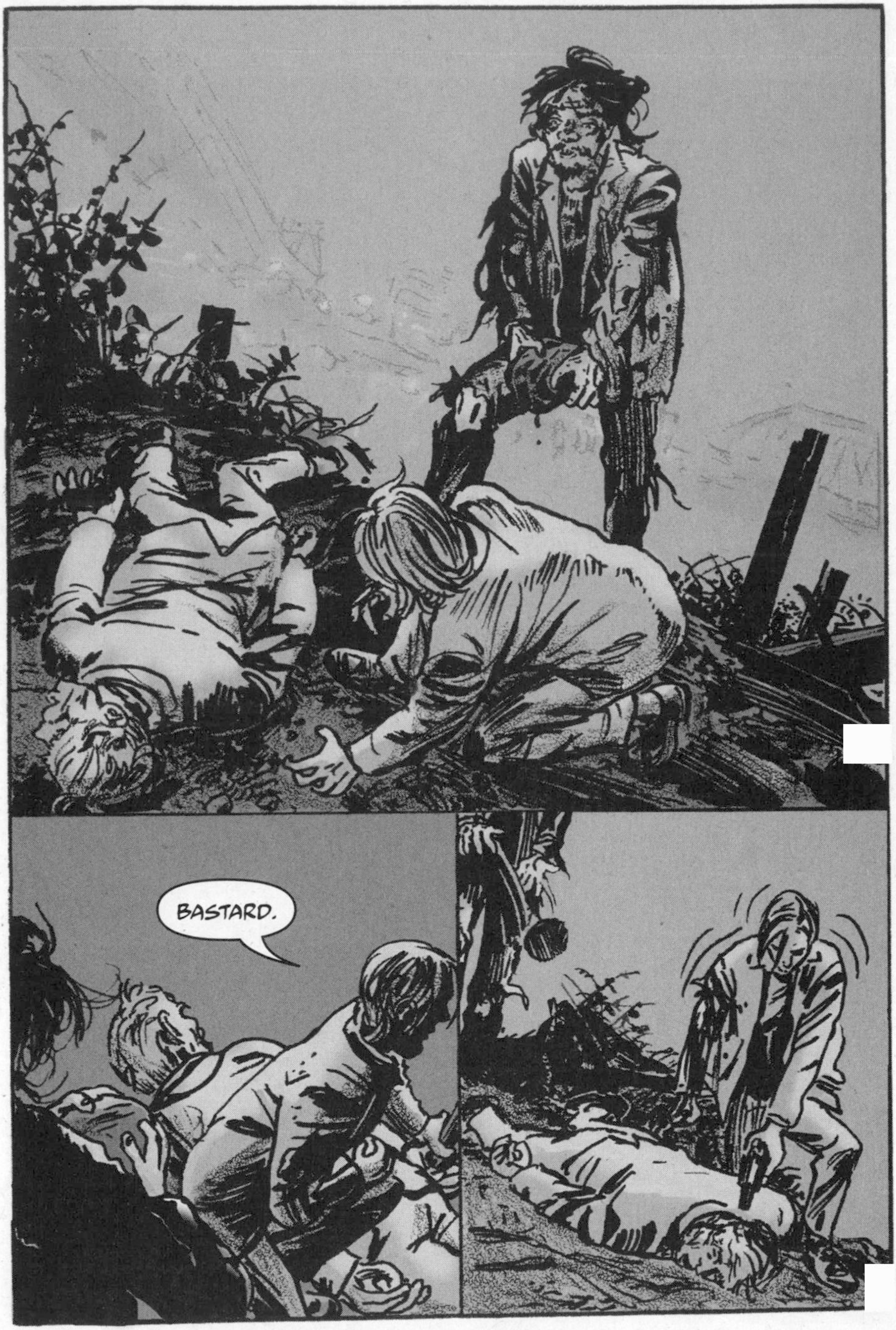
BASTARD.

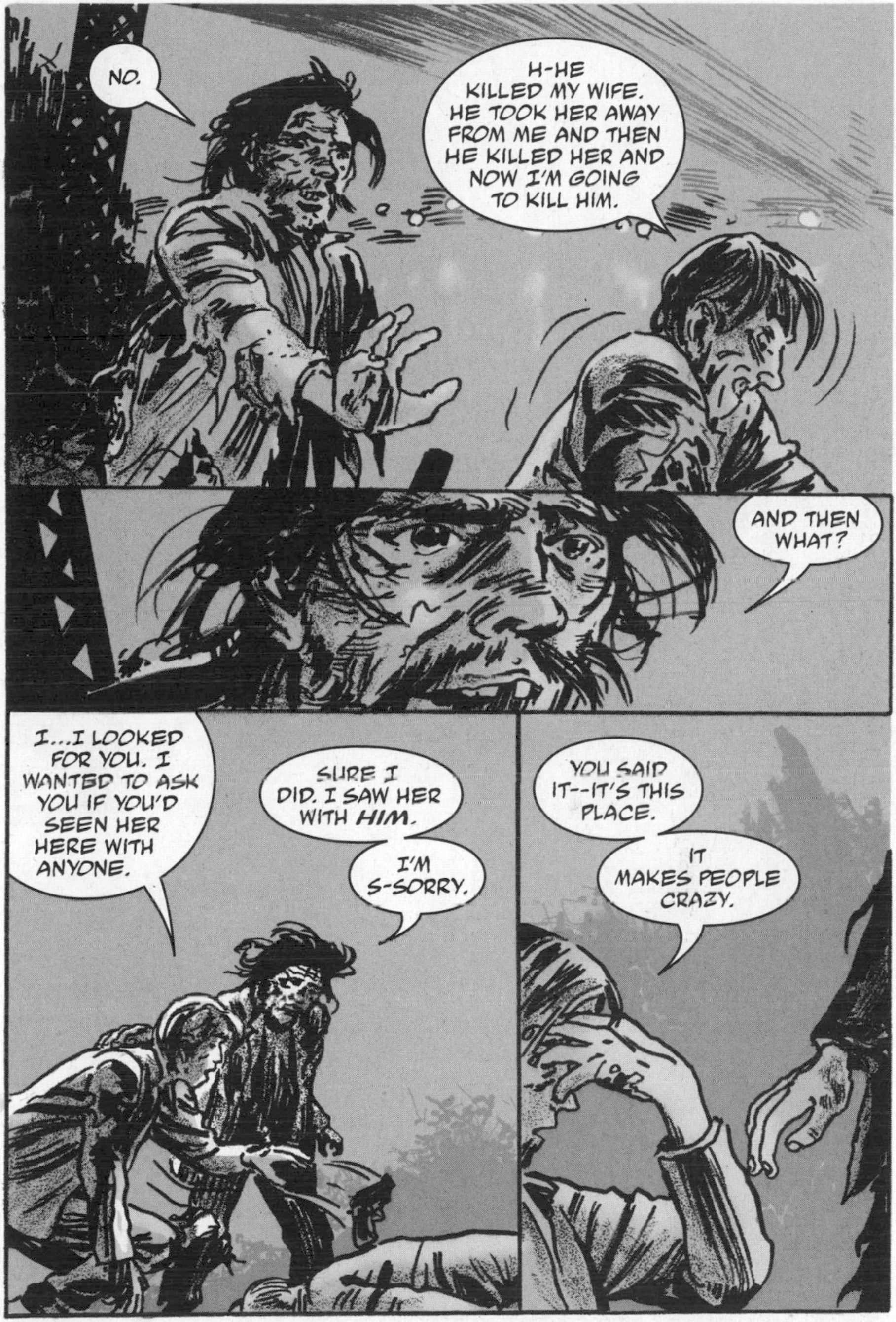
NO.
H-HE KILLED MY WIFE. HE TOOK HER AWAY FROM ME AND THEN HE KILLED HER AND NOW I'M GOING TO KILL HIM.
AND THEN WHAT?
I...I LOOKED FOR YOU. I WANTED TO ASK YOU IF YOU'D SEEN HER HERE WITH ANYONE.
SURE I DID. I SAW HER WITH ***HIM***.
I'M S-SORRY.
YOU SAID IT--IT'S THIS PLACE.
IT MAKES PEOPLE CRAZY.

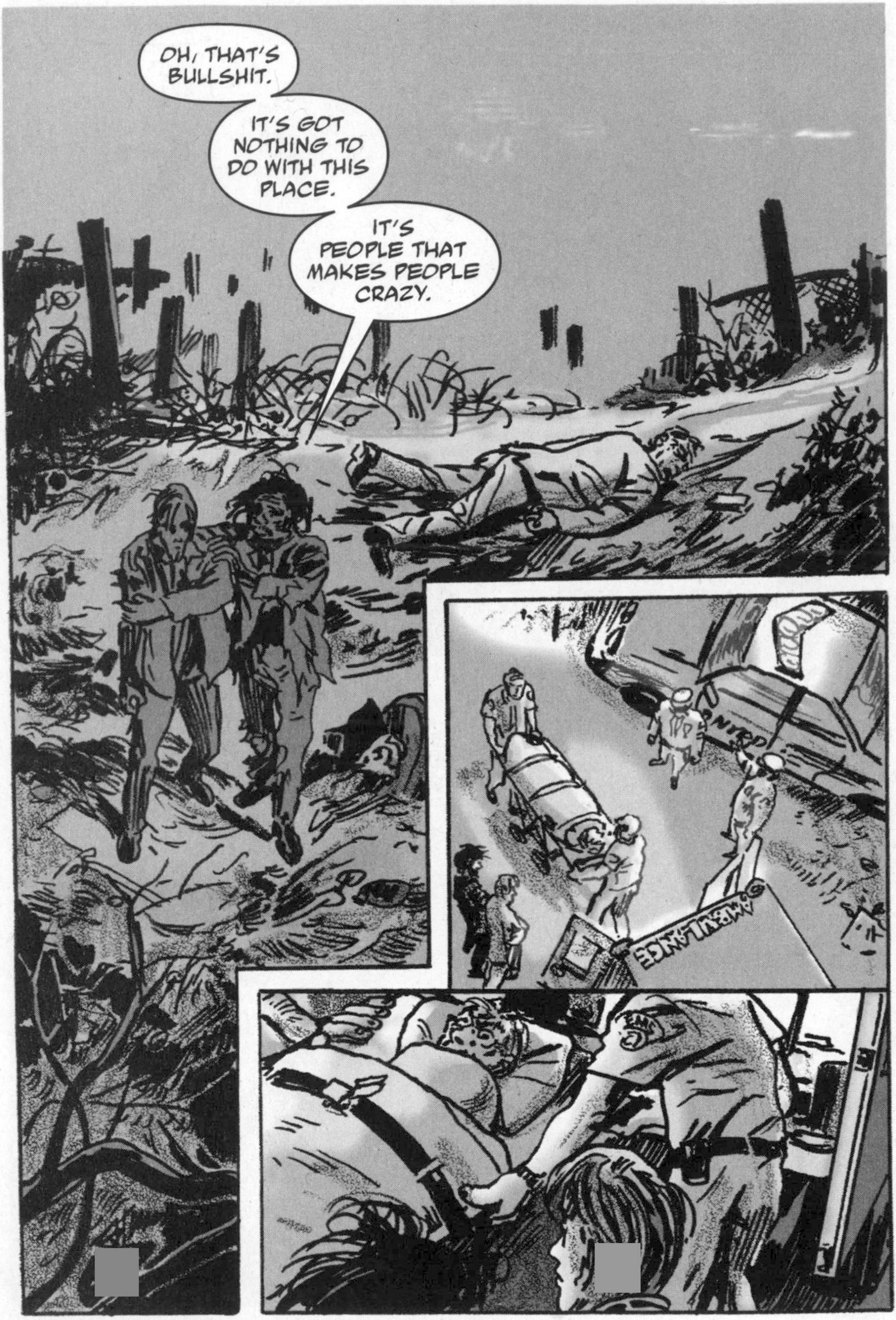
OH, THAT'S BULLSHIT.
IT'S GOT NOTHING TO DO WITH THIS PLACE.
IT'S PEOPLE THAT MAKES PEOPLE CRAZY.

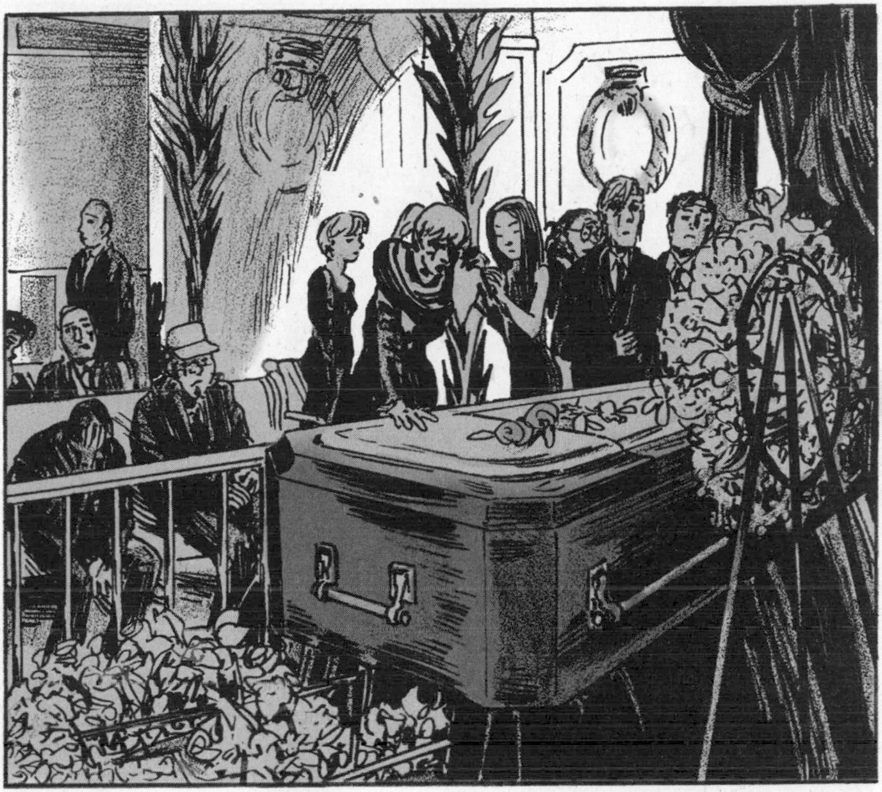

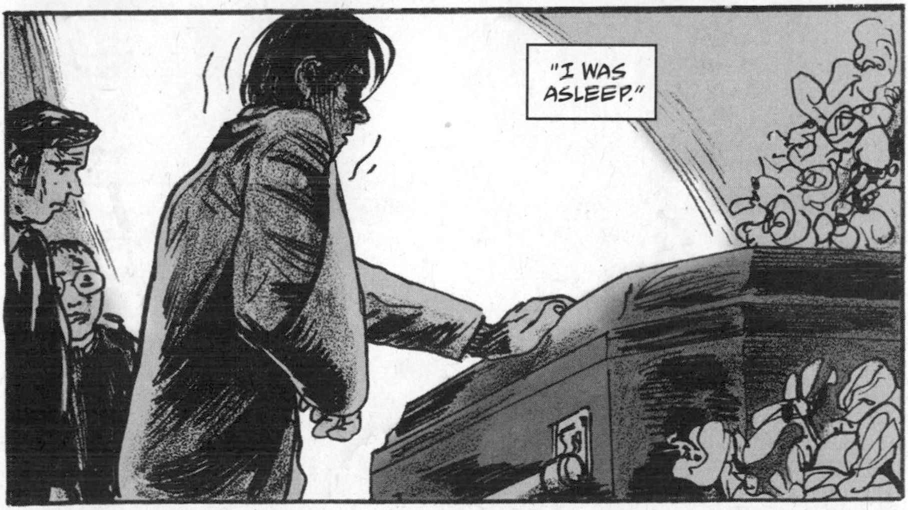
"I WAS ASLEEP."

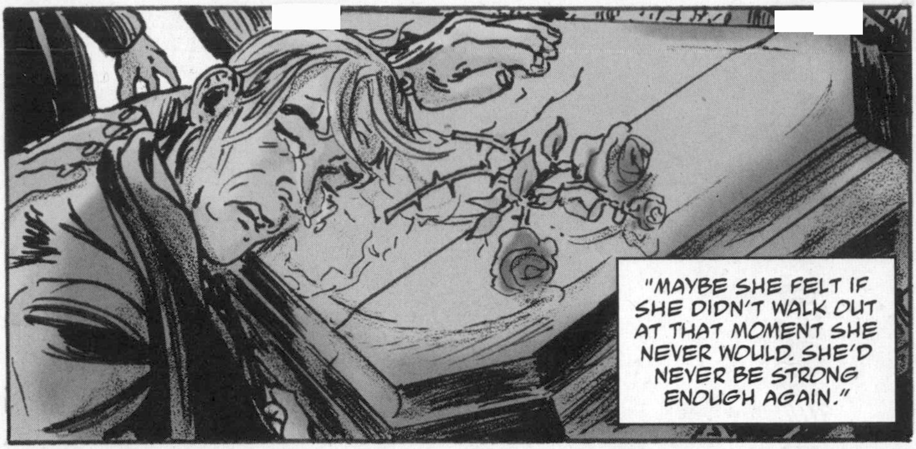
"MAYBE SHE FELT IF SHE DIDN'T WALK OUT AT THAT MOMENT SHE NEVER WOULD. SHE'D NEVER BE STRONG ENOUGH AGAIN."

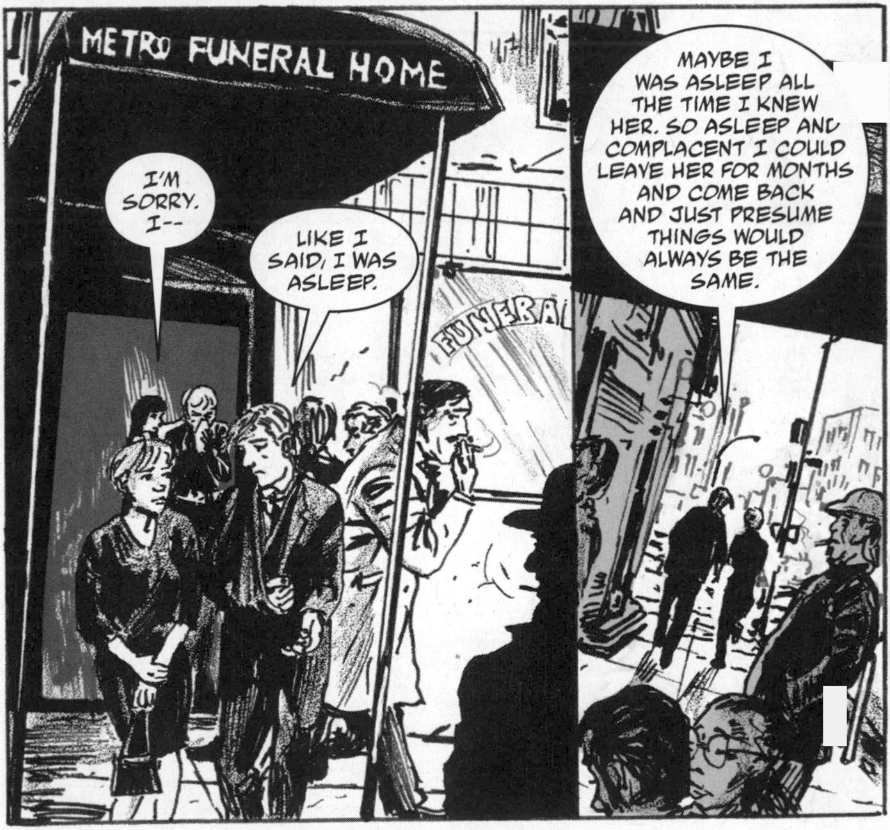
METRO FUNERAL HOME
I'M SORRY. I--
LIKE I SAID, I WAS ASLEEP.
MAYBE I WAS ASLEEP ALL THE TIME I KNEW HER. SO ASLEEP AND COMPLACENT I COULD LEAVE HER FOR MONTHS AND COME BACK AND JUST PRESUME THINGS WOULD ALWAYS BE THE SAME.
FUNERAL

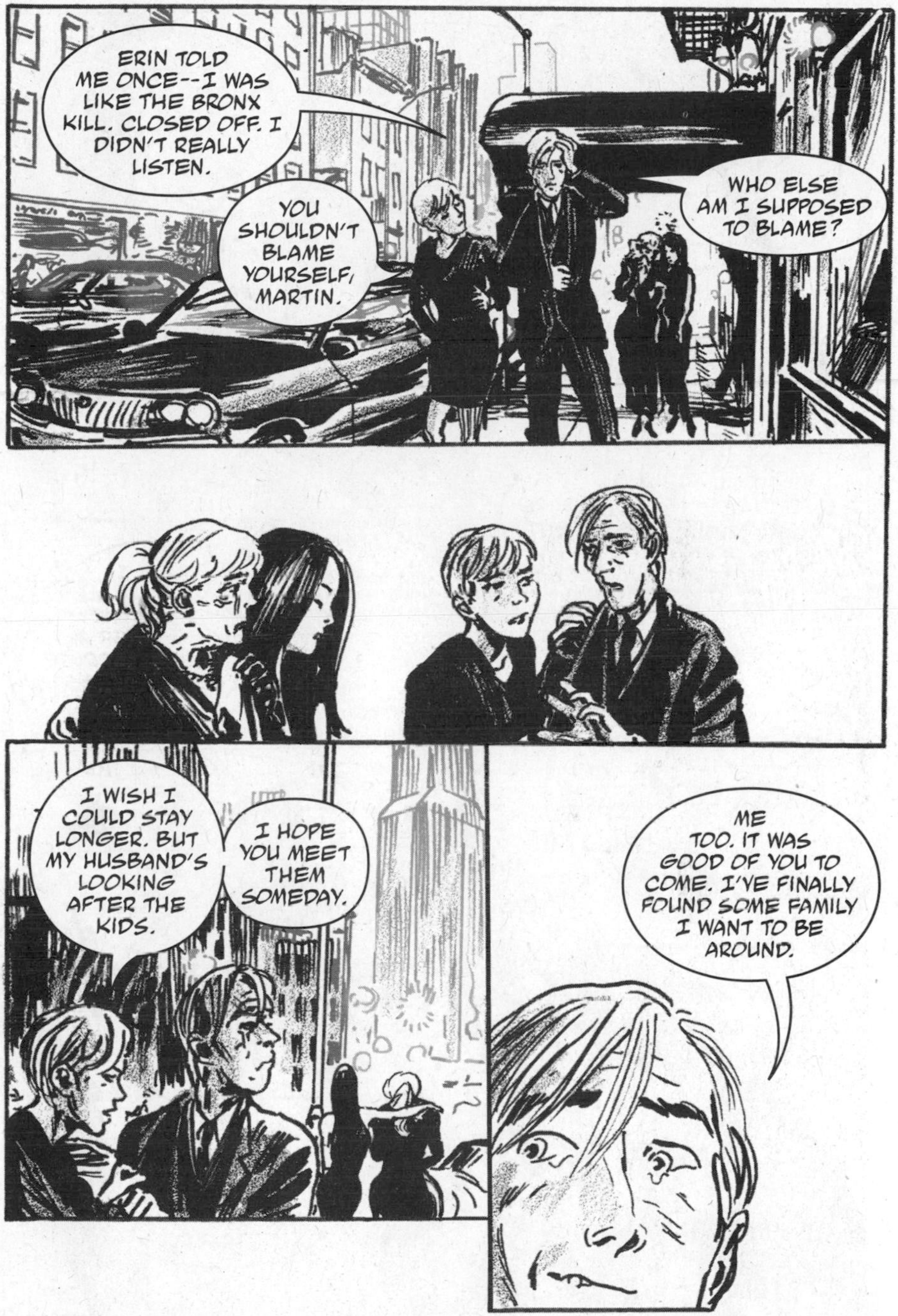
ERIN TOLD ME ONCE--I WAS LIKE THE BRONX KILL. CLOSED OFF. I DIDN'T REALLY LISTEN.
YOU SHOULDN'T BLAME YOURSELF, MARTIN.
WHO ELSE AM I SUPPOSED TO BLAME?
I WISH I COULD STAY LONGER. BUT MY HUSBAND'S LOOKING AFTER THE KIDS.
I HOPE YOU MEET THEM SOMEDAY.
ME TOO. IT WAS GOOD OF YOU TO COME. I'VE FINALLY FOUND SOME FAMILY I WANT TO BE AROUND.

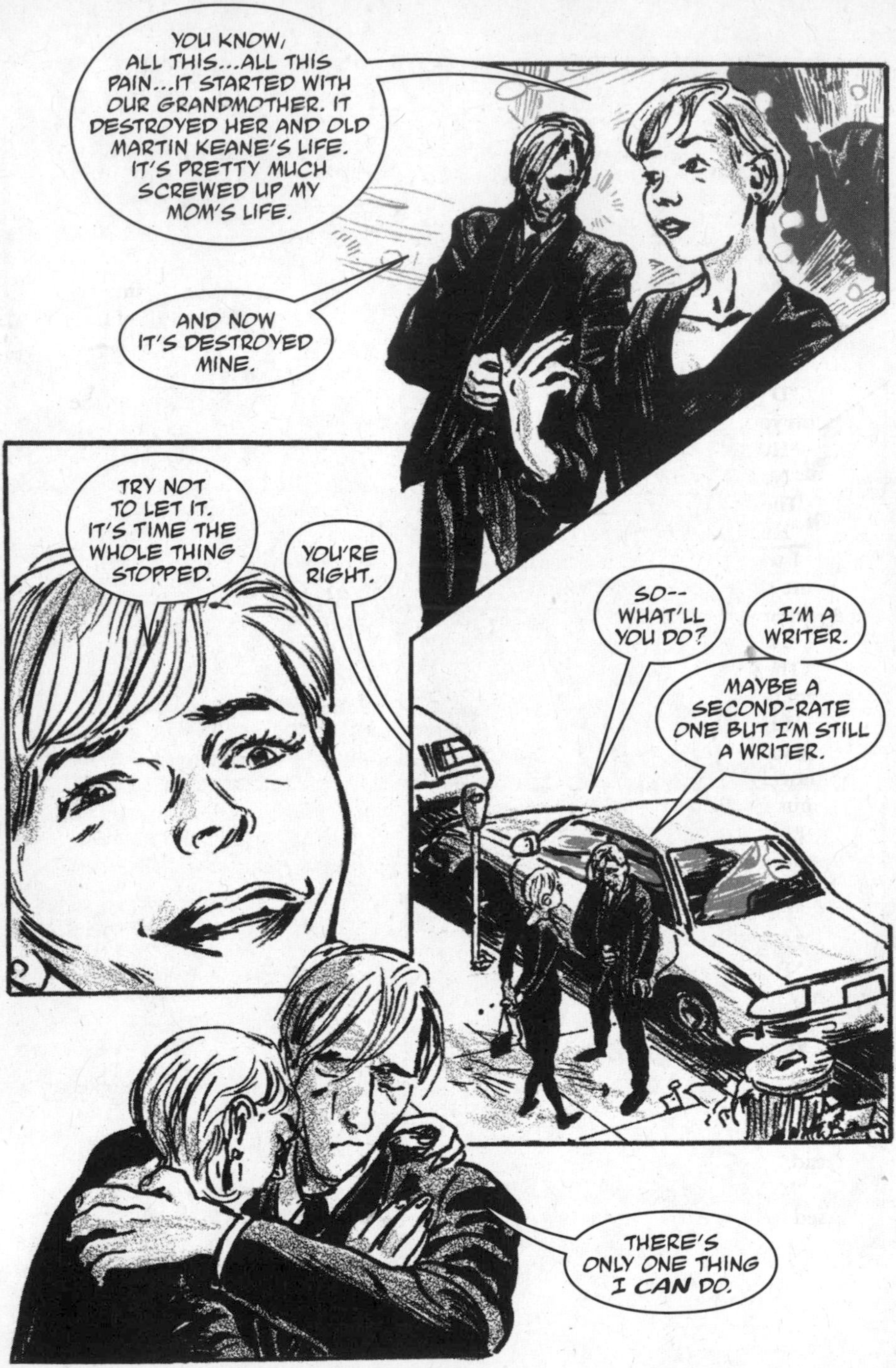
YOU KNOW, ALL THIS...ALL THIS PAIN...IT STARTED WITH OUR GRANDMOTHER. IT DESTROYED HER AND OLD MARTIN KEANE'S LIFE. IT'S PRETTY MUCH SCREWED UP MY MOM'S LIFE.
AND NOW IT'S DESTROYED MINE.
TRY NOT TO LET IT. IT'S TIME THE WHOLE THING STOPPED.
YOU'RE RIGHT.
SO-- WHAT'LL YOU DO?
I'M A WRITER.
MAYBE A SECOND-RATE ONE BUT I'M STILL A WRITER.
THERE'S ONLY ONE THING I *CAN* DO.

Night was setting in, and bats were scooting high overhead by the time my carriage dropped me near the place towards where, it seemed, all my life, and all the lives of all the people I had known, had been moving.

This was what Ann wanted. This is what my wife had told me I must do. Stop running, she'd said. Face the past. Face Hugh.

Easier said than done. *True!*

The lights of Manhattan hung in the distance like a curtain of diamonds and then disappeared behind a bank of cloud, throwing the thin strip of land that led down to the water into blackness. *darkness*

There was a noise to my right. I stood still, feeling my heart pounding.

"D'you remember when we were young and you'd scare the pants off me with your stories about the headless man of Cork?"

"Hugh?"

"Now it's your turn to be scared, Michael."

The voice was coming from the direction of the water.

"Hugh, step out here where I can get a look at you."

instill I tried to instil in my voice all the authority of the elder brother. But it came out thin as water, and it quivered like an old man's. Hugh laughed. I tightened my grip on my pistol but felt no braver, and no safer.

"This has to stop, Hugh."

There was another noise. What was he doing? Slowly a shape emerged from the darkness.

Hugh seemed to have aged at least twenty years. He'd always had a wayward, wild look to him but this had been tempered by some quality, an innocence maybe, an innate goodness. There was nothing innocent or good about the man who stood before me now. He held some kind of knife or blade in his right claw. His left eye was badly swollen. His clothes worn and uncleaned. He would not have been out of place in the hovels of the Old Brewery in Ward Six. He saw my surprise, my *dismay* at his appearance.

"I've lived a hard life, brother."

"That was your decision."

"Things aren't that simple. You always did think things were simple. They're not. Not for people like me, anyhow."

"Why did you do it?"

He flinched and rubbed his sore eye.

"I used to go down to Queenstown and watch those poor starving people lining up on the quays, d'you remember?"

"Aye, I do. That wasn't good for you. I believe it put evil thoughts into your head."

"My evil thoughts had nothing to do with them. I used to envy them, I used to wish I was one of them."

"I don't...understand?"

"It was Papa. The handsomest man in Cork."

"What about him?"

"He showed me an ugly side. He said grandpa made him do the same so there was nothing wrong with it. He made it sound like...like an old family tradition. Like bricks and building."

Hugh sneered at my show of confusion. He took a step closer. I could smell him, the sweet sickly reek of not-quite-death.

"Do I have to spell it out, Michael? The physical act itself?"

It was like a shadow, a cloud, slowly lifting from my past. From father. I shuddered.

"Jesus Christ."

"Oh, I called out for his help. Don't you think I didn't. But Jesus wouldn't help me. So finally I had to help myself. I had to take out those eyes that had seen me so abased."

"But Ann-Marie? Eveline?"

"They could see my shame. I was stained. Stained by what Papa made me do. They could see it, Michael. I knew. So I...I..."

He started crying. I studied the wretched ruined creature before me. I had loved him once. When he had been my strange little changeling brother. I felt ashamed that I found it so difficult to summon up anything like love now.

"I came to America to escape, Michael. Not just from the constables. I came here to get far away from the people who could see the stain on me. But when I got here...it was no different. Some people can see it on me. The filth. The mark. The thumbprint of the devil."

"That's not true, Hugh. No one can see anything on you."

He shook his head, looking at me pityingly.

"You yourself saw it this evening."

"No."

But had I? I had been shocked by how ravaged my younger brother looked. But had there been more than that? Had I seen the thumbprint of something evil? The thumbprint of my Papa?

"Hugh...it's time it ended. It's like...it's like the pain gets handed on and on. And it's time we ended it."

"How? How do we do that?"

His eyes were wide and imploring and for one moment I saw the young man and the boy he once was. For one moment he was my younger brother, the one who used to follow me around Cork, the one I scared witless by tales of the Headless Man. The one Papa sent out to Cunniams for his bloody crubeens.

And then he looked down and his expression changed. The boy sunk back behind the face of the man that he'd become. *at what I held*

This section needs work.

Family tradition

Brickyard

POLICE!!

178

"I see."

"I'm sorry, Hugh."

The pistol weighed heavily in my hand. I had kept it from my days with the Dead Rabbits but had never expected to use it on my own flesh and blood. I fired twice at Hugh's heart, and then reloaded and put a bullet through his head, in the recommended fashion of Baboon Connelly. Afterwards I dragged my poor brother's body towards the water's edge, while a few faint lights glinted on the low hump of Randall's Island.

Hugh's body floated for a moment and then sank beneath the water and darkness of the Bronx Kill. I thought about saying a prayer but decided against it. The truth is I was more inclined to utter a curse. But can we curse those who are already dead? Can we curse the past, in the same way that the past can curse us?

With such thoughts in my head, I turned and headed back for my carriage, resolving never to visit that damned place again.

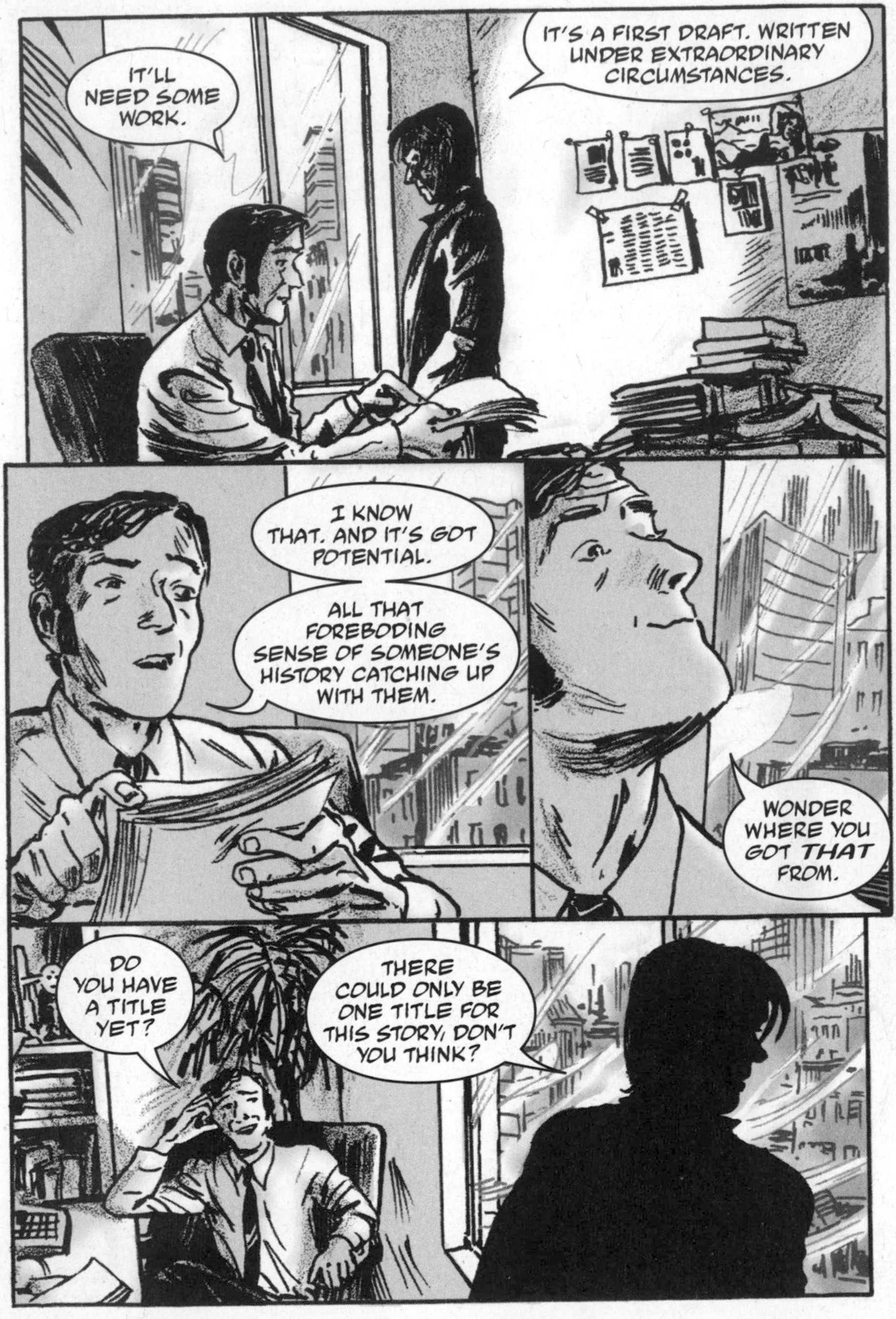
IT'LL NEED SOME WORK.
IT'S A FIRST DRAFT. WRITTEN UNDER EXTRAORDINARY CIRCUMSTANCES.
I KNOW THAT. AND IT'S GOT POTENTIAL.
ALL THAT FOREBODING SENSE OF SOMEONE'S HISTORY CATCHING UP WITH THEM.
WONDER WHERE YOU GOT *THAT* FROM.
DO YOU HAVE A TITLE YET?
THERE COULD ONLY BE ONE TITLE FOR THIS STORY, DON'T YOU THINK?

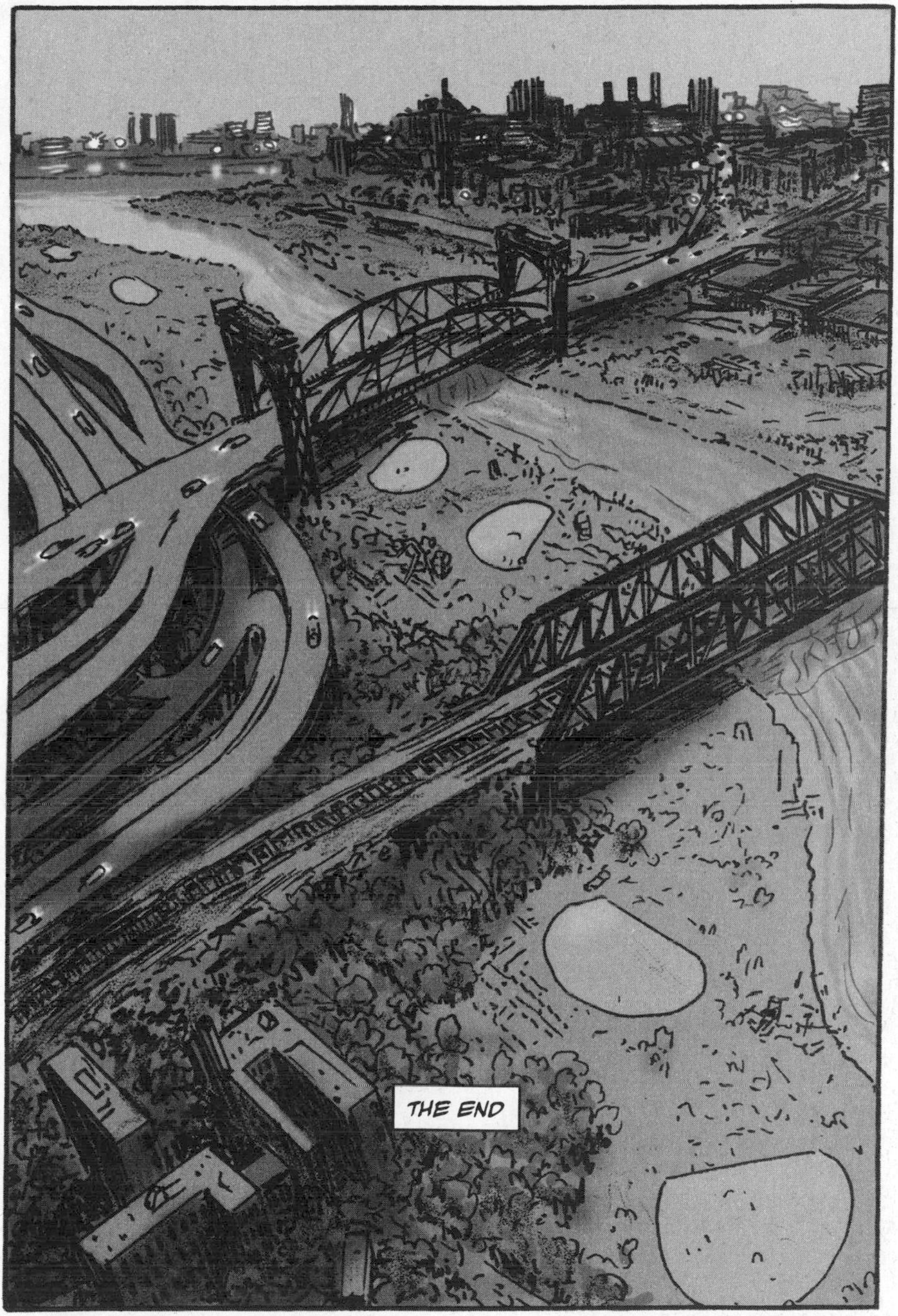
THE END

FILTHY RICH

AVAILABLE NOW

Written by **BRIAN AZZARELLO**
(Best-selling author of *100 Bullets* and *Joker*)

Art by **VICTOR SANTOS**

Richard "Junk" Junkin has always lived on the wrong side of trouble... A former pro football star whose career was cut short by injury (and a nasty gambling problem), Junk now spends his time dreaming of what might have been, selling cars in Jersey and lusting after the boss's unbelievably spoiled, unbelievably sexy and unbelievably rich daughter, Victoria.

So when the boss asks him to be Victoria's personal bodyguard while she tears up the New York City club scene, Junk leaps at the chance. But before long, he finds that Victoria wants a lapdog and not a chaperone, someone who's going to do all of her dirty work – *all* of it – someone who wants to get filthy rich...

BRIAN AZZARELLO
NEW YORK TIMES BEST-SELLING AUTHOR OF JOKER
VICTOR SANTOS
FILTHY RICH

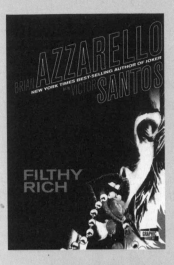

THE CHILL

AVAILABLE NOW

Written by **JASON STARR**
(Best-selling author of *Panic Attack* and *The Follower*)

Art by **MICK BERTILORENZI**

A modern thriller steeped in Celtic mythology – a broken-down cop tracks a seductive killer who possesses the supernatural power known as "the chill." Can he stop her before her next victim dies horribly... but with a smile on his face?

JASON
STARR
MICK
THE CHILL

AREA 10

AVAILABLE NOW

Written by **CHRISTOS N. GAGE**
(*Law & Order: SVU*)

Art by **CHRIS SAMNEE**

When a detective – tracking a serial killer who decapitates his victims – receives a bizarre head injury himself, he suspects a connection between his own fate and the killer's fascination with Trepanation – the ancient art of skull drilling.

AREA 10
CHRISTOS N. GAGE
CHRIS SAMNEE

VERTIGO CRIME